REMARKABLE PLANTS OF TEXAS

Remarkable

UNCOMMON ACCOUNTS

NUMBER SIXTY-TWO

The Corrie Herring Hooks Series

Plants of Texas

OF OUR COMMON NATIVES

MATT WARNOCK TURNER

UNIVERSITY OF TEXAS PRESS  AUSTIN

Copyright © 2009 by the University of Texas Press
All rights reserved
Printed in China
First paperback printing, 2013

Requests for permission to reproduce material from
this work should be sent to:
    Permissions
    University of Texas Press
    P.O. Box 7819
    Austin, TX 78713-7819

http://utpress.utexas.edu/index.php/rp-form

(∞) The paper used in this book meets the minimum requirements of ANSI/NISO Z39.48-1992
(R1997) (Permanence of Paper).

Library of Congress Cataloging-in-Publication
Data

Turner, Matt Warnock, 1960–
    Remarkable plants of Texas : uncommon accounts
of our common natives / Matt Warnock Turner.
— 1st ed.
        p. cm. — (Corrie Herring Hooks series ;
no. 62)
    Includes bibliographical references and index.
    1. Endemic plants—Texas. 2. Plants—Texas.
I. Title. II. Series.
    QK188.T85 2009
    581.6'309764—dc22
                                        2008024440
ISBN 978-0-292-75703-5 (pbk. : alk. paper)
doi:10.7560/718517

Dedicated to the memory of my mother

VIRGINIA RUTH MATHIS TURNER (1925–2006)

who found uncommon beauty in common places.

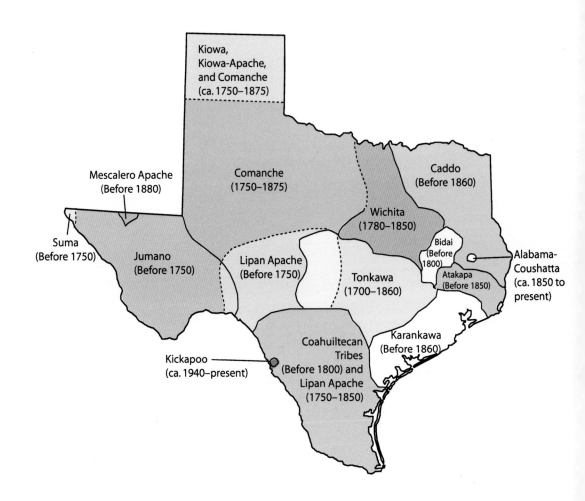

Kiowa,
Kiowa-Apache,
and Comanche
(ca. 1750–1875)

Mescalero Apache
(Before 1880)

Comanche
(1750–1875)

Caddo
(Before 1860)

Wichita
(1780–1850)

Bidai
(Before
1800)

Suma
(Before 1750)

Jumano
(Before 1750)

Lipan Apache
(Before 1750)

Tonkawa
(1700–1860)

Atakapa
(Before 1850)

Alabama-
Coushatta
(ca. 1850 to
present)

Kickapoo
(ca. 1940–present)

Coahuiltecan
Tribes
(Before 1800) and
Lipan Apache
(1750–1850)

Karankawa
(Before 1860)

*Native American Tribes in Texas, ca. 1700 to
present. Locations of major tribes cited in text
that have inhabited the state of Texas. Many
tribes are not contemporaneous. Boundaries and
dates are general approximations to provide a
holistic view over three centuries. (See Glossary
for further information on individual tribes.)*

Contents

Map: Native American Tribes in Texas, ca. 1700 to present   vi
Medical Disclaimer   x
Acknowledgments   xi
Introduction   xiii

TREES

Acacia farnesiana
  Huisache   3

Arbutus xalapensis
  Texas Madrone   7

Carya illinoinensis
  Pecan   11

Celtis spp.
  Hackberry   17

Cornus florida
  Flowering Dogwood   20

Diospyros texana
  Texas Persimmon   25

Diospyros virginiana
  Common Persimmon   28

Juglans spp.
  Black Walnut and
  Texas Black Walnut   32

Juniperus spp.
  Eastern Red-Cedar and
  Ashe Juniper   38

Maclura pomifera
  Osage Orange   45

Morus spp.
  Red Mulberry and
  Little-leaf Mulberry   49

Pinus spp.
  Loblolly Pine and Longleaf Pine   54

Populus deltoides
  Cottonwood   59

Prosopis glandulosa
  Mesquite   64

Prunus spp.
  Wild Plum and Black Cherry   71

Quercus stellata
  Post Oak   75

Quercus virginiana
   Live Oak 80

Sabal mexicana
   Sabal Palm 87

Salix nigra
   Black Willow 91

Sapindus saponaria
   Soapberry 95

Sassafras albidum
   Sassafras 98

Taxodium distichum
   Bald Cypress 102

SHRUBS

Agave lechuguilla
   Lechuguilla 109

Berberis trifoliolata
   Agarita 114

Dasylirion spp.
   Sotol 118

Ephedra antisyphilitica
   Mormon Tea 122

Euphorbia antisyphilitica
   Candelilla 125

Fouquieria splendens
   Ocotillo 129

Ilex vomitoria
   Yaupon 134

Larrea tridentata
   Creosote Bush 139

Rhus spp.
   Fragrant Sumac 144

Rhus spp.
   Sumac 147

Sophora secundiflora
   Texas Mountain Laurel 151

Ungnadia speciosa
   Mexican Buckeye 159

Yucca spp.
   Yucca 163

HERBACEOUS PLANTS, CACTI, GRASSES, VINES, AND AQUATICS

Allium spp.
   Wild Onion 171

Amaranthus spp.
   Amaranth 175

Argemone spp.
   White Prickly Poppy 180

Artemisia ludoviciana
   White Sagebrush 183

Bouteloua spp.
   Blue Grama and Sideoats Grama 187

Capsicum annuum
   Chiltepín 191

Chenopodium spp.
    Goosefoot 195

Coreopsis tinctoria
    Plains Coreopsis 199

Cucurbita foetidissima
    Buffalo Gourd 202

Datura spp.
    Jimsonweed 206

Echinacea angustifolia
    Purple Coneflower 210

Equisetum spp.
    Horsetail 214

Eryngium yuccifolium
    Rattlesnake Master 217

Gaillardia pulchella
    Indian Blanket 221

Helianthus annuus
    Sunflower 225

Hoffmannseggia glauca
    Indian Rush-Pea 229

Lophophora williamsii
    Peyote 232

Lupinus texensis
    Texas Bluebonnet 238

Monarda spp.
    Horsemint 242

Nelumbo lutea
    Yellow Lotus 245

Opuntia spp.
    Prickly Pear 248

Opuntia leptocaulis
    Tasajillo 257

Phoradendron tomentosum
    Mistletoe 260

Phytolacca americana
    Pokeweed 266

Smilax spp.
    Greenbrier 270

Solanum elaeagnifolium
    Silverleaf Nightshade 274

Tillandsia spp.
    Spanish Moss and Ball Moss 278

Typha spp.
    Cattail 284

Verbesina virginica
    Frostweed 289

Vitis spp.
    Wild Grape 293

Glossary 299
Bibliography 311
Index 329

Medical Disclaimer

This book concerns the natural and cultural history of Texas plants; it is not meant to be a guide to plant uses. This is especially true for plants with reported medical or psychotropic properties. Such properties are here reported for their historical value, to enlighten the public about the treatments of an earlier time and, in some cases, about their legacies today. In no way is this book meant to be prescriptive, and it by no means replaces professional medical advice. The medical uses contained herein should not be read as promoting experimental use by individuals, who could do serious harm to themselves. Neither the author nor the University of Texas Press accepts responsibility for the accuracy of the information itself, or for the consequences from the use or misuse of the information in this book.

Acknowledgments

First and foremost I am indebted to Dr. Beryl Simpson and to my father, Dr. B. L. Turner, both of the Section of Integrative Biology at the University of Texas at Austin. Their tireless efforts in reviewing each and every unit of this book provided both words of encouragement and critical comment, while imbuing the text with a scientific precision that is not always the wont of someone with a literary background.

Academic professionals from several scientific disciplines added insights from their areas of expertise to this book. I am very thankful to: Robert Adams (Baylor University), Meredith Blackwell (Louisiana State University), Ted Delevoryas (University of Texas), Phil Dering (Shumla School), Barney Lipscomb (Botanical Research Institute of Texas), Andrew McDonald (University of Texas Pan-American), A. Michael Powell (Sul Ross State University), Alan Prather (Michigan State University), Martin Terry (Sul Ross State University), and Damon Waitt (Lady Bird Johnson Wildflower Center).

I am equally grateful to the personal attention I received from those who are steeped in plant lore through vocation and deep personal interest. Elizabeth Seiler provided copious commentary on junipers, and Landon Lockett, who has vastly broadened our understanding of Texas populations of sabal palms, offered careful insights, a personal tour, and a free specimen. David Sitz, of Matagorda County, also added information on palms. I am most thankful to Ted Gray, a west Texas rancher and subject of a recent biography (Nelson 2000), who allowed me to interview him about his personal "cowboy" experience with the plants of the Trans-Pecos.

Nancy Elder, Head Librarian of the Life Science Library at the University of Texas, deserves my special thanks for her amazing sleuth-work abilities, for her tolerance of my interruptions, and for her genuine enthusiasm for this project. Tom Wendt and Lindsay Woodruff, Curator and Assistant Curator, respectively, of the Plant Resources Center at the University of Texas, receive my continued respect for their assistance with questions and for their excellent management of one of the nation's largest herbaria.

Although I was able to photograph most of the plants in this work myself, I relied on the kindness of others for a few that eluded me. I would like to thank J. L. Neff and also the Dexter Collection of the Plant Resources Center for the loan of two photos for this work (Indian rush-pea and dogwood).

Finally, I must thank the many personal friends whose kind words of support and reassurance provided the courage to make major life changes, the animus to undertake a big project, and the where-withal to see it through: Paul Waller (who gave the manuscript a thorough read), James Robbins, and Leora Lev, as well as Jim Berrong, Richard Connelly, Barry Cravens, Douglas Galloway, Frank Kou-mantaris, Jonathan Lee, Arthur Martinez, T. J. "Tim" Middleton, Scot Rogerson, Richard Schwiner, Hideko Secrest-Rosen-zweig, and Adam Toguchi.

Introduction

The vast majority of books about the native plants of Texas are field guides, in one form or another. Given Texas' extraordinary botanical wealth and diversity, with approximately 6000 species spread across more than 268,000 square miles including several distinct floristic regions, this is entirely understandable. There is a simple need to know the names of the plants, how to recognize them, and how to distinguish them from similar species. But once we know what we are looking at—whether a pecan, prickly pear, or bluebonnet—is there nothing more to know? Is there anything remarkable or noteworthy about the plant? Did it play a role in history? Is it useful to humankind? Does it contain medicinal, psychotropic, or toxic compounds? Is there unusual ecological or biological information about it? Is it particularly important to wildlife—birds, bees, or butterflies? Does it have cultural significance today, and if so, why? In short, what is its story?

These are precisely the questions that this book addresses, the stories it attempts to tell. This work is ethnobotanical in the broadest sense. More than simply a listing of the human uses of plants (though a great many are included), this work explores our vast array of connections to them. These connections come from many fields and disciplines, including the natural sciences (biology, chemistry, ecology, pharmacology, taxonomy), social sciences (archaeology, history, linguistics), and humanities (folklore, legends, and traditions). The peoples involved reflect the historic diversity of Texas, including prehistoric peoples, indigenous tribes who lived in or moved through the state, French and Spanish explorers, Hispanic and Anglo settlers, and contemporary citizens. Sources run the gamut from archaeological findings, chronicles, pioneer journals and diaries, reports from early scientific expeditions, ethnobotanical works on Native Americans, studies of African American folk healers, cowboy ballads, state symbols and place names, current scientific articles, and even interviews with contemporary naturalists, ranchers, and other lovers of the land.

Each plant has its own story to tell and leads where it will. Some plants, such as lechuguilla, sotol, and yucca, are especially rich in the Texan archaeological record, providing documented fiber and foodstuffs for millennia. Other plants, such as jimsonweed and peyote, are known for their psychotropic compounds. Horsemint, sassafras, and yaupon make famous teas, and the fruits of agarita, mesquite, persimmon, and prickly pear provide jellies and preserves. But these stories are by no means one-dimensional, or centered on economic botany. Each narrative makes its twists and turns according to the landscape that surrounds it.

For instance, live oak once provided a source of food, tannin, and ink, but it also is one of the heaviest of American woods, supplying one of the strongest shipbuilding woods available in the world. It gave the USS *Constitution* (Old Ironsides) her military advantage and helped to establish the supremacy of the U.S. merchant marines. Live oak became the first North American tree to be set aside for future use in a forest preserve. A cluster of live oaks on Galveston Island was the greenery that first greeted early Texas immigrants arriving on our shores. Fully half of all the historic trees of Texas are live oaks, commemorating such things as treaties, battles, encampments, trysts, and buried treasure. Live oak leaves, denoting strength, even grace the Official State Seal of Texas.

Such a broad approach reaches beyond mere laundry lists of well-known uses to locate the unusual, the forgotten, the unknown but must-know things about our native flora. Horsetail, for example, is known as the Tinkertoy plant among children, who pull its stems apart and reattach them for sport. Plant enthusiasts may refer to the reedlike herb as scouring-rush on account of its rough, sandpapery surface. How many of us are aware that horsetail is a living fossil, with ancestors dating back more than 350 million years, to when tree-sized horsetails composed some of the earth's first extensive forests? Or take yaupon, an evergreen shrub increasingly used in landscaping throughout the state. Practically every indigenous tribe of the American Southeast drank a naturally caffeinated tea from its leaves, as did many European explorers, colonizers, and settlers. Our knowledge of this native tea has all but vanished, while the tea known as *mate*, from a close relative of yaupon in South America, has remained a common drink and source of regional identity and pride. How many of us know that bald cypress trees were once so large that dances could be held on their stumps, or that cypress shingle-maker camps developed into some of the first settlements of the Hill Country? Who would guess that the fruits of the weedy silverleaf nightshade, ubiquitous in roadway medians, can curdle milk and were originally used to make asadero cheese, a common ingredient of chile con queso?

In choosing which plants to cover, my approach is to take a bird's-eye view of the entire native vascular flora of Texas (including trees, shrubs, wildflowers, grasses, cacti, vines, and aquatics) and ask which of these are the richest and most interesting in terms of their human (and even wildlife) connections. Which are the ones that appear, again and again, in diaries, journals, reports, and scientific research? Then I balance this group against the plant's abundance and distribution in our state, as it would be of little interest to extol the virtues of a plant that readers would rarely encounter in the wild. Conversely, there is little advantage to including a well-known plant that has a comparatively short or uninteresting story. The selection is naturally a subjective decision that I hope readers will indulge, trusting from their own experience that most of the plants included here are major players in the state's flora. Although some would argue that trees, and to a lesser extent shrubs, have the lion's share of ethnobotanic lore, I purposefully include many herbaceous plants, including wildflowers, for the sake of diversity. Even here, only those with particularly interesting stories make the cut. Wherever possible I focus on the stories that most concern Texas, including broader connections to the Southeast, Southwest, or Mexico when relevant, and reaching yet farther (to the east and west coasts or even to Europe and Asia) only when truly remarkable connections merit it.

This book is written for a broad spectrum of people who are interested in Texas native plants, from novices to experts, from casual observers to plant aficionados, from gardeners and naturalists to landscape architects and botanists, from city dwellers and suburbanites to ranchers and park rangers. The book does not presuppose botanic knowledge, and technical terminology is kept to a bare minimum. In 65 entries or units, the book covers more than 80 native plant species in 62 genera among 44 families. Although the accounts can essentially stand alone (that is to say, they can be read independently),

in an effort to give some order to the lot, I have grouped the plants into three main divisions: trees, shrubs, and everything else. Within each division the plants are listed by genus name, in alphabetical order, but the common name is presented in boldface for easier recognition. The origin of the scientific name is provided in the heading, and comments on the common names usually appear in the text. The name of the family to which the plant belongs also appears in the heading, along with a thumbnail description of the plant and its habitat and distribution (in Texas, in the United States, and outside the country). Color photos of each plant are provided.

In most cases there is ample information to devote an entire account to one particular species. In many cases, however, two or more species are discussed under the same heading. This can occur when there is sufficient difference between two species to merit discussion, but enough similarity that splitting them would cause redundancy (as is the case with loblolly and longleaf pine, blue and sideoats grama, and Spanish and ball moss). In these examples, both species appear separately in the heading and are clearly distinguished in the text. In other cases, such as hackberry and sotol, folk wisdom may treat several distinct species of one genus in a similar manner, or as happens with well-known entities like plum, sumac, wild onion, and cattail, historical records report as one entity plants that scientists classify as several species. In these cases several scientific names are provided for only one common name;

here, again, attention is given to the most common species within our state, taking into account both abundance and distribution. Finally, when there are many species that are widespread, difficult to distinguish, or very similar ethnobotanically, as is the case with amaranth, greenbrier, and yucca, the genus becomes the focus and species are mentioned only to make nuanced distinctions.

The many sources involved in the research of this book are found in the bibliography. How to reference these sources throughout the work took some thought. Cluttering the text with parenthetical citations is unappealing to all save the academic researcher, but completely omitting them smacks of fiction and potentially frustrates those who are interested in delving into particulars. The compromise presented here is to list at the end of each account a reference to every work that was consulted in its writing, interrupting the narrative only to cite direct quotations or points that rely heavily on a specific source.

This book will fill a niche that is overlooked in the available literature. The work that is most similar to it, Ellen Schulz's *Texas Wild Flowers: A Popular Account of the Common Wild Flowers of Texas*, is long out of print (1928). Another collection of kindred spirit, Donald Culross Peattie's *A Natural History of Trees of Eastern and Central North America* (1966) and *A Natural History of Western Trees* (1953), is thorough and beautifully written, but it is limited, of course, to trees. The many current Texas field guides are neither meant to provide, nor have the space for, lengthy commentary, though

some exception can be found in Paul Cox and Patty Leslie's concise *Texas Trees: A Friendly Guide* (1999), Zoe Kirkpatrick's beautiful *Wildflowers of the Western Plains* (1992), and John and Gloria Tveten's informative *Wildflowers of Houston and Southeast Texas* (1997). Each of these is limited to a type of flora, a region, or both. Elizabeth Silverthorne's *Legends and Lore of Texas Wildflowers* (1996) centers on flowers and follows a more literary path. Delena Tull's excellent *Edible and Useful Plants of Texas and the Southwest: A Practical Guide* (1987), to which this book is indebted, focuses mainly on edible plants and dyes; as the title suggests, the book is meant to provide firsthand, how-to information. Finally, Scooter Cheatham's formidable work, *The Useful Wild Plants of Texas* (1995), will be the last word on native plant uses, when all twelve volumes of the reference work, covering more than 4000 plants, are completed.

This book then is a one-volume, easy reference for Texas' most common and ethnobotanically interesting plants. It is not limited to a region or a specific type of plant. It can be stowed in the backpack and treated like a field guide, since its structure allows quick access and provides descriptions and photos, and since each plant is treated as a separate entry. It can just as easily be enjoyed as a narrative work, providing the reader with an overview of the natural history of our native plants. Whichever way it is read, I hope this book will open your eyes to the remarkable stories that surround our flora, such that you never look at these plants again in the same way.

TREES

Huisache

Acacia farnesiana (L.) Willd.

Acacia, as classically conceived, is an enormous genus of approximately 1200 species, mainly distributed in warmer areas. Texas has about a dozen species (and many varieties), several of which have different growth forms depending on habitat. *Acacia farnesiana*, locally called huisache or sweet acacia, the most widely distributed species in the genus, is rarely confused with our other species, at least when in flower or fruit. The yellow, puff-like flower balls (each ball is actually a cluster of tiny flowers) are amazingly fragrant and often cover the entire tree. Some compare their scent to a blend of orange blossoms and violets. The short, plump, nearly cylindrical fruit pods are also distinctive. Huisache is more difficult to identify by habit alone. Along the Gulf Coast, it tends to be a single-trunked shrub, with somewhat drooping branches, but inland plants tend to have several trunks with more ascending branches. There is even a population of prostrate trailing huisache from Brazos Island.

ORIGIN OF SCIENTIFIC NAME

The word *Acacia* derives from the Greek *akis*, a sharp point, referring to the sharp spines of many species, including this one. The species honors Cardinal Odoardo Farnese (1573–1626) of Rome, of the famous Farnese family that intermarried with the Borgias and Medicis and filled some of the highest offices of the Church in the sixteenth and seventeenth centuries, including the papacy. Huisache was first introduced to the immense and botanically rich Farnese gardens in 1611 from Santo Domingo.

OTHER COMMON NAMES

sweet acacia, honey ball, cassie, opoponax, popinac, vinorama, guisache, huizache, uña de cabra (and many more)

FAMILY

Fabaceae (Legume or Bean Family)

DESCRIPTION

Flat-topped or rounded shrub or small tree 6–20' tall (max. 30'), deciduous (appearing evergreen in mild winters); branches with pair of straight thorns at each node; small leaves twice compound; very fragrant, yellow-gold flower balls up to 1" across; fruit pods cylindrical and oblong, 2–3" long.

HABITAT AND DISTRIBUTION

More frequent on heavier, wetter clays of low-lying areas in the southern third of Texas, especially the Rio Grande plains, but tolerant of many soil types and scattered in other areas in the lower half of the state; along southern edge of U.S. from California to Florida; Mexico, Central America, and northern South America. Naturalized around the globe: Australia, Africa, Europe, southern South America, China, and India.

The scent-laden blossoms of huisache.

There seems to be a general consensus that in Texas huisache was historically most abundant south of the Nueces River, with scattered populations farther north, and that it has gradually been spread, both intentionally and naturally, all along the Gulf Coast and inland approximately 200 miles. In the early twentieth century there were persistent rumors that the tree was not native to Texas. In one account, a Mexican commissioner to San Patricio County brought the tree to his hacienda, whence it spread to the rest of the state (Schulz 1928); in another it arrived from south of the border only in the twentieth century (Bedichek 1950). These ideas are completely unfounded, as Spanish sources mention the tree all along the route from Laredo to San Antonio as early as 1768 (Foster 1995). They more likely are obser-

vations that huisache, as a fast-growing pioneer plant, thrives in disturbed areas (such as livestock pastures) where, as if from nowhere, a whole thicket suddenly appears. As settlement spread outside deep south Texas, what had been a scattered, occasional tree suddenly became a more dominant feature, giving rise to notions that it was exotic.

Unbeknownst to many Texans, huisache has an amazing history in the European perfume industry. Native plant experts have noted that "huisache is better appreciated where it is not so abundant" (Wasowski and Wasowski 1997). Following this insight, what for south Texas is a spiny shrub that at worst punctures tires, and at best provides shade for cattle at water tanks, is for the south of France a beloved dooryard tree and the basis of exquisite perfumes. First cultivated for perfumery in Rome toward the end of the sixteenth century, *Acacia farnesiana* became industrially important in Provence starting around 1825. Known as *cassie ancienne* in French perfumery, the tree is extensively cultivated on the outskirts of Cannes and near the famous distilleries of Grasse. It blooms in southern France from September through November (as opposed to January–March in Texas). So desirable were the flowers that a new variety was created, *A. farnesiana* var. *cavenia* (sometimes recognized as a species), which blossoms both in spring (primarily) and fall; called *cassie romaine*, its flowers are not as highly prized as those of its progenitor. Cassie extracts are difficult and expensive to produce, since the flowers are hand-collected (amid the many thorns), the quality of the harvest can be easily ruined by violent storms or early frosts, and the delicate perfume is destroyed by steam distillation and must be carefully extracted by volatile solvents. Extrait de cassie, the end result, is one of the more costly scents in the industry and is rarely used in its pure state; instead, it is employed to extend and deepen the notes of other fragrances, especially those involving violet bouquets. Some of the more famous older perfumes using cassie include Buckingham Palace and Jockey Club, and recent additions are Bois de Isles and Roma. Outside France, Algeria, Egypt, Syria, and Lebanon have cultivated huisache for cassie extracts.

The story of huisache use does not end with its aromatic flowers. The wood, bark, and seedpods have all been utilized.

Like mesquite, a member of the same subfamily as *Acacia*, huisache has a heavy, durable, and close-grained wood, which makes it a good choice for posts, plows, hand tools, pegs, and various woodenware articles. The rose-colored wood is reported to be excellent for cabinetry, though it is not likely available in very large widths, because the trunks rarely exceed a foot in diameter. Like mesquite, huisache wood and root wood make an excellent fuel; unlike mesquite, huisache is not good for grilling or barbecuing because it is said to impart a slightly unpleasant taste to food. Immature huisache pods contain 23% tannin, a glucoside of ellagic acid. Mixed with various iron ores and salts, the pods, as well as the bark and fruit pulp, are used for tanning and dyeing leather (especially in India) and for making inks. In addition, the pods yield a gummy material that can be used to mend pottery, and the trunk sap is considered by some to be superior to gum arabic, at least in the arts, if not in the food industry (Duke 1981). Gum arabic, a colorless, tasteless substance and an essential ingredient in soft drinks, beauty products, and pharmaceuticals, is harvested from the branches of *Acacia senegal*, primarily from Sudan, Chad, and Senegal. Attempts to introduce *A. senegal* to Texas did not yield a competitive product, and one wonders if any real attempt has been made to harvest *A. farnesiana* sap as a substitute.

Huisache has been cultivated around the world, in many areas for more than two hundred years, and the reported medicinal uses for the plant are simply too numerous to list here. Some of the more commonly reported uses in our area include: flowers, added to ointment, are rubbed on the forehead to treat headache; a tea from the flowers is imbibed for indigestion; and crushed leaves (sometimes dried) are used to dress wounds and treat skin abrasions and rashes. Kickapoo elders swore that a decoction made from huisache bark, used to treat influenza, was instrumental in preventing the decimation of their village during the 1918 flu pandemic (Latorre and Latorre 1977).

Landowners with stands of huisache may be interested to know that huisache flowers are valuable to beekeepers, and the leaves are a food source for livestock and wildlife. The flowers bloom very early, sometimes as early as December in south Texas, providing a source of pollen to the bee at a time of year when little else is available. Huisache is probably a better supply of pollen than of actual nectar; its cousins *Acacia berlandieri* (guajillo) and *A. greggii* (catclaw) are renowned for their nectar. Late freezes, more common on the northern edge of its distribution, can make huisache flowers unreliable. Young leaves and branchlets are browsed by domestic livestock and white-tailed deer.

Deer and javelina also eat the fruit, and many birds, including quail, feed on the seeds. As with many thorny shrubs, huisache makes a good cover and nesting site for birds.

The name *huisache*, commonly used in Mexico, derives from the Nahuatl word for the same tree (and other spiny trees), *huitzachin*. Weesatche, Texas, a town about 15 miles north of Goliad, is named for the tree, which is common in the area. Its unusual spelling, according to Texas journalist Frank X. Tolbert, is "a monument to the bold, independent phonetic way that Texans often spell their place names" (Roell 2005). The current National Champion huisache, which gains most of its points from its 160-inch girth, is located at the Atascosa County Jail in Jourdanton, Texas.

SOURCES: Alloway 2000; Bedichek 1950; Bray 1904; Clarke et al. 1989; Cox and Leslie 1999; Diggs et al. 1999; Duke 1981; Foster 1995; Groom 1992; Havard 1885; Jessee 1965; Lacey 2004; Latorre and Latorre 1977; Naves and Mazuyer 1947; Peattie 1953; Pellett 1976; Richardson 2002; Roell 2005; Schulz 1928; Seigler et al. 1986; Taylor et al. 1997; Vines 1984; Wasowski and Wasowski 1997; Williams 2004; Wills and Irwin 1961; Wrede 1997

Texas Madrone

Arbutus xalapensis Kunth

By all accounts, Texas madrone is one of the most beautiful trees in the state. Small to moderately sized, evergreen, with pleasingly crooked branches, dark green leaves, clusters of white flowers in the spring, attractive red fruits in the fall, and colorful bark that is a showstopper on any hike, it is a tree that is difficult not to like. When it sheds in the summer, the thin bark exhibits a kaleidoscope of colors. As the old bark peels away in papery layers, the new creamy-colored bark is revealed (hence "lady's leg"). This lovely white slowly modulates through a series of warm colors from orange, apricot, and peach to coral, rusty tan, and Indian red (hence "naked Indian"). Finally, red browns and chocolates appear before the process starts all over again.

For all its beauty, Texas madrone is rarely seen, at least by city folks. It is most common in the mountains of west Texas, such as the Chisos, the Guadalupe, and especially the Davis Mountains, so avid hikers are apt to be most familiar with it. Madrone is uncommon, and perhaps is becoming more so, in central Texas, where it is closer to urban areas, though some outstanding examples

ORIGIN OF SCIENTIFIC NAME
Arbutus is the Latin name for the strawberry tree, most likely applied to *A. unedo*, common throughout the Mediterranean. *Xalapensis* refers to the town of Xalapa (also Jalapa), capital city of the Mexican state of Veracruz, near where the type specimen was collected. Texas specimens were previously recognized as a separate species, *A. texana* Buckley, but recent research suggests that they are best understood as part of a broader concept of *xalapensis*. The common name still reflects the older view and is well ingrained in the literature.

OTHER COMMON NAMES
madroño, madroña, Texas arbutus, lady's leg, naked Indian

FAMILY
Ericaceae (Heath Family)

DESCRIPTION
Small, many-trunked, evergreen tree, 12–20' high (max. 45'), with glossy leaves and distinctive pinkish-red peeling bark; pinkish-white urn-shaped flowers in clusters, followed by small ($1/4$–$1/3$"), fleshy, orange-red fruit.

HABITAT AND DISTRIBUTION
In rocky, igneous, or (especially) limestone soils in wooded hills, canyons, and slopes of Trans-Pecos mountainous regions and hills of the Edwards Plateau; occasional in southern Panhandle; southeastern New Mexico, south through Mexico to Guatemala.

Madrone in fruit.

have been found in this region. In 1848 Viktor Bracht, a German businessman and explorer sent to Texas to represent the interests of German colonists, noticed a "fine specimen" of what was surely a madrone standing close to the road that leads from Austin to Fredericksburg (Bracht 1931). In 1969 the National Champion was located in this general area, northwest of Dripping Springs, but was surpassed in the 1980s by a specimen in the Chisos. As of 2006, the State Champion (with 171 points) is located in Uvalde County, but the National Champion is currently found in the Lincoln National Forest of New Mexico (only 26 feet high, but with a huge circumference of 175 inches and, hence, 214 points). New Mexicans must surely find sport in having the largest *Texas* madrone.

More vexing to Texas gardeners, nurserymen, and ranchers is the difficulty of propagating the plant and its susceptibility to animal disturbance. Although madrone seeds germinate easily, they can be rather difficult to grow beyond seedling stage. As seedlings they seem to require low light and good moisture, with simultaneous excellent drainage. Many suspect that Texas madrone depends on a symbiotic relationship with mycorrhizal fungi (as is the case with the Pacific madrone), but to date this has not been proven (Nokes 2001). Some have had success using juniper mulch and/or soil from the parent tree, but it seems that "growing Madrones from seed is kind of like 'witching' for water. People either can do it or they can't" (Cox and Leslie 1999). To make matters worse, the plants, with their tiny, fibrous roots, can be tricky to transplant, even if one is successful with the propagation, and transplanting from the wild is notoriously difficult. Once

The famous lady's legs of Texas madrone in the Chisos Mountains, Big Bend.

established, the young plants are readily foraged by deer (heavy damage has been reported from the Guadalupes), as well as by goats. Cattle will browse them lightly but often do more damage by trampling. Such difficulties raise concern for the long-term future of the tree. One hopes that good land stewardship and refined propagation techniques will help.

Primarily of ornamental interest, Texas madrone does have a few uses. The fruit, when fully ripe (difficult to acquire if birds are around), is said by the Kickapoo to be "sweet and savory like strawberries" (Latorre and Latorre 1977). This neatly echoes the English common name for the genus *Arbutus*, "strawberry tree" (Spanish: *madroño*), though the best-known species in Europe, *A. unedo*, is thought to have fruit that is rather bland and mawkish (*unedo* from Latin, *unum* + *edo*, "I eat just one"). So we are perhaps blessed with a better-tasting species. The fruit can be eaten fresh, dried, boiled, or steamed, and to quote a longtime Texas conservationist, it makes a "terrific tart jelly that's perfect with roast venison" (Bartlett 1995). The Mountain Pima of Chihuahua, Mexico, still eat the fruits, which are reportedly high in zinc.

Apart from the fruit, Texas madrone's wood, bark, and leaves have also provided miscellaneous uses. Madrone wood is heavy, hard, moderately strong, and close grained, but it is rather brittle and is not durable; it is easily worked and takes a fine finish but seasons poorly. It has been used historically for mine timbers, tools, handles, rollers, and stirrups, as well as for the occasional mathematical instrument.

Other historic wood uses include fuel and charcoal for gunpowder. The Kickapoo made deer calls from madrone. Given the deer's apparent fondness for the tree, one wonders if there is a psychological connection on the part of the Kickapoo hunter. The beautiful bark, presumably on account of its tannins, was used in the tanning industry at one time, and both leaves and bark have been employed as astringents and diuretics in Mexico. Madrone bark and roots have been utilized to make yellow, orange, and brown dyes, not surprising given the bark's colors (Hatfield 1954). All of these historic non-food uses were minor at best, and with the tree somewhat rare today, it is probably wise to leave them to the past.

The West Coast species *Arbutus menziesii*, which extends from Vancouver to lower California, is "as characteristic of the North Coast Ranges of California as the Redwood itself" (Peattie 1953) and has been called "the finest broad-leaved evergreen tree in its native land" (Henderson 1982). Texas should count itself lucky to have its close relative, at the northern tip of its range, grace our mountains and hills with its lovely limbs. We should do our best to preserve and promote this stunning native.

SOURCES: Bartlett 1995; Berry 1964; Bracht 1931; Burlage 1968; Cheatham and Johnston 1995; Cox and Leslie 1999; Haislet 1971; Hatfield 1954; Henderson 1982; Laferriere et al. 1991; Latorre and Latorre 1977; Loughmiller and Loughmiller 1996; Nokes 2001; Parks 1937; Peattie 1953; Simpson 1988; Vines 1984; Wasowski and Wasowski 1997; Whitenberg and Hardesty 1978; Wrede 1997

Pecan

Carya illinoinensis (Wangenh.) K. Koch

Like a seasoned, professional athlete in a room of earnest but average sportsmen, so stands the pecan in historic fame and economic importance among the species of the genus *Carya*. This genus comprises approximately sixteen species worldwide, of which eleven occur in eastern North America and eight are native to Texas. All are species of what is commonly called hickory, and all of our domestic species (save one) have *hickory* in their common name. All eight Texas species of hickory (save one) are difficult to distinguish. This one exception is the pecan, which stands literally and figuratively above the rest. The pecan is the largest, fastest-growing, best-known, most valuable, and one of the longest-lived of all the hickories. In fact, the pecan is probably the best-known native nut tree in the States, and it bears what most would agree is the best-tasting native nut. Its only possible competitor is the black walnut (same family, different genus). The pecan is one of a very few plants native to the United States that has turned into an important agricultural crop, and Texas is home to the most

ORIGIN OF SCIENTIFIC NAME
Carya is from the Greek *karya*, a nut-bearing tree. The name was variously applied in ancient times to walnut, chestnut, and hazel trees. *Illinoinensis* refers to the state of Illinois, at the northeastern edge of the pecan's native distribution, whence eighteenth-century traders brought the nuts to the Colonies, where they were called "Illinois nuts." An alternate spelling, *illinoensis*, has frequently appeared in botanical literature but is not the correct epithet according to the International Code of Botanical Nomenclature.

OTHER COMMON NAMES
nogal morado, nuez encarcelada

FAMILY
Juglandaceae (Walnut Family)

DESCRIPTION
Very large, deciduous tree well over 100' tall with broad and rounded crown and trunk to 4' in diameter; compound leaves with leaflets tapering and curved; nuts in clusters, individual nuts oblong, $3/4$" to 2" in length, with splitting husks.

HABITAT AND DISTRIBUTION
Prefers deep, rich, alluvial soils along streams and river bottoms in eastern two-thirds of state; south-central U.S., including the southern half of the Mississippi River Valley, north to Illinois and Indiana; extensive cultivation beyond these limits in southeastern and southwestern U.S.; scattered in Mexico.

Pecan clusters.

extensive native pecan groves in North America. Aptly designated the official state tree of Texas, the pecan has played a major role in our area from prehistoric times to the present, involving Native Americans, Spanish and French explorers, Anglo colonists, and African American slaves, and livelihoods ranging from hunter-gatherer to farmer, agronomist, entrepreneur, and astronaut. The pecan is one of only a handful of plants so thoroughly rooted in Texas history.

The delicious nut of the pecan tree receives the lion's share of the tree's fame. Pecan shells appear in prehistoric sites in some areas of the country dating back to 6750 BCE, and in Texas they have been unearthed in strata dating to roughly 600 years after that date. Burned rock middens of the second millennium BCE,

abundant in central Texas, are thought to be related to the processing of nut crops such as acorns, walnuts, and pecans. Despite often scant and scattered archaeological evidence, there is little doubt that early peoples took advantage of such a nutritious foodstuff. Pecans, like many nuts, are rich in fats, proteins, and minerals, are highly dependable (i.e., the trees are fixed in space and their fruit ripens at roughly the same time every year), and can be stored for leaner times of the year. Specifically, pecans are rich in linoleic fatty acids (14–38%), which are not readily available in the prehistoric diet. One hundred grams of pecan nut meat has a food energy value of 687 kcal; 9.5% is crude protein, 73.7% is fat, and 12.7% is carbohydrate (Hall 2000). Pecans are also low in sodium, have no cholesterol, and are a good source of calcium, iron, phosphorus, potassium, and magnesium.

Although fats have become so ubiquitous in the modern American diet as to cause alarm, pecan oils contain highly monounsaturated fats, which are now considered important to a healthy diet. In the North American pre-Columbian diet, fats were far scarcer. Before the introduction of European livestock such as cattle and hogs, which had been bred to be fatty, Native Americans relied for meat on such animals as bison, deer, and rabbit, which are comparatively lean. Nuts provided such a critical and easily obtained source of fat and protein that pecans actually influenced migration and settlement patterns of prehistoric people. That is what Cabeza de Vaca described in his account (ca. 1530) of the pilgrimages of south Texas Indians, who would travel more than 100 miles to harvest pecans along the rivers and would subsist on the nuts almost exclusively for two months. He also reported that the pecans saved him from starvation. His account is likely the first written record of the pecan, and it is one of the earliest historical sources for what is now the United States.

Many Texas Indian tribes consumed pecans in historic times, including the Bidai, Caddo, Coahuiltecan, Comanche, Kickapoo, Lipan Apache, and Tonkawa. One of the Coahuiltecan tribes southwest of San Antonio, the Payaya, are known to have stored large amounts of pecans (apparently unshelled) in underground pits, which allowed for pecan consumption for the greater part of each year. A Tonkawa preservation method involved pounding dried venison or bison meat with pecan meal in order to form pemmican, which was especially useful for traveling (or the warpath), when long-lasting, ready-made food was needed. Outside our state, the Choctaw, who lived between the Mississippi and Alabama rivers, are believed to have grown carefully selected pecans even before European contact.

Numerous Spanish explorers commented on the nuts in Texas and elsewhere. Roughly ten years after Cabeza de Vaca's pecan feast, Hernando de Soto stumbled onto pecans in eastern Arkansas, which his chronicler compared to walnuts, only with thinner shells. The Spanish words for pecan at that time were *nogal*, which in Spain referred to the tree of the common or English walnut (true hickories had become extinct in Europe in the Pleistocene), and *nuez* (plural *nueces*), which also designated walnut, though the word has since come to refer generically to many other nuts. America has several species of walnut, too, but we know from the abundance, size, and location of the trees described in Spanish sources that pecan was the tree in question. The Nueces River in Texas was named in 1689 by Alonso De León for its large growth of what were undoubtedly pecans.

The French role in Texas was admittedly small (a small doomed colony on the coast), but it was lasting in that it caused the Spanish to protect their territorial claims by colonizing Texas. Likewise, the French influence with the pecan was minor but enduring. The very name *pecan*, likely derived from an Algonquian word for a hard-shelled nut, was first recorded as *pacanes* or *pecanes* by early eighteenth-century French explorers of the lower Mississippi, an area rife with pecans. It was through the French influence in the region that the name became accepted. The other French legacy is the confection known as the praline, which was named for the French marshal César du Plessis-Praslin, who sugared almonds to make them more digestible. As early as 1762 the "New Orleans praline" was popular and soon became a regional delicacy. Eventually the candy, in various crunchy and chewy versions, spread through the pecan belt, where it became a staple in Tex-Mex (but not Mexican) cuisine.

The late eighteenth century found the pecan in the highest social circles on the East Coast. Traders and fur trappers brought the first pecan nuts from southern Illinois and Indiana, the extreme northeastern limit of the pecan's natural range, back across the Alleghenies to the Colonies, where they were known as Illinois nuts or Mississippi nuts. This accounts for the pecan's scientific epithet, *illinoinensis*. Thomas Jefferson planted pecans at Monticello as early as 1780 and gave them as a gift to George Washington, who planted them at Mount Vernon in 1786, where today they are the oldest living trees on the grounds.

The nineteenth century in Texas saw an increasing awareness of the value of the native nut. The Tonkawa used pecans to barter with early Texas settlers. Enterprising citizens of the early state transported whole wagonloads of the nuts to Houston, where they could be shipped to northern states. By 1857, 200,000 bushels were ex-ported annually, and after the Civil War, pecans in parts of Texas were considered five times more valuable than cotton. San Antonio, which, one mid-century traveler observed, had nothing to export except "pecan-nuts, and a little coarse wool" (Olmsted 1857), soon became the center of pecan activity in Texas, thanks largely to the efforts of one man. Gustave Antonio Duerler, a Swiss-born candy and cracker manufacturer in San Antonio, decided to stimulate the pecan market by shelling the nuts before sale. In June of 1882, having used "friendly Indians" to shell 50 barrels of nuts (Manaster 1994), he distributed the naked nut meats to cities back East where they were apparently very popular. Duerler soon invested in the earliest hand-driven cracking machines, which by 1914 he had modified into power-driven models. The shelling industry thrived in San Antonio because of an enormous supply of native pecans in the region (1.25 million pounds were harvested in the area as early as 1880) and the low cost of Mexican-American labor in the city.

Until almost the twentieth century, native (wild) pecans supplied the majority of the market, but improving the pecan crop through cultivars had already begun and would soon be the rage. The earliest successful pecan graft was made in 1846 and is credited to an African American slave gardener of Governor Telephore J. Roman at the Oak Alley Plantation in Saint James Parish, Louisiana. Antoine (because he was a slave, his last name was not even recorded) trunk-grafted sixteen trees and produced the variety known as Centennial. Hundreds of cultivars have been produced over the years in order to increase yield or nut size, or to emphasize other traits advantageous to agriculture. Much of pecan cultivation took place initially in the Deep South, east of the pecan's native range, often as a backup crop. Texas, with naturally extensive, dense groves of pecans in the central and eastern parts of the state, did not bother as much with cultivation until somewhat later. Edmond E. Risien, an English-born cabinetmaker, was pivotal in changing that picture in Texas. Having settled in San Saba in the 1870s, he developed a ring-budding technique of propagation, greatly increasing the supply of stock available on the market. He also set out to find the best pecan in his region, offering $5 for the best nut brought to his office. Risien purchased 320 acres surrounding the tree that bore the winning nut and planted an orchard with its seeds. Though untrained in horticulture, he used his instincts to breed pecans with maximum meat and minimum shell that thrived in the drier conditions to the west. From his one original tree, called "The Great San Saba Mother Tree," came the famous papershell varieties such as the San Saba Improved, Texas Prolific, No. 60, Squirrel's Delight, and Western Schley, now known simply as Western. Texas grows more Western pecan trees than any other variety, and the Western is second only to the Stuart among all improved varieties. San Saba hosted the first national pecan show in 1927 and still bills itself as the "Pecan Capital of the World."

Given such abundant historic and economic wealth in pecans, the 36th Texas Legislature named the pecan the Texas state tree in 1919. There are at least four famous, must-see pecan trees in our state: three for historical reasons, and one for its size. The first is a Choctaw pecan planted at the head of Governor Jim (James Stephen) Hogg's grave in 1969. Jim Hogg, the first native-born governor of the state, served from 1891 to 1895 and championed the rights of the common man. Before his death in 1906, he asked that, in lieu of a grave monument of stone, a pecan tree be placed at his head and a walnut at his feet. He wanted the nuts of these trees to "be given out among the plain people of Texas, so that they may plant them and make Texas a land of trees" (Manaster 1994). The nut growers who gathered in Austin to decide which trees to plant at Hogg's graveside ended up forming the Texas Nut Growers Association. When the trees bore fruit, the pecans and walnuts were distributed to schools and organizations throughout the state. The original trees, having subsequently died, were replaced in 1969, but clearly there is great sentimental and symbolic value here.

The second must-see pecan is the above-mentioned Great San Saba Mother Tree, located 9 miles northeast of San Saba. This is claimed to be the "most famous pecan tree in the world" (Fowler 1993) and the "source of more important varieties than any other pecan tree" (Haislet 1971). Another famous pecan is the Jumbo Hollis near Bend, Texas (also in San Saba County), which has the distinction of having produced the largest pecan nuts in the world, weighing in at 33 pecans to the pound (70–80 per pound is considered normal). This tree was once cited in Ripley's "Believe It or Not" column. Finally, our State Champion Pecan, once the national champ, is located just north of Weatherford in Parker County. Towering over 90 feet tall, it has a 117-foot spread and a 258-inch girth.

For many decades in the twentieth century, Texas produced more pecans than any other state. Recently Georgia has been the leader, or at least a competitor, in pecan production, but Texas leads all states in pecan consumption. Texas still produces the vast majority of seedling nuts (those from native, noncultivar trees). Recently, a new preference for native pecans has appeared, even in agricultural circles, over our papershell hybrids. Although native nuts are smaller, they are considered tastier, and native trees tend to be healthier and longer lived, with fewer problems. With only about one-eighth of the state's 800,000 acres of native trees under some sort of management, Texas still has a largely untapped resource at its disposal. The pecan grows wild in at least 150 of our 254 counties.

The edible pecan nut practically eclipses all other uses of *Carya illinoinensis*, but other parts of the tree have minor applications. Pecan wood is hard but not strong and is deemed less valuable than other hickories. Historically used for shingles, it has more recently been applied in flooring, veneering, wall paneling, and some furniture. Baseball bats, hammer handles, and farm implements are made from the wood. Both the Bidai and Kickapoo Indians used pecan for bowls, dippers, and ladles. Pecan shells, ground into powder, provide filler for plastics and veneered

wood. Ground pecan shells are also utilized in making metal polish, nonskid paint, dynamite, and jet engine cleaners. The green hulls that cover the pecans yield a strong brown-black dye, especially good for dyeing hair. Native tribes, such as the Comanche, Kiowa, and Kickapoo, have variously employed pecan leaves and bark as a tea, medicinal astringent, and antifungal to treat ringworm. The Kickapoo used the dried roots of pecan for smoking their buckskins, and the Tarahumara of Mexico toss bundles of crushed pecan leaves into rivers to stupefy fish.

The pecan's fame reaches astronomical proportions, literally. The pecan nut has the distinction of being the first fresh snack food to be used in outer space. Seeking an alternative to freeze-dried meals for the *Apollo 13* and *14* missions, NASA needed a tasty, high-energy food that could withstand both extremely hot and subfreezing temperatures. NASA's stringent requirements eliminated most fruits, but the pecan, low in moisture and calorie-packed, won out (Manaster 1994). The pecan well deserves its fame in Texas. From prehistoric foodstuff to modern cultivars, from Cabeza de Vaca to NASA, it is unlikely that any other native Texan plant has such an extensive, unbroken, and thoroughly recorded history of use in our state.

SOURCES: Bolton 1908; Bracht 1931; Burlage 1968; Cabeza de Vaca 1993; Fowler 1993; Garrett 2002; Haislet 1971; Hall 2000; Hester 1980; Hester et al. 1989; Latorre and Latorre 1977; Lewis 1915; Manaster 1994; Newcomb 1961; Newkumet and Meredith 1988; Olmsted 1857; Peattie 1966; Pennington 1958; Roemer 1935; Simpson 1988; Sjoberg 1951, 1953; Tull 1999; Vines 1984

Hackberry

Celtis laevigata Willd.

Celtis reticulata Torr.

For the most part, hackberry is a tree that no one notices. Lacking showy flowers, striking form, or fall color, it is rarely included in landscaping plans, and to most city folk, it is an unremarkable denizen of alleyways and fencerows. At its worst, hackberry is ragged in appearance with crooked branches and warty trunks. Being short lived (ca. 30 years) and prone to twig dieback, broken limbs, root fungus, wood borers, and leaf galls, hackberry is always, in the words of one of Texas' foremost gardeners, "turning brown, dying, or falling apart" (Garrett 2002). These bleak facts, plus the tree's habit of reseeding itself everywhere, have understandably led many people to consider it a weed.

The flipside of a weed is a tough and dependable survivor. Fast growing, indifferent to soil type, and extremely drought tolerant, hackberry is a good candidate for windbreaks and fencerows or any barren area where

ORIGIN OF SCIENTIFIC NAME

The word *celthis* appears in Pliny as a name for a "lotus tree" in northern Africa (*Celtis australis*), which had clusters of bean-sized, saffron-colored fruits that were sweet in taste. Though certainly not a lotus in the modern sense, the genus (formalized by Linnaeus) does vaguely echo the ancient description. *Laevigata* refers to the smooth or polished appearance of the leaves. *Reticulata*, the adjectival form of *reticulum*, Latin for "little net," refers to the netlike, slightly protruding veins on the underside of the leaves.

OTHER COMMON NAMES

For *Celtis laevigata*: sugar hackberry, sugarberry, southern hackberry, palo blanco. For *Celtis reticulata*: net-leaf hackberry, western hackberry, acibuche, palo blanco

FAMILY

Ulmaceae (Elm Family)

DESCRIPTION

Celtis laevigata: Medium-sized tree to 60' (max. 80') with rounded crown, spreading branches, and gray, often extremely warty, bark. *Celtis reticulata*: Small tree to 30', often a large shrub, with open crown and ascending branches.

HABITAT AND DISTRIBUTION

Celtis laevigata: Widespread across the state in almost any soil type; often solitary in vacant lots, along fencerows and streams; southeastern U.S. as far north as Indiana; northeastern Mexico. *Celtis reticulata*: Rolling and High Plains and Trans-Pecos with disjunct populations in east Texas, generally in limestone soils; southwestern U.S.

NOTE

Celtis reticulata, whose leaves are net-veined beneath and rough to the touch on top, is sometimes treated as a variety of *C. laevigata*. Intermediates exist, and the genus is in need of taxonomic revision. For our purposes here, both can be treated together.

shade is required and nothing else will grow. At its best, given deep alluvial soil and plenty of water, it can make a fairly attractive tree; it was once planted for quick shade along streets and in city parks. An early author proclaims that *Celtis* (as a genus) is Texas' "commonest shade tree" (Lewis 1915).

Hackberry wood is mainly sapwood—heavy, somewhat soft, coarse-grained, and weak. Never utilized extensively for lumber, it has been used primarily for fuel and to some extent for fencing, flooring, crating, and sporting goods. Historically, some furniture was made from the wood, since it could take a good polish. Noah Smithwick, pioneer and memoirist, mentioned that the mid-nineteenth-century Mormon settlement near Marble Falls (Burnet County) manufactured chairs, tables, and bedsteads from hackberry wood, which "being so white, required a good deal of washing to preserve its purity" (Smithwick 1983). Indeed, the light-colored sapwood accounts for the Spanish name *palo blanco* ("white wood"). We also know through the riveting memoir of Frank Buckelew, who in 1866 was captured by the Lipan Apache near Utopia at the age of fourteen, that this tribe used hackberry wood for their saddles (Dennis and Dennis 1925), a use which is still reported among the Kickapoo. The Caddo also employed hackberry twigs in their basketry.

The hackberry's real treasure lies in its somewhat inconspicuous and subtly sweet fruit, hence the name *sugarberry*. The smooth round drupes (orange, dull red, or reddish black) are really little more

than a hard pit surrounded by a very thin layer of sweet skin, yet they are an important food source for many animals, especially birds. Persisting long after the leaves fall, hackberry fruits provide a critical winter food for a panoply of resident and migrant birds, including bluebirds, cardinals, cedar waxwings, doves, flycatchers, jays, mockingbirds, orioles, robins, sapsuckers, sparrows, thrashers, thrushes, titmice, turkeys, vireos, warblers, and woodpeckers. White-tailed deer, raccoons, and other small animals avail themselves of the fruit as well. Apart from the fruit, hackberry trees also provide larval food for a number of butterflies, including the question mark, mourning cloak, pale emperor, snout, and hackberry butterflies.

The tiny stony fruit has a storied human connection as well. Sugarberry pollen has been isolated in human coprolites dating to 500 BCE, and seeds have been found in archaeological digs that may be considerably older. In fact, if the controversial Lewisville site in southern Denton County dates to 10,000 BCE, then the many hackberry seeds found there could represent some of the oldest plant remains utilized by humans in North America (Banks 2004). In historical times the Kiowa frequently ground the prized berries into a paste, which was molded on a stick and baked on an open fire. The Comanche added fat to the paste before cooking. A Comanche tale of sharing, giving, and receiving revolves around these roasted sugarberry balls (Canonge 1958). Recently, a simple recipe for sugarberry syrup has emerged (Tull 1999), and an expert on desert survival suggests grinding the fruit

The frequently unnoticed fruits of the hackberry.

with water and baking the paste on hot stones, like crackers (Alloway 2000).

A few minor uses are worthy of note. The shallow, spreading roots of hackberries have been used for cordage and for making a yellow dye; the bark has been used in tanning. Texas folk tradition holds that hackberry wood makes a good toothbrush. I find this personally satisfying since one of my first remembrances of an ethnobotanical connection came (at the age of eight) from a bus driver who, constantly chewing on a hackberry stick, extolled the virtues of what others, he maintained, considered a weed tree.

On the vast plains of north Texas, the landmark for what is now Plainview (Hale County) was once twin groves of hackberries. The town almost chose *Hack-berry Grove* as its official name but decided to emphasize the vast treeless plain instead. Nonetheless, three small towns and more than a dozen creeks in Texas have been named for the hackberry. Weed or not, this tough and nurturing tree has made some inroads into the common psyche and deserves at least a second look.

SOURCES: Alexander 1970; Alloway 2000; Banks 2004; Bray 1904; Bryant 1974; Canonge 1958; Carlson and Jones 1939; Cox and Leslie 1999; Damude and Bender 1999; Dennis and Dennis 1925; Fletcher 1928; Garrett 2002; Haislet 1971; Harrar and Harrar 1962; Latorre and Latorre 1977; La Vere 1998; Lewis 1915; Mattoon and Webster 1928; Simpson 1988; Smithwick 1983; Taylor et al. 1997; Tull 1999; Turner 1954; Vestal and Schultes 1939; Vines 1984; Wauer 1999

Flowering Dogwood

Cornus florida L.

Flowering dogwood is probably our most ornamental native deciduous tree because it offers something aesthetic for each season. In spring its showy masses of white flower bracts are so stunning that they are, like bluebonnets, the object of annual pilgrimages. The spreading and layered foliage is appealing in the summer months, and landscapers no doubt appreciate a flowering tree that does well in shade. The autumn brings dark red, wine-colored leaves and bright scarlet berries that remain at the ends of the branches into winter, long after the leaves have fallen. It is not surprising that flowering dogwood was brought into cultivation as early as 1731, and that George Washington planted wild specimens at Mount Vernon, as did Thomas Jefferson at Monticello. As if to show how intimately the tree and its blossoms are interconnected, the flowering dogwood is the state flower of North Carolina but the state tree of Missouri, and both state flower and state tree of Virginia. Despite flowering dogwood's well-deserved renown for aesthetic appeal, its abundant and diverse benefits to humans, wildlife, and forest actually merit equal attention. This beautiful tree is one of a hand-

ORIGIN OF SCIENTIFIC NAME

Cornus is the Latin word for at least two species of European dogwood, the cornelian cherry (*C. mas*) and the bloodtwig dogwood (*C. sanguinea*). It is also assumed that the word relates to *cornu* (horn) on account of the wood's hardness and the connection with cornel spears, renowned for their strength among both Greeks and Romans. *Florida* means rich in flowers or freely flowering.

OTHER COMMON NAMES

Virginia dogwood, Florida dogwood, arrowwood, boxwood, false box, white cornel

FAMILY

Cornaceae (Dogwood Family)

DESCRIPTION

Small deciduous tree to 30' tall (max. 40'), with somewhat flat and spreading crown and short, often leaning or crooked trunk, rarely exceeding 1' in diameter; tiny green-yellow flowers surrounded by 4 large (2 ½" long), white, notched bracts; clusters of red, shiny drupes, to ½" long.

HABITAT AND DISTRIBUTION

Rich, moist, well-drained soils of woods and streams in eastern third of state, where it is a shade-tolerant understory tree of pine forests; Southeast and Mid-Atlantic states to southern New England; southern Ontario and northeastern Mexico.

ful of native plants in which practically every part affords rich discussion.

Take the quality of its wood, which is all but forgotten today. At first glance the wood of *Cornus florida* is inimical to use as lumber. It is difficult (especially nowadays) to obtain in large, straight pieces; it is hard to cut and shape; it seasons poorly and is prone to shrinkage; it does not glue easily; and it is not resistant to decay. But this wood has an unusual set of properties not often found together. It is heavy (64 pounds per cubic foot when green), strong, but not stiff. Although it is very hard, it also has an extremely high resistance to sudden shock; that is, it resists cracking. Even after repeated whacks, the wood will not split, mushroom out, or broom. Instead, the wood, being very fine textured, just smooths out, as if polished. Walnut is said to wear even smoother, but it is rather weak. Hickory is stronger, but becomes rough with use. Dogwood strikes the perfect balance and so was used for specific items that had to take repeated hard knocks without splitting or chipping, such as golf-club heads, mallets, mauls,

chisel handles, turnpins, wedges, and shoe lasts. Dogwood was highly desired for any process in which a small wooden object had to keep its shape and take continual wear without diminishing in size, breaking, or splintering. Basically, the more dogwood is rubbed, the smoother and more satiny it becomes, hence, its use to make things that turn all the time or take continual wear, like bobbins, spool heads, pulleys, and knitting needles. Combining its resistance to shock and its ability to take wear are items such as yokes, hay forks, rakes, and sledge runners.

By far the most frequent industrial use of dogwood was in shuttles for the textile industry, which were more critical than they might seem, since their absence meant a lack of fabric and clothing. With the slow speed of hand weaving, shuttles could be made from almost any wood, but with mechanization, shuttles were shot back and forth across the taut warp threads at high speeds. The slightest tendency of the shuttle wood to roughen would render it useless. Before 1880, Turkish boxwood (*Buxus sempervirens*) was

The stunning floral bracts of dogwood.

the shuttle wood of choice, but a sudden craze for roller-skating, of all things, placed such heavy demands on boxwood that dogwood (along with persimmon) were found to be excellent substitutes. Of course, dogwood, which acquired the name *American boxwood*, began to feel the pressure, too. Approximately four million dogwood shuttle blocks were produced annually in the mid-1920s. Since it took about a cord of dogwood to produce 400 shuttle blocks (an amount that supplied 100 looms on full-time production for one year), 10,000 cords were needed in a year. The total stand of commercially available dogwood in the States in 1926 was 231,000 cords, which meant the country had enough trees for only 23 years, and that was not counting dogwood timber cut for uses other than shuttle blocks (Cuno 1926). By the time World War II came along, Appalachian sources of dogwood were markedly reduced. With increased production of textiles for war use, the demand for dogwood shuttles increased, and the U.S. Department of Agriculture encouraged woodland farmers to check their timber for any suitable trees. Since the war, plastic shuttles have rapidly replaced wooden shuttles, relieving the pressure on dogwood timber but simultaneously leaving its merits in obscurity.

Native Americans who lived within dogwood's distribution were well aware of the wood's properties. The Lipan Apache, for instance, preferred dogwood for fire drills, since the wood could withstand the wear of the hard and fast rotations. The Caddo, who among Texas tribes lived most consistently within the range of *Cornus florida*, had more varied uses for

the wood, such as for basketry and bed construction. By far the predominant use of dogwood among Indians in our area was for making arrows. In addition to the Caddo, the Apache, Comanche, Wichita, Kiowa, and Tonkawa all preferred dogwood for these weapons, doubtless for the same reasons: it is a hard, shock-resistant wood that holds up under repeated use. The Wichita even had allusions to dogwood arrows in their mythology. It is likely that dogwood is here understood to include other species, such as *C. drummondii* (rough-leaf dogwood), which has a wider distribution in Texas than *C. florida*, extending across the eastern half of the state. Many dogwood species share similar wood affinities.

Medicinally, dogwood bark offered treatments in historic times. The Caddo and many Appalachian tribes used the inner bark of root and smaller branches, dried and powdered, as a tonic, stimulant, antiseptic, and astringent. The Cherokee chewed the bark as an analgesic for headaches, and the Alabama boiled the inner bark in water to treat dysentery. Cornin or cornic acid is the active ingredient in the bark. Dogwood bark acquired some renown as a substitute for Peruvian bark (the source of quinine) as early as 1728 in Virginia and was especially valuable in the Confederacy during the naval blockades of the Civil War. Malarial fevers and chills were a major problem in southern lowlands, and even though some believed dogwood to be less effective, it was the best treatment available given the circumstances. Many thought that fevers might be avoided by chewing on dogwood twigs. Dogwood was removed from the *U.S. Pharmaco-poeia* around the turn of the twentieth century, having been judged a "feeble, astringent bitter" (Bush 1973).

Roots and root bark of both flowering and rough-leaf dogwood, according to several sources, are said to yield a red dye, but these sources are vague on specifics, sometimes attributing the use to Native Americans (without mention of tribe), sometimes not. A well-known horticul-turist, L. H. Bailey, reported that when the scarlet dye of the root bark was mixed with sulfate or iron, a good black ink could be obtained (Bush 1973). A Texas native dye expert has managed to obtain a rusty brown dye from roots, bark, and prunings, and a bright yellow from leaves and twigs (Tull 1999).

Dogwood twigs and bark once offered Native Americans and pioneers a re-spected supply for twig toothbrushes and a source of dentifrice. Peeled twigs were chewed on until frayed, which provided a brush of sorts. The sap was thought to inhibit dental problems and harden the gums. This is also recorded among Afri-can Americans in Virginia, who substitut-ed dogwood for a West Indian shrub used for the same purpose. Pioneers also made occasional use of powdered dogwood bark as a toothpaste.

Flowering dogwood is beneficial to native wildlife and is recommended as a wildlife attractor. The red fruits, which are high in fat (15–35%) and calcium (1.1%), are eaten by at least 42 species of birds, half of which (especially woodpeckers and thrushes) make heavy use of the fruit; sev-eral, such as the wild turkey, treat the fruit as a preferred food. At least 12 species of

mammals, including deer, bears, raccoons, foxes, and squirrels, consume the fruit or browse the wood, twigs, and foliage. Dogwood foliage is also high in fat (val-ues range from 2% to 13%), and especially high in calcium (1.45–3.25%). The browse is particularly important to white-tailed deer on account of its nutritional value and widespread occurrence; it has been known to constitute from 13% to 20% of deer diets in April and May. Where cattle share woodland range with deer, they are also known to consume up to 50% of the available browse. Dogwood browse is rich in other minerals such as potassium, phos-phorus, magnesium, manganese, sulfur, iron, cobalt, fluorine, and aluminum; it accumulates 10 to 30 times more alumi-num than maple and oak.

When these mineral-rich leaves turn russet and fall to the ground, they return their riches to the forest floor. Flower-ing dogwood is considered "one of the best soil improvers among eastern North American trees" (Nesom 1998). Its leaf litter contains more than twice the cal-cium of most of its associates. It also de-composes more rapidly than that of most other species: three times faster than hick-ory; four times faster than yellow poplar, eastern red-cedar, and white ash; and ten times faster than sycamore and oak. This rapid decomposition ensures ready avail-ability of the minerals to the soil and thus to roots, and the calcium helps to mod-erate soil pH. The presence of dogwood trees indicated good farmland to pioneers, not only because they tended to grow in rich, well-drained soils but also because they especially enriched the soils beneath them. Flowering dogwood's generosity to wildlife and forest soils has earned it a place of respect in forestry circles.

The blooming of the dogwood signals springtime, of course, but it was used as a marker for other events. In the Deep South it signaled the beginning of the mating season for the wild turkey, and turkey hunters were frequently known to have dogwoods in their yards. In Texas in 1940, the Young Democrats of Travis County proclaimed April 13 (Thomas Jefferson's birthday) to be Dogwood Day. Hearkening somewhat sardonically to an alleged statement of the late Governor James Stephen Hogg ("The political dogs begin to bark loudest and longest about the time the dogwood begins to bloom"), Dogwood Day seems to have been the day by which political candidates were expected to announce their intentions to run for office (Adair and Hunt 1940). Today, the flowering of the dogwood for most people in our area means a time for annual revels and sight-seeing tours, such as the Dogwood Festival of Tyler County, which was first celebrated in 1940 (apparently a watershed year in Texas for the dogwood).

In an age of increasing global commerce and transport, many tree species are vulnerable to imported diseases. Flowering dogwood has recently been attacked by a serious disease, known as dogwood anthracnose. Trees affected by the fungus responsible, *Discula destructiva*, drop their leaves prematurely; cankers develop on the trunk that girdle and kill the tree within a year or two. First noted among Pacific dogwoods (*Cornus nuttallii*) in 1976, the fungus is believed to have been brought to North America on imported plants of Japanese flowering dogwood (*C. kousa*),

which is fairly resistant to the fungus. The disease then appeared in the early 1980s among flowering dogwood on the East Coast and gradually spread over the next decade into the Southeast. It would appear likely that the disease, with high mortality rates, will come our way, and some are predicting dire consequences. One hopes that the resistant horticultural strains that are being developed will keep this magnificent and magnanimous tree from ruin.

Several origins have been proposed for the name *dogwood*. One asserts that a decoction of bark from the English dogwood was once used to treat mangy dogs (Vines 1984). Another maintains that *dog* comes from *dag*, from the Old English *dagge*, a dagger or sharp pointed object. European butchers once used the wood of *Cornus sanguinea* for skewers, *skewerwood* being a common name for the tree. A recent researcher contends that neither of these claims has any real support. He maintains that the earlier word for *C. sanguinea* was *dogtree,* a bearer of dogberries, "worthless little fruits" fit only for dogs, and cites convincing evidence from Renaissance sources (Eyde 1987).

SOURCES: Adair and Hunt 1940; Bush 1973; Carlson and Jones 1939; Carr and Banas 2000; Cox and Leslie 1999; Cuno 1926; Dennis and Dennis 1925; Diggs et al. 1999; Dorsey 1904; Eyde 1987; Fernald 1950; Foreman and Mahoney 1849; Greene 1972; Grimé 1976, Hamby 2004; Harrar and Harrar 1962; Hatfield 1954; La Vere 1998; Mayhall 1962; McLemore 1990; Mitchell et al. 1988; Moerman 1998; Nesom 1998; Newkumet and Meredith 1988; Peattie 1966; Schulz 1928; Silverthorne 1996; Sjoberg 1953; Tull 1999; USDA 1942; Vestal and Schultes 1939; Vines 1960, 1984

Texas Persimmon

Diospyros texana Scheele

The most noteworthy feature of Texas persimmon is its fruit, which, at least in the opinion of one author, is the "sweetest natural Texas fruit on the range" (Reiff 1984). This fruit, which at maturity is a small ball, 1 inch in diameter, purplish black in color, and tasting like a sweet prune, has fed man and beast for millennia. The seeds and fruit were the third most abundant plant remains found in an ancient cooking pit in Val Verde County dating to approximately 7000 BCE. Both the coastal Karankawa Indians and the Comanche of the Plains consumed the fruit and that of its cousin, the common persimmon, which grows more to the east. Spanish conquistadores, calling them "nísperos," compared them to medlars in Spain. The famed early nineteenth-century botanical explorer Jean Louis Berlandier mentions that the chapote was "greatly esteemed" along the Frio River south of San Antonio (Berlandier 1980), and the mid-nineteenth-century explorer Viktor Bracht says a tasty preserve was made from it (Bracht 1931). Like many fruits, the Texas persimmon has been, and continues to be, made into jellies, jams, puddings, pies, and quick breads. Not surprisingly, a varietal wine can be coaxed from it. Please note that we are here discussing the fruit when ripe (somewhere between

ORIGIN OF SCIENTIFIC NAME

The genus name *Diospyros* translates loosely as "fruit of the gods" (from the Greek *Dios* "of Zeus" or "of Jove," and *pyros* "grain"), referring to the sweet edible fruits of the type species *D. lotus*.

OTHER COMMON NAMES

Mexican persimmon, black persimmon, chapote, chapote prieto

FAMILY

Ebenaceae (Ebony or Persimmon Family)

DESCRIPTION

Shrub or small tree usually under 10' (occasionally reaching 40'), intricately branched with small leaves, seemingly evergreen in its most southern range and generally deciduous in the northern (i.e., north of San Antonio).

HABITAT AND DISTRIBUTION

In ravines and canyons in central, south, and west Texas, forming heavy thickets on the Edwards Plateau and Rio Grande plains; Nuevo Leon, Coahuila, and Tamaulipas, Mexico.

The delicious black fruits of our native Texas persimmon.

July and November). The unripe fruit, on account of its tannins, is quite astringent and will leave a horrible, puckering taste in the mouth.

A host of native animals depend on the fruit: deer, coyote, common gray fox, red fox, ringtail, raccoon, javelina, turkeys, and other birds. In the case of the raccoon, ringtail, red fox, and common gray fox, the Texas persimmon composes a large portion of their fall diet. These animals, in turn, become dispersal agents for the tree through the considerable number of unchewed and unharmed seeds in their feces. The fragrant early blooms of the tree (as early as February), each with abundant nectar, make the persimmon an excellent early honey plant.

The fruit is also famous for its ability to stain things; indeed, one of the troubling things about eating the fruit is the seemingly indelible black stain left on one's fingers. The stain is put to good use as a dye, and Mexican and Texan Hispanics alike dyed leather, sheep- and goatskins, and even their hair with the fruit or, occasionally, with the seeds. Colors vary from tan to reddish brown. There is even a report of the fruit's use as an ink.

Leaving the fruit aside, another useful product of *Diospyros texana* is its wood. The small tree belongs to the ebony family, and the renowned strong, black wood used in piano keys and cabinetry comes from a tropical relative in the same genus, *D. ebenum*. It should come as no surprise to learn that our Texas ebony, so to speak, provides a smooth, hard, even-grained wood, which takes a high polish and is suitable for turning, tool handles, engrav-

ing blocks, curtain rings, furniture, penholders, picture frames, walking canes, and even fiddle keys.

Texas persimmon makes a lovely ornamental and should be used more extensively in native gardens. It has lustrous foliage, sweet-smelling flowers, dark fruits, and especially gorgeous bark. The bark is thin, reddish gray, and on mature trees (ca. 10 years) peels off in strips, exposing a white or gray trunk beneath. Landscape gardeners compare the beauty of its trunk to that of the Texas madrone and the nonnative crepe myrtle. The plant is easily grown from seed, grows well in most well-drained soils, and, once established, is drought tolerant. It can be left as a bush or pruned into a more treelike shape. It is the larval host plant for gray hairstreak and Henry's elfin butterflies. The late Benny Simpson, Texas tree expert, justifiably called the Texas persimmon "one of Texas' premier small trees" (Simpson 1988).

The current National Champion Texas persimmon, at 26 feet high, is in Uvalde County. The north entrance to Big Bend National Park, Persimmon Gap, is so named because of an abundance of the shrub in the area.

SOURCES: Berlandier 1980; Bracht 1931; Carlson and Jones 1939; Chávez-Ramírez and Slack 1993; Damude and Bender 1999; Dobie 1928; Fletcher 1928; Foster 1995; Gatschet 1891; González 1998; Havard 1885; Hester 1980; Mielke 1993; Parks 1937; Powell 1988; Reiff 1984; Simpson 1988; Spongberg 1977; Standley 1920–1926; Tull 1999; Warnock 1970; Wasowski and Wasowski 1997; Wauer 1980; Wrede 1997

Common Persimmon

Diospyros virginiana L.

There are only two species of *Diospyros* in the United States, and Texas is the only state where both are native. The smaller, black-fruited Texas persimmon inhabits the southern half of the state and northern Mexico, and the much larger, orange-fruited common persimmon grows in the eastern half, which is the southwestern corner of its distribution. For hundreds of years, the common persimmon was prized for its fruit. Even through the first half of the twentieth century, the tree was "too well known to need comment" (Parks 1937), and its fruit was popular, being consumed "in great quantities in the southern states," according to the American tree expert of the time (Sargent 1947). Today it is probably safe to say that few of us are familiar with this fruit or have any idea what to do with it. The hegemony of commercial crops tends to homogenize demand and to obscure regional foodstuffs, no matter how tasty. The persimmon as fruit has more or less become a quaint relic of a grandparent's pantry. As a tree, it is known as a well-shaped ornamental with perfumed flowers and lustrous leaves or, with its deep and suckering roots, as a means to control erosion.

Part of the reason for the failure of the persimmon to

ORIGIN OF SCIENTIFIC NAME

For the generic name, see *Diospyros texana*. *Virginiana* refers to the colony of Virginia, so named in honor of Elizabeth I, the Virgin Queen.

OTHER COMMON NAMES

eastern persimmon, persimmon tree, simmon, possumwood, date plum, Jove's fruit, winter plum, American ebony

FAMILY

Ebenaceae (Ebony or Persimmon Family)

DESCRIPTION

Small to medium, slow-growing, deciduous tree to 50' high with trunk 1' in diameter (historically to twice these dimensions); crooked, drooping branches forming round-topped crown; reddish-orange fruit 2" in diameter, remaining on tree after leaf fall.

HABITAT AND DISTRIBUTION

Tolerates a diversity of soils and habitats, growing in acid to neutral sand, sandy loam, and heavy alkaline clay, in shaded forests and river bottoms, open woodlands, dry uplands, prairies, and clearings. Mainly eastern half of Texas; southeastern two-thirds of U.S. (minus southern Florida), northwest to Iowa, east to Connecticut.

The not-quite-ripe fruits of the common persimmon.

attract attention lies in the difficulty of discerning when the fruit is fully ripe, because until that moment, its taste offers one of the most sour and puckering sensations known among our native plants. Captain John Smith, one of the founders of Jamestown, Virginia, having tasted the fruit, said, "If it be not ripe, it will draw a man's mouth awrie with much torment" (Peattie 1966). Everyone agrees that the fruit is unripe if green, but the orange-red colors do not necessarily guarantee full ripeness. When fully ripe, persimmon fruit is amazingly sweet and luscious. Two schools of opinion, both equally adamant, have formed over the magic moment of maturity. The first, with roots in the mid-nineteenth century, states that one must wait to harvest the fruit when yellow-brown, after the first or second sharp freeze, when the astringent tannins have dissipated. The late Benny Simpson, beloved Texas tree expert, noted that the botanist Donovan Correll would leave the fruits overnight in the ice-tray compartment of his refrigerator to reproduce this effect artificially (Simpson 1988). The other school maintains that the only-after-frost theory is a myth, contending that it is merely a coincidence that the late maturity date of the fruits, especially those from certain trees in the Deep South, happens to occur after freezes. In the end, full ripeness is highly variable. Experts have noted that adjacent trees, growing under the same conditions, can reach maturity at different times, with or without frost. Some advise to wait until the skin is wrinkled and the fruit very mushy.

Historically, persimmon fruits were

enjoyed throughout their range. Native American tribes of the southern Appalachians, such as the Cherokee, and our own Caddo of east Texas, consumed the fruit raw. In order to make the fruit last beyond its season, native peoples employed a variety of preservation techniques. One of the most common was simply to dry the fruit like a prune. Indeed, the word *persimmon* comes from the Algonquian (Delaware) word *pasimenan*, which refers to artificially dried fruits, and the common name *date plum* follows suit. Hernando de Soto encountered dried persimmons in 1539 in his bellicose explorations of the South. Another technique, practiced by the Comanche, was to beat the ripe fruits to a pulp, removing seeds and skins, and then allow the substance to dry to a paste or cake, which could later be rehydrated. Louisiana natives followed a very similar method to make foot-long rectangles, like flatbread, one finger thick, that were oven- or sun-dried. These they traded extensively with the French. Native Americans also mixed persimmon pulp with various grains, such as corn and other meal, to make something closer to what moderns would call a bread. De Soto was, in fact, offered persimmon loaves in the vicinity of Memphis. Colonists were preparing persimmon breads in the South in the nineteenth and twentieth centuries. By adding hops, corn, or wheat bran to fermenting fruits, they managed a kind of persimmon beer. Persimmon wines were also produced, as was a type of brandy. William Bollaert, who traveled through Texas in 1842–1844, mentioned a beer

produced from a fermented mixture of persimmon juice and sweet potato. Contemporary tastes will likely limit the fruit's use to jams, pies, sweet breads, or puddings (see Tull 1999 for recipes).

Persimmon wood once had a good reputation, albeit in a small circle. Very similar to dogwood, persimmon wood is dense, heavy, strong, close grained, smooth, even textured, and able to withstand shock without splitting. These qualities make the wood desirable for turnery and tool handles. Persimmon wood was used to make objects that had to stand up to repeated wear, such as mallets, gavels, billiard cues, shoe lasts, spinning wheels, and parquet flooring. The majority of persimmon wood went to make golf-club heads and shuttles in the textile industry, where it was a close second to dogwood.

Persimmon provided several other resources in the nineteenth century. The puckering qualities of the tannins in the unripe fruits are also found in the tree's inner bark. Both fruit and bark were used extensively in the latter part of the century as an astringent to treat fevers, sore throats, diarrhea, dysentery, and hemorrhages. Settlers likely picked up these uses from Native Americans. The Caddo, for instance, used the tree and root bark for sore throats and to wash and dress wounds. The Cherokee made a persimmon syrup for hemorrhoids and bloody stools. Civil War doctors of the South, always looking for a good substitute for hard-to-obtain drugs, recommended syrup made from unripe persimmon fruits boiled in sugar as an easily used preventive for dysentery in camps. Apart from medicinal uses, immature persimmons, mashed and boiled in water, provided the basis for an indelible ink and black dye during this time; the juice also served as a tanning agent for leather, said to be preferable to oak bark (Porcher 1869). The seeds, dried and roasted, were employed as a substitute for coffee, though recent attempts to recreate this have been disappointing (Tull 1999).

As one might expect of any native tree bearing tasty fruit, the persimmon is a favorite of wildlife and livestock. At least sixteen species of birds, notably bobwhites and wild turkeys, relish the fruit. Native mammals that consume persimmons include deer, foxes, raccoons, skunks, rabbits, squirrels, and especially opossums, which have a strong affinity for the fruit, at least according to folklore. The Caddo include in their oral tradition a story about an opossum in a persimmon tree who outsmarts the gullible coyote. In one of Audubon's well-known illustrations, North America's only marsupial is de-

picted in the branches of the persimmon, about to devour the fruit. Folk tradition maintains that "most 'possum hunts end at the foot of a 'simmon tree" (Peattie 1966), and the common name *possumwood* bears testimony to the connection. Livestock, such as horses, cattle, and especially hogs, are known to forage the fallen fruit. Some care should be taken in the amounts consumed. Persimmons are known to cause phytobezoars, rounded gastric concretions composed of vegetable skins, seeds, and fibers that lodge in the stomach or intestines, causing colic in horses and intestinal distress in humans.

SOURCES: Bracht 1931; Carlson and Jones 1939; Core 1967; Cox and Leslie 1999; Cuno 1926; Diggs et al. 1999; Dorsey 1905; Foreman and Mahoney 1849; Griffith 1954; Halls 1990; Hollon and Butler 1956; Kellam et al. 2000; Lewis 1915; Mattoon and Webster 1928; Moerman 1998; Newkumet and Meredith 1988; Parks 1937; Peattie 1966; Porcher 1869; Sargent 1947; Simpson 1988; Tull 1999; Vines 1984; Zarling and Thompson, 1984

Black Walnut

Juglans nigra L.

Texas Black Walnut

Juglans microcarpa Berland.

Despite the fame of its wood, or rather because of it, black walnut may be the most valuable tree you've never seen. At a distance it is easily confused with the ubiquitous pecan or even the weedy nonnative *Ailanthus* (tree of heaven), both of which have similar compound leaves. So it is easy to pass one by without recognizing it. In addition, the tree tends to grow sporadically in its range, rarely forming more than small groves, being well represented in one area but completely absent from an adjacent area of similar habitat. But mainly, it was the centuries of heavy cutting of mature specimens for timber that left the black walnut more talked about than actually seen. It has become one of the scarcest and most coveted of American native hardwoods.

ORIGIN OF SCIENTIFIC NAME

Juglans, the classical Latin name for *J. regia* (the common or English walnut), is a combination of *jovis*, "of Jupiter," and *glans*, "acorn" or "nut." *Nigra*, "black," refers to the dark brown heartwood of this species. *Microcarpa* is a straightforward Greek compound meaning "small fruit," referring to the particularly small nuts of this species.

OTHER COMMON NAMES

For *Juglans nigra*: eastern black walnut, American black walnut. For *J. microcarpa*: Texas walnut, little walnut, dwarf walnut, river walnut, nogal, nogalillo, namboca

FAMILY

Juglandaceae (Walnut Family)

DESCRIPTION

For *Juglans nigra*: Deciduous tree with rounded crown, stout branches, and straight trunk, historically reaching 100–150' in height, with trunk 4–6' in diameter (now rarely exceeding 80' and 3', respectively); smooth, round fruits, 1 1/2–2 1/2" in diameter. For *Juglans microcarpa*: Small deciduous tree or many-trunked shrub, historically to 50' tall (now rarely 30'); fruits 1/2–3/4" in diameter. Both species with compound leaves.

HABITAT AND DISTRIBUTION

Juglans nigra prefers deep, rich, alluvial soils with constant moisture in bottomlands and along streambeds in roughly the eastern half of the state; outside Texas in approximately eastern half of U.S.; southernmost Ontario. *Juglans microcarpa* is scattered along dry, rocky streams and gullies in central, south, and west Texas; southeastern New Mexico, western Oklahoma; also northern Mexico.

The somewhat elusive black walnuts.

Walnut, as most people know, makes an excellent wood for carpentry and furniture, and black walnut is one of the finest American woods for this purpose. Its wood, like that of many walnuts, is heavy, hard, strong, close grained, easily worked, and takes a high, satiny polish. It resists warping and checking, and it glues easily. Black walnut's real attraction lies in its dark, beautifully grained, purple-brown heartwood, which is unique among American commercial hardwoods. Like wild cherry wood, its only competitor for most-desired carpentry lumber, it becomes more beautiful with age. As a bonus, most pieces made from the wood are mildly but distinctively aromatic.

No wonder, then, that from the earliest moments of colonial America black walnut was coveted and commanded high prices. Black walnut wood had already been sent to England as early as 1610. The tree was introduced there by the middle of the seventeenth century and was in cultivation by 1686. Master craftsmen of the William and Mary and Queen Anne periods frequently relied on the wood for large pieces of furniture such as desks, bureaus, tables, cupboards, and chests. Smaller items included cradles, chairs, boxes, clock cases, and candlesticks. Among articles of ceremonial value were pulpits, altar rails, and coffins. The wood's strength and durability made for excellent waterwheels, tool handles, carriage hubs, and various ship parts. The Caddo of east Texas, still fairly populous in colonial times, recognized the black walnut for the same virtues. They made mortars and pestles from the wood, as well as hoes, which were cut from the trees during a special winter ceremony for crop prognostication.

Despite black walnut's esteem during this period, some colonial uses seem wasteful in hindsight. Since the timber resisted decay and was easily split, it was chosen extensively for the more pedestrian uses of fence posts and shingles. In the indiscriminate clearing of land for cultivation, much of the wood was squandered or simply burned for fuel. So abundant was the wood in the Colonies in the first half of the eighteenth century that the early Swedish botanist Pehr Kalm remarked, "Several times I visited places where black walnut was the only wood used in the fireplace" (Kalm 1942).

In the nineteenth and twentieth centuries, walnut wood grew in popularity as it became scarcer. The wood was in high demand at several points in the nineteenth century, notably in the so-called rage for walnut (1830–1860), in which furniture factories turned out machine-made Empire, Victorian, and Revival styles, "ruin[ing] many a fine piece of wood," in the words of one natural historian (Peattie 1966). Musical instruments, such as piano cases, and sewing machines were also manufactured from the wood. By the turn of the twentieth century, the supply of easily available, valuable timber had almost been exhausted. Nonetheless, World War I created a need for black walnut for airplane propellers, among other war items, and many walnut plantations were started in the United States and Canada in the decades between the

two world wars. The wood continued to be popular for office furniture, both solid and veneered, as well as for radio, television, and phonograph cabinets. Black walnut was also sought after as an interior finish for cafes and public buildings. Despite tree farms, market demand often exceeded supply, and ruthless cutting eliminated the tree from certain localities. Still the most popular wood for furniture into the 1960s, black walnut became so valuable that the price for a single mature tree could exceed $20,000, more than the value of a house at the time. As veneering techniques improved to the point where wood could be shaved to $1/36$ of an inch, beautiful walnut grains and burls could decorate any piece of furniture, and fewer trees needed to be felled per unit of furniture. Black walnut trees were still equally valuable, however, and they were often rustled from private land. The taller specimens toward the end of the twentieth century were usually less than 80 feet tall, and the primary value of the lumber today is in veneering.

The use of black walnut wood for gunstocks requires separate discussion. The wood's ability to season in place, without shrinking or warping, its fine machining properties and absence of splintering, its strength without excessive weight, and especially its ability to withstand shock, such as recoil, all make black walnut the gunstock wood par excellence. The wood's uniform texture combined with a slight coarseness that renders it easy to grip is particularly conducive to this purpose. Black walnut lumber was already employed for gunstocks in the eighteenth century, but the pressing needs of the Civil War, and especially of the two world wars, placed heavy demands on the tree and increased its value. Even today, the more expensive shotguns and sporting rifles are still made from the wood.

Of all the nut trees native to the United States, black walnut has one of the best-tasting nuts, probably second only to pecan. The nut meats are high in protein and in the much-touted omega-3 fatty acids. Practically all Native Americans and colonists who lived in the tree's distribution consumed the nuts raw and stored them in various ways for future use. Since walnut oils can become rancid quickly, some pioneers, likely following indigenous habits, boiled the nuts before drying them and molding them into cakes. Others pickled the nuts (hull and all). The Mescalero Apache of our area kneaded walnuts into mescal (cooked *Agave* spp.), along with piñon seeds and the berries of juniper and fragrant sumac. It may seem strange to us today, but many eastern tribes prepared a sort of nut milk from walnut and various hickories. The kernels were removed, ground into flour, and mixed with water, or in a Creek version, pounded nuts were added to boiling water from which a thick, oily liquid was later strained, "sweet and rich as fresh cream," to be added to other foods (Havard 1895). Archaeologists have found black walnut seed and hull fragments in many sites across Texas dating back thousands of years. Walnuts of *Juglans microcarpa* were the single most abundant plant remains from a 9000-year-old hearth in the rockshelter known as Baker

Cave along the Devils River (Hester 1980).

Various parts of the black walnut tree yield excellent dark dyes. Naturally rich in tannins, the leaves and green hulls that cover the nuts produce the deepest shades of brown, which can be used to dye wool, cotton, leather, or even hair. The dyebath of hulls and leaves, usually boiled, can be left to steep indefinitely, and the dye becomes increasingly stronger until it approaches black. Even the fresh hulls by themselves will stain the hands (or sidewalks) for weeks. The Caddo used the leaves for a basket dye, the Apache made a black paint from the hulls, and the Kiowa boiled the roots to make a blue-black dye for their buffalo hides.

Medicinally, black walnut is known primarily as an astringent, fungicide, and vermifuge. Hispanic folk medicine employs the aromatic, bitter leaves in a tea to treat irritable bowel syndrome, colitis, and dysentery. Civil War soldiers applied the leaves and bark externally as a styptic to stop bleeding and used the green hulls to treat ringworm fungus. The Comanche, as well as African American folk healers, utilized juice from the leaves or the green hulls for ringworm. Given this antifungal track record, a current naturalist and tree expert recommends walnut tannins for the treatment of athlete's foot (Pasztor 2003). The Kiowa made a decoction of the root-bark "to kill worms" (Vestal and Schultes 1939), which finds a parallel among the black residents of Georgia's postbellum Piedmont who used the green hulls to kill "maggots," which probably in part referred to screwworms on livestock (Cadwallader and Wilson 1965).

Possibly related to its medicinal constituents, black walnut has a somewhat unusual ability known as allelopathy, "the inhibition of one plant by another via the release of chemicals into the environment" (Diggs et al. 1999). The tannic acid known as juglone washes from the black walnut's leaves during rains and is also believed to be emitted by the roots, creating a zone, sometimes 80 feet from the trunk, in which many plants simply will not grow. Affected plants include pine trees, apples, cherries, azaleas, rhododendrons, and crabapples, but especially members of the potato family, including tomatoes, peppers, tobacco, and potatoes. Even other black walnut seedlings will not flourish around their parent tree. Allelopathy may help keep certain forest competitors at bay and ensure that offspring grow only at a distance from the parent plant. Walnut's allelopathic powers have been noted from the time of Pliny (first century) onward, and today organic gardeners still avoid adding walnut leaves to their compost on account of them. Pioneers claimed that the fragrant leaves repelled ants and flies, and black walnut sawdust is sometimes effective in deterring fire ants. Horses have been known to suffer toxic reactions when walnut shavings or leaves are strewn in their stalls, and people occasionally report contact dermatitis from handling the leaves.

A few other items are worthy of mention in connection with this already storied tree. The Caddo manufactured a rope and cord from black walnut bark fiber, which they apparently used to bind the framework of their houses. Current industrial uses of the black walnut include the addition of the nut oil to soaps and paints and the grinding of nutshells as an abrasive to clean jet engines and to smooth precision gears. Ground walnut shell products are used as additives in oil drilling, as air-pressured propellants to strip paint, and as filter agents in smokestack scrubbers. As a native tree whose propagation should be encouraged, *Juglans nigra* is a larval plant for the spectacular luna moth, the even larger walnut moth, and the walnut sphinx moth, "known for its squeaking cries" (Wasowski and Wasowski 1997).

As is often the case with trees native to the eastern half of Texas, there is a smaller cousin, adapted to drier conditions, in the western half. *Juglans microcarpa*, the Texas black walnut, is common in mountain arroyos of west Texas, where it sometimes hybridizes with *J. major* (Arizona walnut); it mirrors the eastern *J. nigra* in many respects. It once boasted specimens reaching 50 feet, but most of those trees have been felled. Now it is rarely seen over 30 feet and often is common only at half or even a quarter of that height, sometimes considered a big shrub (hence the name *little walnut*). Texas black walnut also produces highly desirable, dark wood, though rarely in any width useful for lumber. It, too, was used for fence posts and fuel, and the Kickapoo made pipe stems, ladles, bowls, bows, gunstocks, and ax handles from the wood. Its tiny fruits, the smallest of all walnuts, are sweet and tasty but take much labor to obtain; only indigenous tribes, and native wildlife such as javelinas and rock squirrels, seem to bother. One naturalist recommends obtaining the nut meat by a flotation method: the nut is crushed and added to water, and the hulls then sink while most of the nut meat floats to the top (Alloway 2000). The hull juice also can be used to treat ringworm. Particular to this western cousin, however, are the use of its stock for the grafting and budding of English walnuts and the use of its crushed leaves and bark by the Tarahumara Indians of Mexico for fish stupefaction.

SOURCES: Alloway 2000; Basehart 1974; Betts 1954; Black and McGraw 1985; Bolton 1987; Bray 1904; Burlage 1968; Cadwallader and Wilson 1965; Carlson and Jones 1939; Castetter and Opler 1936; Cox and Leslie 1999; Diggs et al. 1999; Fletcher 1928; Garrett 2002; Griffith 1954; Hamby 2004; Harrar and Harrar 1962; Havard 1885, 1895; Hester 1980; Joutel 1998; Kalm 1942; La Vere 1998; Latorre and Latorre 1977; Lewis 1915; Mattoon and Webster 1928; Moore 1990; Newkumet and Meredith 1988; Pasztor 2003; Peattie 1953, 1966; Pennington 1958; Pinchot 1907; Sargent 1947; Simpson 1988; Tull 1999; Vestal and Schultes 1939; Vines 1984; Walker 1996; Wasowski and Wasowski 1997; Williams 1990; Wrede 1997

Eastern Red-Cedar

Juniperus virginiana L.

Ashe Juniper

Juniperus ashei J. Buchholz

Eastern red-cedar is common throughout the eastern half of our state, where it avoids the limestone soils of the western half, being one of the least alkali-tolerant of the drought-hardy trees and shrubs. In the nineteenth century early travelers reported dense "sombre forests of cedar" (Taylor 1936) in the La Grange area and bare trunks up to 60 feet high along the San Jacinto River near Galveston Bay. We should keep in mind that current stands of cedar, like all trees in highly disturbed areas, reflect neither their density within pristine forests nor typical measures of mature height and girth. Eastern red-cedar is an aggressive species that quickly invades disturbed sites. It tolerates many soil types but attains its

---

ORIGIN OF SCIENTIFIC NAME

Juniperus is the Latin name for the genus since classical times. *Virginiana* refers to the colony of Virginia, which in turn was named for Elizabeth I, the Virgin Queen. *Ashei* honors William Willard Ashe (1872–1932), a senior forest inspector for the U.S. Forest Service and a pioneer in forest research and economics. Ashe planted one of the first commercial stands of longleaf pine in North Carolina.

OTHER COMMON NAMES

For *Juniperus virginiana*: red juniper, red cedar, Virginia juniper, Carolina cedar, red savin, Baton Rouge, juniper bush, pencilwood, pencil cedar. For *J. ashei*: mountain cedar, rock cedar, post cedar, Mexican juniper, brake cedar, Texas cedar, enebro, tascate, taxate, cedro

FAMILY

Cupressaceae (Cypress Family)

DESCRIPTION

Evergreen trees or large shrubs. *Juniperus virginiana*: 20–50'; (up to 120';) with variable shape, but often with single main trunk and pyramidal in form; young specimens often resemble Christmas trees. *Juniperus ashei*: 10–15'; high (historically to 50';), many-stemmed when young and frequently bearing gray-white splotches, usually maturing to a single trunk.

HABITAT AND DISTRIBUTION

The most widely distributed conifer of tree size in this region, *Juniperus virginiana* inhabits the eastern half of the state and is found throughout the entire eastern U.S. (in every state east of the hundredth meridian). *Juniperus ashei* occurs in Texas almost exclusively on the limestone soils of the Edwards Plateau, where it inhabits hillsides, canyons, and ravines, often forming extensive thickets; smaller populations in the Arbuckle Mountains of Oklahoma, and in the Ozarks of Arkansas and Missouri; northern Mexico.

greatest size in deep alluvial soils receiving annual rainfall of 35 inches or greater. It also makes a great windbreak and is often planted on the Great Plains for its ability to withstand drought, heat, and cold. An authority on Texas gardening points out that the tree, "once established, can withstand more abuse than almost any other tree we grow" (Sperry 1991). Reportedly the species has been in cultivation since 1664, and many cultivars are now available through the nursery trade.

One of the dominant woody plants of the Edwards Plateau, Ashe juniper blankets many of the steeper hillsides and canyons of the Texas Hill Country, such that the shrub and the region are almost inseparable in the mind's eye. Groves on the eastern edge of the Edwards Plateau were noted for their growth in the nineteenth century, and the current National Champion Ashe juniper, at 41 feet high with a spread of 49 feet (as of 2007), is found in the same area in New Braunfels. Ashe juniper commonly has a gray-white fungus, possibly a lichen-forming fungus, growing in splotches on its branches (especially on younger specimens of 20–40 years old). This phenomenon has led some to believe the tree's name comes from the ashen color of the fungus instead of the forest researcher, Mr. Ashe.

Careful research has shown that eastern red-cedar does not hybridize with Ashe juniper even when it overlaps in distribution in the central part of the state. Eastern red-cedar will approach Ashe juniper in habit and appearance, especially when growing on thinner and more alkaline soils; conversely, mature individuals of Ashe juniper with unbranched trunks may occasionally resemble eastern red-cedar.

Among the Anglo settlers of Texas, *Juniperus* wood (a.k.a. cedar) was favored for housing construction in the mid-nineteenth century, even in east Texas towns that were surrounded by pines. Although log buildings were constructed in Texas out of almost every native timber tree, cedar was used preferentially wherever it was available. Many of the early houses of New Braunfels and Fredericksburg and the crude huts, or jacales, of San Antonio were constructed of cedar. The main reason for this preference lies in cedar wood's durability and fragrance. The wood of both species contains a high level of cedrol and related compounds; these aromatic oils naturally inhibit rot and repel insects, such as termites and moths.

Since eastern red-cedars are usually taller and straighter, and since the color combinations of their red heartwood and white sapwood are unique and striking, their wood was favored in the construction of houses, fences, furniture, closets, and hope chests. Given its softness, straight grain, and freedom from defects, the heartwood was preferred for lead pencils through the early part of the twentieth century, later replaced by incense cedar (*Calocedrus* sp.) of the western United States. Few now recall that Henry David Thoreau, the nature philosopher of Walden Pond, was involved in his family's cedar-pencil business, which collected its eastern red-cedars in the vicinity. Through Thoreau's research and improvements, his family's pencils were recognized as America's best.

Ashe juniper berries, technically cones.

Ashe junipers, usually shorter, more branched, and with higher levels of cedrol in their wood, lent themselves to slightly different purposes. Their wood made especially excellent fence posts, railroad ties, telegraph poles, house blocks, and pier materials. *Old-growth* Ashe junipers, however, can also attain tall heights (50 feet) and are generally single-trunked. So the many houses, barns, and smokehouses built by early settlers along the eastern edge of the Edwards Plateau, where the distributions of the two species of *Juniperus* approach each other, probably also contain Ashe juniper. Generally, Ashe juniper wood was utilized for ties and fence posts, since contact with the soil would not cause it to deteriorate, in many cases even after a century of use. In the late

nineteenth century, central Texas was one of the main exporters of this wood for these purposes throughout the western United States. Ashe juniper wood was also used historically for fuel (not surprising, given its abundance and the great heat generated by its charcoal). Even as late as the early twentieth century, communities such as Austin were largely dependent on this wood for warmth in winter months.

Cedarwood oil, obtained from both species (but especially Ashe juniper), is commercially important as a fragrance. It is used to scent soaps, room sprays, disinfectants, cosmetics, and especially perfumes, where it is a standard additive not only for its smell but also for its ability to prolong other fragrances. The Texas cedarwood oil industry began in Rock Springs in 1929. There are now several extracting factories in the Hill Country, and cedarwood oil is shipped all over the world.

Native Americans have used juniper wood, bark, and foliage for a variety of purposes over the millennia. The wood of a juniper species was identified from a 7000 BCE hearth in Baker Cave (Val Verde County). Interesting finds in the Shumla caves of the same area included limestone and reed pipes with juniper foliage (instead of tobacco) still within the bowls, as well as a pouch (made from prickly pear pads) stuffed with juniper foliage, which still retained its aromatic fragrance centuries later. The Kiowa and many other Plains Indians have used the smoke of various species of juniper for purification and cleansing, usually placing cedar twigs and leaves on coals to produce the smoke. The long bark of Ashe juniper was also incorporated into softer baskets, cradles, or mats, and it is reported that the Lipan Apache mixed the smaller twigs of cedar foliage with grasses to form a bedding material, on which hides were laid.

Many Indians revered the eastern red-cedar as a "tree of life," using its aromatic leaves, which contain camphor, in sweat lodges and in purification rites. In the Kiowa and Comanche peyote rituals, there was even a "cedar man" dedicated to keeping the cedar-twig incense burning. The Kiowa also carved "love flutes" from the red heartwood (Vestal and Schultes 1939). This tribe also employed small trees and branches, together with cottonwood,

to form a screen behind which the performers of the sacred sun dance prepared themselves. Both Kiowa and Comanche used the long straight poles of red-cedar for their tepees, since the wood was durable and unlikely to warp. The Wichita used the wood extensively for posts and poles in the construction of their circular grass lodges, which could reach 30 feet in diameter. The tall-statured Karankawa of the coast made long bows (reaching from foot to chin) of the red-cedar, which were beautifully crafted, and kept them well oiled and polished.

The tribes of the Caddoan Federation of east Texas echoed these uses by employing red-cedar as incense (their infirm were "smoked" with cedar) and as a building material. Intriguing, though, were the nuanced ways in which red-cedar was tied into their religious and ceremonial beliefs. The doors of their houses, for instance, faced only east and west and were preferentially constructed of cedar. According to Caddoan lore, if rites for the dead were not properly conducted, the deceased was in danger of rising up and running away, in which case only a fire of cedar and mulberry could prevent the dead person from becoming a monkeylike "lost timber spirit" (Dorsey 1905). Early Europeans also reported that Caddoan tribes started their fires with fire drills of cedar and mulberry.

There are reports that juniper berries (technically they are fleshy cones) were eaten by Native Americans, but it is likely that these were the fruits of western species of *Juniperus* and only rarely those of the two species under discussion, which are frequently bitter to the point of being unpalatable, if not inedible. That having been said, German immigrants used Ashe juniper berries very sparingly (one or two berries to a pot) to flavor sauerkraut, sauces, and stews, and current suggestions include crushing a few berries on salmon just before grilling. In larger numbers, the berries are claimed to be an excellent diuretic. The Kiowa chewed eastern red-cedar berries for canker sores in the mouth. The fruits of both species are also eagerly devoured by a large variety of native mammals and birds. The berry of the common juniper of Europe (*J. communis*) is one of the main flavoring ingredients of gin, which is reflected in the somewhat bitter taste of the alcohol.

Ashe juniper always seems to find itself at the center of an ecological debate. At many sites in its distribution, especially on the eastern edge of the Edwards Plateau, one can stand at an overlook and behold nothing but a vast sea of juniper occasionally interrupted by a grassy knoll or a ribbon of oak. The shrubby tree's prevalence has led to heated debates over its natural (usually understood as pre-European) distribution and density.

On one side are those who maintain that much of the Hill Country, especially its valleys and other areas with good topsoil, should be filled with native prairie grasses, which thrive in such soils. They point out that when the Europeans began to keep livestock within restricted, fenced areas, the practice quickly led to overgrazing. Grasses, with their many fibrous roots, thrive in deep topsoil where their ability to absorb moisture promotes rapid and dense growth, against which few trees and shrubs can compete. At the same time, grasses hold the soil in place; overgrazing reduces grasses, causing soil erosion. This in turn allows juniper seedlings (and those of other woody plants) to compete where once they could not. Ashe juniper, capable of flourishing in rocky limestone with little topsoil (some say it can germinate on bare rock), was able to gain a foothold. Contributing to this new situation was the cessation of fire (whether natural or man-made). The absence of fire allowed woody plants to mature more easily to adulthood, since fast-burning prairie fires destroy seedlings and saplings, sparing more mature trees that can withstand them.

This viewpoint, which has strong merits, can be carried to an extreme, leading people to believe that the entire Hill Country should be a rolling grassland, that Ashe juniper should grow only on a few isolated ledges, or even that it is not native to central Texas at all. So, on the other side, there are those who have begun to point to evidence that juniper has thrived here, even in extensive thickets, or brakes, for a very long time. Numerous reports, from the Spanish explorers of the seventeenth and eighteenth centuries to the Anglo settlers of the nineteenth, describe vast, almost impenetrable thickets of juniper throughout this area, even before any extensive cultivation or grazing took place. Many of the largest specimens were felled for buildings, so that what remained by the latter half of the nineteenth century was not necessarily indicative of the size or density of these groves.

Furthermore, it is well known that the rare golden-cheeked warbler migrates every spring from its wintering grounds in southern Mexico and Central America to the Texas Hill Country to nest in mature stands of Ashe juniper, whose long fibers of shredded bark, together with spiderweb silk, provide its sole nesting material. It does not seem plausible that the warbler only discovered the Ashe juniper and the Edwards Plateau in the last couple of hundred years. Finally, one might point out that grazing or farming was rarely attempted on the steeper slopes of the Edwards Plateau, and the arboreal vegetation present there is likely to be, more or less, what it has always been.

Clearly the truth lies somewhere between the two positions. Although there is little doubt that farmers and ranchers of the mid-nineteenth century had a strong impact on the local ecology, a good deal of the general flora of the Edwards Plateau was likely to be at least somewhat (if not fairly) similar to what is found now. It is likely that grasses, extending in from the prairies, did dominate the valleys and river plains, but it is also clear that Ashe juniper naturally inhabited the slopes and rocky ledges where there was little topsoil. In many areas of the Hill Country, such topography allowed for very extensive thickets of the little tree, providing shelter to deer, turkey, and anyone wanting to escape detection. (There are numerous accounts of Native Americans fleeing into these thickets of cedar, at which point their pursuers usually gave up.) The myth of the Hill Country as pure rolling grassland, into

which cedars only recently invaded, stems from early twentieth-century observers, who did not realize that the cedars were, in part at least, reclaiming land that had been theirs all along (Weniger 1984).

The pollen of Ashe juniper, produced only on the male trees (the females produce the fruit), is notorious for causing allergies (cedar fever) during pollination season in December through mid-February. Reportedly, a single tree can produce several pounds of pollen (Seiler 2005). Its identification with allergies, together with somewhat exaggerated notions about the shrub's thirst for water, has given the tree a bad name in certain circles. One should always keep in mind the good with the bad. Surely an evergreen, drought-hardy tree that provides shelter and nourishment for many wild animals as well as a highly useful resource for humans should not be condemned lightly. The Ashe juniper is one of the quintessential trees of the Texas Hill Country, one of its most prominent and very native inhabitants.

The names *cedar* and *juniper* require comment. Frequently one overhears discussion—sometimes heated—about whether the eastern red-cedar is a "real cedar." Some argue that it is not, while others maintain that it is, especially when compared with Ashe juniper of the Hill Country, which allegedly is not a cedar but rather a juniper. The problem here is one of common names. The biblically famous cedars of Lebanon are members of the genus *Cedrus*, an Old World genus. If this is what is meant by *cedar,* then neither the Ashe juniper nor the eastern red-cedar qualifies. Following this logic, neither the Pacific red-cedar nor the yellow cedar (both of the Pacific Northwest) is a cedar, since they belong to the genera *Thuja* and *Chamaecyparis*, respectively. Indeed, no tree native to North America is then a cedar, since no member of *Cedrus* is native to this continent. Such confusion is what led botanists to adopt the Linnaean binomial system. Scientifically, both eastern red-cedar and Ashe juniper are members of the same genus, *Juniperus*, and you can call them informally cedar or juniper or anything you wish. Common names, after all, reflect local oral traditions and hand-me-down metaphors; they are not intended to convey scientific precision.

With that in mind, *cedar* is clearly sovereign in common parlance. Texas can boast of almost 60 place names (towns, mountains, hills, lakes, hollows, sloughs, springs, etc.) that contain the word. At least 36 streams are known as Cedar Creek, ranging from Angelina County in east Texas to Brewster County in the Trans-Pecos. Yet there is not a single entity named for juniper. Clearly, the word *cedar* is ubiquitous and is deeply ingrained in our everyday vocabulary. It is likely that as pioneers from the eastern United States settled the state, the only member of *Juniperus* with which they were familiar was the eastern red-cedar, and so they used the term *cedar* indiscriminately for any of the several species of the genus. A final point of interest: Louisiana's capital, Baton Rouge (French for "red stick"), is named for the eastern red-cedar.

SOURCES: Adams 1987, 1991, 2004; Adams and Turner 1970; Banta and Caldwell 1933; Battey 1876; Berlandier 1980; Bracht 1931; Bray 1904; Canonge 1958; Carlson and Jones 1939; Castetter and Opler 1936; Dennis and Dennis 1925; Dorsey 1904, 1905; Foster 1917; Gatschet 1891; Goodrich and Wiley 1834; Griffith 1954; Guenther 1973; Hall 1952; Hart and Kemp 1974; Heald and Wolf 1910; Hester 1980; Holley 1836; Hollon and Butler 1956; Jordan 1978; Kindscher 1992; La Vere 1998; Lawson 1990; Martin 1933; Mattoon and Webster 1928; Newcomb 1961; Newkumet and Meredith 1988; Nye 1962; Olmsted 1857; Pulich 1976; Roemer 1935; Seiler 2005; Shafer 1986; Simpson 1988; Smithwick 1983; Sperry 1991; Taylor 1936; Tull 1999; Van Auken 1993; Vestal and Schultes 1939; Vines 1984; Weniger 1984; White 1907; Wrede 1997

Osage Orange

Maclura pomifera (Raf.) C. K. Schneid.

Osage orange is a paradox among Texas trees. Seldom used in city landscaping on account of its thorns, large fruit, and sometimes scraggly appearance, and not being part of any forest tree community, it rarely appears in groves or even in large groupings outside the Red River Valley. Unless the observer is beneath a female tree in fruit or close enough to note its telltale orangish bark, one is apt to mistake the mature tree for an elm. And yet, probably no other native Texan tree has been so widely disseminated across the nation or shares richer historical connections to humans. Osage orange is all around us but rarely noticed; steeped in history, it is all but forgotten.

For the first seven centuries of the last millennium, Osage orange was the source of a treasure, prized by locals and traded afar. This was its extremely hard and flexible wood, little affected by humidity, which local Indian tribes fashioned into excellent bows. Osage orange bows with draw weights of 70 pounds appear in archaeological sites as far back as 1050 CE, and in historic times the Caddo fashioned bows from the wood that were the envy of their day. These durable and resilient weapons, and perhaps the wood itself, were traded as far west as Ari-

ORIGIN OF SCIENTIFIC NAME
The person honored by the generic name is William Maclure (1763–1840), a Scottish-born American geologist and educational reformer. President of the Academy of Natural Sciences of Philadelphia for 22 years, Maclure made major contributions to his field, including the first true geological map of any part of North America, and was also a strong advocate for universal education,

especially for women. *Pomifera* is Latin for pome-bearing, referring (imprecisely) to the fruit.

OTHER COMMON NAMES
bois d'arc, bodark, horse apple, hedge apple, naranjo chino, bow wood

FAMILY
Moraceae (Mulberry Family)

DESCRIPTION
Moderate-sized, deciduous tree, 20–40' tall (max. 60'), with a low, rounded, ragged crown and soft-

ball-sized, exotically wrinkled lime-green fruit (on female specimens).

HABITAT AND DISTRIBUTION
Along stream bottoms, ravines, waste places, and fence lines. Native (pre-1800) distribution disputed, but generally conceded to be northeast and north-central Texas, southeastern Oklahoma, and southwestern Arkansas. Current distribution includes most of eastern two-thirds of the U.S. and southeastern Canada.

zona (Yaqui tribe), as far north as Montana (Blackfoot), and throughout the Great Plains (Pawnee, Omaha, and Osage tribes). Tribes of the southern Plains, such as the Kiowa and Comanche, had access to the trees themselves and could fashion their own bows. Tribes without such access, however, would barter a horse to obtain one, so highly valued was a bow of this wood. As early French explorers of the Mississippi Valley came upon this trade, they called the wood *bois d'arc* ("bow wood"), which was corrupted into the English *bodark*. It is likely that the distribution of the tree, as outlined above, expanded during these times as various tribes sought to ensure a constant supply by planting seeds in propitious places. This may explain the tree's odd appearance at desert seeps in the Trans-Pecos and in opportune spots throughout the southern Plains; it also complicates attempts to understand the tree's natural range. Archers today still consider bois d'arc one of the two best bow woods in existence, the other being yew, which in the United States grows only in the Pacific Northwest.

Bois d'arc's fame might well have faded were it not for some unusual and historic circumstances. Around the turn of the nineteenth century, an inhabitant of the Great Osage Village of southwestern Missouri acquired bois d'arc trees from an undisclosed location 300 miles to the west (which confirms that the trees were growing and being traded well beyond their native range). This individual gave samples to Mr. Pierre Chouteau, of the prosperous fur-trading family of Saint Louis,

who in turn gave cuttings from his garden to Captain Meriwether Lewis of the Lewis and Clark Expedition. Lewis, in turn, sent the cuttings to Thomas Jefferson in 1804 in the first shipment of specimens from west of the Mississippi on that remarkable journey. In what constituted his first description of a plant unknown to science, Lewis commented, "So much do the savages esteem the wood . . . for the purpose of making their bows, that they travel many hundred miles in quest of it" (Jackson 1962). Having made it to the East Coast in such good hands, the "Osage apple" (Lewis's term) began to be distributed among friends, with rumors that it made a good hedge. It is said that the huge tree at Patrick Henry's home in Brookneal, Virginia, was from one of these very cuttings. This venerable Osage orange is currently the National Champion, measuring 60 feet high and 27 feet in circumference. By 1818 Osage orange was under cultivation, and about the same time it began to be used as a natural hedge plant in south-

The bizarre, mammoth-sized fruit of Osage orange.

ern states. Sam Houston even planted
these hedges in Huntsville.

The real transformation of Osage orange into the tree known simply as *hedge*
came in the early 1850s, when the *Prairie
Farmer* actively promoted the plant as a
way to fence the prairie. Without access
to cheap wood and lacking stone, farmers
of the prairie had no way to enclose livestock or protect crops. Hedge apple was
a perfect solution and made agricultural
settlement of the prairies truly possible.
Given its tolerance of drought, heat, and
wind; rapid growth of thorny, zigzagging
branches; and ability to sucker prolifically
when cut, hedge apple could be pruned
in four or five years into a hedge that was
"pig tight, horse high, and bull strong"
(Webb 1931), that is, too dense for a pig
to squeeze through, too tall for a horse to
jump, too strong for a bull to push over.
In Illinois, as early as 1855, contractors
were paid $1 per mile to tend the hedges,
and various midwestern counties fur-
nished free trees to encourage their planting. Horse apple seed prices reached $50
a barrel, and east Texas farmers started
hauling the fruits along with their cotton to the steamships at Jefferson. Tens of
thousands of miles of hedges were planted throughout the Midwest and Plains,
providing an American answer to Europe's hawthorn hedges. Because of these
efforts, hedge apple has been planted in
greater numbers than almost any other
tree species in North America.

The final chapter in this saga is filled
with irony. In efforts to come up with a
better wire fence, one inventor, according to some sources, used hedge apple as

*Bois d'arc thorns, said to be the inspiration for
barbed wire.*

his inspiration, and barbed wire was the
result. So the hedge provided the model
for its own demise, as barbed wire in the
last quarter of the nineteenth century was
ultimately easier and cheaper to install
and maintain. But wire needed posts,
and hedge apple got the last laugh by
providing the very wood on which the
wire would be strung. It was chosen for
more than just convenience. Hedge apple
is well known to be the most decay-resistant wood in North America, and it is
immune to termites. Prairie farmers even
today clear-cut hedges every decade or
so, producing 4000 fence posts per mile
of hedge. The wood is so hard that fence
staples must be inserted while the wood
is green; otherwise, they must be tied on
with hay-baling wire.

Eventually people found other uses
for bois d'arc's extremely durable wood.
Charles Goodnight, the famous early Texas cattleman, built the first chuck wagon
in history out of the seasoned wood so

it could withstand the abuse of his huge Panhandle spread (Peattie 1953). The wood was coveted for house piers, street paving blocks, and railway ties. Bois d'arc limbs were even used in lieu of rebar for the reinforcement of concrete. Other uses included bridge pilings, insulator pins, treenails, and pulley blocks. Bois d'arc wood, though very hard to work, takes a fine polish and is beautifully iridescent, reminiscent of tigereye. It is also considered to have good tonal qualities, and for that reason is employed in duck and goose calls and is preferred for some musical instruments, such as harps.

The lime-green, brainlike fruits require at least passing comment. Although they are not eaten by humans and are generally avoided by most wildlife, horses do seem to take to them naturally. That oddity, plus a series of fruit characteristics and a seeming lack of dispersal agents, invites the startling theory that bois d'arc fruit may be an anachronism. It is theorized that mammalian megafauna of the Pleistocene (such as horses, ground sloths, and mastodonlike creatures) may have once been prime agents of its dispersal. Pollen samples indicate that the plant had an extensive range in phases of the Cenozoic, but with the extinction of those animals roughly 10,000 years ago, *Maclura pomifera* slowly shrank in distribution to the relatively small area known today. The reintroduction of modern horses by the Spaniards, plus the strong human intervention described here, may have reinvigorated its expansion (Janzen and Martin 1982; Barlow 2001).

There is one bois d'arc characteristic that any Texan will appreciate: bois d'arc fruit is proven to repel cockroaches. For a long time this was folk knowledge, but recently the chemical 2,3,4,5-tetrahydroxystilbene has been shown to be the agent responsible (Ball 2000). The root bark and sapwood yield a yellow-brown dye that once was used for the khaki coloring of army uniforms; trunk bark was used in tanning leather. The leaves have been used as a substitute food for silkworms, which normally feed on mulberry (*Morus* sp.), a member of the same family.

Bois D'Arc Creek, a sizable tributary of the Red River on the border of Fannin and Lamar counties, is considered by many to be the epicenter of the plant's range, given the dense growth of the tree in this area. David Crockett, who thought about settling there, called the lush area "Bodark Bayou." The Fannin County seat, Bonham, was previously named Bois D'Arc. At least two other small Texas towns, a creek, and dozens of city streets in the state bear the name. In south Texas in Brazoria County, a particular tree receives unusual recognition. Known as the Freeman's Bois D'Arc, it was one of the trees under which the slaves from fourteen plantations assembled in 1865 to be informed of their official freedom from slavery.

SOURCES: Ball 2000; Barlow 2001; Biffle 2000; Burton 1990; Cox and Leslie 1999; Haislet 1971; Jackson 1962; Janzen and Martin 1982; Kumler 2005; La Vere 1998; Marcy 1853; Nesom 1998; Newkumet and Meredith 1988; Peattie 1953; Schambach 2000; Simpson 1988; Smith and Perino 1981; Vestal and Schultes 1939; Vines 1984; Walker 1996; Webb 1931; Weniger 1996; Wrede 1997

Red Mulberry

Morus rubra L.

Little-leaf Mulberry

Morus microphylla Buckley

Red mulberry never quite gets the respect it deserves. It offers many obvious advantages to the native landscape gardener: it has an attractive form, grows moderately fast, resists drought and disease, and bears a delicious, juicy fruit. Yet, for all this, red mulberry is somehow always in the background, on the periphery of attention, a second runner-up. Its fruits are tasty, but they go unnoticed and litter our sidewalks. Its leaves provide fodder for silkworms, but they are inferior to those of the white mulberry (*Morus alba*). Its wood is strong and durable, but not quite as much as that of juniper, Osage orange, or bald cypress; nor is it as abundant as those trees. Its bark yields cordage and paper, but it never quite reaches the degree of fame of other cordage and paper plants. Often confused with the imported *M. alba*, it suffers the added

ORIGIN OF SCIENTIFIC NAME

Morus is the Latin word for mulberry tree, and *rubra* is "red," for the immature fruit of this species. *Microphylla* is a Greek compound (*micro* for small, *phyllon* for leaf) referring to the unusually small leaves of this southwestern species.

OTHER COMMON NAMES

For *Morus rubra:* American mulberry, moral. For *M. microphylla:* Texas mulberry, Mexican mulberry, mountain mulberry, western mulberry, dwarf mulberry, wild mulberry, mora, moral

FAMILY

Moraceae (Mulberry Family)

DESCRIPTION

Morus rubra: Small to medium-sized, often understory tree, 30–40' tall (max. 50'), with short trunk and rounded broad crown; leaves 3–9" long, rough-hairy on top, soft-hairy below; fruits resemble oblong blackberries, usually red when immature and dark purple when ripe, edible, sweet, and juicy. *Morus microphylla:* Shrub to small tree to 20' tall, leaves 1 $1/2$–2 $1/2$" long, sandpapery rough

on both surfaces; fruit red (immature) then black at maturity, edible, but with scant juice.

HABITAT AND DISTRIBUTION

Morus rubra prefers the rich, moist soils of stream bottoms of mainly southeast and east Texas; practically the entire eastern half of the U.S.; Ontario. *Morus microphylla* is scattered on rocky slopes, limestone hills, and canyons of the western two-thirds of the state; Arizona, southern New Mexico; northern Mexico.

indignity of being considered nonnative or a mere cultivar. Red mulberry is always just beyond the pale of our esteem.

And deserving of our esteem it is. Red mulberry's strongest asset, its fruit, has been a boon to humans and wildlife alike for centuries. Native Americans of Virginia brought quantities of the fruit to their meetings with colonists as early as 1607; in effect, red mulberries were among the first fruits native to America that English settlers tried. These Indians actually grew mulberry trees near their dwellings, and the fruits were an item of trade. Colonists quickly recognized the berries as good fodder for poultry and hogs and (like many fruits) as a source of fermented drink. Native Americans of the Appalachians, where the trees are abundant, consumed the fruit, as did, closer to home, both the Caddo and Comanche. The French and many of the Spanish expeditions to Texas noted mulberry trees, and some of the earliest books on Texas in English make mention of the fruit, "on which we regaled ourselves, by only riding under the shade, and picking the mulberries sitting in our saddles" (Goodrich and Wiley 1834). Modern uses for the fruit include jellies, preserves, pies, and a pleasant drink. Mulberries can also be dried, in which case they taste a bit like raisins.

Possible reasons for our seeming indifference to the fruit these days are our lack of access to *ripe* mulberries and the consequences of eating the unripe berries. The fruit, at almost any stage of development, is eaten by a host of animals, including opossum, raccoon, squirrels, and at least 21 kinds of birds. It may be the case that the fruit is largely devoured before people take notice. In addition, fruit maturation on an individual tree is usually staggered over a period of about a month; rarely are large numbers of fruit on the same tree ripe at the same moment. People may mistake the immature red color as an indication of ripeness and then find that unripe mulberries, like many fruits, are fairly unpalatable. They can cause gastrointestinal distress and may, in fact, cause hallucinations and central nervous disorders.

Another unsung asset of red mulberry is its wood. Fairly strong, light, and compact, it is best known for its durability when in contact with soil or water. Like its relative of the same family, Osage orange, which is renowned for being the most decay-resistant wood in North America, red mulberry wood was used for fence posts and railway ties. Like bald cypress, it was also utilized in cooperage and in various parts of ships, yachts, and boats (such as knees and dowels). As early as the American Revolution, large numbers of red mulberries were felled in areas of shipbuilding. When worked, red mulberry wood is reddish, has a fine grain, and takes a high polish. Colonial carpenters considered it one of the best woods for cabinetwork, along with black walnut. Mulberry wood was never used extensively, likely because it was relatively infrequent in the forests and its short trunks yielded few decent-sized boards. The Caddo of east Texas used mulberry wood for fire drills.

Long replaced by synthetics and more economical materials, bark as a source of cloth, cordage, and paper may seem peculiar. The women of the Choctaw tribes of the Deep South, however, wore cloaks

Mulberries of Morus rubra, *which turn a dark purple-black color when ripe.*

made from the inner bark of mulberry trees. Harvesting young shoots that rose from roots of felled trees, they sun-dried the stems, pounded them, removed the woody bits, pounded the remaining threads a second time, and allowed them to bleach, "exposing them to the dew" (Peattie 1966). When whitened, the coarse threads were ready to be woven. In our area, socially prominent Caddo women wore skirts of the same material, and the Tonkawa of central Texas, possibly influenced by the Caddo, manufactured a similar cloth. It is notable that one of the prime historic clothing materials of the Polynesians of the South Pacific was a cloth, called tapa, made from the inner bark of the paper mulberry, *Broussonetia papyrifera*, which has also been introduced to the United States as an ornamental and grows in many parts of Texas. Tapa is still made in Fiji, Samoa, Tonga, and other islands, where it is largely used as paper for traditional paintings. South

of our border, the Otomí of San Pablito, in the state of Puebla, Mexico, still use little-leaf mulberry (*Morus microphylla*), among many other trees, as a raw material for their famous bark paper paintings.

Mulberry fibers can also be extracted to make cordage. Jamestown colonists noted in the early seventeenth century that mulberry bark made "good linen cloth and Cordage" (Hatch 1957). Half a century earlier, in the winter of 1542–1543 in the Deep South, the remaining Spaniards of the de Soto expedition made mulberry bark fiber into the rope they needed for their handmade boats, which they would use to reach Mexico. In Texas, the historian of the La Salle expedition in 1687 noted that mulberry ropes "leathery and fine" were used among the indigenous tribes (Joutel 1998), and there is one report of the Tonkawa making a mulberry rope (Sjoberg 1953); it would seem likely that such use was known among many native tribes of the South.

Perhaps oddest among the red mulberry's attributes is the use of its leaves as a food source for humans, animals, and especially insects. New shoot growth can be eaten as a vegetable if cooked for about 20 minutes, and colonial Americans used the boiled leaves to fatten their swine. The most important historic use of the leaves was as a fodder for silkworms. Sericulture was all the rage in Europe from at least the seventeenth through nineteenth centuries and was particularly championed by James I of England, who hoped that the climate of the Colonies would be more propitious for silkworm culture. The early colonists attempted to raise silkworms on red mulberry leaves, with partial success, and by the mid-1600s landowners were being asked to plant ten mulberries for every 100 acres they owned.

Various problems prevented this industry from thriving in the Colonies. The tree best suited for sericulture is *Morus alba*, the white mulberry, which is native to China. Although this species was introduced into Europe in the twelfth century, into England by the late sixteenth century, and into Virginia before 1650, it took some time and some disappointing results for the colonists to recognize that there was much difference between the white and the red species. Technical expertise was also lacking, leading to inadequate cleaning and weaving. The main issue was labor, which was expensive in the Colonies, and the special attention that sericulture required just as farmers needed to do their spring planting. Without a cheap and exploitable labor force, colonial sericulture could never quite compete economically with that of other countries.

Silk culture was also not as profitable as the burgeoning tobacco industry. This notwithstanding, sericulture was attempted again and again across the continent, as late as the early twentieth century, following various technical, horticultural, and economic changes. Mary Austin Holley, in her promotional book *Texas*, for instance, still hints at the possibilities at a time of particular upswing in sericulture speculation: "The various kinds of mulberry are common forest trees throughout Texas, and afford every facility that can be desired for the rearing of silk-worms" (Holley 1836). Fifty years later, Julius Schütze, a German Texan from a silk-growing family, recognized that our wild mulberries were unsuited for sericulture but thought a prosperous silk industry could still be achieved locally using the (related) Osage orange (Schütze 1884).

White mulberry was introduced to Texas in the 1870s and 1880s, mainly for windbreaks in the Panhandle, where "unsightly groves" still attest to these attempts (Parks 1937), or as fruit trees elsewhere, although its fruit is less tasty than the red mulberry's. Like many introduced plants, it escaped cultivation and now appears to be wild in many areas across the state, where it is commonly mistaken for our native red mulberry. The white is distinguished by its leaves, which are smooth on both surfaces and tend to be more deeply lobed; also, the fruit is white to pink when fully ripe. Identification is complicated, however, by the many horticultural varieties and hybrids that render these key characters useless.

Our other native mulberry, little-leaf mulberry (*Morus microphylla*), frequently referred to as Texas mulberry, is a diminutive, southwestern brother to the red. Much shorter (often a big shrub), with small, very rough leaves, it is not easily confused with the other mulberries. The current National Champion, at 30 feet tall, is in Presidio County in the ghost town of Shafter. In light of what we have already seen with red mulberry, little-leaf shows its relation to the genus both in its fruits and in its wood. Its berries, which are nearly black when ripe, are much smaller than red mulberries. Some have found them "very palatable" (Havard 1885), but others think they are "rather sour and dry" (Fletcher 1928). The Chiricahua and Mescalero Apache of New Mexico and Texas ate the fruits fresh, as well as pressing them into pulpy cakes, which they dried and stored for winter use. The Tohono O'odham of southern Arizona and the Havasupai of northern Arizona still eat the fruit; the Havasupai tend a grove in the Grand Canyon, which they are believed to have planted long ago.

Often mentioned in the literature is the little-leaf mulberry's use for bow wood, which is reported among the Chiricahua, Mescalero, and Lipan Apache, as well as the Tohono O'odham, in short, the main tribes who dwell in the tree's distribution. Although Osage orange is considered the premier wood for bow making, these tribes lived largely west of its range and probably had access to it only through trade or the occasional planted tree. Not surprisingly, they chose a member of the same family whose wood, though soft and sappy, is quite resilient. These bows were about 5 feet long by 2 inches thick and were bent by plac-ing the wood in hot ashes. The Seminole of northern Florida also used red mulberry to make bows.

The name *mulberry*, in various forms, is well rooted in Texas history. Two towns, both in northeast Texas, have or once had this name. So have at least six creeks in Texas, one of which forms Mulberry Canyon, part of greater Palo Duro Canyon and one of the main divisions of Charles Goodnight's famous JA Ranch. The ranch headquarters sat near the canyon, which is now part of the Mulberry Ranch. *Las moras*, Spanish for mulberries, and *el moral*, mulberry tree, appear in the names of several Texas creeks, as well as of the well-known springs in Brackettville and so-called mountain just to the town's north. Rancho de la Mora, once located near Falls City (Karnes County) on the San Antonio River, was an eighteenth-century ranch that belonged to the San Antonio de Valero Mission. It ran 4000–5000 head of cattle in the early 1770s on its pastures. Place names in the eastern third of the state likely refer to the red mulberry, and those of the western third recall the little-leaf. Those in the middle third could go either way, depending on the specific locality.

SOURCES: Burns and Honkala 1990; Carlson and Jones 1939; Castetter and Opler 1936; Core 1967; Cox and Leslie 1999; Crosswhite 1981; Fletcher 1928; Goodrich and Wiley 1834; Griffith 1954; Hardin and Arena 1974; Hatch 1957; Havard 1885; Holley 1836; Joutel 1998; Kalm 1950; Lewis 1915; Matsui 1930; Mattoon and Webster 1928; Moerman 1998; Mueller 1884; Neich and Pendergrast 1997; Newcomb 1961; Parks 1937; Peattie 1953, 1966; Peters et al. 1987; Robertson 1993; Schütze 1884; Sjoberg 1953; Tull 1999; Vines 1984

Loblolly Pine

Pinus taeda L.

Longleaf Pine

Pinus palustris Mill.

Loblolly and longleaf pine are Texas' most famous pine trees, for different reasons. The rapid-growing loblolly is exceptional for the large quantity of timber it provides. The stately longleaf is renowned for its sheer beauty and for the quality of its wood, despite its relative scarcity. The two trees yield some of the most important and valuable timber in the United States.

Loblolly is one of the most prominent forest trees in America, especially in terms of the amount of timber it produces. It once ranked near the top in terms of amount cut; it still is the most abundant pine tree in Texas and the most aggressive in terms of growth, composing much of the dense and impenetrable forest of the Big Thicket. Faring well in both clay and sandy soils, it grows more rapidly over long periods of time than any of

ORIGIN OF SCIENTIFIC NAME

Pinus is the Latin word for pine tree. Forming a somewhat redundant name, *taeda* is Latin for (especially resinous) pine wood. *Palustris*, meaning marshy or boggy, is an unfortunate choice since *P. palustris* prefers dry, sandy hills; ironically, *P. taeda* is often found at swamp edges.

OTHER COMMON NAMES

For *Pinus taeda*: old-field pine, rosemary pine, bull pine, torch pine, swamp pine. For *Pinus palustris*: longleaf yellow pine, southern yellow pine, hill pine, hard pine, heart pine

FAMILY

Pinaceae (Pine Family)

DESCRIPTION

Tall, evergreen, resinous, aromatic trees with straight to slightly tapering trunks, and with both male (pollen) and female (seed) cones on the same tree. *Pinus taeda* reaches just over 100' tall (historically almost twice this height) and bears pale green, stiff needles, 6–9" long, and cones, 3–5" long. *Pinus palustris* attains 125' and has bright green, soft, and flexible needles, 8–18" long, and cones, 6–10" long, often slightly curved.

HABITAT AND DISTRIBUTION

Pinus taeda inhabits both the poorly drained lowlands as well as the dry uplands of the eastern third of Texas as far west as Bastrop County; southeastern coastal states, Arkansas, Oklahoma, and Tennessee. In Texas *Pinus palustris* prefers the low sand ridges of a fairly restricted area encompassing ten southeastern counties; outside Texas along strictly coastal, southeastern states.

the other southern yellow pines, averaging 3 ½ feet in height and ½ foot in diameter per year in its youth, and reaching 60 feet in 20 years given good conditions. On account of its quick growth, loblolly is the most commonly planted timber pine in Texas.

Historically, loblolly approached heights of 200 feet with trunks up to 5 feet in diameter, earning it the name *bull pine.* Known to reoccupy abandoned fields and clearings quickly, it also acquired the name *old-field pine.* The odor of its resinous boughs encouraged the moniker *rosemary pine. Loblolly,* the most common name applied to the tree, was originally British sailor slang for a thick gruel. The term was later applied in America to mudholes and swampy areas, with which the pine, often growing in low-lying, wet areas, became associated.

Loblolly wood, usually sold as "yellow pine" in Texas, is light, rather weak and brittle, very coarse grained, and not durable. Still, it has a wide range of uses where strong and durable wood is not essential. In the late nineteenth and early twentieth centuries, this meant pulpwood, barrel staves, box shooks, doors, mine props, pilings, ties, and fuel. By the end of the twentieth century, the wood was used primarily in the manufacture of plywood, brown paper (called kraft, used in packaging boxes), newsprint, and rayon fiber.

The so-called Lost Pines of Bastrop County are famous for their relative isolation, lying about 100 miles west of the east Texas pine forest, where most of the *Pinus taeda* populations are found. Shorter and more drought tolerant than

Loblolly pines in Bastrop State Park.

Loblolly pine cones.

their eastern relatives, the trees of the Lost Pines represent the western edge of the distribution of *Pinus taeda*. They have been the subject of much controversy. During the Pleistocene glaciation, when our climate was cooler and moister, loblolly forests may have extended as far west as the Edwards Plateau. As the climate became drier and warmer during the Holocene, the loblolly population contracted in the Bastrop area into a population disjunct from populations farther east. Recent genetic investigations suggest that our Lost Pines represent, in fact, an ancient refuge for *P. taeda* and that all extant east Texas loblollies may actually descend from these pines (Al-Rabab'ah and Williams 2004).

Longleaf pine, though greatly limited in number, is praised and revered by naturalists, lumbermen, and woodworkers throughout its distribution. Variously called the "largest and most important of the southern yellow pines" (Harrar and Harrar 1962), the "aristocrat of southern pines" (Simpson 1988), or in the glowing religious terms of the nineteenth century, "one of the great gifts of God to man" (Porcher 1869), longleaf is one of our most stately and striking trees. With a tall and gently tapering trunk and long supple needles bunched at the ends of its heavy twigs, it is majestic in size and shape. Impressive, too, is its timber, which is the most valuable of all American pine for heavy construction.

Pure stands of longleaf pine compose some of the most spectacular forests in the state, especially where repeated fires have been allowed to eradicate the under-brush. The relative uniformity of these parklike woods (with their well-spaced pines among a thin understory of dogwood, wild azalea, American holly, and grasses, relatively free from undergrowth and brambles) is natural and easily explained. Longleaf pines are adapted to deep, well-drained sands, where they have an advantage over other plants. Their huge taproots, which are able to reach water far below the surface, allow the trees to flourish, even through summers and droughts, on the dry sandy hills that are inimical to other trees.

Another factor contributing to solid stands of longleaf pine is fire. Longleafs are marvelously adapted to forest fires. As seedlings, they begin life in what is called the grass stage, in which the plants, while spending their energies below ground in extensive root systems, do very little above ground, looking like clumps of evergreen grass only a few inches high. During this stage, which may last 3–25 years, wildfires pass quickly over them, leaving the root systems and terminal buds (protected by a thick bundle of needles) unscathed. Once the roots are well established, longleaf pines end their grass stage by putting energy into their trunks, shooting up 3–6 feet per year, gradually tapering to 1 foot per year. This period of growth is the only time when longleaf is susceptible to fire damage. Once attaining a height of 10–15 feet, the pine becomes a veritable "asbestos tree" (Walker 1996). Enveloped by a corky bark, and with terminal buds held sufficiently aloft, they cannot be harmed by most grass fires; in fact, fire helps longleaf forests by eliminating competition and keeping various fungal diseases in check. Unfortunately, the pure, open stands of longleaf ensured easy clearance and historic overcutting, and the stubbornly long and unpredictable grass stage still challenges reforestation efforts.

Longleaf timber is one of the finest woods to be found east of the Rockies. The wood is durable, heavy, hard, stiff, and very strong. The lumber is full of resin, and its even grain and distinct growth rings are easily recognized in furniture. So hard and resinous is the wood that early settlers would leave longleaf buildings unpainted for generations. Historically, the timber was used in all kinds of building and construction, especially in trusses and frames where long lengths of strong wood were needed. Longleaf trunks could once be easily attained in dimensions of 60 feet long by 40 inches in diameter, making excellent bridge wood, ship masts, keels, keelsons, and spars, as well as poles and pilings. Other uses included flooring, planking, and decking. More recently, the wood has been used in pulp and paperboards.

Being easily accessible in locations with mild winters, longleaf pine was intensely exploited, and in the absence of good reforestation plans, it has greatly declined in numbers. As early as colonial times, some of the choicest stands were already reserved for exclusive use of the British Navy for masts and spars. Extensive clearing came about toward the end of the nineteenth century as northern lumbermen exhausted supplies of white pine and looked to the South for new sources of wood. The lumber industry built its own

railroads for easier access to timber, reaching Texas longleaf forests before 1900. By 1909 the South had become the lumber hub of the nation, and approximately half the total annual cut came from longleaf pine, which "set standards of excellence that had no equal among the world's tree species" (Walker 1996). Throughout the South, the pines were floated down rivers to ports where they were shipped to destinations as far away as Europe. An early Texas forest expert, noting that the state's annual cut of longleaf exceeded 750 million feet in the early twentieth century, estimated that virgin longleaf pine would last only another 20 years (Bray 1904). Indeed, by 1915 the forests of the older Gulf states had been largely cleared of the wood, and by 1940, true longleaf forests were largely a memory. Having at one time occupied as many as 60 million acres, by 1985 longleaf forests inhabited less than 4 million acres, only 6% of their original coverage, mainly in small, isolated, second-growth stands. Quite possibly no virgin stands of longleaf remain.

The very long and supple needles of longleaf pine have aesthetic and practical uses. The Alabama-Coushatta Indians, who came to east Texas in the late eighteenth century, continue an old artistic tradition by using longleaf pine needles to create baskets and other containers as well as animal effigies depicting real and legendary forest creatures. Also called pine straw, the needles are frequently used as garden mulch in the eastern part of the state.

Both longleaf and loblolly pines have contributed heavily to the naval stores industry (which refers to products obtained from pine resin, especially rosin and turpentine). Longleaf pine was once the world's leading source for this industry; currently about a dozen species of *Pinus* are used worldwide. The term *naval stores* originates from the use of pitch and tar in waterproofing wooden sailing ships, and it is still commonly used today in the trade. Originally, gum (or resin) was tapped from the living pine tree to be distilled into rosin, a brittle, transparent solid, and turpentine, a clear liquid with a pungent odor. Rosin was used as a preservative for rope and a caulk for ship timbers. It is still used in adhesives, inks, rubber compounds, surface coatings, chewing gums, soaps, and detergents. Baseball pitchers use rosin to make the ball less slippery, and violinists rely on rosined bows to make their strings sing. Turpentine was once used for lamp oil and as a preservative painted on posts, but today it is mainly used in chemical industries as a solvent for paints and varnishes and in the synthesis of cleaning agents, fragrances (anything with a pine odor), flavors, and vitamins.

These two outstanding pine trees commonly hybridize in nature, producing what is called the Sonderegger pine (*Pinus* x *sondereggeri* H. H. Chapm.). Loblolly and longleaf flower at roughly the same time each year, and hybrids are frequent in Louisiana and east Texas. Notable in the hybrid is the absence of the grass stage; the seedling attains height in the first year of growth. This is the only named southern pine hybrid, though other hybrids have been observed.

SOURCES: Al-Rabab'ah and Williams 2004; Baker and Langdon 1990; Boyer 1990; Bray 1904; Coppen and Hone 1995; Cox and Leslie 1999; Desmond 1919; Harrar and Harrar 1962; Lewis 1915; Mattoon and Webster 1928; Peacock 1985; Peattie 1966; Porcher 1869; Simpson 1988; Stanley 2004; Walker 1996; Wasowski and Wasowski 1997; Wauer 1999

Cottonwood

Populus deltoides Bartram ex Marshall

Little surpasses the alluring beauty of an enormous, solitary cottonwood on the prairie, which beckons with its shade, rustling leaves, and promise of nearby water. Easy to propagate, fast growing, and reaching a huge size, the cottonwood surpasses all other contenders for the tree most planted on the plains and prairies east of the Rockies. The tree's utility to humans, however, is somewhat strained. It generally does not make a good tree for urban settings, and its resources in the way of lumber and medicinal properties are middling at best. For all that, the cottonwood has rooted itself deeply as both a literal and figurative marker, a landmark of the prairie as well as of the heart.

Cottonwood's assets are readily apparent to anyone who has spent much time around the tree. Like the willow, which belongs to the same family, it is astonishingly easy to grow. Saplings, several inches in diameter, can be transplanted with only a few bare roots intact and still

ORIGIN OF SCIENTIFIC NAME

Populus (feminine) is the Latin name for the poplar tree, which is a member of this genus. *Populus* (masculine) is Latin for "people" or "public," which has led to the speculation that the poplar got its name from its growth around public squares or meeting places. *Deltoides* means shaped like the Greek letter delta, an equilateral triangle, in reference to the leaves.

OTHER COMMON NAMES

eastern cottonwood, Carolina poplar, necklace poplar, water poplar, southern cottonwood, yellow cottonwood, álamo

FAMILY

Salicaceae (Willow Family)

DESCRIPTION

Large, deciduous tree with broad, open crown, massive branches, and often short trunk, historically reaching almost 200' in height, with trunk 4–8' in diameter (now rarely exceeding 100' high and 3–4' in diameter).

HABITAT AND DISTRIBUTION

Various soils along ditches, streams, rivers, stock tanks, and lakes (but not in permanent, standing water), and along dry riverbeds and draws where roots can still reach moisture; all parts of Texas, though scarce on the Edwards Plateau and in south Texas; entire U.S., east of the Rockies, minus southern Florida; outside U.S. in southern Quebec and Alberta.

NOTE

No distinction is here made between several varieties of *Populus deltoides*, sometimes considered separate species, such as var. *monilifera* of the Panhandle and var. *wislizeni* of the Trans-Pecos.

The enormous cottonwoods of Fort Davis, Texas.

survive. Fence posts made of cottonwood have been known to sprout and take root when placed in moist earth, which is what happened with the Fort Davis corral, where the trees are still standing. Cottonwood is an amazingly fast grower. In its early stages, the tree can increase 4–5 feet in height and an inch in diameter each year, reaching a height of 60 feet in only fifteen years, making it the fastest-growing commercial forest species in North America. Cottonwood is a big tree, reaching well over 100 feet, qualifying it as the largest tree in the central United States between the Appalachians and the Rockies. Moreover, the tree's presence invariably indicates water, whether running aboveground in a stream, spring, or seep or lying in underground pools. A mature cottonwood needs upward of 50 gallons of water a day; although the tree's roots are extensive, they are shallow, so the water must be fairly close to the surface, a clue not lost on early travelers and pioneers.

These same growth factors, however, offer a downside from the human perspective. Fast growth in a tree often implies two disadvantages, a short life and weak wood, and cottonwood suffers from both. It is relatively short-lived, often counting a full life between 30 and 60 years of age, and is considered old at 75. Its wood is generally brittle, and whole branches frequently come tumbling down, which poorly recommends the tree for residential planting. The extremely shallow roots, so adept at finding water, are skilled at locating and clogging drain pipes and have a habit of lifting and cracking foundations and sidewalks. The cottony seeds released by the female trees like summer snow in May and June, although beautiful, are considered by some to be a nuisance. A single large cottonwood may release as many as 48 million seeds, and these tend to form drifts that interfere with air conditioners and machinery. For all these reasons, some cities have actually prohibited the planting of the tree.

As one might suspect from the weak branches, cottonwood lumber is not very well rated. The wood is light, soft, and not very strong. Once cut, it is extremely difficult to season, and its boards warp and crack. Even one of the earliest promotional books on Texas found little to recommend the wood, calling it "the least valuable of forest timbers" (Holley 1836). That said, woodworkers manage to find many uses for cottonwood lumber, such as for the interior parts of furniture (drawers, backs, and partitions), and for all sorts of containers, from piano crates to cigar boxes. The lightweight wood commends itself for ox yokes, saddletrees, and (among the Puebloans) drums; and its softness makes it easy to carve and easy on knives, hence its use for cutting boards. Cottonwood is particularly good for excelsior (wood shavings for stuffing and packing), and its pulp makes an excellent paper, which is lightweight but opaque, used in high-quality magazines and books. Cottonwood, in fact, is one of the few hardwood species that is grown specifically for its pulp.

Although less than perfect for lumber,

Cottonwood leaves, renowned for their music.

cottonwood actually makes decent beams and posts. If stripped of its bark and kept dry and out of the sun, the wood is actually quite durable. Mexican and southwestern churches have cottonwood rafters, or vigas, sometimes intricately carved, that have held up for centuries. The wood was frequently used in New Mexican houses, corrals, and shelters. Pioneers on the Plains built some of the first cabins, fences, and stables from the wood, especially as it was often the only tree present and the only lumber available before the arrival of the railroads. Many indigenous tribes of the Southwest, such as the Jumano of west Texas, utilized the wood in house construction. The Kiowa of the Plains (including our Panhandle) had a special relationship to the tree. According to Kiowa origin legends, the progenitors of their people emerged from a hollow cottonwood log. The Kiowa sun dance involved the construction of a circular medicine lodge, roughly 60 feet in diameter, built with many long logs of cottonwood, especially cut for the temporary structure.

Similar to the medicinal uses of willow, cottonwood's main application for illness involved the relief of pain, fever, and inflammation. Containing varying amounts of salicin, the precursor to aspirin (see black willow), a tea made from the dried inner bark was widely used for these purposes in folk medicine of the Southwest. Externally, the leaves and sometimes bark were utilized as a disinfectant and pain reliever, in the form of a decoction applied to lesions and wounds, or as a poultice applied to swellings, aching teeth, and skin abrasions. The famous Texas rancher Charles Goodnight boiled the inner bark into a strong tea to treat the gastric distress of his men who had drunk "gyppy water" (water containing gypsum), which was common in the area (Peattie 1953). Indigenous and Hispanic traditions once used the cylindrical outer bark to make bone splints, and a thick syrup made from the bark was used with cloth to make a cast for setting bones.

Miscellaneous uses of cottonwood include food, forage, stuffing, and fuel. Many southwestern tribes consumed the catkins (of both sexes), raw or added to stews, as a welcome first green of spring. In the winter, when supplies of grass were exhausted, Plains Indians, such as the Mandans, fed their horses on cottonwood bark. The Caddo of east Texas stuffed pillows with the fluffy seeds of cottonwood and cattail, along with goose down. The wood, like many softwoods, burns with an intense, clean heat, but the fire is of short duration; some Puebloans prefer it for firing pottery. The wood makes a decent fire drill as well.

These many attributes of cottonwood add to its historic renown, but the tree's most salient feature is its sheer beauty and stature, especially on the Plains, where it stands as a sentinel in an otherwise featureless landscape. Cottonwoods came to be used as markers, such as the one that Captain McClellan blazed in 1852 where the Red River meets the hundredth meridian (Marcy 1853), or the one now called the Landmark Cottonwood, near the South Canadian River, that guided Indians, pioneers, military units, and stagecoaches to a safe crossing (Haislet 1971). Since they could be seen for miles away, cottonwoods became meeting places, sites of rendezvous, where hunters, travelers, mail carriers, even picnickers, found respite. On a hot treeless prairie or in a desert draw, the tree offers coolness and shade, and the leaves, which rustle in the slightest breeze, make a mesmerizing white noise, like waves at the beach or rain. Cottonwood leaves are famous in their own right. Cowboy songs praise their lovely sounds: "Where the cottonwood leaves are whisperin' in the evenin' soft and low, / 'Tis there my heart's a-turnin' and homeward I must go" (Lomax and Lomax 1948). J. Frank Dobie spins the tale of a drought-stricken squatter who, having mistaken the cottonwood's "sweetest music" for rain, felt mocked when he discovered the truth. He chopped the tree down with an ax, only to feel regret and despair at the loss of his faux rain (Dobie 1928).

Evidence for the cottonwood's resonance in the Texas psyche is found in proper names and place names. The first that comes to mind is perhaps the most famous Texas landmark of all, the mission of the Alamo, which bears the Spanish name for cottonwood, after the trees nearby. The historic San Antonio street La Alameda (Spanish for cottonwood grove or walk) is now called East Commerce Street, but its old, half-alive cottonwoods were depicted in the mid-nineteenth-century painting by the German-Texan landscape painter Hermann Lungkwitz (Pinckney 1967). According to the *Handbook of Texas*, there are 44 different creeks in the state that bear the name *Cottonwood*, which is more than for any other tree. When one considers the towns named Cottonwood and other place names that refer to the tree,

including the many Spanish terms for it (*alamosa*, "full of cottonwoods"; *alamocito* and *alamito*, "little cottonwood"), there are about 75 proper names statewide that directly name or allude to this tree. This total is exceeded only by cedar (86 entries) and oak (95), but these last two trees are considerably more abundant, have more practical uses, and, in the case of oak, include many species (pin oak, post oak, red oak, and others). It is fair to say that the ubiquity of the cottonwood name reflects something more than the tree's abundance or its utility.

The cottonwood, official state tree of three states (Kansas, Nebraska, and Wyoming), is steeped in associations. It is a giant where trees are few, offering wood where there is little or none. It marks and delineates the landscape, serving as signpost and guide. It offers a gathering place of refuge and comfort, a place where one knows where one is and is glad to be there. The cottonwood's fame is greater than the sum of its parts, and its spiritual resonance—not its size, horticultural merits, or practical uses—is what endears the tree to many.

SOURCES: Alloway 2000; Ambrose 1997; Betts 1943; Bray 1904; Castetter and Opler 1936; Cooper 1990; Cox and Leslie 1999; Curtin 1965; Dobie 1928; Dunmire and Tierney 1995; Fletcher 1928; Garrett 2002; Haislet 1971; Hicks 1966; Holley 1836; Kindscher 1992; La Vere 1998; Lomax and Lomax 1948; Marcy 1853; Mattoon and Webster 1928; Moerman 1998; Moore 1990; Mueller 1884; Nesom 1998; Newcomb 1961; Nye 1962; Peattie 1953, 1966; Pinckney 1967; Powell 1988; Sargent 1947; Standley 1912; Vestal and Schultes 1939; Walker 1996; Wasowski and Wasowski 1997; Wauer 1999

Mesquite

Prosopis glandulosa Torr.

"To find shade under a mesquite tree is like dipping water with a sieve" (Roemer 1935). Mesquite's dappled shade—some would call it stingy—together with its fierce thorns and a fruit that is generally deemed unpalatable today, probably kept this hardy tree from serious consideration for State Tree of Texas. Indeed, none of the southwestern states selected *Prosopis glandulosa*, or any *Prosopis* species, to be its state tree, despite the major historical role that mesquite has played in the region. The extension of the tree's once restricted range to become, in the eyes of many, an invasive menace did not bolster its case. Still, at the back of the Texan mind, there is always a grudging respect for mesquite. Able to withstand a harsh environment, actually thriving in heat and drought, providing wood, fuel, and food on the otherwise treeless plain, the tree acquires symbolic status for its perseverance and generosity. Whether for its strong and beautiful wood, the scent of its smoking fires, its nectar-rich flowers and nutritional fruit, or simply the reliability of its springtime leafing as a signal of the end of winter, the mesquite endears itself to Texans more than they are sometimes willing to admit. No other plant,

ORIGIN OF SCIENTIFIC NAME

For reasons not understood, the generic name stems from a Greek name for a kind of prickly fruit, especially that of burdock (*Arctium lappa*). *Glandulosa* refers to the glandular anther connections of the flowers.

OTHER COMMON NAMES

honey mesquite, algarroba, algarrobo

FAMILY

Fabaceae (Legume or Bean Family)

DESCRIPTION

Shrub or small tree, usually under 40', with open crown and short trunk to 1 1/2' in diameter; feathery, twice-compound leaves; flowers white, in compact elongate racemes, turning yellow with age; pods slender, 4–10" in length, constricted between seeds.

HABITAT AND DISTRIBUTION

In various soils throughout most of the state, rare toward eastern border; Oklahoma, New Mexico, Arizona, and more limited in California, Nevada, Utah, Colorado, and Kansas; northern Mexico.

Mesquite at San Juan Capistrano Mission, San Antonio.

with the exception of the prickly pear, so quickly comes to mind when one thinks of plants characteristic of the land and culture of the state.

Texans are usually reluctant to praise the mesquite outright, which has much to do with the tree's relatively recent invasion of ranchland and stubborn resistance to control. Native to most of western Texas, the tree originally was much more scattered, especially on the prairie, where grasses were thick and grass fires common. Mesquite grew in thick stands only on well-drained hillsides or in the dry creeks and river bottoms of south Texas. With the introduction of cattle by the Spanish, however, mesquite was able to spread quickly into new areas, and with the fencing of land and the gradual sup-

pression of prairie fires, it was able to reach heretofore unknown densities. A single cow chip may contain 1600 mesquite seeds, all the more ready to germinate after passage through the cow's gut. In the absence of fire, which would kill mesquite saplings but rejuvenate grasses, a mesquite invasion was set in motion. By the early nineteenth century, the grassy plains surrounding San Antonio had already turned into a mesquite thicket that encircled the city for several miles, providing concealment for Indian attacks. With the famous cattle drives to the north toward the end of the century, mesquite was able to expand its range considerably, and with overgrazing on fenced land, it became very dense. By the end of the twentieth century, the tree had infested more than 60 million acres of Texas rangeland.

As a love-hate relationship between the rancher and the mesquite developed, the downside was soon apparent. Mesquite was forming impenetrable thickets from which it was difficult and time-consuming to extricate wayward cattle. Its growth was beginning to crowd out grasses and shrubs, and the plant was too thirsty in its use of precious water. Mesquite, once established, was virtually impossible to eradicate. Many landowners made the mistake of cutting back single trunks to the ground, only to find multitrunked trees growing back from the stem crown. Eventually, though, a silver lining was found. The trees provided shade, timber, and fuel in a landscape largely devoid of the same. They offered fodder for livestock, allowing ranches to survive severe droughts, which grass alone would not have permitted. The trees also enriched the soil with organic matter and nitrogen, which actually made for more productive grassland. The trick was to keep the mesquite in balance with grassland, as on a savannah, where trees are occasional and spread out. One naturalist maintains that the mesquite is less a tree and more an "elemental force, comparable to fire—too valuable to extinguish completely and too dangerous to trust unwatched" (Peattie 1953).

A major asset of mesquite, which landowners have begun to appreciate more and more, is its remarkable wood. Mesquite wood is heavy, very hard (nearly twice as hard as oak and walnut), durable in contact with soil, and extremely resistant to shrinkage or warping (about four times more so than competing woods),

Mesquite pods, single most important plant food source for Native Americans of the Southwest.

which is a property highly prized in the furniture and flooring industries. For these reasons mesquite has seen extensive use throughout Texas history. Native American tribes, such as the Coahuiltecan, used the wood for bows, for a variety of tools such as digging and stabbing sticks, and for war clubs. Hispanic rustic houses (jacales) of the San Antonio area in the eighteenth and nineteenth centuries were erected with vertically arranged mesquite logs; palisades of these logs also made typical yard enclosures of the period. San Antonio and other cities later used mesquite to make hexagonal street paving blocks, which would last for several decades. Anglo settlers used the wood extensively for posts, rails, and fences, as well as for wagon wheels. Smaller pieces of wood were employed by everyone for axes, hoes, plows, tool handles, and gunstocks. Mesquite wood is usually difficult to find in large pieces, but it has long been recognized as an excellent hardwood for furniture, comparable to cherry and walnut. With its dark reds and purples,

Wild Plum

Prunus angustifolia Marshall

Prunus mexicana S. Watson

Black Cherry

Prunus serotina Ehrh.

Prunus is an important genus that includes all the wild and cultivated forms of apricots, peaches, plums, cherries, and almonds. Given the many species of wild plum and at least one edible cherry in Texas, the genus deserves attention in a book such as this. In the case of wild plums, it is difficult to single out one major species. There are about half a dozen species that are commonly called "plum" in the state (and they are all more or less edible), but historical comments are usually too vague to identify the particular species involved. Given that plum trees are basically used for a singular purpose (i.e., edible fruit), we will limit our brief discussion to the two most

ORIGIN OF SCIENTIFIC NAME

Prunus is the classical Latin name for the plum tree. *Angustifolia* means narrow-leaved; *serotina* means late-coming, probably referring to the fruit. *Mexicana* is self-evident.

OTHER COMMON NAMES

For *Prunus angustifolia*: Chickasaw plum, sandhill plum, mountain cherry. For *P. mexicana*: Mexican plum, big tree plum, inch plum. For *P. serotina*: wild black cherry, mountain black cherry, rum cherry, whiskey cherry, capulín

FAMILY

Rosaceae (Rose Family)

DESCRIPTION

Prunus angustifolia: Suckering shrub or small tree to about 12' tall with dense, zigzagging, and sometimes spine-tipped branches; fruits red or yellow, approximately 1/2" in diameter. *P. mexicana*: Single-trunked tree to 25' tall (max. 40'); fruits reddish purple, about 1" in diameter. *P. serotina*: Medium-sized tree to 50' tall, with trunk 1.5' in diameter (but historically reaching twice these dimensions); flowers in racemes; pea-sized fruits dark red, ripening to purple-black.

HABITAT AND DISTRIBUTION

Prunus angustifolia inhabits the sandy open woods, roadsides, and fencerows of the eastern two-thirds of the state, plus the Panhandle; southeastern United States. *P. mexicana* prefers creek bottoms, moist woods, slopes, and canyons of the eastern half of the state; plains and southeastern U.S.; northern Mexico. *P. serotina* grows in Texas in three distinct areas according to variety: woods and thickets of east Texas (var. *serotina*); slopes, canyons, creek bottoms of Edwards Plateau (var. *eximia*); mountain canyons, and streams of the Trans-Pecos (var. *virens*); the species grows in the eastern half of the U.S.; eastern Canada, Mexico, and Guatemala.

Mexican plum in bloom.

widespread and abundant species in the state.

Prunus angustifolia, the Chickasaw plum, has round red or yellow fruits, so small that one of the shrub's common names is mountain cherry. The fruits, whether plums or cherries, are said to be juicy and delicious, well worth the effort of gathering them from the dense and thorny branches. Clumps of Chickasaw plum were frequently found around Indian villages (hence the Indian name), and although not exactly cultivated, these small trees may have become the forerunners of some of the numerous horticultural forms later produced from this species for southern orchards. Chickasaw plum was extensively introduced to the south Atlantic and Gulf states from the western portion of its distribution; some naturalists claim that the tree is rather difficult to locate in the wild, and it is usually found

around dwellings. The spring blossoms are fragrant and appear very early in the season, so early that in north Texas they are frequently nipped by the last freezes of winter and subsequently do not bear fruit. The plums, when available, are made into jelly, preserves, and wine, though they are rarely seen at market in any quantity.

Mexican plum is more a beautiful specimen tree and less a fruit tree. Single-trunked and taller than the Chickasaw, it is a scattered understory tree that lacks the habit of suckering and makes a good garden specimen. Its early bloom, coinciding with the redbud's, is both visually spectacular and fragrant, bearing a "uniquely pervasive aerial perfume" (Gehlbach 2002). The blossoms give way to reddish-purple fruit, about twice the size of Chickasaw plums, approaching one inch in diameter (hence the name *inch plum*). In the autumn the tree often puts on a beautiful show of yellow and orange leaves. Despite these ornamental advantages, the plums are less tasty than the Chickasaw's, being usually tart, if not somewhat bitter. They are best added to other foods and are prized for making jams and jellies. Being somewhat drought resistant and lacking a suckering base, Mexican plum has been used as a root-grafting stock.

The Spanish explorers who began to establish their missions and presidios across Texas toward the close of the seventeenth century frequently noted plums on their journeys, as it was important to record any useful food source. Many Native American tribes in our area, such as the Apache, Kiowa, and Wichita, availed themselves of the fruits wherever they could be obtained, either eating them fresh or drying them for storage. The Comanche in the winter actually tracked pack rats to their nests to find hoarded plums. The Caddo of the twentieth century sometimes gathered unripe plums for drying, to be later boiled and sweetened; perhaps this was a technique to gather fruit before wildlife could beat them to it. The earliest Anglo pioneers, when cultivated fruit was still unavailable, gathered wild plums for pies.

Many Texans today would be surprised to learn that we have a native cherry tree. Black cherry represents the opposite scenario from plums; that is, there is only one species called cherry that is edible in our area, but its uses are diverse. Nineteenth-century commentators found *Prunus serotina* to be "undoubtedly one of the most valuable of [the South's] indigenous plants" (Porcher 1869), not only for its ornamental qualities, similar to those of

Mexican plum, but also for its edible fruit, medicinal properties, and beautiful wood.

Like the fruit of the Mexican plum, black cherries are edible but tend to be rather tart or bitter (this varies widely from tree to tree). Although sometimes eaten raw, they were much more popular made into pies, jellies, and wines. Appalachian pioneers created a bitter drink known as cherry bounce, made from the juice of black cherries mixed with brandy or rum. Southerners made cherry cordials by soaking the fruit in whiskey or brandy (hence the tree's common names involving alcohol). Eventually black cherry was used to make a flavoring, such as that used in the manufacture of soft drinks.

Medicinally, black cherry bark (from twigs, trunk, and especially roots) was renowned as a tonic and astringent with "the property of calming irritation and diminishing nervous excitability," according to nineteenth-century medicine (Porcher 1869). It was used to soothe coughs, especially the chronic coughs associated with tuberculosis, but also for general colds and fevers. Native American tribes, such as the Cherokee and Kickapoo, employed the plant to treat a variety of ailments from colds, dysentery, and hemorrhoids to excessive menstrual flow. African American folk medicine echoed several of these uses, adding sore throats to the list of ailments treated. The seeds, bark, and leaves have the distinct odor of bitter almond, a signal that they contain the cyanogenic glycoside amygdalin (found in many *Prunus* species), which hydrolyzes to form hydrocyanic (prussic) acid. The prussic acid seems to be responsible for the medicinal effects. Medicinally, the (usually inner) bark was the only part used, and then in cold, not boiled, infusions.

The leaves and seeds were ignored for medicinal purposes, which is understandable given their toxicity. *Prunus serotina* is considered the most toxic of the eastern wild cherries. Fresh leaves contain more than 10 times the minimal amount of hydrocyanic acid considered dangerous, and as little as a quarter pound of leaves is toxic to a 100-pound animal. All classes of livestock have died from consuming the leaves. Humans usually avoid the bitter leaves, but the seeds cause problems to those who swallow them with the fruit. Black cherry kernels, like peach and apricot pits, are highly toxic.

Black cherry's real economic clout was found in its lumber, which provided the most precious cabinet wood in the rose family and one of our best furniture woods, second only to black walnut. Black cherry wood is a rich, reddish brown (with yellowish sapwood) and is heavy, hard, and strong, has a fine grain, and takes a beautiful polish. It does not warp, check, or split while seasoning, a trait greatly esteemed among carpenters. It also bends and works well, glues easily, and is shock resistant. Historically the wood found ample use in the manufacture of furniture, cabinets, boats, veneer, paneling, and trim, in addition to printer's blocks, handles, scientific instruments, gunstocks, and various woodenware items.

When there were still many decent-sized black cherry trees in our forests, cherry lumber had a greater unit value than any other hardwood of the eastern United States, with the exception of wal-

nut. Unfortunately, the high value of the wood led to the disappearance of commercially useful trees. In the eighteenth and nineteenth centuries, the attack came from two fronts; forest lands with rich soil (where the largest specimens grew) were cleared for agriculture, and fine specimens elsewhere were sought for the sawmill. As early as the turn of the twentieth century, forest experts were noting that the best specimens of black cherry had already been felled throughout the entire eastern United States, and that even small trees were being sought by cabinetmakers. Around 1900 a city could still order a fleet of streetcars with superb cherry paneling, but what was routine soon became extravagant. As was the case with many timber trees, the best cherry lumber came from the tall, straight, relatively slow growth that dense forest conditions produced. With the forests fast disappearing, field-grown black cherries were next in line, but these tended to be short-trunked, full of limbs, and knotty. Black cherry lumber quickly sank to twenty-eighth place among native trees in the amount cut. Once near the top, black cherry was soon at the bottom of our native cabinet woods.

SOURCES: Basehart 1974; Bolton 1908; Bray 1904; Cadwallader and Wilson 1965; Carlson and Jones 1939; Cox and Leslie 1999; Diggs et al. 1999; Gehlbach 2002; Hamby 2004; Hardin and Arena 1974; Harrar and Harrar 1962; Havard 1895; Kingsbury 1964; Kirkpatrick 1992; La Vere 1998; Lampe and McCann 1985; Latorre and Latorre 1977; Mattoon and Webster 1928; Moerman 1998; Newcomb 1961; Peattie 1966; Porcher 1869; Simpson 1988; Smithwick 1983; Thomson 1978; Vines 1984; Warnock 1977

Post Oak

Quercus stellata Wangenh.

Arguably the most abundant and widest-ranging oak in Texas, post oak is the dominant tree of the Cross Timbers of the north-central part of the state and of the Post Oak Savannah in the east-central portion. It is also abundant in many other sandy areas, such as the Coastal Plains, the Pineywoods, the Central Mineral Region of the Edwards Plateau, and the sand belts (Carrizo Sands) that run from south-central to northeast Texas. Post oak, like many oaks in our state, is sometimes difficult to identify on account of its many growth forms, which some taxonomists treat as varieties. On mature specimens, however, the 5- to 7-lobed leaves with stellate hairs on the underside, plus the frequently gnarled habit with branches nearly at right angles to the trunk, help to distinguish the tree. Another oft-noted feature is the shape of the leaf lobature. The middle two lobes are frequently pronounced and perpendicular to the midvein, seemingly forming the arms of a Maltese cross. Post oaks are slow-growing and long-lived; ages of trees in north-central Texas have been obtained of 200–300 years, but others have been found going back four centuries. On account of their slow growth, longevity, and ability to produce well-defined annual growth rings, post oaks are excellent candidates for dendroclimatological studies, al-

ORIGIN OF SCIENTIFIC NAME

Quercus is the Latin name for the English oak, *Quercus robur*. *Stellata*, "star-shaped," refers to the stellate hairs on the underside of the leaves.

OTHER COMMON NAMES

iron oak, cross oak, branch oak, rough oak, box oak

FAMILY

Fagaceae (Oak or Beech Family)

DESCRIPTION

Deciduous shrub to medium-sized tree with dense rounded crown, generally 20–40' tall with trunk 1–2' in diameter in most of Texas, but twice this size with good conditions, especially in the south-

eastern U.S.; leaves usually 5-lobed, shiny dark green above, hairy and gray-green beneath.

HABITAT AND DISTRIBUTION

Eastern two-thirds of the state, in gravelly-silty and, especially, sandy soils; throughout the Southeast: north to Iowa, east to Pennsylvania, hugging the coast to Massachusetts.

The sand-loving post oak.

drained, neutral to slightly acidic, sandy soils, where they usually become the dominant overstory tree, especially in upland areas. They do poorly in heavy clays, since presumably their sensitive roots are accustomed to the easy water infiltration that sand allows. When construction crews inadvertently compact or remove topsoils beneath their driplines, altering the environment of their feeder roots, post oaks routinely die. Thousands perish every year from these practices. All tree experts advise that if you have a decent specimen of post oak in your yard, *leave it alone.* These hardy natives are adapted to grow under the poorest conditions and do not respond well to synthetic fertilizers or herbicides. Many experts also discourage branch trimming. Noted nature writer Roy Bedichek quotes General Beck, who was in charge of landscaping at the University of Texas campus for many years: "The more you trim a post oak the unhealthier it becomes" (Bedichek 1994). Calling the post oak a "picturesque roughneck," Bedichek urges that the trees be left to their own devices, and any attempt to make the sometimes gnarled branches conform to artificial notions of tree design will have disappointing results. Post oaks are perfect shade trees for parks or for any place where a permanent tree is needed that requires little care or service. They are particularly good for soil stabilization on dry, sloping sites where few other trees flourish. They are even more resistant to oak wilt than most other oaks. The only problem with post oaks for the landscaper, other than soil preference and slow growth, is that they

lowing reconstructions of annual precipitation over several centuries.

Given the right habitat and if left undisturbed, post oaks make beautiful and rugged shade trees, but they are picky about their soil, intolerant of disturbance, and notoriously difficult to transplant. They are exquisitely adapted to well-

basically have to be grown in place from acorns. They are so difficult to transplant that very few nurseries will stock them.

It is impossible to mention the post oak in Texas without discussing the Cross Timbers. The Cross Timbers are thick bands of forest, rising up out of the prairie as if from nowhere, that extend north from just above Waco to southern Kansas. In Texas there are two main north-south belts of woods, the East (or Lower) Cross Timbers, which divides Dallas and Fort Worth, and the West (or Upper) Cross Timbers, which lies to the west of the Fort Worth Prairie. It is thought that the name *Cross Timbers* may have come from the complaints of westward settlers who, having left the forests of the east and entered the prairie for the first time, had "to cross yet another body of forest before entering the grasslands" (Diggs et al. 1999). Indeed, from east to west, one goes from Post Oak Savannah, to prairie, to East Cross Timbers, to more prairie, to West Cross Timbers, to the Rolling Plains. The Cross Timbers are, in the words of an authority on the subject, a "forested archipelago largely surrounded by a sea of prairie" (Francaviglia 2000). Fingers of woods, largely confined to sandy soils, extend up to the clayland prairie. The contrast between the two vegetational types is sharpened by their position in a climactic ecotone between forest and grassland. The reduced tree diversity of the Cross Timbers represents the last gasp of the eastern deciduous forest, and the grasses appearing in their midst are the first breath of the true prairie.

In the Cross Timbers, and the Post Oak Savannah to the east, post oak is generally considered the dominant wood. In the Cross Timbers, post oak and blackjack oak (*Quercus marilandica*) together

Variation in leaf lobature from a single post oak; note the Maltese cross of the leaves toward the right.

make up about 75% of the trees and 90% of the forest canopy. The two oaks are found in sandy soils from New England all the way to the Cross Timbers, where their distribution ends at the beginning of the West. In some places the Cross Timbers is densely timbered, with thick mats of briers and grapevines forming seemingly impenetrable walls. In others, the woods are more like a savannah, lacking underbrush and arranged such that "wagons can without difficulty pass between [the trees] in any direction" (Marcy 1853). In some cases roads were placed through the open woods for "summer shade and dry uniform footing" (Olmsted 1857). Since many parts of the Cross Timbers were less suited to cultivation than the surrounding prairie, and since the generally smaller trees were less desirable for timber than others, many remnants of virgin forest still exist, especially in less developed areas outside Texas. The Cross Timbers "is one of the largest relatively unaltered forest vegetation types in the eastern United States" (Stahle and Hehr 1984).

Post oak wood is heavy, hard, and close grained, but difficult to cure. This, plus the tree's relatively small stature, slow growth, and unruly growth form (knots, holes, rotted limbs, etc.), made the timber commercially rather uncompetitive. Occasionally the wood has been used for furniture and in construction, such as for lathing, siding, veneer, particle board, building and mine timber, molding, and flooring. Pioneer log cabins were constructed from the wood, and in the Cross Timbers region these tended to be smaller, with timbers sometimes vertically arranged, on account of the shorter lumber of this region. Two qualities of post oak wood, however, have earned it respect. One is the wood's impermeability. Like other white oaks (in fact, it is often marketed as white oak), post oak has a reddish-brown gum that plugs the pores of its wood, making it useful for storing liquids and desirable in cooperage. Like another white oak cousin, live oak, post oak was sometimes used in shipbuilding. The second and better-known quality of post oak wood is its durability, being considered moderately resistant to decay. Although not as durable as Osage orange or Ashe juniper, post oak is one of the most abundant durable woods in the eastern half of the state. Resisting decay for up to two decades or more when in contact with soil, the wood was widely used for fence posts (hence the name *post*) as well as for railroad ties. Some of the first rails in America were laid on the lumber; its short lengths and sometimes crooked shapes were less problematic for this purpose. Cheaper, creosote-treated lumber began to replace them, but post oak ties were still used well into the twentieth century. In the Post Oak Savannah, east of the Blackland Prairie, where the less timbered lands were more easily cleared and the sandy soils more easily cultivated, vast numbers of post oaks were felled for timber and for fuel in the latter half of the nineteenth century.

Like those of other white oaks, post oak acorns have relatively low levels of tannins and are edible. The Kiowa (and doubtless many other Texas tribes) dried and pounded acorns of this species, as well as making a coffeelike drink from them. An early visitor to Texas claimed he "was tempted to gather and eat a handful of these acorns . . . they were nearly as sweet as chestnuts. Of all oaks of the forest perhaps the post or iron-oak yields the richest and most abundant nuts" (Taylor 1936). Although tannins can vary a great deal between species and even within populations, it is difficult to imagine that one could eat the acorns as is, without boiling them or otherwise leaching out the tannins. Native wildlife can tolerate the tannic acids without problem, and post oak acorns are relished by deer, javelina, wild turkeys, squirrels, and many other rodents. Livestock, on the other hand, are not so tolerant of the acids, and post oak toxicity is reported among cattle, sheep, and goats, though most frequently in drought years when other forage is scarce.

Post oak does not command quite the acclaim of live oak, but it is still well respected in Texas cultural history. At least 22 historic and contemporary places in the state bear its name, including ten towns and nine creeks. Historic post oak trees include the Old North Church Oak near Nacogdoches, where the first Baptist church in Texas was organized in 1838, and the Cattle Raisers Oak in Graham, under which 40 Texas ranchers formed the Texas and Southwestern Cattle Raisers Association in 1877.

SOURCES: Bartlett 1995; Bedichek 1994; Bray 1904; Cox and Leslie 1999; Diggs et al. 1999; Francaviglia 2000; Garrett 2002; Haislet 1971; Lewis 1915; Marcy 1853; Olmsted 1857; Parks 1937; Peattie 1966; Simpson 1988; Stahle 1996–1997; Stahle and Hehr 1984; Stein et al. 2003; Stransky 1990; Taylor 1936; Vestal and Schultes 1939; Walker 1996; Ward and Nixon 1992

Live Oak

Quercus virginiana Mill.

Texas is blessed with oaks. In fact, we have more species of oak than of any other tree. Approximately three-fourths of all U.S. oak species grow in our state, thanks to its size, geographic diversity, and proximity to Mexico, which itself boasts nearly 60% of all New World species. Of all the Texas oaks, perhaps none is as well known, beloved, or venerated as the live oak. In part, live oak is respected for its incredibly strong wood, which played a critical yet all-but-forgotten role in American maritime history. Live oak has also provided a historic source for food, tannin, and ink. Ultimately, however, veneration for the tree centers on an aesthetic appreciation for its beauty and stature, together with cultural perceptions of its virtues and longevity.

Live oak wood is renowned for its strength and durability. Hard, strong, tough, and close grained, the wood is exceedingly heavy and dense. At about 59 pounds per cubic foot (nearly 75 pounds if green), it is the heaviest of all oak wood and among the heaviest of all American woods; a single large branch of 70 feet is weighed in *tons*. Live oak timbers are known to sink in water with surprising frequency. The wood's density is due in part to a waxy gum that fills vessels in the tree's vascular sys-

ORIGIN OF SCIENTIFIC NAME

Quercus is the Latin name for the English oak, *Quercus robur*. *Virginiana* refers to the colony of Virginia, so named for the Virgin Queen, Elizabeth I.

OTHER COMMON NAMES

southern live oak, coastal live oak, Virginia live oak, encino

FAMILY

Fagaceae (Oak or Beech Family)

DESCRIPTION

Rhizomatous shrub to very large evergreen tree to 60' tall; stocky trunk, 3–6' in diameter, frequently dividing a few feet above ground into massive horizontal branches; low, wide-spreading, closed crown to more than 125' in diameter.

HABITAT AND DISTRIBUTION

Thrives in sandy loam on hummocks, ridges, and along river bot-

toms of the Coastal Plain; tolerates a variety of soils farther inland in south-central and southeastern Texas, where it is thought to hybridize extensively with *Quercus fusiformis* (escarpment live oak); southeastern coastal plain, east to Florida, north to Virginia; westernmost Cuba.

The amazingly strong branches of live oak.

tem, as the heartwood forms, that would otherwise contain air. The wood is infamous for dulling saws and axes. A traveler in the late nineteenth century reported, "Let [a live oak] be seasoned, and then attempt to cut it with an axe: '*hic opus, hic labor est*' [This is work, this is labor]. I have seen the strongest man strike it the heaviest blow that he could, and the only token was a sharp, metallic ring and the rebound of the axe" (Taylor 1936). In many respects, a live oak tree was a nightmare for the lumberjack of yore. Requiring the constant resharpening of blades, it was time-consuming to fell, difficult to transport, and, with its short trunk and curving branches, stingy in yielding long, straight timbers.

A nightmare for the woodsman was the shipwright's dream. In the age of wooden ships, live oak was the strongest and most durable shipbuilding wood that grew in the nation, possibly second only to teak for the best maritime wood worldwide. In addition to its strength, it resisted decay, even when exposed to alternate wetting and drying, and lasted up to five times longer than the more commonly used white oak. Live oak also was lacking in odor, an important consideration for wood used in the holds of ships, where odors could nauseate passengers. The tree's short trunk and massive, contorted limbs, although inimical to timbers and planking, were superb for frames, below-deck stanchions, and especially for knees (braces for the ship's framework and supports for the deck beams). Knees required wood that formed a sharp angle yet was reliably strong. Live oak provided

An example from Lockhart, Texas, of the massive trunks that live oaks can attain with age.

many such angles at the junctions of the trunk with the horizontal limbs and buttressed roots. Because of the unusual cohesion of interwoven grains at these junctions, live oak knees were "stronger than any artificial joint a shipbuilder could devise" (Weekes 1979). Enormous knees, weighing up to half a ton, hewn in a solid piece, were not uncommon.

The boon of this uniquely American resource and its effects on U.S. history should not be forgotten. As far back as 1670 and throughout the first half of the eighteenth century, live oak's properties were recognized and its timbers incorporated into colonial vessels. During the Revolutionary War, the success of such live-oak ships as the privateer *Hancock*, a brigantine that captured a record nine British vessels within three months in 1776, led to the wood's widespread fame in our emerging maritime nation. With the establishment of the U.S. Navy in the last decade of the eighteenth century, massive amounts of southern live oak were used to build the Navy's first frigates. Among them was the 44-gun USS *Constitution*, which earned the nickname *Old Ironsides* when British shot reportedly bounced off her sides in the historic victory over HMS *Guerrière* during the War of 1812. The *Constitution* is the oldest commissioned warship afloat in the world today.

After the Louisiana Purchase (1803) and the acquisition of Florida (1819), the nation held a virtual monopoly on the world's supply of live oak, which is the most characteristic tree of the lower coastal plains of the southeastern United

States. *Virtual* is necessary because the supply was perhaps overestimated (the trees grow mainly in a narrow belt hugging the coast), and the tree was exceedingly difficult to obtain, given malarial conditions and the local lack of infrastructure. It was even more difficult to protect from plundering, and the demand was great. A ship of the line, for instance, easily required 34,000 cubic feet of live oak (approximately 680 trees), and European countries, having long depleted their own forests, were on the search for new sources of timber. In light of the demand, Congress had already agreed to buy two small islands off the Georgia coast for live oak reserves in 1799; consequently, live oak became the first North American tree to be set aside for future use in a forest preserve. Over subsequent decades, presidential proclamations added to these lands, totaling 268,000 acres in five southern states by 1868. Although the lands suffered much illegal plundering (Congress did not set aside sufficient funds to protect them), many northern shipwrights earned money by "live oaking" in the South in the eighteenth century and the first half of the nineteenth century (Wood 1981). When Sam Houston claimed in 1837 that four-fifths of the live oaks of the world grew in Texas (Muir 1958)—a forgivable exaggeration—this was a comment of serious economic potential.

When at the beginning of the Civil War the inconclusive duel between *Merrimack* and *Monitor* proved that ironclads were the way of the future, the demise of the wooden ship was imminent. Given that live oak was never useful for timber, the end of the wooden ship industry spelled the end of the live oak market, and it is still one of the few woods that has decreased in use for reasons other than sheer scarcity. Nonetheless, for more than a century live oak reigned supreme. It built the world's finest whaleships, clippers, and packets; helped to establish the supremacy of the U.S. merchant marine; and encouraged Congress to create public preserves that would become the foundation for current laws dealing with trespass timber cutting.

There were a few uses for live oak outside the shipbuilding industry. Wagon axles, hubs, cartwheels, mill-wheel cogs, as well as submerged piles, docks, and waterwheels, were often manufactured from live oak wood. Carpenters generally avoided the wood, as it was simply too hard to work. Live oak bark was used in the tanning industry, and an astringent bark tea was reported to treat diarrhea and dysentery. Oak galls, the swellings produced by the tree in response to parasitic insects, especially gall wasps, were an important ingredient in iron gall ink, arguably the most important ink in Western history. Most permanent records between the Middle Ages and the twentieth century, including such notables as Leonardo da Vinci's notebooks, manuscripts of J. S. Bach, and the U.S. Constitution, were written in some version of iron gall ink, which included galls from various species of oak, iron sulfate, gum arabic, and water. Although live oak galls were probably not major components in American inks, they were likely used to some extent.

As odd as it may seem to us today, live oak acorns were once an important source of food. Many acorns are rich in protein, fat, calcium, and other minerals, but they also contain bitter tannins, which are time-consuming to remove. Unlike acorns from the red oak group, which take two years to mature and are very bitter from extra tannins, acorns from the white oak group, in which live oak is usually included, take only one year to mature and are fairly sweet, tasting like chestnuts. Shelling live oak acorns and boiling the kernels several times to remove the tannins is difficult work, but the results can be rewarding. One native plant specialist claims, "Once you've tried acorn waffles, you'll have trouble settling for plain old waffles again" (Tull 1999).

Native American groups throughout the country made heavy use of acorns, including those of live oak, from which a sweet oil was also obtained for cooking. In Texas many tribes processed acorns for consumption, though historical records frequently neglect to designate the species. The coastal Karankawa, and probably also the Bidai of southeastern Texas, consumed live oak acorns that grew in their homelands, but it is not entirely clear if the Caddo and Tonkawa, both acorn eaters, consumed this species. Acorn preparation methods varied but usually involved the removal of tannins followed by various sorts of cooking. The Bidai leached their acorns of tannins by burying the kernels in pits filled with ashes and damp earth. The Karankawa made ash cakes of acorn meal, cooking them over live coals. The Apache, who used

gray and gambel oaks, roasted the acorns first and then pounded them into a meal, which was mixed with dried meat and fat. Archaeological records date live oak acorn use in Texas to at least 390 BCE, though many experts think the burned rock middens dating to 2000–1000 BCE likely reflect acorn processing.

Anglo settlers were more apt to see acorns as livestock feed, especially for pigs. Gideon Lincecum, in his travels through Texas in 1835, spoke of the lands of south-central and southeastern Texas as "everywhere surpass[ing] any country for hogs I have ever heard of . . . the post oak prairies . . . [are] covered with acorns, the live oak groves also afford fine acorns for hogs" (Lincecum 1949). In Europe, oak forests had long been esteemed for hog mast, and they were often valued by the number of swine they could feed; one pig usually needed 2.5–4 acres. Forest floors littered with acorns would have been viewed as a boon to early Texas settlers. Of course, local fauna were already well aware of the food source; bears, javelina, deer, squirrels, and turkeys are just a few of the many animals known to consume the nuts.

Currently, live oak is divorced from practically all these historical connections, save one: its continued aesthetic and cultural value as a monarch of trees and as a long-lasting memorial. Oaks have been praised and eulogized wherever they are found throughout the ages. In Europe, oaks have been venerated from the Druids onward. Stateside, and specifically with live oak, we find Walt Whitman referring to the tree as the "loving lounger in my winding paths" (*Song of Myself*), and famed Texas naturalist Roy Bedichek calls the live oak "the noblest tree of Texas soil" (Bedichek 1994). Perhaps no other description is more revealing of the live oak's allure than one published by an anonymous traveler in 1834:

> I never shall forget my feelings at the sight of an object I saw near the banks of the Brazos. Through the misty morning air, a singular sight. . . . There stood before me . . . an almost unbroken veil of white and matted moss. After admiring and wondering for a time, and approaching a little nearer, I perceived that this singular appearance was caused by a full grown tree of considerable age, with trunk and boughs which seemed as firm as iron, and laden with luxuriant foliage of a peculiar depth and darkness, overspread with lichens, hanging in bunches from the extremity of every branch, and twig. . . . When the light fell upon it strongly, the whiteness of the moss . . . offered a striking resemblance to the hoary head of a venerable old patriarch. . . . I could hardly have persuaded myself, without the experience, that any object in the vegetable world could have produced an effect on my mind so much like that excited, under ordinary circumstances, by the presence of a dignified human being. I was gratified when I learned that this noble tree was a live oak. (Goodrich and Wiley 1834)

Live oak boughs laden with Spanish moss, so emblematic of the South, awaken a sense of awe, and like all great trees,

these are seen as ancient and strong, tenacious, steadfast, and indestructible. "The lone live oak is, of all the images of a tree, the closest to an image of nature, a nature that is larger and longer-lived than humans" (Anderson 2003).

For these reasons, live oak is the commemorative tree par excellence in its region. No other tree memorializes military, political, historical, and cultural events as nobly as this tree. Throughout the South as well as Texas, famous old specimens are acknowledged as cultural icons. The live oak known as the Old Senator of Saint Augustine, Florida, allegedly witnessed the landing of Juan Ponce de León in 1513. The Evangeline Oak of Saint Martinville, Louisiana, is memorialized through Longfellow's epic poem of two lovers separated in the expulsion of the Acadians from Nova Scotia. There is even a Live Oak Society, under the auspices of the Louisiana Garden Club Federation, whose sole members, aside from one human chairperson, are live oaks at least 8 feet in girth; currently, there are 5067 members in fourteen states, and even Hurricane Katrina did little to reduce these numbers. In Texas, some of the more historically famous live oaks include the Runaway Scrape Oak near Gonzales, under which Sam Houston and nearly 400 Texans camped on their historic retreat a week after the fall of the Alamo; the oak under which General Santa Anna surrendered to Sam Houston after the Battle of San Jacinto, apparently no longer standing but memorialized in a painting by William H. Huddle; and the Treaty Oak of Austin, under whose boughs Stephen F. Austin is reputed to have signed the first boundary-line agreement with native tribes. The poisoning of Treaty Oak in 1989 led to national and international coverage, public outcry, and a blank check from Ross Perot; currently about 35% of the tree survives, and it is still an icon.

With all this said, we have only barely touched on important live oaks in the state. The Texas Forest Service's *Famous Trees of Texas* includes 96 trees, fully 50 of which are live oaks (Haislet 1971). The events to which these trees were sentinel are manifold: outdoor church services, weddings, auctions, Masonic meetings, midnight trysts, buried treasure, county charters, court trials, duels, hangings, burials, and encampments of all kinds. The first Texas tree species that many early maritime immigrants saw was the live oak, since, being resistant to salt spray, it was one of the only trees reported growing on the barrier islands of the coast; the Three Trees at the center of Galveston Island in the mid-1800s could be seen far out at sea. The Big Tree at Goose Island State Park near Rockport, though no longer State Champion live oak, is one of the best-known trees in the state. The official state seal of Texas includes a branch of live oak leaves, symbolizing strength, and at least 30 Texas place names (of counties, towns, communities, creeks, etc.) honor this tree. It is safe to say that although the live oak is renowned throughout the South, it sets its roots as deeply in Texas as anywhere.

SOURCES: Anderson 2003; Babb 1985; Bedichek 1994; Bolton 1987; Castetter and Opler 1936; Cox and Leslie 1999; Dart 2007; Dering 1982; Desmond 1919; Eusman 2005; Goodrich and Wiley 1834; Haislet 1971; Hatfield 1954; Havard 1895; Hester et al. 1989; Hollon and Butler 1956; Kephart 1972; Lewis 1915; Lincecum 1949; Mattoon and Webster 1928; McAlister and McAlister 1993; Miller and Lamb 1985; Muir 1958; Ricklis 1996; Simpson 1988; Sjoberg 1951, 1953; Stein et al. 2003; Taylor 1936; Taylor et al. 1997; Tull 1999; Vines 1984; Walker 1996; Weekes 1979; Wood 1981

Sabal Palm

Sabal mexicana Mart.

Texas is fortunate to be among a handful of states that have native populations of tree-sized palms. Our arborescent palm, *Sabal mexicana*, can reach 50 feet, and is one of the most common palms of lowland tropical Mexico, where it is often found in habitats disturbed by humans. Unlike our other, much more common native palm, the shrub-sized dwarf palmetto (*Sabal minor*), sabal palm is not salt tolerant and tends to grow on coastal flatlands and along inlets several miles from the sea. Texas represents the northernmost limit of its distribution, but where that limit falls in the state has been the topic of some excellent research. The Sabal Palm Audubon Center and Sanctuary, a unique subtropical community that affords food and shelter to many species of animals and plants rarely seen in the United States, is located just southeast of Brownsville. Until recently, it was assumed that a few dozen acres of the sanctuary's densest palm growth represented the northernmost outpost of what was considered essentially a Mexican palm. In the nineteenth century sabal palm was reported growing in sparse clumps along the Rio Grande as far as 80 miles inland from the sea, but agricultural clearing eradicated most

ORIGIN OF SCIENTIFIC NAME

The origin of the word *sabal* is unfortunately not known. Michel Adanson (1727–1806), a French naturalist of Scottish descent, proposed the name in 1763 in his *Familles des Plantes* without comment. It is possibly derived from an American vernacular or Indian name. The specific epithet is self-evident.

OTHER COMMON NAMES

Texas palm, Texas palmetto, Mexican palmetto, Rio Grande palmetto, palma de mícheros, palma real, palma redonda, palma llanera, palmito, apachite, guano

FAMILY

Arecaceae (Palm Family)

DESCRIPTION

Robust palm, 20–50' tall, with large fan-shaped leaves forming a rounded crown; leaves 5–7' long and equally wide; fruit round, dull black, 1/2–3/4" in diameter.

HABITAT AND DISTRIBUTION

Coastal flatlands and inland rivers of south-central and southern Texas; throughout Gulf coastal Mexico, including Yucatan; one collection from El Salvador.

of these palms, leaving only the population at the Sanctuary and a few scattered individuals. Although the palm had been planted here and there as an ornamental, the sanctuary, so it was thought, represented the only natural population of *S. mexicana* left in Texas.

Enter Landon Lockett. A linguist by training, a naturalist by inclination, Dr. Lockett carefully examined historic botanical literature where he found reports of tree-sized palms in the city of Victoria. With the help of local citizens, he was able to find a population of sabal palms (many 20–25 feet tall) along Garcitas Creek, approximately 4 miles upstream from Lavaca Bay (Lockett and Read 1990). This just so happens to be the same area where La Salle in 1685 established the first European colony in Texas, the ill-fated Fort Saint Louis, in the account of which Lockett found further evidence for palms. Lockett's assiduous and careful research and many field trips uncovered historic evidence for a natural population of sabal palms in San Antonio, as well as a living population south of Houston in Brazoria County (approximately 30 trunked palms plus an uncounted number of younger, trunkless specimens) of what may be hybrids between sabal palm and dwarf palmetto, or possibly between the sabal and an as-yet-unidentified palm (Lockett 1991 and pers. comm.). Currently protected on 46 acres of the San Bernard National Wildlife Refuge, these palms, if hybrids, represent not only the first known hybrids of any *Sabal* species but also the only known naturally occurring palm hybrids in the country. It is

Sabal palm at the San José Mission in San Antonio.

also possible that these palms constitute a new species altogether (DNA studies are in progress). Further literary sleuthwork has bolstered Lockett's case for a much more extensive Texas distribution of sabal palm than had been recognized for years (Lockett 1995). Unfortunately for the sabal palm, its wood was found to be immune to shipworm; in the nineteenth century this meant that the tree was highly sought after for wharf docks and pilings. In a grievous case of overharvesting, these native south-central populations were all but obliterated. Many were also transplanted from the wild as prized ornamentals. From Lockett's research, it seems probable that sabal palm once inhabited the thick bottomland forests along many Texas rivers extending inland dozens of miles from the Gulf Coast.

Sabal palm has a rich history in material culture use, especially along the Gulf coastal plain of Mexico, including the Yucatan; its presence in the Yucatan may be due, in part, to the activities of pre-Columbian peoples. Sabal palm trunks, which are durable in contact with soil and are said to last a lifetime, are occasionally used in the construction of rustic houses in rural areas of these regions. Far more common is the use of the leaves for roof thatching. In the Yucatan, the palm is grown in plantations, where it is the mainstay of the thatch industry. Throughout its range in Mexico the leaves are employed in the manufacture of various woven items such as chair seats, hats, handbags, and briefcases. Leaf petioles and the fibrous trunk bark are also sources of weaving and stitching materials. In terms of sabal palm material use in Texas, other than references to trunks used in wharf construction, there is one early comment (1828–1829) that the Karankawa adorned their heads with palm leaf wreaths (Berlandier 1969). Given that both *Sabal mexicana* and *S. minor* were in the heart of Karankawa territory (approximately between Corpus Christi and Matagorda bays), it is difficult to say which plant this references.

Sabal palm fruits are edible. Again,

A young sabal palm showing the strong downward curve of the leaves as seen from the side.

most of our information comes from Mexico, where these are called *mícheros* and are occasionally found in the markets of Matamoros and Brownsville. The Kickapoo Indians of Mexico (once, also, of Texas) eat the fruit. Delena Tull reports that the sweet pulp surrounding the seeds has a datelike flavor, which is not surprising, since dates come from date palms. She recommends softening the pulp with boiling water in order to use the fruit in sweet breads (Tull 1999). The more common use of the (unpitted) fruit in Mexico, however, seems to be for fodder for hogs, cattle, and fowl. Although the seeds are low in protein and oil, they do contain unsaturated fatty acids beneficial for cattle feed. Native wildlife such as coyotes, raccoons, chachalacas, and rodents also eat the fruit.

The terminal buds of sabal palm, called *palmitos* (*palm hearts* in English), are consumed on a small scale in Veracruz and San Luis Potosí and are comparable in taste to those of other species imported from Costa Rica, Brazil, and Paraguay. In northeastern Mexico *palmito* is also the name for the whole tree. Some have proposed pursuing a palmito industry in Mexico based on the sabal palm, but since the trees are slow growers and removal of the terminal bud usually kills the tree, profit would appear marginal at best. That being said, the Kickapoo formerly dried and pounded the terminal buds into a meal, as doubtless did other native tribes within the tree's distribution.

Although there is little direct historical evidence in Texas for these various uses of sabal palm, one can assume that our indigenous tribes were aware of at least some of them. The tree is generally less abundant and more localized in Texas than it is in Mexico (where it grows in extensive groves), and the coastal Indian groups were extirpated early on, which would explain the paucity of evidence.

Texas sabal palms can be distinguished from many imported palms by the lack of spines on the leaf stems; by the strong downward curve of the leaves, which, seen from the side, appear to form semicircles; and by leaves that have many marginal threads and are V-shaped when viewed from the end. These palms deserve our respect and protection, and new populations should be sought. Like those recently found, they should be protected from felling or poaching. Plantings should be encouraged, especially along waterways in the southern half of the state. Although they grow slowly in the wild and are somewhat difficult to transplant from the ground, they start easily from seed, grow quickly in cultivation, and transplant easily from containers, given extra care in handling their fibrous roots and ample water until they are established (the first couple of years). Unlike nonnative palms, they are entirely adapted to Texas winters in approximately the southern half of the state. These beautiful and stately natives deserve much wider attention in native landscaping, as well as in the wild.

SOURCES: Bartlett 1995; Berlandier 1969; Cox and Leslie 1999; Havard 1885; Joutel 1998; Latorre and Latorre 1977; Lockett 1991, 1995, 2004; Lockett and Read 1990; Olvera-Fonseca 2004; Piña Lujan 1972; Small 1927; Standley 1920–1926; Tull 1999; Vines 1960; Wasowski and Wasowski 1997; Zona 1990

Black Willow

Salix nigra Marshall

When H. B. Parks published *Valuable Plants Native to Texas* in 1937, he did not include a single member of the genus *Salix,* not one willow. Although *Salix nigra* is the largest willow in the nation and likely the world (specimens in our Pineywoods reach 100 feet, but those of the lower Mississippi are reported at 125 feet), and despite its standing as the only commercially important willow out of approximately 90 species represented in the country, its omission from *Valuable Plants* likely reflects a common attitude that willows are weeds. Black willows certainly grow like weeds, averaging 4 feet per year, which, in Parks's defense, makes for a weak, soft, and brittle wood, prone to breakage. As a pioneer species, they are supposed to be the first denizens of recently disturbed areas, such as freshly scoured streambeds or sloughs. Here they will flourish and eventually, save in the lowest-lying areas, give way to other trees such as cottonwoods. Consequently, they are short-lived, averaging 55 years but often reaching only half that. Their extensive, shallow roots, capable of breaking pavement, are so adept at finding water that they are infamous for clogging drains and sewers. This hydrophilic trait makes their presence a good indicator of hidden water in semiarid regions. A short-lived, brittle tree that invades pipes does not commend itself to landscapers; however, as with all native plants in the right (i.e., natural) habitat,

ORIGIN OF SCIENTIFIC NAME
Salix is the classical Latin name for willow; *nigra,* "black," refers to the sometimes black appearance of the bark on mature specimens.

OTHER COMMON NAMES
Gulf black willow, swamp willow, Gooding willow, western black willow, southwestern black willow, Lindheimer black willow, scythe-leaved willow, pussy willow, sauz, jarita

FAMILY
Salicaceae (Willow Family)

DESCRIPTION
Fast-growing, medium-sized, multi-trunked, deciduous tree to 30–60' in our area (max. 100').

HABITAT AND DISTRIBUTION
In wet soils, standing water, flowing streams, and periodic streams throughout the state; eastern half of the U.S.; New Brunswick, Canada, and northern Mexico.

Black willow leaves.

they have much to offer, in this case, soil stabilization and the aesthetics of their red and yellow winter branches. Historically, the black willow and its cousins have offered much more; they have been extraordinarily generous to humankind.

From a naturalist's point of view, black willow is best at that for which it is naturally adapted, erosion control. Its interlacing, far-reaching roots form mats that buffer riverbanks from the scouring action of fast-moving water. Engineers often use what is called riprap (usually heaps of stones) to protect banks from erosion, and willow roots perform the same function naturally. Willows establish themselves with ease along waterways, reproducing vegetatively from their shallow but long roots (up to 75 feet) or from the implanting of dislocated twigs and branches. Willows are easily propagated by inserting green posts into moist soil; in large numbers they have a good survival rate and compare favorably with artificial riprap.

Another soil stabilization method, once used on the lower Mississippi but now replaced by asphalt (!), involved weaving green willow stems into pads, like huge mattresses; weighted down with earth, they soon produced willow thickets.

Although black willow wood is weak, it has the advantages of being pliant, tough, lightweight, and resistant to twisting while drying. It also resists splitting when nailed; its springy fibers actually hold on to nails better than most woods. These assets, plus an abundant, seemingly ubiquitous supply, have made willow the wood of choice for baskets, hampers, panniers, crates, and fish weirs. Willow branches, bark, and bast could be used in both foundation and sewing elements for baskets, and willow basketry was practiced by the Caddo of east Texas and the Jumano of west Texas. The Jumano, like other tribes of the Southwest, made grain storage baskets of willow, which, if they resembled those of the Akimel O'odham of southern Arizona, were so large that the weaver had to stand inside them to complete them. Immigrant settlers were already familiar with willow baskets from their respective homelands. Mormons were making willow baskets in Texas in the mid-nineteenth century. Slender willow branches, called withes or osiers, were the basis for wicker furniture. In northern states where wickerwork centers were located, willows were grown expressly for this industry. Fences, orchard props, and vineyard trellises were common wicker structures.

Willow withes were frequently used among Texas Indian tribes for house construction and various household furniture items. Standard lodge construction used willow not for the frame, which required thicker, sturdier wood, but for the transverse lathing, which held up the grass thatch that formed the roof and walls of the domed structure. Wichita, Caddo, and Mescalero Apache lodges were constructed in this manner, as were the summer shelters of the Kiowa. Sometimes the willow poles themselves formed the frames for smaller or more temporary structures, such as the shelters of the Karankawa or the sweathouses of the Kiowa; the sweathouses were igloo-shaped and covered with robes. In addition, willow withes were used to make cradleboards and cradles among the Kickapoo and Wichita. Around the interior of their thatched lodges, the Wichita also placed beds, raised several feet off the floor, which were constructed of willow rods covered with buffalo hides. Many species of willow were doubtless used in these efforts, but black willow would have been predominant by far.

Black willow wood is lightweight, only 27 pounds per cubic foot, or about half as heavy as post oak and live oak. The wood also tends not to splinter, crack, or warp (if properly seasoned), which accounts for its historic use in the manufacture of artificial limbs. Various Indian tribes, French guides, and trappers tended to make travois poles from willow wood, and the Kiowa used it for arrow shafts and drum frames. Willow saddle trees were also known, which may have been common among the Comanche and Lipan Apache. Willow is the preferred wood for divining rods, not only because it is light and springy but also doubtless because of the tree's connection to water.

Medicinally, the bark, roots, and leaves of willows around the world have been used as an analgesic and for the relief of fever. In North America willow infusions and poultices were known to treat fevers, headaches, pain, and swelling among the Cherokee, Alabama, Chickasaw, Cree, Crow, and Thompson tribes, among others. In our area, the Kiowa chewed willow bark for toothache and used an infusion of leaves on the body for pneumonia and rheumatic aches. Hispanic folk tradition of the Southwest also recommends willow tea for fevers, headaches, and arthritis and, given willow's antiseptic properties, for an astringent gargle for sore gums and throat. The Comanche actually used willow ashes to treat sore eyes.

It should not come as a surprise then to learn that *Salix*, as the name intimates, is the original source of salicin, the natural compound used to make aspirin. The discovery of salicin is one of the more famous stories in medicobotanical literature. The word *discovery* here applies only to the more recent European perspective. Willow's history of pain and fever relief extends around the globe and across millennia. The very earliest recorded medicinal use of willow dates from around 3000 BCE among the Sumerians. Subsequently, its medicinal use is noted among the Egyptians, the classical Greek and Roman authors, and the Chinese of the sixth century. European Medieval and Renaissance folk tradition was aware of the willow's medicinal applications, but use of its analgesic properties slowly waned as the tree became more appreciated as a building material.

Then a certain Reverend Edward Stone in rural Oxfordshire, England, decided one summer day in 1758 to chew on the bark of the *Salix alba* trees in his yard, and it changed the world. Noting its bitterness, he immediately likened the taste to the bark of the Central American cinchona tree (the original source of quinine), which, expensive and difficult to obtain, was the only successful treatment known for ague, or malaria, at the time. He performed an initial experiment on 50 ague sufferers and reported his successful treatment to the Royal Society in 1763. It took but a short while to catch on. In 1828, a German pharmacy professor, Buchner, refined and named the yellowish bark extract *salicin,* which was produced in pure crystalline form only a year later by a French pharmacist, Leroux. In 1838 the Italian chemist Piria produced a potent acid from the crystals, which he dubbed salicylic acid. Further refinements were made by Felix Hoffmann working for Bayer and Company in 1894, who managed to buffer the drug's harsh effects on the stomach

through acetylation, and the rest is history. Now synthetically produced, aspirin is probably the most widely used medicinal drug in the world. Our black willow was not the original inspiration for aspirin, but it shares the same or very similar constituents and, like willows the world over, has its own tradition as an analgesic.

Willow wood generally makes poor fuel for cooking. Like other softwoods, it burns brightly and quickly and does not produce the hot coals generally needed for baking and roasting. Cowboys on the range preferred hardwoods, such as oak and mesquite, if possible (Ted Gray, pers. comm.). Curiously, willow charcoal, because it is largely mineral free, has a long history in the manufacture of gunpowder (a complicated mixture of saltpeter, sulfur, and charcoal). The crack willow (*Salix fragilis*) has been the main source of gunpowder charcoal from early times, but no doubt many species have been tried. Historically, dogwood tended to be used for rapid-burning, small-grain powder for rifles and shotguns, and willow and alder were employed for slower-burning, coarse-grained powder used in larger guns and for blasting.

SOURCES: Ball 1949; Basehart 1974; Brown 1998; Carlson and Jones 1939; Cox and Leslie 1999; Crosswhite 1981; Dorsey 1904; Garrett 2002; Gatschet 1891; Greene 1972; Harrar and Harrar 1962; Jeffreys 2004; La Vere 1998; Latorre and Latorre 1977; Mayhall 1962; Moerman 1998; Moore 1990; Newkumet and Meredith 1988; Nye 1962; Parks 1937; Peattie 1966; Pitcher and McKnight 1990; Simpson 1988; Smithwick 1983; Vane and Botting 1992; Vestal and Schultes 1939; Vines 1984; Walker 1996; Watson et al. 1997; Wrede 1997

Soapberry

Sapindus saponaria L.

[*Sapindus saponaria* L. var. *drummondii* (Hook. & Arn.) L. D. Benson]

Soapberry provides a rare instance in which a plant's common, generic, and specific names all highlight the same distinguishing feature, in this case the fruit's use as a soap or detergent. The waxy berries contain up to 37% saponins, which are surfactants (surface-active agents) that reduce surface tension and foam when shaken, as in the case of soap. Mash the fruits in water to produce a good lather, or simply rub one fruit with a little water over the hands for an instant soap (water is essential, or you'll have a sticky mess). My personal experience with this left my hands surprisingly clean, supple, and smooth, though there are a few reports of contact dermatitis, so caution is advised. According to Havard, a botanist who collected heavily in west Texas in the late nineteenth century, soapberry has a neutral pH, which indicates it would be particularly good for washing fabrics that are too delicate for strong lye-based soaps (Havard 1885). Indeed, other species of *Sapindus* have been used in China and Japan for laundering silk. Mexicans and Hispanics throughout the Southwest have used soapberry as both a laundry detergent and shampoo (*jaboncillo* is Spanish for "little soap"). Soapberry is still a significant botanical source for industrially utilized surfactants.

ORIGIN OF SCIENTIFIC NAME

Sapindus combines the Latin *sapo* (soap) with *indus* (Indian, of the Indies), referring to the many Native Americans who used the genus for soap. The addition of *saponaria* (soapy) yields the emphatic, if not redundant, epithet "soapy Indian-soap."

OTHER COMMON NAMES

western soapberry, wild china (-berry), Indian soap-plant, jaboncillo, amole de bolita, cherioni

FAMILY

Sapindaceae (Soapberry Family)

DESCRIPTION

Small to medium-sized, deciduous, broad-topped tree to 30' tall (max. 45') with pinnately compound leaves and showy clusters of flowers followed by yellowish translucent fruit.

HABITAT AND DISTRIBUTION

Scattered throughout the state (but rarely abundant) in a wide range of soils, along stream bottoms, forest margins, and disturbed areas; southwestern U.S., south-central Plains; northern Mexico.

Soapberry in flower.

Soapberry fruits are generally considered poisonous, but they do have some medicinal applications. Folk traditions have employed them as a fever remedy and to treat rheumatism and renal disorders. The Kiowa made cuts into soapberry stems in order to gather the latex, which they used as a healing agent for wounds. The late Barton Warnock, well-known botanist of the Trans-Pecos, included this cryptic one-liner in one of his floras: "For a sore stomach one may squash the leaves in water and drink the liquid" (Warnock 1974). Drinking a soapy substance may sound misguided, but recent evidence indicates that soapberry leaves (and especially the fruits) do reduce hydrochloric acid in the stomachs of rats and are potentially useful for the treatment of gastric ulcers (Albiero et al. 2002).

Soapberry fruits in winter.

Sapindus saponaria provides a few material uses as well. Each yellow fruit contains a single, round, shiny black seed. These seeds were popularly used for beadwork, necklaces, rosaries, and buttons. The tree's wood, which is heavy, strong, and close grained, has been occasionally used by the Kickapoo for fleshing stakes and ax handles. Given that the wood splits easily into thin, pliant strips, others were more apt to integrate the wood into cotton baskets and packsaddle frames. Apparently little used for lumber, the wood makes an excellent fuel.

A few other odd uses are worthy of note. The fruit pulp can be used in the manufacture of varnish and floor wax, and it yields a bright yellow dye on wool. There are several reports that native peoples of the Southwest and Mexico cast soapberries into streams to stun and stupefy fish for easy capture. This is surely the case, given the ability of saponins to disrupt membranes. Biological applications range from fish and snail poisons to the control of disease-bearing waterborne organisms. Saponins also have commercial uses, beyond soaps and detergents, in fire extinguisher foams and in emulsification agents for fats and oils.

Western soapberry makes a very decent landscape tree, but perhaps not for the garden or lawn. Self-sufficient, tolerant of many habitats, moderately fast growing, and dependable in its yellow fall foliage, the tree has been cultivated since 1900 and is widely planted in shelterbelts and as a shade tree. The Texas Department of Agriculture once pronounced this *the* tree for Texas landscaping (Cox and Leslie 1999). That being said, soapberry doesn't tend to live very long, it suckers freely (creating little groves), and its fruits are potentially poisonous, though not to birds such as cedar waxwings, bluebirds, and robins, which freely devour them. As with many natives, soapberry has its own connection to the insect world. The soapberry hairstreak butterfly times its emergence to the tree's flowering, and its caterpillars rely solely on its foliage for food. Texas boasts the current National Champion western soapberry, 61 feet tall and 9 feet in circumference, located in Aransas County.

Soapberry in older literature is frequently called "wild china," presumably to distinguish it from the cultivated, loosely similar chinaberry (*Melia azedarach,* an Asian import that quickly naturalized here). So early was chinaberry's introduction to Texas that the trees were planted in Austin's colony (San Felipe de Austin) as early as 1828. Unfortunately, because the names are easily confused, it is often difficult to designate with certainty the tree behind the many Texas geographic names that contain the word *china* (China Springs, Grove, Creek, Draw, etc.).

SOURCES: Albiero et al. 2002; Balandrin 1996; Berlandier 1980; Cox and Leslie 1999; Damude and Bender 1999; Haislet 1971; Hatfield 1954; Havard 1885; Latorre and Latorre 1977; Mattoon and Webster 1928; Nokes 2001; Parks 1937; Schulz 1928; Standley 1920–1926; Tull 1999; Vestal and Schultes 1939; Vines 1984; Warnock 1974

Sassafras

Sassafras albidum (Nutt.) Nees

Many of our economic plants suffered sudden reversals of fortune, such as when a synthetic drug or dye offered a better or cheaper alternative, or when supposedly tastier (or more easily acquired) commercial foodstuffs replaced them. Sassafras offers a unique trajectory. It went from obscurity to celebrity status, plateaued for several centuries with a more sober and steady reputation, and then, suddenly, plummeted into oblivion. A natural historian accurately asserted, "no other American tree was ever exalted by such imaginary virtues, in expectation, as sassafras, or has fallen so far in esteem" (Peattie 1966).

As was frequently the case with our flora, Native Americans first brought the virtues of the sassafras to the attention of Europeans. Indian tribes who inhabited Florida used sassafras root bark to treat fevers and many other disorders and shared this knowledge with the Spanish in the early part of the sixteenth century. Nicolás Monardes, Spanish physician and botanist (see horsemint account), championed the plant as a remedy for malarial fevers and as a panacea for practically any illness. For a while, around the turn of the seventeenth century, sassafras was all the rage in Europe as a cure-all and spring tonic, and sassafras root tea, called saloop, was sold in street stalls

ORIGIN OF SCIENTIFIC NAME
The genus name is believed to derive from an American Indian name for the plant, which was written by Spanish settlers as *salsafras*, later becoming *sasafrás*. *Albidum* is Latin for whitish and refers to habital forms of the species that appear lighter in color.

OTHER COMMON NAMES
white sassafras, red sassafras, ague tree, cinnamon wood, smelling stick

FAMILY
Lauraceae (Laurel family)

DESCRIPTION
Medium-sized, deciduous, aromatic tree to 50' tall with trunk 2' in diameter (historically twice these dimensions); leaves often mitten shaped but lobes vary widely, even on same tree; oblong fruits, dark blue to black, $1/4$–$1/2$" long, inside scarlet cups at ends of pedicels.

HABITAT AND DISTRIBUTION
In sandy soils of forest margins, abandoned fields, and fencerows of east Texas; widespread and abundant on wastelands of eastern third of U.S. (minus northern New England and southern Florida); southernmost Ontario.

Sassafras leaves in early autumn.

throughout London. Because of its alleged medicinal benefits, sassafras was not only one of the first plants from the New World to reach the Old but was also among the first plants from North America to be exported from the Colonies. Captain John Smith of the Jamestown Colony sent sassafras to England among his first shipments, and sassafras was demanded among the colony's tribute as late as 1610. As early as 1603, a group of merchants from Bristol, England, formed a company with the sole purpose of collecting sassafras along the New England coast.

Shortly after this period, when people realized that sassafras, like so many other plants, was no panacea, the tree lost its sensational appeal but retained a modest renown for particular uses. Native Americans of the Northeast used sassafras to treat rheumatism and as a postpartum tonic. Southeastern tribes, such as the Cherokee, used sassafras bark infusions to treat worms, colds, diarrhea, and rheumatism. It was also used to treat skin diseases and to poultice wounds and sores. As a mouthwash and gargle for sore throat, sassafras tea was widely touted among the Choctaw, Creek, Delaware, Houma, Iroquois, and Seminole. American colonists and African American folk healers picked up these uses, and nineteenth-century medical practices recommended the tea to bring on sweats, to increase the flow of urine, and to treat indigestion, bowel and bladder troubles, menstrual issues, and skin disorders. The mucilaginous tea was thought especially beneficial to treat fever, pneumonia, bronchitis, and other respiratory problems.

The biggest appeal of sassafras tea, however, lay simply in its pleasant taste. Sassafras wood and root are aromatic, smelling like fennel, and they have a sweetish, spicy taste. Sassafras tea was a favorite substitute for black or green tea in the South during the Civil War, and for coffee in the early days of Texas statehood. Lightly fermented root beers were made from sassafras roots in the South, in combination with greenbrier roots and other ingredients. Like other native teas (such as yaupon), sassafras tea and its consumption developed a somewhat rural and backwater reputation. A frontier folk song, "The Texian Boys," warns that in marrying a good-for-nothing, "your doom will be / Hoecake, hominy, and sassafras tea" (Lomax and Lomax 1948). Sassafras root tea and a jelly made from the same remained popular in the Appalachians well into the second half of the twentieth century.

Most people outside Louisiana are unaware that the filé of the famous Cajun stew known as filé gumbo is nothing other than dried, ground sassafras leaves. The Choctaw and Chippewa dried and pounded the leaves, which have a lemony odor when fresh, and used them to impart a flavor similar to bay leaf to their meat soups. The Cajuns simply followed their lead. The leaves also contain mucilage, which serves as a thickening agent for gumbo, especially at times of the year when okra, the preferred thickening ingredient, is unavailable (*gumbo* derives from a Bantu word for okra). Today filé tends to be used sparingly as a spice sprinkled on top of gumbo at the table.

The twentieth century valued sassafras mainly as a flavoring agent, though traditional herbalists continued to respect its purported medicinal qualities. Sassafras oil, derived from roots and root bark, found extensive use in flavoring candies, chewing gums, toothpastes, mouthwashes, soaps, skin lotions, and perfumes. Sassafras extracts were used to disguise bitter-tasting medicines. Sassafras fragrance was added to insecticides and insect lotions, both as an aromatic and as a repellent. Sassafras mucilage was used in the manufacture of postage stamps. But sassafras oil was perhaps best known as a flavoring ingredient of carbonated beverages, especially root beers, many of which owe their characteristic odor to the plant. Sassafras oil was usually manufactured in small, rather primitive homemade stills scattered throughout the Appalachians and southern Midwest. Annual production of the oil reached 200,000 pounds by mid-century.

Then came the crash. Researchers found that the major constituent of the steam-distilled sassafras oil, safrole, caused liver cancer in rats and mice. As a consequence, the Food and Drug Administration banned sassafras volatile oil as a food and flavoring additive in 1960 and further prohibited the interstate marketing of sassafras bark for tea in 1976. Although sassafras continued to be collected and the tea consumed (at a greatly reduced level), a centuries-old tradition largely fell by the wayside. There are those who feel this was unnecessary. Some studies suggest safrole toxicity differs in humans and lab animals (Tyler 1993), and others maintain that safrole itself is not found in the rootbark tea, which, they claim, is safe to drink (Moore 1990). A long tradition of sassafras tea drinking would seem to be in their favor (never mind that tradition could be used to support tobacco smoking as well). Safrole occurs in many essential oils derived from botanical sources, such as black pepper and nutmeg, but in small amounts. It is interesting that sassafras is rarely included in books about poisonous plants, even those published after 1960 (Kingsbury 1964; Hardin and Arena 1974; Lampe and McCann 1985), and recent works on edible plants still include instructions for preparing the tasty tea (Tull 1999). Sassafras leaves do not contain safrole, allowing filé to be free from restrictions. Commercial, safrole-free sassafras extracts are still made for root beer, and artificial flavoring agents have also been developed.

Rarely used today, sassafras tree lumber was once utilized for special purposes. Although the wood is soft, weak, and brittle, it has the advantages of being very durable and fragrant, and it shrinks less than almost any other hardwood. The lumber was once used for posts, fences, cross-ties, and occasionally for boat-building, cooperage, and cabinetry. The aromatic wood was reputed to repel bedbugs and moths, and many bedsteads and occasionally hope chests were made from it. Cabin floors, as well as hen roosts, were sometimes made from sassafras to keep vermin and lice out.

Today, the historically rich sassafras tree is largely considered a fast-growing ornamental, whose deeply furrowed, red-brown bark, beautiful fall colors, and freedom from pests recommend it for landscape planting. Its fruits are relished by native wildlife, and the spicebush swallowtail butterfly favors the tree for its egg laying.

SOURCES: Anderson 1955; Banta and Caldwell 1933; Cadwallader and Wilson 1965; Carter and Feeny 1999; Cox and Leslie 1999; Diggs et al. 1999; Grande and Dannewitz 1987; Hall 1948; Hamby 2004; Hardin and Arena 1974; Harrar and Harrar 1962; Havard 1896; Hocking 1997; Hussey 1974; Kingsbury 1964; Lampe and McCann 1985; Lomax and Lomax 1948; Mattoon and Webster 1928; Moerman 1998; Moore 1990; Peattie 1966; Porcher 1869; Sievers 1947; Thomson 1978; Tull 1999; Tyler 1993; Wigginton 1977

Bald Cypress

Taxodium distichum (L.) Rich.

Whether lining our rivers and lakes with their stately columns or thronging the swamps in soldiered ranks festooned with moss, bald cypress is one of our most magnificent trees. Long-lived, massive, straight-trunked conifers, they are a southern (admittedly modest) answer to California's redwood. Unlike other conifers in our area, their needles are soft and featherlike, arranged gracefully along the length of each branchlet. Oddly, they are deciduous; their fine needles turn russet before falling and leaving their crowns bald. Pyramidal in shape when young, they eventually attain a more open form, with branches in near-horizontal layers with large spaces between them. Especially in areas where water levels fluctuate, they tend to form knobby protuberances, called knees. These outgrowths from the lateral roots sometimes reach 12 feet in height, but their precise function—whether support, food storage, or aeration—is unknown. Though usually found growing along permanent water, bald cypresses are fairly drought tolerant, and some of the largest specimens are actually found in drier areas; apparently they need constant moisture only for germination. Savvy landscapers have begun planting cypress in seemingly unnatural habitats to great advantage. The

ORIGIN OF SCIENTIFIC NAME

The generic name combines *taxus*, Latin for yew tree, with the Greek suffix *-oides*, "like" or "resembling." *Distichos* is originally a Greek poetic term for two lines of verse; in botanical usage *distichous* denotes vertical rows on opposite sides of an axis, as in the leaf arrangement here.

OTHER COMMON NAMES

southern cypress, white cypress, gulf cypress, yellow cypress, red cypress, black cypress, swamp cypress, ahuehuete, sabino(a), ciprés

FAMILY

Taxodiaceae (Taxodium Family)

DESCRIPTION

Deciduous conifer reaching 150' with trunk diameter of 8', often with swollen and buttressed bases

and forming growths upward from the roots known as knees.

HABITAT AND DISTRIBUTION

In muck, clay, or finer sands of swamps, seeps, stream and river courses; primarily in southern portions of the eastern two-thirds of Texas; coastal southeastern U.S., extending up the Mississippi and Ohio river valleys to Indiana.

Bald cypress in fall color.

tree clearly impressed early colonists, as it was one of the first North American trees introduced to British gardens in the early 1600s. It is also the state tree of Louisiana.

Few trees in Texas attain the size and age of bald cypress. Ordinarily, mature cypress reaches 100–120 feet, occasionally topping out at 150 feet. The tree grows as fast as 1 foot per year for the first 100 years, then tapers off during the next century while its girth expands. Diameters are commonly 4–5 feet, but historical reports of 8–10 feet are not uncommon. Virgin stands once contained many trees 400–600 years old, though reports of much older specimens abound. A Tennessee bald cypress, called the Tennessee Titan, was reported to be more than 1300 years old before it was struck by lightning in 1976. The oldest documented trees in eastern North America are found in a stand of bald cypress along the Black River, North Carolina; they are more than 1600 years old. Bald cypress can be easily misdated because of the appearance of false rings, and many accounts of age have likely been unintentionally exaggerated; this notwithstanding, the tree lives to a venerable age. The germination requirements and longevity of bald cypress have given it a significant role in recent litigation in Louisiana and Texas. Since bald cypress seeds will not germinate underwater, and flooding over the tops of seedlings kills them, the location and age of the trees can be used to determine low- and high-water levels of streams and lakes, which in turn demarcate state-owned from private land, thereby settling disputes over surveys and land ownership.

The size and beauty of bald cypress were noted by early explorers and passed into local lore. The German geologist Ferdinand Roemer noted in his travels along the Guadalupe River in 1846 that cypress trees were 10 feet in diameter. A decade later in the same area, the founder of American landscape architecture Frederick Law Olmsted reported a fallen trunk with a diameter of 14 feet. Much impressed by the cypresses at Sisterdale on the Guadalupe, Olmsted waxed poetic:

> I have rarely seen any resort of wood-nymphs more perfect than the bower of cypress branches and vines that overhang the mouth of the Sister creek at the ford near the house. You want a silent canoe to penetrate it; yet would be loth to desecrate its deep beauty . . . the cypresses rise superbly from the very edge, like ornamental columns. (Olmsted 1857)

Folklorist J. Frank Dobie mentioned a cypress stump, "Ingram's snag," with a hollow "ample enough to camp in" (Dobie 1928). Another Texas folklore enthusiast heard reports that "folks used to saw down a big cypress and give a dance on the stump," the veracity of which she did not doubt after seeing the giant cypresses at Chapultepec, Mexico (Hatfield 1954). Indeed, an individual of a Mexican species of cypress (*Taxodium mucronatum*, also native to southernmost Texas) is famous for having the largest trunk circumference of any tree in the world, over 150 feet—ample room for a dance, were it to be felled. Known as the Arbol del Tule, in Santa María del Tule, Oaxaca, the ancient

Cypress knees in Big Cypress Bayou, Jefferson, Texas.

tree is more than 30 feet in diameter and is believed to be more than 2000 years old. Currently, the largest tree in Texas is a specimen of *T. distichum* in Real County with a modest trunk circumference of 36 feet.

Apart from size and aesthetics, bald cypress is well known for its lumber. Its wood is light, soft, close and straight grained, moderately hard, but not strong. Both the light sapwood and the dark-brown heartwood are easily worked, but only the heartwood is decay resistant. So durable and immune to rot is this heartwood that cypress came to be called the "wood eternal." It was in demand for its long-lasting qualities, and toward the end of the nineteenth century many cypress swamps throughout the coastal South were cut and later drained for ag-

riculture. In Texas, many mills and mill towns sprang up along Hill Country rivers and creeks where cypress trees could be lumbered for shingles and housing materials. Both Bandera and Kerrville, for instance, began as shingle-maker camps in the early 1850s, boasting some of the area's first grist- and sawmills. Exceptionally wide cypress boards can still be seen in the oldest buildings of San Antonio and the Hill Country. Given the wood's resistance to rot, cypress is used extensively for items exposed to water or soil, such as exterior trim, shingles, siding, doors, flooring, posts, poles, pilings, dock timbers, and railroad ties. Bridge builders and, to a lesser extent, boat manufacturers have relied on the durable wood. In the nursery industry, cypress is the preferred wood for greenhouse planking and seed flats. It is not surprising that the wood is also used for water tanks, silos, caskets, laundry tubs, and stadium seats. Nationally, cypress production peaked in 1913, with the milling of one billion board feet, but gradually declined thereafter. By the early twentieth century, most merchantable trees had been felled; usable cypress remained uncut only in places difficult to access. Except for chestnut, which was decimated by blight, bald cypress "probably has had the greatest reduction in volume over the past century of any American tree" (Walker 1996). Fortunately, there is some evidence that second-growth cypress may replenish the lowland forests over the long term.

Bald cypress is steeped in Texas history and place names. A bald cypress limb is credited with saving the life of Martín de Alarcón, governor of the province of Texas, who almost drowned in the Guadalupe River near New Braunfels in 1718. The upper reaches of the Guadalupe were called Alarcón for a short while thereafter (Foster 1995). Ben Milam, entrepreneur and soldier for the Texas cause

in the Battle of Bexar (1835), was killed by a Mexican sniper who, according to legend, was concealed in a bald cypress on the San Antonio River. This towering twin cypress is now called the Ben Milam Cypress in his honor. The Sabine River, which partially forms our border with Louisiana, comes from the Spanish name *Río de Sabinas* (River of the Cypresses); hence, the name *Sabine* graces a county, a lake, a pass, and at least two towns in Texas. *Sabinal*, Spanish for cypress grove, is bestowed on both a town and an intermittent river near Uvalde. The cypress lends its name to more than a dozen creeks and towns throughout the state, revealing the ubiquity and fame of the stately tree.

SOURCES: Bartlett 1995; Bray 1904; Brown 1984; Diggs et al. 1999; Dobie 1928; Dorado et al. 1996; Foster 1917; Foster 1995; Haislet 1971; Harrar and Harrar 1962; Hatfield 1954; Kernell and Levy 1990; Langdon 1958; Lewis 1915; Mattoon and Webster 1928; Olmsted 1857; Roemer 1935; Stahle 1996–1997; Sternitzke 1972; Vines 1984; Walker 1996; Watson 1985; Wrede 1997

SHRUBS

Lechuguilla

Agave lechuguilla Torr.

Agave lechuguilla, one of the most abundant plants of the Trans-Pecos, is not easily forgotten by those who neglect to keep a respectful distance from it. Lechuguilla has one of the most extensive distributions of any member of the *Agave* genus, approximately 1000 miles, and is considered by many to be an indicator species of the Chihuahuan Desert, where it is the dominant perennial on roughly 40 million acres. Its density of growth is truly remarkable; the number of individual rosettes, averaging 8500 per acre, can reach a density of more than 12,000 per acre. Given this extraordinary abundance, it is believed that there are more rosettes of lechuguilla in the wild than of any other of the more than 200 species of *Agave.* Thick stands of lechuguilla, armed with their stiff, needle-sharp spines, can impede both human and animal movement. The spines of the wryly named "little lettuce" easily stab human legs and animals, and horses unfamiliar with the country can actually be lamed by them. Early Spanish explorers complained that lechuguilla prevented them from traveling at night, highly desirable in hostile territory. Today the plant is a hazard to the tires of off-road vehicles. Ranchers also dislike the plant because it is dangerous

ORIGIN OF SCIENTIFIC NAME

Agave is Greek for "noble" or "illustrious"; Linnaeus chose it when naming the first-described century plant (*A. americana*). Lechuguilla, Spanish for "little lettuce," is the common name for the plant on both sides of the U.S.-Mexico border and was employed directly for the specific name. The author of this name (J. Torrey) accidentally misspelled the specific epithet as *lech-eguilla*, which was later corrected by subsequent workers following the International Code of Botanical Nomenclature. It is common to see the scientific name with both spellings.

OTHER COMMON NAMES

None, so far as known.

FAMILY

Agavaceae (Agave Family)

DESCRIPTION

Small, trunkless succulent composed of basal rosette of stiff, yellow-green, sideways-curving leaves, 12–20" long, each armed with marginal teeth that slant down, and terminating in a stout, sharp, 1" spine; flower stalk to 15'.

HABITAT AND DISTRIBUTION

Open, arid, calcareous rocky slopes in mostly west Texas (Trans-Pecos); southern New Mexico; Chihuahuan Desert of north-central Mexico as far south as the state of Mexico.

The stiff, spined leaves of lechuguilla.

for livestock to consume; cows, goats, and sheep have died from feeding on the leaves. Goats, in particular, are susceptible to lechuguilla fever, a condition that occurs when the indigestible fibers clog an animal's digestive tract.

It may come as a surprise, then, that *Agave lechuguilla* is an important succulent in our state, ranking with sotol and prickly pear historically as one of the most utilized plants. Lechuguilla is likely Texas' best native fiber plant, though practically no Texan is aware of this. Across the border in Mexico, lechuguilla is the most widely harvested agave currently used for fiber (Nobel 1994). More than 10,000 tons of fiber per year were produced in the later decades of the twentieth century, when its harvest or processing provided at least temporary em-

ployment to more than 200,000 people. Obtaining the fiber at a commercial level is time consuming. The leaves are gathered by hand, and only the central buds of unopened leaves (called "cogollos") are harvested, since their fibers are finer and more easily twilled. The young leaves are stripped of their spines, pounded, and then scraped several times with a dull knife, which removes the pulp and exposes the fibers. These are cleaned and placed in the sun, which both dries and bleaches them. Little of this process has been successfully mechanized, since apparently the fibers are easily crushed and lose their resiliency. Also, unlike *Agave fourcroydes* (from which henequen fiber is produced) and *A. sisalana* (which yields sisal), *A. lechuguilla* has not been successfully grown in plantations.

Lechuguilla fiber is called *ixtle* or *istle* (a Nahuatl term for fiber), but in the export trade, it is known as tula istle, tula fiber, Mexican fiber, or Tampico fiber (Tampico being the major port of export). Although all agave fibers are in a weak competitive position with abaca and the synthetics (such as rayon and nylon), they retain niche markets owing to particular properties. Lechuguilla fiber has a certain resiliency, texture, and water absorbency that qualifies it for certain commercial purposes, such as power-driven cylinder brushes, steel mill brushes, and rotary floor scrubbers and polishers. It is also widely used in mats, brooms, dusters, roofing brushes, and pastry brushes. Domestic utilization in Mexico, in addition to brushes, revolves around cordage, rope, and twine, and it is employed in myriad products such as clotheslines, harnesses, bridles, tethers, sacks, and baskets.

As one might suspect, lechuguilla fiber extraction is not modern in origin. Its commercial history dates only to the nineteenth century, but the folk tradition of its use goes back centuries. Archaeological evidence, in fact, indicates its usage in north-central Mexico as far back as 8100 years ago. On our own side of the border, west Texas caves reveal equally ancient use of lechuguilla fiber for similar purposes. The principal material for cordage, the fiber was used extensively in making sandals, baskets, and mats. Texas Indian tribes, such as the Jumano, Coahuiltecan, and Lipan Apache, continued such uses into historic times. The Coahuiltecan were known to employ the twisted fibers for bowstrings, one of many uses that

the late desert survivalist David Alloway encouraged, and for which he provided careful instructions (Alloway 2000).

Another major use of lechuguilla, again almost unknown north of the Rio Grande, is for soap. There are two sources for this: the rootstock and the leaves. The rootstock (the bottom of the basal rosette) and shallow roots are crushed and then soaked in water for several minutes. The water is stirred into a lather that can be used as a shampoo, body wash, or detergent. The Tarahumara Indians of northern Mexico, calling it *amole* (Nahuatl for soap), are fond of employing the suds to clean white clothes, especially woolen items. The leaves provide another source of soap, obtained especially during the fiber removal process. The large quantity of leaf pulp (including marginal spines), called *guishe* or *shite,* is naturally soapy and can be used to scrub pots, pans, and dishes, as well as clothing. The suds come from a saponin (a sapogenin glucoside), which, like most saponins, has membrane-disrupting properties. Not surprisingly, the leaf pulp has been used to poison arrow tips, as well as to pour into rivers to stun fish for easy capture. Along these lines, recent research has found that extracts from lechuguilla roots are active against many microbes, including yeasts, molds, and bacteria. Like other saponin-containing plants, lechuguilla also contains a steroidal precursor; however, given its resistance to cultivation and mechanical processing, obtaining the required substances in quantity and transporting them from often remote and inaccessible locations make the plant

Lechuguilla's flower stalk, about 12 feet high; Big Bend National Park.

economically infeasible as a source for steroids.

Lechuguilla flowers are a sight to see, as are so many of the agaves in bloom. Blooming on average only after 20 years of growth (reports vary from 3 years to 35), the plant sends up an inflorescence that can grow as much as 8 inches per day, in its initial stages, slowly decelerating as it approaches its maximum height of 8–15 feet in three to four weeks, at which point about 40% of the plant's total biomass is invested in the flower stalk. Blooming in May and June, the yellowish-purple flowers offer an exceptional source of energy for various insects and other animals during the height of the dry season. Coprolite evidence from the lower Pecos suggests that even prehistoric humans partook of the flowers. When the bloom is finished, the plant dies, survived by its many offshoots. The dried stalks, together with those of sotol, provide one of the few desert substitutes for wood; they have been variously used for roof materials, basket frames, spear shafts, and knife handles.

As with sotol, lechuguilla hearts, the starchy white meristem of the basal rosette, historically played a role as a food staple. Nomadic tribes of north-central Mexico were reportedly boiling them for food before the Spanish arrived in the New World (Sheldon 1980), though most sources agree that the hearts were more often consumed only after baking in pit ovens (see sotol account). The Jumano, Coahuiltecan, and Lipan Apache made extensive use of lechuguilla and other agaves as a food staple in historic times. As the Lipan moved farther south into the plant's range, *Agave lechuguilla* likely became their most important wild-plant staple, in the same way *A. parryi*, and the starchy foodstuff called *mescal* made from it, became the signature plant of the western branch of the tribe, the *Mescalero* Apache. According to current sources, baked lechuguilla, although edible, is considerably less palatable than sotol and other agaves (Alloway 2000).

SOURCES: Alexander 1970; Alloway 2000; Belmares et al. 1979; Bryant 1986; Dewey 1943; Freeman and Reid 1985; Gentry 1982; Loughmiller and Loughmiller 1996; Martin 1933; Nelson 2000; Newberry 1887; Newcomb 1961; Nobel 1994; Nobel and Quero 1986; Pennington 1958; Powell 1988; Reyes-Agüero et al. 2000; Shafer 1986; Sheldon 1980; Silverthorne 1996; Standley 1912; Verástegui et al. 1996; Wauer 1980; Williams-Dean 1978

Agarita

Berberis trifoliolata Moric.

[*Mahonia trifoliolata* (Moric.) Fedde]

Looking at a dusty agarita growing through a barbed-wire fence in the midsummer heat, one would hardly imagine that this prickly, hollylike shrub could serve any purpose other than sheer orneriness. Nothing could be farther from the truth. Its roots, stems, flowers, and fruits have variously served insects, animals, and humans for millennia. Indeed, agarita compares favorably with Texas' most eminently useful plants.

The bright yellow, saffron-scented flowers are especially attractive to bees. The early blooming period of the plant (as early as January and February) provides copious amounts of pollen and nectar for the bees at a time when there is precious little to be had. Agarita is preceded only by mistletoe in the annual blooming cycle of bee plants in Texas. Its flowers are also unusual in having stamens with touch-sensitive bases, which, when triggered, strike the nectar-seeking bee on the head, covering it with pollen. The fresh flowers of all Texas species of *Berberis* are also entirely edible.

The fruits that develop from the pollinated flowers bring the plant its renown. The bright red berries provide fodder for quail and other birds, and probably any animal willing to withstand the prickles, including humans.

ORIGIN OF SCIENTIFIC NAME
Berberis is the latinized form of *berberys*, an Arabic name of the fruit. Some workers place the species in the genus *Mahonia*, named in honor of Bernard M'Mahon (1775–1816), a prominent American horticulturist. *Trifoliolata* refers to the compound leaves of three leaflets.

OTHER COMMON NAMES
algerita, agarito, agrito, wild currant, currant-of-Texas, desert holly, chaparral berry, palo amarillo, Laredo mahonia

FAMILY
Berberidaceae (Barberry Family)

DESCRIPTION
A small evergreen shrub, usually 2–6' high, with prickly, hollylike, gray- or blue-green leaves.

HABITAT AND DISTRIBUTION
Western two-thirds of state, plus coastal south Texas, generally on dry, rocky hillsides and slopes, but also on pastureland and along fence lines; Arizona and New Mexico; northern Mexico.

Agarita flowers, among spring's earliest.

Agarita in fruit.

In fact, there is evidence going back to 7000 BCE (Baker Cave, Val Verde County) that early Native Americans ate the berries. Ripening in May and June, the berries are one of the earliest fruits of the season, but even when ripe, they are highly acidic (hence the name *agrito*, Spanish for "little sour"). Few present-day folk are likely to eat more than a handful straight from the bush. As with cranberries, the addition of sugar greatly expands the fruit's culinary virtues, and agarita berries make excellent jellies, pies, cobblers, cool drinks, wine, and even an agarita margarita (Cheatham and Johnston 2000). The Apache are known to have made a type of jelly from the fruit as well. The roasted seeds have even been used as a substitute for coffee (though in hard times, many seeds were so employed).

Since the berries are well protected among the prickly leaves, getting them to the kitchen in any quantity is no love affair. There seems to be general agreement, from an early popular book on Texas wildflowers through J. Frank Dobie's childhood recollections to a recent work on a border healing woman, that the best way to collect agarita fruit is to place a sheet (or upturned umbrella) around the base and to whack the bush with a stick or broom (Schulz 1928; Dobie 1967; Babb 1985). The opinions offered on how to separate the berries from the leaves, twigs, and other chaff vary from manual picking to winnowing the berries in the wind like grain to rolling them down a wet tow sack (since the chaff will stick to the sack).

Moving down the plant to the stems and roots, a myriad of uses prevail. Take a knife to the bark of any stem and one will find a surprisingly bright yellow flesh beneath. This yellow coloring, present in both stems and roots, was prized by Native Americans and early settlers as a source for a yellow to tan-orange dye. Berlandier, one of the earliest trained botanists to collect in Texas, noted in 1828 that the pounded roots were used to make a yellow dye, and rarely is agarita mentioned in subsequent publications without noting this use. Current-day craftsmen also use the yellow wood in carvings and for beads.

Perhaps less well known is the antimicrobial alkaloid contained in the roots. Aptly named berberine, it has been employed as a dressing for impetigo and ringworm. A decoction of the roots was also used in frontier times for toothache. Berberine, which can be derived from many species in the genus, has a weak physiological effect, but in sufficient quantities it can cause fatal poisoning. As late as the 1940s it was rarely used in the United States except as a bitter stomachic; in the form of berberine salts, it did have some longevity as an ingredient in eyedrops on account of its astringent properties, a use that echoes the Mescalero Apache's eyewash made from *Berberis haematocarpa*, which is found in west Texas. Currently, however, even this use has ceased, and berberine does not appear to be favored in any drug therapy.

The plant as a whole, with its armory of spiny evergreen leaves, provides perfect shelter for small wildlife (birds, rodents, rattlesnakes). As larger animals tend not to browse the foliage, agarita is a good nurse plant, providing a safe haven for vulnerable seedlings, which might otherwise be quickly eaten.

Three other species are known in Texas, all of which have five or more leaflets per leaf (as opposed to three). *Berberis repens*, creeping barberry, has purple berries and rarely exceeds a foot in height. It is common in the Rocky Mountains, extending all the way to British Columbia, but just barely finds its way into Texas in the Guadalupe Mountains. Red barberry (the *B. haematocarpa* mentioned above) can reach 6–8 feet in height; in Texas it is largely confined to the mountains of the Trans-Pecos (the Guadalupe, Davis, Sierra Diablo, and Chisos ranges). Its red berries are said to be less tasty than those of *B. trifoliolata*. Finally, *B. swaseyi*, Texas barberry, is distinctive in having the largest (up to half an inch in diameter), juiciest, and sweetest berries of the four species; the berries tend to be orangish red in color. Endemic to the Edwards Plateau, it is reported to hybridize with agarita, though the blooming periods of the two species just barely overlap, being January–March for agarita and March–May for Texas barberry (Harms 2007).

SOURCES: Babb 1985; Basehart 1974; Berlandier 1980; Castetter and Opler 1936; Cheatham and Johnston 2000; Dobie 1967; Durand 1973; Enquist 1987; Harms 2007; Hester 1980; Hocking 1997; Kirkpatrick 1992; Pellett 1976; Powell 1988; Schulz 1928; Standley 1920–1926; Tull 1999; Wasowski and Wasowski 1997; Wills and Irwin 1961; Wood and Osol 1943; Wrede 1997

Sotol

Dasylirion leiophyllum Engelm.

Dasylirion texanum Scheele

Dasylirion wheeleri S. Watson

Sotol deserves high marks both for its beauty and its rich ethnobotanical history. In the words of one early naturalist, it is "the most striking botanical feature of the country" west of the Pecos (Havard 1885). With its tight cluster of many leaves, it adds architectural form to any area in which it grows, dotting landscapes with distinct mounds and making an excellent foundation plant around buildings. One would hardly suspect that this shrub once constituted one of the great semiarid staples in our state, for in its region, sotol was more responsible for food and material culture than almost any other plant, with the possible exception of lechuguilla and other *Agave* species.

All Trans-Pecos ranchers know that in times of need they can rely for cow fodder on the heart of sotol, the short trunk and leaf bases that form a cabbagelike, basal rosette. With the leaves burned or chopped off and the hearts cleaved, cattle are able to reach the sugary

ORIGIN OF SCIENTIFIC NAME
The genus name is a combination of the Greek *dasys* (thick, rough, bushy, shaggy) with *lirion* (a type of lily). The genus used to be placed in the lily family. *Leiophyllum* is Greek for smooth-leaved, *texanum* needs no explanation, and *wheeleri* honors Lieutenant George M. Wheeler of the Army Corps of Engineers, who led the U.S. Geographical Survey West of the 100th Meridian.

OTHER COMMON NAMES
For *Dasylirion leiophyllum*: smooth sotol, desert candle. For *D. texanum*: Texas sotol, saw yucca. For *D. wheeleri*: desert spoon, Wheeler sotol

FAMILY
Nolinaceae (Nolina or Beargrass Family)

DESCRIPTION
Shrubs composed of dense basal rosettes of stiff, slender, ribbon-like, spiny leaves, 1–3' long; usually trunkless, with stem mostly subterranean; flower stalk unbranched, 5–15' high.

HABITAT AND DISTRIBUTION
Locally abundant on dry, rocky slopes, hillsides, mesas, and desert grasslands of western and central Texas. *Dasylirion leiophyllum*, the most common species of the Trans-Pecos, extends into New Mexico; *D. texanum* reaches from the Trans-Pecos to the Edwards Plateau; *D. wheeleri* appears in Texas only in El Paso and Hudspeth counties, the eastern edge of a range that stretches west to Arizona; all three extend into adjacent parts of Mexico.

Dr. B. L. Turner between two sotols in bloom.

and starchy pith, which they relish. It is thought that they would generally make short work of sotol plants were it not for the armada of saw-edged leaves. During severe droughts, many sotols between Del Rio and Sanderson and across the Big Bend succumbed to this practice.

Few now know that sotol heart was a major staple food for many tribes of the region. As far back as 4000 BCE early Native Americans had discovered that the spongy sotol hearts, although edible raw, were more palatable if roasted slowly. The preferred method for roasting was in a pit oven. A fire was started in a rock-lined

pit several feet deep and allowed to burn down to coals; more rocks were added on top of the coals; sotol hearts (as well as lechuguilla and other agaves) were placed on top of the rocks and covered with plant matter (such as sotol leaves) for moisture; then the entire pit was covered with earth and left for up to 48 hours. This slow cooking caramelizes the starchy pulp, rendering it soft and sweet, easier to extract and tastier to consume. The leaf bases could be eaten like artichoke bracts. These pit ovens sometimes contained hundreds of sotol hearts and could reach dimensions of 5 feet deep by 10 feet or

Sotol as it appears most of the year.

more in diameter. The numerous fire-pit rocks—often split from the heat—were left in large piles, which help archaeologists to identify these sites.

From the seventeenth through nineteenth centuries, several tribes were known to have consumed sotol extensively, especially in times of emergency, such as in drought or when pursued. As early as 1684 it was noted that the Suma, along the Rio Grande near El Paso, relied heavily on them. The Comanche, but especially the Lipan, Chiricahua, and Mescalero Apache, also partook of the plant. Roasted in the same ancient manner, sotol hearts could be consumed on the spot, but apparently the tribes preferred to pound the hearts into a paste and sun-dry them. Dried sotol could be mixed with nuts and fruits or ground into a flour, rehydrated, and baked into ash cakes as needed in the winter. Given the prevalence of sotol where these tribes lived, it was virtually impossible for

them to starve. Several agaves may have been considered superior for roasting, but they were often not available or were less prevalent in this region. By the latter half of the nineteenth century, sotol was one of the Lipan's most important foodstuffs and, whether or not a sign of duress, was in constant use.

Just as tequila is made from agave, a potent alcohol called sotol mescal, or simply sotol, is also made from the hearts of *Dasylirion* species by the Hispanic peoples of this region. Roasted in the manner described above, or simply boiled, the hearts are mashed with water, the juices allowed to ferment, and the liquid distilled. The result, in Havard's words, is a "limpid, colorless liquor of penetrating smell and peculiar taste not unlike the smoky flavor of Scotch whisky" (Havard 1885), though a current naturalist compares the drink to a "mixture of hair oil and gasoline" (Wauer 1980). Sotol mescal was a common alcoholic beverage and the dominant spirit among the frontier population of west Texas at the end of the nineteenth century; it became a leading article of contraband along the Rio Grande in the years of Prohibition. During World War II, an alcohol from sotol was apparently produced commercially in Val Verde County, and sotol mescal was still noted as the most popular alcoholic beverage among the Kickapoo in the late 1970s. It is still enjoyed all along the Rio Grande in the Trans-Pecos.

Dasylirion leaves are one of Texas' native sources of plant fiber; along with lechuguilla, beargrass, and *Yucca* species, they have a rich history of use. Caves in the southwestern part of the state have provided abundant archaeological evidence for sotol leaf use over many millennia in such articles as sandals, mats, baskets, and many varieties of twisted cordage. The Lipan Apache used the dried leaf bases as cigarette papers. Additional modern uses for the leaves in the area include ropes, rough hats, and roof thatching. Called "ixtle" by Hispanics of the region, the fibers are best extracted by heating the leaves over coals, pounding them with stone, and scraping the pulp off the fibers with a knife.

In a land with few or no trees, it is not surprising that sotol's 15-foot flower stalks would be used for such a variety of needs. Ancient uses included basket frames, spear shafts, fireboards, fire tongs, knife handles, and digging sticks. Historical (mainly Apache) uses include tepee poles, cradleboards, ceremonial headdresses, and one-string fiddles. Sotol stalks even enter into Lipan mythology as a source of hunting arrows (Opler

1940). Perhaps the most frequently cited use of the stalks, past and present, is for fire drills and fireboards for starting fires. Sotol stalk fireboards, also called hearth boards, were the bottom pieces of wood into which fire drills were rapidly drilled to create friction. Spent fireboards have been found in ancient sites and were so abundant in historic times that early pioneers, finding them scattered about the land, thought they must be Indian bullet molds. Modern guides still argue that sotol stalks, which are fairly soft and produce ignitable dust quickly, make the best fireboards in the area. More recently, sotol stalks have been used as walking sticks and to construct porch and house roofs, corrals, and other structures.

There are a few other odd uses. Sotol flower stalks, especially when they first emerge, can be roasted and eaten. The central edible portion is white, sweet, and palatable. There is also evidence that sotol flower ingestion was common among archaic peoples in the area. Dead and dried whole plants make excellent fuel, burning rapidly and brightly, like paper. Even live plants usually have a ring of dead leaves at the bottom, and these can be lit for emergency signaling (the green leaves above providing smoke), an old Mexican and cowboy trick that also provides warmth after sudden thunderstorms (Alloway 2000).

SOURCES: Alexander 1970; Alloway 2000; Basehart 1974; Bement 1989; Bolton 1908; Bryant 1974; Dennis and Dennis 1925; Fletcher 1928; Greene 1972; Havard 1885, 1895; Latorre and Latorre 1977; Martin 1933; Newberry 1887; Newcomb 1961; Opler 1940; Parks 1937; Powell 1988; Schulz 1928, Shafer 1986; Tull 1999; Warnock 1970; Wauer 1980

Mormon Tea

Ephedra antisyphilitica Berland. ex C. A. Mey.

Mormon tea has an unusual if not striking appearance. With a mass of thin, jointed green twigs, which somewhat resemble pine needles, the plant has been compared to a "shrubby squat conifer" (Wasowski and Wasowski 1997). This is not far from the truth. As the name *joint-fir* suggests, the genus *Ephedra* belongs to the gymnosperms, which are plants that lack true flowers and have exposed seeds, like those of a pine cone. All the conifers (pines, firs, junipers, etc.) are gymnosperms, as opposed to the majority of trees, shrubs, and wildflowers in this book, which are angiosperms, having true flowers and fruits that enclose their seeds. *Ephedra* actually holds a unique position between the two groups. On the one hand, it bears its seeds in cones and is definitely a gymnosperm; on the other hand, it has (highly specialized) reproductive features that are in line with angiosperms. *Ephedra* is the only genus in its family. It contains about 60 species in temperate and warm regions worldwide (save Australia).

The species of greatest economic importance occur in Asia. The stems and roots of *Ephedra sinica*, *E. equisetina*, and *E. intermedia* are all sold under the Chinese market name *ma-huang*, which is the source for ephedrine, the principal active constituent of the herbal medicine. Tradi-

ORIGIN OF SCIENTIFIC NAME
Ephedra is a Greek name for a plant mentioned in Pliny with numerous rushlike, jointed branches and a few slender leaves; in Pliny's day this name was also applied to *Equisetum* (horsetail), though the two are not related. The word may derive from *ep-*, "upon," and *hedra*, "seat," since the segments of the stems appear to sit on one another. *Antisyphi-litica*, "against syphilis," refers to the use of this species to treat the disease.

OTHER COMMON NAMES
joint-fir, clapweed, desert tea, squaw tea, teamster's tea, cowboy tea, kidney weed, popote, tepo-pote, popotillo, cañatilla

FAMILY
Ephedraceae (Mormon Tea Family)

DESCRIPTION
Erect or spreading shrub to 3' tall with many vertical, jointed stems; appears leafless; male, pollen-producing cones on separate plants from female, seed-producing cones; female cones less than 1/2" long, often turn red at maturity.

HABITAT AND DISTRIBUTION
Arid soils and rocky slopes and ravines across western two-thirds of state; southwestern Oklahoma; northeastern Mexico.

Mormon tea.

tional Chinese medicine has recommended ma-huang for almost 5000 years to treat asthma, nasal colds, fevers, coughs, and joint pains. In this country ma-huang is taken as a stimulant, performance enhancer, and appetite suppressant, although only limited clinical data support these uses. More than 200 diet supplements contained the herbal ingredient before the FDA, concerned over rising reports of insomnia, hypertension, heart attacks, strokes, and seizures, banned the sale of dietary supplements containing *Ephedra*.

North American species of *Ephedra* in our area contain only minute amounts of ephedrine, though they do contain tannins and pseudoephedrine, the latter being the active ingredient in commercial decongestants. Native peoples and folk healers of the Southwest have employed local species of *Ephedra* to treat a host of conditions very similar to those treated by ma-huang. Hispanics of this region have prepared a tea of the stems to treat head colds, hay fever, and hangovers. Anglos of the Southwest used the tea to treat arthritis and rheumatic pains, and various Pueblo tribes have used the tea as a cough medicine. Contemporary desert naturalists still recommend the tea as a stimulant and to increase bronchial dilation for easier breathing. Southwestern species of *Ephedra* provide some uses not usually attributed to ma-huang. Traditional *curanderos* have employed the tea as a laxative and to treat jaundice. The idea that the tea cleanses and purifies the blood and organs (such as the liver and kidney) was popular among frontiersmen. Poultices of the macerated stems, on account of their astringent qualities, were applied to snakebites. The stems, simply chewed, are considered excellent thirst quenchers.

By far the most frequently mentioned medicinal application for species of the

American Southwest is for urinary and kidney disorders. Mormon tea (a.k.a. kidney tea), as well as ma-huang, were well known as diuretics, substances that stimulate and ease urination. For this reason, Hispanic peoples from California to Texas and indigenous tribes of this region, such as the Navajo, Mescalero Apache, and many Puebloans, have used the tea to treat urinary disorders and kidney pain.

Mormon tea's diuretic properties are likely responsible for the notion that southwestern species of *Ephedra* were useful in treating venereal disease. *Ephedra antisyphilitica*, as the name suggests, was used extensively to treat syphilis. Throughout the Southwest, Anglos, Hispanics, and Native Americans (Akimel O'odham, Apache, and Zuni, among others) variously used teas and decoctions of the stems and entire plants of this and other local species to treat both syphilis and gonorrhea (hence the name *clapweed*). Men traveling with teams of draft animals in the desert Southwest allegedly contracted these disorders from the locals. So common were the diseases that the teamsters carried quantities of *E. antisyphilitica* with them as a matter of course, hence the name *teamster's tea*. *Cowboy tea* may have a similar derivation, or perhaps, like *desert tea*, the name indicates that it was simply one of the few drinks available in the wilderness. Although *Ephedra* teas likely helped to relieve the painful urination of gonorrhea, they could not cure it. Effective cures for venereal disease came only after the invention of antibiotics.

All medicinal purposes aside, *Ephedra* species simply make respectable teas. Again, numerous indigenous tribes and Hispanic peoples of the Southwest use these teas as refreshing drinks. The Navajo sometimes roast the stems before preparing the tea, but usually the stems are simply used fresh or dried. The Apache, Havasupai, Tohono O'odham, and Zuni, among many others, enjoy this beverage, though the Puebloans seem to prefer the flavor of their Indian tea (*Thelesperma megapotamicum*). Early Mormon settlers, for whom alcohol, coffee, and tea were proscribed, found that they could imbibe the mildly stimulating *Ephedra* teas without violating the letter (though perhaps the spirit) of their law. As tradition would have it, their liberal use of the drink led to the name most commonly applied to the genus (and many species).

In the wild, *Ephedra antisyphilitica* often appears gnarled and weather-beaten. This is partly because the plant is heavily browsed by deer and cattle, and in times of drought, it may be nibbled to a state where it is almost unrecognizable. The plant offers nesting and cover for small animals, and quail feast on its seeds. In the garden, it is a good specimen or accent plant, though it may be difficult to grow and is usually not offered in the nursery trade. The many bunches of thin twigs are the basis for the Spanish common names *popote* (broomstraw), *popotillo* (little broomstraw), *tepopote* (broomstraw tea), and *cañatilla* (little reed).

SOURCES: Alloway 2000; Burlage 1968; Curtin 1965; Dunmire and Tierney 1995; Friedman 1990; Hicks 1966; Hu 1969; Kirkpatrick 1992; Moerman 1998; Moore 1990; Palmer 1878; Smithers 1964; Stevenson 1993; Taylor et al. 1997; Tull 1999; Warnock 1970, 1977; Wasowski and Wasowski 1997

Candelilla

Euphorbia antisyphilitica Zucc.

This hardy desert perennial with its clumps of rodlike stems is basically a Mexican species that just crosses the Rio Grande into Texas, growing in real abundance only in several counties of the Trans-Pecos. Its relative scarcity in our state, however, is offset by the unusual resource it offers and the unique industry that has developed around it.

Euphorbia antisyphilitica was named in the early nineteenth century for its reported medicinal properties. The white sap, or latex, of the species, common throughout the genus, was extensively used in Mexico to treat venereal diseases; whether the treatment was successful is unknown, but unlikely. The Kickapoo Indians, who now live primarily in Mexico, still prepared a decoction of the plant to treat syphilis as late as the 1970s. They drank the tea and applied it externally to syphilitic sores. The plant was also known as a purgative, which is not surprising given the toxicity of many plants in this family.

Apparently, it was not until the twentieth century that candelilla became recognized for something that it was very adept at producing: wax. The stems of candelilla are covered with a thick, flaky coat of wax, which helps the plant conserve water (a device found in many desert

---

ORIGIN OF SCIENTIFIC NAME

As related in Pliny's *Natural History*, King Juba II of Mauritania (52 BCE–23 CE), a scholar-king and natural historian, discovered on Mount Atlas a rodlike plant with milky sap of medicinal properties and named it in honor of his physician and friend Euphorbus. *Antisyphilitica* alludes to this species' historical use in treating venereal disease.

OTHER COMMON NAMES

wax plant

FAMILY

Euphorbiaceae (Spurge Family)

DESCRIPTION

Stiff perennial herb, rarely exceeding 3' in height, forming clumps of numerous erect, pale green, pencil-like stems; tiny, drought-deciduous leaves present only on new growth; tiny, pinkish-white flowers cluster at stem tips usually following rains.

HABITAT AND DISTRIBUTION

Scattered to locally abundant on gravelly and rocky limestone slopes, ridges, and hills of the Trans-Pecos and south Texas, usually within 50 miles of the Rio Grande; extreme southern New Mexico; desert mountains of northern and central Mexico.

Typical clump of candelilla.

Close-up of candelilla showing flowers.

plants); the wax becomes especially abundant during prolonged periods of heat and drought. Mexican rural folk mix this wax with paraffin to make excellent candles, said to burn brightly and with a pleasant odor, and the name *candelilla* (Spanish for "little candle") may reflect this use, or it may simply refer to the shape of the plant's stems. It so happens that candelilla wax, which consists mainly of long-chain hydrocarbons, is one of the highest-quality waxes known, and in commerce it became one of the best-known vegetable waxes, second only to carnauba palm wax. In its heyday, the wax was used extensively for such things as acid-proofing agents for metal etching, adhesives, carbon paper, chewing gum, cosmetics, crayons, electrical insulating, inks, leather dressings, linoleum, lubricants, phonograph records, polishes (for floors, shoes, furniture, and automobiles), sealing waxes, and varnishes. During the world wars, the wax was in high demand for waterproofing military tents and tarpaulins and for the manufacture of explosives. In general, the majority of candelilla wax in the United States has been utilized in coating and polishing preparations and in chewing gum. The companies most directly involved are Johnson Wax, American Chicle, and Wrigley. Trident chewing gum still contains candelilla wax to this day.

The collection of the wax provides an insight into an almost extinct cottage industry of the west Texas border region. Since candelilla tends to grow in remote and inaccessible areas, the wax has historically been obtained through small teams, each usually comprising no more than half a dozen men, who move from area to area as supplies are depleted. Wild plants are pulled up by the roots and loaded onto donkeys and mules for the trip back to a temporary processing camp. Here the plants are boiled in water with sulfuric acid in large vats until the wax floats to the surface, where it is skimmed off and allowed to solidify. The crude wax obtained represents about 2% of the weight of the plant material used; in general, one ton of candelilla plants yields about 50 pounds of wax. This wax is loaded onto mules and taken to the nearest refiner, where it undergoes the final purification required for commercial use. The majority of candelilla plants are collected in the hottest and driest states of northern Mexico, such as Chihuahua, Coahuila,

and Nuevo Leon, but families and small teams north of the border in Brewster, El Paso, Hudspeth, Jeff Davis, Presidio, Terrell, and Val Verde counties also have profited from the industry. Unfortunately, the practice of removing candelilla plants by the roots, the only effective harvesting method known, causes candelilla populations to recover very slowly, and whole areas become quickly denuded of growth.

The candelilla wax industry flourished for only a short while, though it is still not entirely extinct. The wax was known to commerce as early as 1912, but did not receive real attention until around World War I, when vegetable oils became scarce. The 1920s, '30s, and '40s saw the heyday of the wax as it developed into a multi-million-dollar industry, and hundreds of wax camps were scattered up and down the Rio Grande. By 1937 production was beginning to reach excessive levels, the candelilla supply was growing thin, and Mexico began to impose taxes to keep the industry in check. But World War II raised the value of the wax, and production more than tripled during the war years.

After the war, two things weighed heavily on this rural industry. The first was that the Mexican government, fearing extinction of the quickly dwindling candelilla, continued to impose taxes and quotas and actually prohibited wax production in 1947–1948 and again in 1953–1954. Although these measures had some positive results, an unintended consequence was intense smuggling, since U.S. buyers had more available cash and would pay more than could be obtained in Mexico. Plants along the Mexican border were harvested and smuggled to adjacent parts of Texas for processing. The second was that after World War II, petroleum-based synthetic waxes were produced at about one-fourth the cost of candelilla wax, which spelled the sure demise of a viable candelilla wax industry. Despite these setbacks, a handful of candelilleros continue to make the wax in the time-honored tradition for a small market in the cosmetics and chewing-gum industries.

Only time will tell whether candelilla wax will continue to have economic value. On the one hand, it is an excellent wax, and the plants offer a potential arid-land crop in regions where little else will grow. On the other hand, efforts to make the harvest and production of the wax economically competitive have not been successful to date. Candelilla grows on difficult terrain distant from population centers and roadways. Mechanizing its harvest has not worked, except on flat land, which amounts to only a tiny percentage of the plant's habitat. Cultivation has yielded disappointing results. The plants produce the greatest amounts of wax when growing slowly under drought-stressed conditions. Cultivation encourages fast growth, but little or no wax. Traditional methods are actually as efficient as can be expected given the terrain and conditions, but labor costs on the U.S. side make the industry cost-prohibitive. None of these disadvantages is necessarily insurmountable, and it is conceivable that the wax may one day rise again.

SOURCES: Babb 1985; Balandrin 1984; Graham 1975; Hodge and Sineath 1956; Latorre and Latorre 1977; Mielke 1993; Pliny 1938–63; Powell 1988; Schulz 1928; Tull 1999; Tunnell 1981

Ocotillo

Fouquieria splendens Engelm.

One of the most distinctive shrubs of the desert Southwest, ocotillo inhabits Texas only in the Trans-Pecos, where it is on the eastern edge of its distribution. Its peculiar array of slender, spiny stems, seemingly leafless and appearing all but dead for most of the year, gives one the impression of a cactus. Actually, *Fouquieria* is the only genus in its own family, the Fouquieriaceae, which bespeaks its distinctiveness. The genus contains only eleven species, all of which are endemic to Mexico except *F. splendens.* The most widespread member of the genus, *F. splendens* also occurs in the deserts of Texas, New Mexico, Arizona, California, and the southern tip of Nevada. In Texas ocotillo is considered a characteristic species of the Chihuahuan Desert; that is, when you see it, you know you have entered what floristically comprises this desert. Ocotillo's candelabra form is unforgettable; its cluster of 6 to 30 (but up to 75) arching branches can occasionally reach 30 feet in height. These shrubs typically attain 60–100 years of age, but they have been reported to live more than 200 years. Their brilliant clusters of reddish-orange tubular flowers bloom from March to June, in time for the northward migration of hummingbirds, which along with

ORIGIN OF SCIENTIFIC NAME
The generic name honors Pierre Edouard Fouquier (1776–1850), a Parisian medical professor and naturalist who was a beloved teacher and friend to C. S. Kunth, one of the authors of the genus. Kunth helped to describe hundreds of plants from Alexander von Humboldt's voyage through Latin America. The specific epithet is Latin for glittering or shining (or figuratively, magnificent, splendid), referring to the flowers.

OTHER COMMON NAMES
candlewood, coachwhip, Jacob's staff, devil's walking stick, slimwood, vine cactus

FAMILY
Fouquieriaceae (Ocotillo Family)

DESCRIPTION
Trunkless (or nearly so), spiny shrub composed of vertical to ascending wandlike branches arising from a root crown; branches 3–20' long (max. 30'), but only 1–2" in diameter; leaves ephemeral, following rains; clusters of scarlet, tubular flowers at stem tips.

HABITAT AND DISTRIBUTION
Desert flats, rocky slopes, and mesas throughout the Trans-Pecos; west to California; northwestern Mexico including Baja California.

The wandlike branches of ocotillo, with Dr. B. L. Turner.

Ocotillo's short-shoot leaves.

carpenter bees are their prime pollinators. The plant's overall shape, together with its flamelike clusters of flowers, may have given rise to the name *candlewood* (but a more likely possibility is its use as fuel).

One of ocotillo's most discussed features is its extraordinary leaves, which is surprising given their frequent absence. The shrub actually has two types of leaves. The first is referred to as the long-shoot leaf, which occurs only on new terminal stems in the wet season. As this spatula-shaped leaf matures, the lower portion of the long stalk (petiole), and sometimes also the midportion of the leaf blade, hardens into the sharp, stiff, persistent spine that is the plant's main defense. The second type, the short-shoot leaves, grows from buds in the axils between the main stem and the spines. This leaf has a short petiole, is obovate in shape and rather soft, and grows in clusters of two to twelve. They are most remarkable, as they appear within 24–48 hours after a rain, last but a few weeks, and fall off again. Studies have shown that even rootless segments of ocotillo stem, when watered, will leaf out in this fashion, seemingly overnight. Stems purposefully defoliated five times still produced these leaves at 90% of their nodes when watered (Killingbeck 1990). In nature these ephemeral leaves have been noted up to seven or eight times during a season, depending on moisture; they are, thus, quite reliable indicators of recent rains. Ocotillo's ability to produce leaves quickly and irrespective of root absorption is a remarkable, possibly unprecedented, example of desert adaptation.

Ocotillo as a living fence by the ruins of the Misión del Sagrado Corazón in Ruidosa, Texas.

Ocotillo stems provide a substitute for timber in a nearly treeless landscape. Their most common use is for fencing, and their armature of thorns makes for a natural substitute for barbed wire. A very simple method, employed by the Co-copah Indians of Baja California, is to tie several stems horizontally between posts; this is said to prevent even "the most persistent burro" from passing (Barrows 1967). The most commonly used ocotillo fencing in Texas and adjacent Mexico, however, is what is accurately called a living fence. Stems are cut to the desired height and then aligned vertically side by side, with little space between, usually tied together with wire for support. The bottoms can be lightly buried in a shallow trench. The stems will flush with leaves, depending on rains, and will eventu-

ally take root, sometimes even flowering. Yards and small corrals are enclosed with such fences all along the U.S.-Mexico border where ocotillo grows, either to keep coyotes out and livestock in, or simply for privacy. One desert naturalist even describes how one can make a quail trap using the stems (Alloway 2000).

With only a bit more effort, ocotillo fencing can be turned into a housing material. Simply by adding a liberal coating of adobe to an ocotillo stem fence, a crude type of hut known as a "jacal" can be constructed. Other plant materials, such as candelilla, were sometimes stuffed in the spaces between the stems before plastering. The dried and trimmed flowering stalks of sotol were sometimes used for roof thatching. The jacales of west Texas, once used for housing by both

Hispanic and Anglo settlers, may be the direct descendants of the pit houses of the Jumano, a little-known Puebloan-like farming people along the Rio Grande south of El Paso. The Kickapoo during long hunting expeditions also constructed temporary shelters from ocotillo stems. Contemporary people still occasionally build ocotillo structures, but usually only for sheds or storehouses. More commonly seen today are ocotillo stems, stripped of spines, used for walking sticks. One should be aware that ocotillo, like many desert plants, grows slowly, and harvesting it from the wild, especially in the amounts needed for architectural projects, is discouraged. The ornamental appeal of ocotillo in southwestern gardens has unfortunately increased the collection of large, mature plants from native populations, which is especially unfortunate given the ease with which ocotillo can be propagated from seeds and cuttings.

Ocotillo flowers are edible. The Cahuilla Indians of southern California are known to have consumed both the flowers and seedpods; in addition, they prepared a sweet, tangy beverage by soaking the nectar-laden flowers in water. The flowers and seeds are still consumed in rural areas of northern Mexico, and a current native plant enthusiast recommends eating the flowers fresh or dipping them in batter for frying; either way, their nectar makes for a sweet treat (Tull 1999). The Tohono O'odham of southern Arizona press the nectar from the blossoms and harden it, somewhat like rock candy, to be consumed as a delicacy. Ocotillo seeds were traditionally parched and

ground into a flour by the Cahuilla to make mush or cakes, though our modern palates would find the flour disagreeable; it tastes like alum and is full of tiny hairs.

Several diverse medicinal uses are reported for ocotillo, but no single use is particularly frequent or dominant in the literature. The Apache relieved fatigue by bathing in a decoction of the roots; the Hualapai of northern Arizona made a soothing bath of the same for sore feet. A tea from the flowers was used by the Cahuilla for coughs, and Hispanic folk medicine still uses the same to treat coughs, sore throat, and late menstruation, also employing a tincture made from the stem to treat lymph circulation, pelvic congestion, bladder infections, and tonsillitis. The dried and powdered root was also applied by the Apache to wounds and swellings.

Other uses for ocotillo revolve around the waxes and resins naturally produced on the stems. Usually these are not present in sufficient quantities to be commercially valuable, but they have found occasional use in cleansing, waxing, varnishing, and waterproofing leather products. Because of the resins, the stems make an excellent fuel for starting campfires; they burn for a long time, but with an intense, black, oily flame. The most frequent use of ocotillo in rural areas of Coahuila is as fuel for rustic stoves. Fuel use is the likely origin for the name *candlewood,* a generic English term for any resinous wood. In fact, the word *ocotillo* may be related to fire. The Spanish-American word *ocote* derives from the Nahuatl *ocotl,* both referring to pitch pines (such as *Pinus teocote* and *P.*

oocarpa), which are known to be excellent sources of fuel. Fire-starting sticks are currently marketed from various Mexican pitch pine species. There seems to be a general consensus that ocotillo, with its diminutive ending, denotes something approximating "little torch."

SOURCES: Alloway 2000; Barrows 1967; Henrickson 1972; Killingbeck 1990; Latorre and Latorre 1977; Mills 1996; Mitich 1970; Moerman 1998; Moore 1990; Newcomb 1961; Powell 1988; Reiff 1984; Reyes Carmona and García Gil 1982; Standley 1920–1926; Tull 1999; Vines 1960; Warnock 1970; Waser 1979

Yaupon

Ilex vomitoria Aiton

One of the most widely used evergreen landscape shrubs in Texas and one of the most frequently grown native plants in the state, yaupon appears in front yards, along highways, and in landscaped parking lots throughout the eastern half of the state. Its bright red berries in winter are an attractive feature that not only feeds many species of birds but also invites comparison to the traditional English or Christmas holly (*Ilex aquifolium*). In fact, sprigs of the berry-laden yaupon have been used for years in Christmas decorations wherever it grows.

Yaupon's hidden claim to fame, almost entirely eclipsed in the twentieth century, is its potential as a tea, and not just any tea, but one containing caffeine—the dried leaves contain 0.27% of the stimulant. Of all the species of holly native to North America, yaupon is the only one known to contain caffeine, and it is the only wild tea in Texas with the stimulant. Despite this apparent advantage, and despite a venerable past both in Texas and throughout the South, yaupon is currently overlooked as a tea plant. Almost every indigenous tribe of the south-

ORIGIN OF SCIENTIFIC NAME
Ilex is an ancient Latin name for the holm oak, an evergreen tree from southern Europe, which still bears the name at the specific level (*Quercus ilex*). *Ilex* as a genus name was probably applied to members of the holly family because their leaves resemble the leaves of the holm oak. The rather unpleasant species name refers to the belief that tea made from the plant's leaves, often employed by Native Americans of the South-

east in ritualistic purging, was itself an emetic.

OTHER COMMON NAMES
evergreen holly, cassine, cassina, evergreen cassena, emetic holly, Indian black drink, cassio berry bush, Carolina tea, Appalachian tea, South Sea tea, Christmas berry, yopon del indio, chocolate del indio

FAMILY
Aquifoliaceae (Holly Family)

DESCRIPTION
An evergreen, thicket-forming shrub 12–15' high with many

stems from the base or, given rich bottomland, a small tree to 25' (rarely 40–45') with a diameter of 6" (rarely 1').

HABITAT AND DISTRIBUTION
Eastern half of state in various soils, reaching largest size in southeastern portion; from Edwards Plateau eastward through Gulf states to Florida, northward along coast to Virginia.

eastern United States drank yaupon tea, and many of the early European explorers, colonizers, and settlers enjoyed and commented on the beverage, which they also adopted. Yet, by the beginning of the twentieth century yaupon tea was consumed by only a handful of rural folk.

Practically all the southeastern American Indians consumed the tea, referred to by early observers as "black drink" even though its color is really yellow or green (it does turn dark in strong decoctions with prolonged boiling). Tribes that were known to drink the tea outside what is now Texas include the Timucuan of Florida, the tribes of the coastal Carolinas, the Cherokee, Yuchi, Alabama, Chickasaw, Choctaw, Natchez, and especially the Creek Confederacy. In fact, black drink was one of their defining cultural traits. It was consumed for at least three different purposes: as a stimulating beverage, like coffee; as a medicine; and possibly as an emetic, to induce vomiting, especially in the context of ritual purity. In many groups it was drunk only by adult males of high social standing, and it was often drunk in copious amounts and usually piping hot. Many of the southeastern Indians drank the tea from marine shells, which were often decorated and used ceremonially. These have appeared in burial ceremonials as far back as 1000 CE.

Spanish colonists in Saint Augustine, Florida (founded 1565), adopted the drink from the Timucuans and quickly became addicted to it. Francisco Ximenez in 1615 reported, "Any day that a Spaniard does not drink it, he feels that he is going to die" (Sturtevant 1979). In Spanish Florida and in South Carolina, black drink was referred to as cassina; in North Carolina and England the beverage was called yaupon tea (a Catawba Indian name), Appalachian tea, and Carolina tea. Black drink was made by first roasting, then boiling the leaves. Yaupon clearly filled the same beverage niche for these early inhabitants as coffee does for Americans today.

Thanks to the shipwreck that stranded Alvar Núñez Cabeza de Vaca on Galveston Island in 1528, Texas can boast of being the source for possibly the first reference by a European to the use of this drink. The passage from Cabeza de Vaca's report is interesting and bears citing in full:

They [coastal Indians of Texas, especially the Karankawa] also drink a tea made from the leaves of a tree that resembles the live oak, which they toast in vessels on a fire. After the leaves are toasted, they fill the vessel with water and keep it on the fire. When it has twice come to a boil, they pour it into another vessel and cool it with half a gourd. When it is very foamy, they drink it as hot as they can stand it. From the time they take this tea out of the vessel until they drink it, they shout, asking who wants to drink. When the women hear these shouts they stand still without daring to move. Even if they are carrying a heavy load they do not dare move. If by chance a woman moves during this time, they shame her and beat her and very angrily pour out the brew they were about to drink. They vomit the beverage that they have drunk, quite easily and without embarrassment. They give the following reason for their custom, saying that if a woman within earshot moves when they want to drink, something terrible enters their body through the tea and soon thereafter causes them to die. The whole time that the water is boiling, the vessel is supposed to be covered. If by chance it is uncovered and a woman passes by, they throw it out and do not drink any of it. The tea is yellow and they drink it for three days without eating. Each day each person drinks one arroba and a half of it. (Cabeza de Vaca 1993)

The passage highlights many of the Native American traditions surrounding yaupon tea: it is drunk hot, it is imbibed in large quantities, vomiting or emesis is sometimes connected with the drink, ritualism or other superstitious belief may be involved, and it seems to be relegated to men. Clearly the species name *vomitoria* seems fitting. As many have pointed out, however, the source of the emesis is very likely not the tea itself. Any piping hot beverage (even water) drunk in sufficient quantities can cause emesis. Cabeza de Vaca points out that an "arroba and a half" was drunk per person per day. An arroba was an old measurement of wine, reported to be anywhere from two to four *gallons*, so this is an astounding amount of liquid. Add to this the caffeine in the drink and the period of fasting, and it is easy to see how one could vomit forth the drink almost at will. Imagine a similar amount of hot coffee being taken on an empty stomach.

Yaupon in full fruit.

Continuing with Texas connections, exactly 300 years later (1828) the French biologist Jean Louis Berlandier, one of the earliest trained scientists to collect and describe Texas plants, noted that the tea was still in common use in a Tonkawa village in south-central Texas:

> The chief had us enter his cabin, where he was seated by the fire employed in making a decoction of the leaves from a tree of the Tetrandria Monogynia known in Texas as chocolate or té del Indio [*Ilex vomitoria*]. They use this decoction as a panacea for all scourges, while some tribes, such as the Texas, Cad[d]os, Carancahueses [Karankawa], etc., make it a daily drink. It is a powerful emmenagogue [assists with menstrual flow] and an excellent stomachic. The Indians stew the leaves in water and use a bundle of small pieces of wood to make the decoction foam like chocolate. This extract is placed in another vessel or reduced a second time to a liquid state. This is their favorite drink. (Berlandier 1980)

From this passage it seems obvious that yaupon tea was not just employed ritualistically or even for medicinal reasons, but almost as an everyday beverage. In another work Berlandier mentions that "Texas women, both Creoles and natives" use the tea (Berlandier 1969), which clearly indicates that women, Europeans, and natives all partook of the beverage. He also notes that the Comanche and Lipan did not use the tea, entirely reasonable given that these tribes inhabited the western and northern sections of Texas, where *Ilex vomitoria* approaches the limits of its distribution and grows only sporadically.

Additional sources support yaupon's extensive use by Native Americans in Texas. A young girl whose family had moved to Matagorda Bay in 1838 unwittingly became one of the last original sources on the Karankawa, who by this point (300 years after Cabeza de Vaca lived among them) were near extinction. She mentions that the tea whisked into a yellowish froth was "very bitter and said to be intoxicating, but . . . it never seemed to produce any visible effect upon the Indians" (Gatschet 1891). William Bollaert, who visited Texas in 1842–1844, also confirms that yaupon tea was "much relished" by the Karankawa (Hollon and Butler 1956). The tea received special attention from this tribe at a celebration held at the time of each full moon and after successful hunting or fishing expeditions. This use finds an echo in the Caddoan tribes, who employed the drink after the new moon in September when the crops had been harvested. In short, the major Texas Indian groups who originally inhabited areas in which *Ilex vomitoria* grew (the Karankawa, Caddo, and Tonkawa) all imbibed yaupon tea.

Just as in Florida and elsewhere in the South, immigrants to the areas of Texas where yaupon grew adopted the habit from the natives. Stephen F. Austin's cousin Mary Austin Holley, who first came to Texas in 1831 and wrote two early books to encourage immigration to the region, points out that the tea had already become commonplace:

Among these the Yawpan or tea tree deserves a special notice. Its leaf is very similar, in form and flavor, to that of the veritable Chinese shrub, and is dried and used as a substitute for the latter, by many of the inhabitants of Texas. It is not at all inferior to the black tea or bohea, used among us, in its quality. It is abundant and furnishes to the backwoodsman a very acceptable and cheap beverage, in lieu of the pure chinese article, which is frequently not only costly but difficult to be obtained, especially at a distance from the more populous and commercial towns of the province. (Holley 1836)

Nonnative adoption of the tea is not surprising given that at least some of the immigrants coming to Texas would have come from southern states in which there had been knowledge of yaupon (or yapan) tea from the eighteenth century. By the late 1700s, yapan tea was the customary breakfast drink of the North Carolina coastal region. By the end of the nineteenth century, however, only rural folk (derisively called "yeopon-eaters" by mainlanders) still drank the tea on the Outer Banks. Nags Head resorts, probably thinking of yaupon as a quaint curiosity, boasted of the "refreshing tea" in 1949, and at least one restaurant on Ocracoke Island was still serving the tea as a local specialty as late as 1973.

What's astonishing is that a parallel story of a similar tea describes such a different outcome. Another member of the same genus grew in the New World, this time in the Southern Hemisphere. It, too, contained caffeine and was already used as a tea by the local natives, the Guaraní Indians of Paraguay. It, too, was discovered by the Spaniards at about the same time in the mid-sixteenth century. But *Ilex paraguariensis*, whose dried leaves provide the tea known as yerba maté, was collected and even exported throughout the region. By the nineteenth and twentieth centuries, maté had become the national drink of Uruguay, Paraguay, southern Brazil, and Argentina. The paraphernalia of the decorated gourds (also called matés) and metal straws (bombillas) with which one drinks the tea are objects of great craftsmanship, regional identity, and pride. One wonders if our yaupon tea was perhaps less palatable, or if the disdain for tea after the American Revolution and the ensuing dominion of coffee was simply too great. Perhaps, too, the absence of promotion and marketing had something to do with it (the Jesuits cultivated and exported maté in the early seventeenth century in South America). It probably does not help that the plant bears the specific name *vomitoria*. How odd it is to think that this ubiquitous landscape shrub so steeped in history might have been, but for whim and fate, the basis of a great southern tradition.

SOURCES: Berlandier 1969, 1980; Burlage 1968; Cabeza de Vaca 1993; Core 1967; Diggs et al. 1999; Dyer 1916; Fairbanks 1979; Gatschet 1891; Holley 1836; Hollon and Butler 1956; Hudson 1979; Merrill 1979; Milanich 1979; Schulz 1928; Simpson 1988; Sturtevant 1979; Vines 1984; Wasowski and Wasowski 1997

Creosote Bush

Larrea tridentata (Sessé & Moc. ex DC.) Coville

Creosote bush is one of the most common and underappreciated plants of the arid Southwest. Covering a quarter of Mexico and 70,000 square miles in the United States across three deserts, often dominating the landscape in uninterrupted stands, *Larrea tridentata* is one of the most widespread and characteristic woody plants of the warm deserts of North America. Marvelously adapted to its dry environment, it is one of the most drought-tolerant higher plants on our continent. Its leaves, copiously covered with a sticky, strong-smelling resin, which reminded early settlers of creosote (a derivative of wood tar), naturally lose little water through evaporation. The plant's odor is distinct and memorable but difficult to describe, something fresh and antiseptic, but not sweet or perfumed. Many people find the scent pleasant and penetrating, especially after a desert rain, but others find it rather unappealing (*hediondilla* means "little stinker" in Spanish). The resinous substance, together with a panoply of chemicals, largely prevents creosote bush from being browsed by livestock, and drought-starved sheep have died from eating its leaves. Without the virtue of edible leaves or fruit, creosote bush tends to be seen as a hard-scrabble weed, a sign of useless land. Nonetheless,

ORIGIN OF SCIENTIFIC NAME

The genus honors the Spanish clergyman Juan Antonio Pérez Hernández de Larrea (1730–1803). As dean of Zaragoza Cathedral and, briefly, bishop of Valladolid, Larrea was known as an enlightened promoter of science. *Tridentata* is Latin for "three-toothed," in reference to very obscure features of the petals and staminal scales.

OTHER COMMON NAMES

greasewood, gobernadora, hediondilla, chaparral

FAMILY

Zygophyllaceae (Caltrop Family)

DESCRIPTION

Evergreen perennial shrub, 4–6' high (max. 10'), with small, strongly scented, resinous leaves; stems arise from central base giving open, airy appearance; solitary yellow flowers with clawed petals.

HABITAT AND DISTRIBUTION

Abundant on dry alluvial and gravelly soils of flats, mesas, and ridges of the desert regions of the Trans-Pecos and southwest Texas along the Rio Grande; throughout Chihuahuan, Sonoran, and Mojave deserts of New Mexico, Arizona, California, Nevada, Utah; northern Mexico and Baja.

Creosote bush in bloom.

the plant has many remarkable attributes and uses worthy of recognition.

Biologically, creosote bush is a rugged survivor in a harsh climate. Its long and shallow roots are able to maximize the capture of a meager supply of water and nitrogen. People have long marveled at how abundant and evenly spaced the plants appear. In fact, the Spanish name *gobernadora* ("governess") likely refers to the shrub's dominance and seemingly precise arrangement over large tracts of land. Recent study suggests this may be a result of its root system, which arranges itself spatially to avoid overlap with neighbors in an intensely competitive environment of scarce resources (Brisson and Reynolds 1994). Following this line of thought, the relatively barren bits of land between individual plants are simply evidence of creosote's ability to thrive where others cannot and to capture nutrients more successfully. Others have suggested (and this is hotly debated) that creosote bush poisons the surrounding soil with its phenolics, tannins, and acids, inhibiting the germination and growth of other plants (Elkavoich and Stevens 1985; Hyder et al. 2002). Either way, other plants can and do grow around and under creosote bush, apparently if given propitious conditions.

Creosote bush is amazingly hardy and long-lasting. Ten years after a thermonuclear explosion at Yucca Flat, Nevada, in 1962, 20 of the 21 creosote bushes growing at the blast site's center had resprouted. A few decades later, creosote bush again created surprise when scientists discovered that the shrubs, or rather their clones, are extremely long-lived. Creosote shrubs develop by radial growth,

with new stems arising at the periphery of old stem segments. The central part of the basal crown slowly splits and decays, as the clonal stems continue to develop outward in irregular circles, later becoming ellipses, which may exceed 65 feet in length. Through radiocarbon dating and extrapolation from growth rates (averaging 0.66 mm per year), the age of a certain creosote bush clone in the Mojave Desert was estimated at 11,700 years (Vasek 1980), ranking it among the oldest living higher organisms on the planet. Of course, it is important to remember that no one stem is itself this old, and clonal reproduction raises philosophical questions about how we define age.

Larrea tridentata has an interesting heritage. The genus *Larrea* has an amphitropical distribution, which means that populations exist on both sides of the tropics but nowhere in between. Four species of *Larrea* grow in South America (Argentina, Bolivia, Chile, and Peru); the fifth species, ours, appears almost 2500 miles to the north. Recent molecular analyses confirm that our creosote bush originated in South America and was likely brought north by long-distance dispersal, such as by birds. The South American species that is likely the progenitor of our species is *L. divaricata*, which is so similar to ours that the two were sometimes considered one and the same. The original dispersal event is believed to have occurred quite long ago, between four million and eight million years ago. The extraordinary number of insects and spiders that rely on the plant provides supporting evidence of creosote bush's venerable presence in North America. Thirty species of insects (in five orders), including beetles, praying mantises, and grasshoppers, are associated with *L. tridentata*, the majority of which are monophagous, that is, they feed only on this plant. Twenty-six species of spiders are also associated with the shrub, as are many species of bees. The diversity and specialization of these creosote-loving arthropods strongly suggest a long history of coevolution.

Creosote bush offers little in the way of foodstuffs to man or beast, on account of its foul-tasting resins. Some indigenous groups reportedly pickled the buds in vinegar and ate them like capers. Attempts to remove the resins in order to make a palatable livestock feed have been successful, though economic factors prevent wide-scale utilization. A single specimen of the shrub may contain 49 kinds of volatile oils. The leaf resins contain 19 flavonoid aglycones, as well as several lignans, one of which is a noted antioxidant. Other chemical compounds isolated from the bush include alkaloids, sapogenins, and waxes.

These chemical compounds offer rich medicinal resources. More than 50 illnesses have been treated with creosote bush in the traditional medicine of Mexico and the American Southwest. The two principal uses for external application are as an all-purpose antiseptic and as a treatment for arthritis and rheumatism. As an antiseptic, the plant has been widely acclaimed among cowboys and ranchers as a treatment for saddle sores and minor cuts, bruises, and bites on both themselves and their animals. Methods of treatment include boiling the twigs and leaves in water to make a simple solution to dress the wounds, or

boiling the leaves in lard to make a salve. Sometimes the leaves (either dried and powdered or fresh) were crushed into a poultice and applied directly to chronic sores. Research has confirmed that creosote bush has antifungal properties, giving credence to a host of treatments that include ringworm, screwworm, athlete's foot, and jock itch. The plant has shown good results as an agricultural fungicide to prevent corn pathogens, such as those that produce aflatoxins. For the treatment of rheumatism, stiff joints, and chapped skin, creosote bush has an equally solid history in Native American and Hispanic folk traditions. Here the standard method is to soak the patient in a very hot bath of boiled creosote tea, though applications of the lard salve are also used. Like white sagebrush, creosote bush is occasionally added to steam baths for personal cleanliness and good health, though no more than two such treatments per year are recommended (Hicks 1966). The fumes from burnt leaves have been used in Mexico as a general disinfectant in the home.

Internally, creosote bush used to be consumed for a number of ailments, though this practice has begun to be considered dangerous and is generally not recommended. Indian, Mexican, and folk medicines employed teas, again from the leaves and twigs (called "chaparral" in the herbal supplement trade), to treat everything from simple colds, stomachaches, and gas pains to cancer and tuberculosis. Many uses of the tea centered on bladder, kidney, and liver disorders, such as urethritis, and especially kidney and gallbladder stones, which were said to dissolve from liberal use. Unfortunately, cases of toxic hepatitis and renal disease, probably exacerbated by overconsumption of creosote tablets as dietary supplements (a nontraditional use), were reported by the medical community. In 1992 the U.S. Food and Drug Administration issued a warning (but no regulatory action), and most manufacturers withdrew their chaparral products voluntarily. However, many supporters, such as the nonprofit organization International Larrea Medical Society, feel these actions were premature.

Many of creosote's medicinal claims are connected to a lignan deposited on the surface of the leaves, a powerful and valuable antioxidant known as nordihydroguaiaretic acid, or NDGA. This substance prevents the oxidation of unsaturated fatty acids in vegetable oils during processing. Approved as a food antioxidant by the U.S. War Food Administration in 1943, NDGA was used to protect refrigerated and frozen foods, especially meat, poultry, and fish. It also slowed spoilage of lard and bacon. For a few decades creosote bush was the best source of NDGA, until more effective antioxidants were introduced. In 1970 the FDA prohibited the substance as a food additive since it was found to inhibit several beneficial enzymes; however, it is still used in preserving natural and synthetic rubbers and to stabilize polymers and perfumery oils. NDGA has occasional use as a developer in photography and as a rust-prevention agent. Other industrial applications of creosote bush include use of a strong decoction of the plant to remove scale

from boilers, to unplug pipelines, and to clean rifle barrels.

Larrea tridentata is known historically as a source of glue, dye, and fuel but is little used today. Three species of scale or lac insects inhabit the bush, depositing a brownish lac on the stems. This sticky substance makes a decent cement, which southwestern tribes used to mend broken pottery, waterproof their baskets, and affix arrowheads. Suggested preparation for the cement includes mixing the lac with pulverized rock and then heating the mixture before application. The Apache used the plant's sticky gum as a styptic. An infusion of the leaves, perhaps also the lac, was once used by Mexican shoemakers to dye leather red. Settlers of Utah obtained a greenish-yellow dye from the plant, which imparted the creosote odor to whatever it colored, and Hispanics of the Big Bend Country used the roots to dye blankets brown. Accounting for its common name *greasewood*, creosote's resinous leaves and stems, even when green, will ignite easily and burn with an intense heat. The plant was once much used in local limekilns and can still be employed for a hot cooking fire.

SOURCES: Alloway 2000; Arteaga et al. 2005; Berlandier 1980; Brisson and Reynolds 1994; Curtin 1965; Elkavoich and Stevens 1985; Fletcher 1928; Havard 1885; Hicks 1966; Hocking 1997; Hunziker et al. 1972; Hyder et al. 2002; Latorre and Latorre 1977; Lia et al. 2001; Moerman 1998; Moore 1990; Palmer 1878; Powell 1988; Schultz et al. 1977; Schulz 1928; Simpson et al. 1977; Smithers 1964; Taylor et al. 1997; Timmermann 1977; Tweit 1995; Vargas-Arispuro et al. 2005; Vasek 1980; Wasowski and Wasowski 1997; Wills and Irwin 1961

Fragrant Sumac

Rhus aromatica Aiton

Rhus trilobata Nutt.

Fragrant sumac is less ostentatious than its flame-leaf and smooth sumac relatives. Considerably shorter and lacking the multiple lance-shaped leaflets of its cousins, it is more often than not a straggly shrub partly hidden by larger bushes or tightly nestled among other woody plants and vines in tree mottes. Although for much of the year it is easy to overlook, several key features stand out. First, its flowers are eye-catching. The buds appear in winter, resembling soft red spikes; in spring these open into numerous small yellow blooms, which are clustered at the ends of naked branches before the leaves appear. In addition, its leaves and branches have a peculiar scent, descriptions of which run a gamut of opinion from "offensively scented" to "pungently fragrant" to "spicy." A glance at the common names below will confirm the panoply of views. However one classifies the distinct aroma, the fall color of the leaves is a real bonus; they turn orange, red, and sometimes yellow, displaying a much-relished touch of autumn in the Texas landscape. Given its red fruits in late sum-

ORIGIN OF SCIENTIFIC NAME

Rhus is the classical name (used by Greeks and Romans) for a European species of sumac (*R. coriaria*). *Aromatica* refers to the aromatic foliage and stems.

OTHER COMMON NAMES

skunkbush, polecat bush, sweet-scented sumac, squaw bush, squaw berry, skunk berry, three-leaved sumac, lemita, lemonade sumac, agrillo, ill-scented sumac, quail bush

FAMILY

Anacardiaceae (Sumac or Cashew Family)

DESCRIPTION

Clump-forming, straggly to upright deciduous shrubs, usually to 6' (rarely 12'), with slender, spreading, crooked branches; their three leaflets readily distinguish them from other sumacs in our area.

HABITAT AND DISTRIBUTION

Widespread across Texas; in many types of well-drained soil from the West Coast to Quebec and New England. Considered as two separate species, *Rhus aromatica* would represent collections from the eastern half of the U.S., and *R. trilobata* would inhabit the western two-thirds, Mexico, and southwestern Canada.

NOTE

These two species are very similar and are here treated together. Some botanists consider *Rhus trilobata* to be a variety of *R. aromatica*. Both are highly variable, and several varieties have been proposed.

The trifoliate leaves of fragrant sumac.

mer, fragrant sumac deserves to be planted more frequently in larger landscapes.

Fragrant sumac provides a number of resources, as do other members of the genus. Its fruit, ripening in August and September, is forage for at least 25 species of birds. Tasting much like lemons, the acidic drupes can be mashed with sugar, which is how the twentieth-century Kiowa consumed them, or they can be made into a refreshing drink, still enjoyed among certain New Mexican pueblos today. The Apache historically ground the fruit with mescal (the baked crowns of *Agave* spp.) to be dried and consumed later, and like many post-Contact southwestern tribes, they made a jam from the fruit. Various parts of the plant are also utilized for a dye material; the twigs yield a yellow dye used in coloring the coils of basket designs, and the leaves have provided black dyes for cloth. There is evidence that both the Comanche and the Kiowa mixed the leaves with tobacco for smoking.

Medicinal uses for this species, and many of the other species of the genus, are manifold; space allows only a few to be mentioned here. The Kickapoo use a decoction of the leaves to cure colic and stomach ulcers and to stop diarrhea; such uses make sense given the astringent nature of the sumac's gallic acids. The Kiowa recommend the fruit for stomach trouble and influenza. The Comanche inhale the steam rising from fragrant sumac bark immersed in hot water in their sweat lodges; in addition, they chew the bark for colds. Giving weight to some of these claims, a recent pharmacological study confirmed that *Rhus aromatica* extract shows free-radical scavenging abilities and demonstrated anti-inflammatory properties (Chakraborty and Brantner 2000).

Squaw bush is valued for two unique claims to fame; one involves ancient art, and the other historical tradition. Well known throughout ethnobotanical literature is the plant's use in basketry and other material arts requiring supple wood. Along with willow, squaw bush was one of the most important materials used in Indian basketry in the Southwest. Its peeled branches were especially prized for the warp (or foundation rods) of baskets and water jugs but could also serve wherever a nonbreakable, supple wood was needed, such as in the curved hoods of cradleboards or in the split-twig animal effigies found in remote caves in the Southwest dating back to at least 3500 BCE. If one has seen squaw bush in the summer, with its often crooked and seemingly rigid branches, it is difficult to envisage how the plant supplied flexible material for these projects. The secret lies in its new shoots and suckers, which grow straight, tall, and supple. When dried, these stalks become rigid, making for good basket rods, as well as arrow shafts. Unnatural lengths of squaw bush shoots are so widespread in historic southwestern artifacts (up to 6 feet) that it has been proposed that early American Indians learned how to set fire to the plant to stimulate new shoots (Bohrer 1983). In effect, squaw bush may have been a managed plant, that is, one that is not domesticated but rather encouraged and manipulated (Dunmire and Tierney 1995).

Because of its implication in a historic battle, skunk berry sumac is at the center not only of a particular tribal custom but also of a Pan-Indian revitalization of sorts, which brings us to its second claim to fame. According to Kiowa tribal lore, a group of Kiowa warriors succeeded in winning a four-day battle against a group of Cheyenne and Arapaho raiders in 1838. Tradition maintains that the battleground was covered with skunk berry bushes in fruit (called "tdei-pei-ah-gah" by the Kiowa). In memory of this battle, the Kiowa Gourd Dance Society was formed, also called the T'äñpéko, which roughly translates as "Skunk berry people." This society is one of the oldest of the Kiowa warrior societies, and it was the only one to police the annual Sun Dance encampment. Proper attire for the Gourd Dance includes a blanket that is half blue and half red; the red symbolizes the blood of the Kiowa warriors who fell in battle, as well as the red berries of skunk berry sumac. When reservation authorities began to prohibit the Sun Dance in the last decade of the nineteenth century, the Gourd Dance was performed as a substitute and helped to preserve Kiowa culture in the reservation era. Although the dance had almost disappeared by the middle of the twentieth century, the resurrection of the Kiowa Gourd Dance Clan in 1957 ensured its ceremonial resurgence among the Kiowa and eventually its widespread popularity as a Pan-Indian institution that "celebrates the common heritage of all Indians" (Ellis 1990). Current membership in this clan, also known as the Tiah-pah Society (a direct reference to T'äñpéko), numbers approximately 300 people, including civil servants, doctors, educators, and the Pulitzer-prizewinning novelist and professor N. Scott Momaday.

SOURCES: Basehart 1974; Bohrer 1983; Carlson and Jones 1939; Castetter and Opler 1936; Chakraborty and Brantner 2000; Curtin 1965; Dunmire and Tierney 1995; Ellis 1990; Hocking 1997; Kindscher 1992; Latorre and Latorre 1977; Schulz 1928; Vestal and Schultes 1939; Vines 1984; Wasowski and Wasowski 1997

Sumac

Rhus copallinum L.

Rhus lanceolata (A. Gray) Britton

Rhus glabra L.

Strikingly colorful fall foliage, with a few notable exceptions, does not number among Texas' natural blessings. All the more reason that sumac is revered locally for its faithful displays of oranges, scarlets, and rusty maroons, regardless of a given year's weather. Landscape architects and anyone engaged in park, ranch, or roadside maintenance would do well to give the plant more consideration. Because of the tendency to spread by underground stolons, the plants should be given ample space and are excellent in mass plantings. As pioneer species they are useful for revegetating denuded areas and for preventing

---

ORIGIN OF SCIENTIFIC NAME

Rhus is the classical name (used by Greeks and Romans) for a European species of sumac (*R. coriaria*). *Copallinum* refers to copal gum and means gummy or resinous. *Lanceolata* refers to the lance-shaped leaves. *Glabra* means glabrous or hairless and refers to the plant's smoothness.

OTHER COMMON NAMES

For *Rhus copallinum*: flame-leaf sumac, winged sumac, dwarf sumac, shining sumac. For *R. lanceolata*: prairie flame-leaf sumac, prairie sumac, lance-leaf sumac, prairie shining sumac, Texas sumac, tree sumac, limestone sumac, black sumac. For *R. glabra*: smooth sumac, scarlet sumac, red sumac, white sumac, shoe-make, vinegar tree, Pennsylvania sumac

FAMILY

Anacardiaceae (Sumac or Cashew Family)

DESCRIPTION

Deciduous shrubs to small trees, 4 1/2–30' tall, often forming thickets, with pinnately compound leaves and fruits in dense pyramidal panicles. *Rhus copallinum* often shorter (4 1/2–9') and more shrubby, with fewer leaflets, and with "wings" on the central leaf stem. *Rhus lanceolata* tends to be taller, sometimes forming a small rounded tree; wings present, but narrower. *Rhus glabra* lacks wings altogether.

HABITAT AND DISTRIBUTION

Rhus copallinum prefers the well-drained soils of hillsides and valleys in the eastern third of the state; through the midwestern states to New England. *Rhus lanceolata* primarily inhabits the western two-thirds of Texas, usually in calcareous soils; Oklahoma, New Mexico; Mexico. *Rhus glabra* occurs in East Texas, and is widespread across the entire U.S. in generally moist and rich soils. All three species tend to appear in scattered patches, along fencerows or edges of woodlands.

NOTE

In order to include a gamut of commentary that was not always specific enough to position definitively in one species, I am here treating three separate species under one heading. Superficially, they are similar in habit, leaf structure, and fruit and would not be easily distinguished by the novice.

Autumn fruit clusters of prairie flame-leaf sumac.

erosion. Sumacs as a whole are probably not the best choice for an unsupervised small yard, but some of our foremost native gardeners advocate their inclusion, having found that their tendency to sucker decreases in the absence of grazing, mowing, and burning. Both *Rhus copallinum* and *R. lanceolata* are larval host plants for the red-banded hairstreak butterfly.

Sumac fruit, which resemble erect bunches of tiny dusky red grapes, add to the shrub's appeal. The fruit ripen in August but stay in place all winter, providing a reliable food source for the gallinaceous birds (such as quail, grouse, prairie chicken, and ring-necked pheasant) and for white-tailed and mule deer. The maroon clusters also make excellent accent pieces in fall and winter bouquets. In addition,

the tough and chewy fruit, which is quite sour, can be enjoyed as a natural candy or Sour-Tart. Comanche children were once very fond of the fruit, and a coprolite from the Ozarks proves that indigenous peoples have enjoyed sumac fruit for at least two to three millennia. The drupes contain malic acid; when gently bruised and soaked in warm water, they produce a cooling drink or tea, sometimes referred to as sumac-ade or *Rhus* juice (see Tull 1999 for a recipe). Knowledge of this use was widespread among Indian tribes, who used several species of *Rhus*. At a time in Europe when salt and pepper were precious commodities, Greek and Roman herbalists recorded the use of the fruit and seeds of *R. coriaria* to powder and season meats, which finds a New World echo among the Apache, who used sumac as a seasoning and relish. Today sumac as a spice is still common in the eastern Mediterranean region and is even considered an essential ingredient of Arabic cooking.

Sumac leaves have historic uses that would probably surprise the modern-day reader. Many species of *Rhus* contain high amounts of tannic acid, which is used in the tanning of hides and leather. The European species, *R. coriaria,* or currier's sumac (both terms derive from the Latin *corium,* for hide or leather), was reported as early as the third century BCE in Greece by Theophrastus as a means to whiten leather. As late as the early twentieth century, this European species, commonly known as Sicilian sumac, was still the preferred tanning material for bookbinding and for glove and hatband leathers, where the leather needed to be durable and last indefinitely.

Oddly enough, Americans continued to import foreign tannins despite an abundant supply of domestic sumacs that would have been equally efficacious and much cheaper. As early as 1887, Colonel Nathaniel Taylor, who traversed Texas on horseback, was surprised that San Antonio did not manufacture leather and shoes, given the abundance of leather and "since the mesquite and sumach offer . . . illimitable resources of tannin" (Taylor 1936). In 1892 Dr. George Kalteyer, in a geological survey of Texas, argued that local sumac, if properly dried and prepared, contained just as much tannin and was equally capable of producing good leather as imported sumac. He urged Texans to stop sending leather to New York for dressing and to take advantage of the "im-

mense fields of fortune" awaiting them in what should be a local industry. In the early twentieth century, a U.S. Department of Agriculture examination of *Rhus copallinum, R. glabra,* and *R. hirta* found that all contained 25–35% tannin and that American sumac extracts cost only three-fifths as much as Sicilian extract. By mid-century, World War II had disrupted the export of European sumac, and the main sources of vegetable tannins in the United States were either foreign trees that were likely to be soon exhausted (the quebracho trees of South America), American trees that were dead or dying from blight (the American chestnut), or foreign trees and shrubs that were not readily available (wattle, various species of *Acacia* from Australia and Africa). Again, experts recommended that American sumacs be considered as tanning agents (Katz et al. 1950).

As recently as the 1970s, researchers were exploring the possibility of developing the sumac crop to help rural agricultural communities, given that contemporary sources of tannin were foreign. Although twentieth-century chrome tanning has largely made vegetable tanning obsolete, there is still demand for vegetable tannins in the production of heavy leathers, such as those used in shoe soles, belting, saddlery, upholstery, and luggage. Vegetable tannage also produces embossed and tooled leathers found in handicrafts. Despite the increasing use of synthetic tannins in the industry, American sumac would still appear to be an underexploited resource.

American Indians did not seem to employ sumac in the preparation of their hides, but they found the leaves to be a good additive to their smoking tobacco. Berlandier noted that the Waco, Tawakoni, and Comanche in their "first fruits" ceremony used ayumé (the local Hispanic term for *Rhus* leaves) along with tobacco in consecration activities (Berlandier 1969). In a separate work, Berlandier observed that ayumé, which the Comanche called "temaichia," was harvested only in autumn "when the leaves are generally red and very rusty" (Berlandier 1980). From the ensuing description, it is likely that Berlandier is discussing *R. lanceolata*. Although *Rhus virens* (an evergreen shrub with shiny, leathery leaflets, common in the Edwards Plateau and Trans-Pecos) is frequently singled out as the "tobacco sumac," it is clear that various Texan tribes, such as the Comanche, Kiowa, and Kiowa-Apache, employed several species of *Rhus* in their smoking mixtures.

Rhus species have provided excellent sources of dyes, used by Indians and non-Indians alike. The Cherokee made a black dye from the drupes, which were also noted in the twentieth century as a dye source for wool. In fact, the majority of American sumac at the turn of the century was used for dyeing cotton. *Rhus* gained some fame in dyeing leather black as well, as this comment from a collection of Texas folklore relates: "Sumac dyes leather black. I've often wondered if that weren't the reason it is called 'shoe-make'"

by everybody except botanists" (Hatfield 1954). Delena Tull expands on the various dyeing possibilities of *Rhus* species. She points out that the tannins in sumac act as a natural mordant, so that fibers do not need to be chemically treated in order to absorb the dyes. The colors range from tan to a rich reddish brown, but grays, purples, and gold can also be obtained (Tull 1999).

As tempting as it is to draw a folk etymology from *shoe-make* to *sumac* (also *sumach*), the word apparently derives from the ancient Arabian *sommaq* and the Byzantian *soumaki* (Barkley and Barkley 1938).

Blanket, Texas, in Brown County, ten miles northeast of Brownwood, allegedly gets its name from a distant connection to sumac. Blanket Creek, by some accounts, received its name from a surveying party that encountered a band of Tonkawa Indians who, having been caught in a sudden rainstorm, spread their blankets over sumac bushes for shelter.

SOURCES: Barkley 1937; Barkley and Barkley 1938; Basehart 1974; Berlandier 1969, 1980; Carlson and Jones 1939; Damude and Bender 1999; Doorenbos 2004; Hatfield 1954; Kalteyer 1892; Katz et al. 1950; Kindscher 1992; Lively 2005; McAllister 1949; Moerman 1998; Schulz 1928; Simpson, Beryl (pers. comm.); Smithwick 1983; Taylor 1936; Thorstensen 1993, 1995; Tull 1999; Turner 1996; Turner et al. 2003; Veitch and Rogers 1918; Vestal and Schultes 1939; Vines 1984; Wasowski and Wasowski 1997

Texas Mountain Laurel

Sophora secundiflora (Ortega) Lag. ex DC.

Some of our native plants are so rich in historical commentary and anecdotes of interest as to deserve their own separate book. Lechuguilla, mesquite, pecan, prickly pear, yaupon, yucca, and wild grape immediately come to mind, and several of them are already the subject of book-length works. The lovely Texas mountain laurel, used extensively in recent years in Xeriscaped parking lots and other landscape plantings, might seem an unlikely cohort with these others, but among Texas plants with continuously documented human connections, it clearly ranks among our most venerable. As is the case with Mexican buckeye, when all the evidence is examined, the reasons for these connections are somewhat elusive.

Most gardeners know Texas mountain laurel as a slow-growing, drought-tolerant, evergreen shrub that is somewhat difficult to transplant. For most of the year it provides a stable green backdrop of shiny leaves. Two things are remarkable about this plant: the luxurious flowers and the conspicuous seeds. Early in the spring it bursts forth in gorgeous purple blossoms, which resemble wisteria, proof to its many admirers that in bloom the plant is unequaled in beauty among our native Texan shrubs. The heavy perfume of the blossoms

ORIGIN OF SCIENTIFIC NAME
Sophora comes from the Arabic name *sophera,* used for a tree with pealike flowers. *Secundiflora* means that the flowers all originate from one side of the inflorescence.

OTHER COMMON NAMES
mescal bean, mescal-bean sophora, frijolito, frijolillo, patol, patolito, big-drunk bean. Through confusion with *Erythrina* spp., coral bean and colorín are sometimes seen.

FAMILY
Fabaceae (Legume or Bean Family)

DESCRIPTION
Slow-growing evergreen shrub or small tree 4–15' (but up to 35'), usually with multiple trunks; shiny, leathery compound leaves; bluish-purple, strongly fragrant blossoms followed by large (to 5"), gray-brown, semi-segmented pods.

HABITAT AND DISTRIBUTION
Central, south, and west Texas, usually on well-drained limestone soils of canyons, bluffs, and slopes; southeastern New Mexico; northern and central Mexico, south to Oaxaca.

has evoked many comparisons. Ferdinand Lindheimer (1801–1879), often called the father of Texas botany, thought the scent was "nearly the fragrance of violets" (Gray 1850). Recent comparisons are more mundane, usually referencing grape flavoring, such as grape soda, grape bubblegum, and grape Kool-Aid. Some caution that the odor is "icky sweet" (Wasowski and Wasowski 1997); the botanist Valery Havard went so far as to warn that the blossoms had "a strong, nauseating and very offensive smell" (Havard 1885), which has led some to discourage their use as cut flowers. Some believe the flowers can actually give you a headache (Schulz 1928). Bees love the blossoms, but at least one gardening expert cautions that the honey is said to be mildly toxic (Garrett 2002). These comments gain significance in light of the known toxicity of most parts of the plant and in light of what we know about that second remarkable feature, the seeds.

Most Texans know about the mountain laurel's large, pebble-sized, bright red seeds. *Sophora secundiflora* is a member of the bean family, which is obvious when the seedpods form. Each contains two to five scarlet (sometimes yellow-orange) beans, whose hard seed coats make the beans great candidates for beadwork (once pierced by a heated needle or ice pick) and for the hot-bean game enjoyed by children who heat the beans by rubbing them energetically on clothing (or on the sidewalk) before applying them to a victim's arm. The famously tough seed coat is also responsible for the bean's presence in the archaeological record, and it likely helps to prevent poisoning by in-

A particularly good bloom of Texas mountain laurel on the University of Texas campus.

A pod and the infamous red mescal beans.

gestion, since an unbroken seed can apparently pass through the digestive tract without harm.

The seeds or beans form the basis for a fascinating journey through Texas history. Texas' archaeological record is replete with *Sophora secundiflora* seeds. One of the earliest such records is from the Bonfire Shelter on the lower Pecos River (Bone Bed II, carbon-dated to 8440–8120 BCE), where Pleistocene Paleo-Indian hunters used a cliff stampede to hunt the now-extinct giant bison. *Sophora* seeds were found well preserved among the Folsom and Plainview projectile points and bison bones. By the late 1970s, these seeds had been recovered from at least sixteen prehistorically inhabited caves and rockshelters. Two sites are in Coahuila, Mexico, one in southeastern New Mexico, and thirteen in southwest Texas. The majority of the Texas sites are in Val Verde County near the confluence of the Pecos River and the Rio Grande; the remainder are on the Edwards Plateau. Only two of these many sites have yielded evidence of preferential treatment of *Sophora* beans, including a loincloth with the beans on the fringe, and a twined bag containing a large quantity of beans and what may be ritualistic paraphernalia (see Mexican buckeye). Nevertheless, many people have been led to speculate that the persistence of what are known to be toxic beans in these sites suggests a prehistoric hallucinogenic use. If this is the case, then "*Sophora* . . . has given us the oldest documented evidence for hallucinogenic plant use, not just in the Americas, but throughout the world" (Furst 1986). It

has been suggested that there was a cult or some other highly ritualized use of the bean, perhaps a deer hunting cult, and even that the pictographs and rock art of the area reflect this ceremonialism. Most of the evidence for shamanistic use and artwork is highly anecdotal (the result of taking historic data and working backward to make assumptions about prehistory), but it is, nonetheless, provocative and interesting.

The first likely recorded evidence in historic times that *Sophora* seeds were still highly valued some 10,000 years later came from Alvar Núñez Cabeza de Vaca, who unintentionally became the first European explorer of the land that would later become Texas. Held captive by coastal tribes on or near Galveston Island in 1528, he eventually escaped and made his way inland, where he survived as a traveling trader and healer. He lived for a while with a tribe of Native Americans called the Charruco, and he described their use of *Sophora* beans: "The main items of my trade were pieces of sea snails and their insides, and seashells which they use to cut a certain fruit that looks like a bean, used by them for medicinal purposes and for dances and festivals (this is the thing they value most), sea beads and other things" (Cabeza de Vaca 1993). Many commentators think this passage refers to *Sophora secundiflora* because of its tough bean pod and its long history of ritualistic use. Mesquite beans have also been proposed, but they were primarily eaten for food, and the pods would not need to be cut with seashells. Another possible candidate is coral bean (*Erythrina herbacea*), but its pods tend to open naturally on their own, and its beans do not command near the historical significance of *Sophora*. As is the case with so many of the plants mentioned in Cabeza de Vaca's *Account*, the botanical description suffers from a frustrating lack of detail; yet, the key elements that almost surely point to *Sophora* are that it was an item of trade; it resembled a bean; it was used for medicine, dances, and festivals; and it was highly valued. Although it would be almost two centuries before another report mentioned *S. secundiflora* in Texas, the stage had already been set with ample archaeological records and proof of pre-Contact use.

The first incontrovertible evidence of *Sophora* seed consumption comes from Spanish missionaries, who intimated that the seeds were consumed in conjunction with the cactus peyote. Francisco Hidalgo as early as 1716 noted that the Hasinai Caddo of east Texas were using the "frixo-lillo," or frijolillo ("little bean") together with peyote to procure visions. Among the Coahuiltecan bands in the San Antonio missions, Bartholomé Garcia in 1760 referred to both plants in his confessional: "Have you eaten peyote? / Did it intoxicate you? / Have you eaten frixolillo? / Did it intoxicate you?" (Troike 1962). Since peyote contains documented psychoactive compounds, consuming the cactus with *Sophora* seeds makes it difficult to ascertain to what extent (if any) the seeds are adding to the psychoactive effects. Given that *Sophora* seeds are extensively used as paraphernalia in many of the Plains peyote ceremonies (as beads

in necklaces, bandoliers, fringed leggings, and other ritual items), some anthropologists have been led to believe that the *Sophora* bean cult was the direct ancestor to the peyote cult. Others have argued that one did not actually give rise to the other but rather that tribes who already used the *Sophora* bean blended aspects of their existing ceremonies into their adoption of peyote. At least one recent researcher finds that there is little more than a "cautious opinion," instead of hard evidence, for a cult around the *Sophora* bean per se, and wonders whether the only relationship between the beans and peyote is that the former is used in jewelry and to decorate clothing (Stewart 1980).

Regardless of the peyote connection, a bewildering number of Native American groups used the seeds of Texas mountain laurel. The Caddo confined consumption of the seeds to ceremonies in which clairvoyance or divination was a central feature. One of their three main schools of healers was called *daitino* (the Caddoan word for the seed). Since *Sophora secundiflora* does not grow naturally in east Texas where the Caddo lived, it is thought that the Tonkawa of central Texas were the main trade source. The use of the bean seems to have come to an end just before World War I, and the Caddo no longer use it. A Caddoan informant in the 1930s recalled that once a month the Caddo and Comanche used to get drunk on a *Sophora* bean liquor (beans soaked in water). "They called it 'Jesus Talk' for they claimed when they drank it they could hear Jesus talk" (La Vere 1998).

Before 1872 the Wichita, who likewise

had a *Sophora* bean medicine society, celebrated a deer dance that was held four times a year. A special feature of the ceremony was giving a novitiate a *Sophora* bean, "which produced a violent spasm, and finally unconsciousness, the condition being indicated by the inability of the novitiate to suffer pain when the jaw of a gar-pike was drawn over his naked body" (Dorsey 1904). The Tonkawa had their own deer dance in which the bean was also consumed. The Kiowa, likewise, consumed the bean, danced all night and into the morning until exhaustion, at which point they would go to sleep, "and whatever the Chief dreamed while asleep they would do after they waked up" (La Vere 1998). The Lipan Apache, who themselves rarely ingested the seeds, were aware of the bean's alleged intoxicating effects. One of their many Coyote trickster myths revolves around the mischievous Coyote fooling a group of Indians to ingest the *Sophora* seeds for the sake of longevity. When they become "dizzy and drunk," Coyote cuts their hair short and rolls them around in the pale dust. Having thus succeeded in making them appear to be Anglos, he tries to get neighboring Indians to attack them (Opler 1940).

Several tribes that are loosely part of the Wichita group (Waco, Tawehash, Tawakoni) were all observed by the early botanist Jean Louis Berlandier to use the Texas mountain laurel as a purgative and emetic. In what Berlandier called the "feast of the new fruits," which was generally practiced among the agricultural peoples, the tribe could not partake of the

new fruits of the season without a mass purging. As soon as some new fruit was spotted (such as the first beans or maize or watermelon) a date was set for the ceremony. Committees were appointed to grind the mountain laurel seeds and throw them into a great pot of warm water; then all drank of this potion several times, sipping it through a reed or straw. The rest of the day was spent in singing and purging, or as Berlandier adroitly noted, "At this time you may see a whole nation gathered together in one building, there to vomit and be purged in order to earn the right to eat of the new fruits" (Berlandier 1969). The Comanche, calling the seed *aincapu*, as well as the Caddoan tribes, partook in a first fruits ceremony. The Caddoans (indeed, Native Americans throughout the entire southeastern United States) were well known to use yaupon for similar purposes in what is known in the literature as "black drink." *Sophora* beans may have been a substitute.

Perhaps most interesting about Texas mountain laurel seeds is their extensive use in Indian material culture and trade. More than 30 North American Indian groups were familiar with the red beans. "Without question, the most widespread and continuous purpose for which North American Indian groups have employed [the beans] is as seed beads attached to a wide variety of articles such as shirts, leggings, dresses, and pouches or strung into bandoleers, necklaces, and bracelets" (Merrill 1977). Tribes as far away as the northern Great Plains (such as the Dakota Sioux, Meskwaki, Ojibwa, Winnebago and even the Blackfoot of Montana) employed the beans in this way, without any attention to ingesting them. Since the Texas mountain laurel is predominately located in what is now Texas, it is fair to say that as a trade export item, the little *Sophora* bean enjoyed perhaps the most extensive Native American trade distribution of any item originating in what is now Texas, with the possible exception of peyote. The red beans were likely one of the few natural objects so colored. They were aesthetically pleasing and desirable in themselves, but even more so if imbued with ritualistic significance. Edwin James of the Stephen Long expedition to the Rockies in the early 1820s remarks that a member of his team, upon seeing a pint of *Sophora* beans in an Arapaho medicine bag, exclaimed that the beans were "in such high request among the Oto Indians, that a horse has been exchanged for eight or ten of them" (James 1823). Incredible as this sounds, it is not improbable. Simple glass trade beads were a major source of gifts and bartering throughout the American West. Many a white explorer was astonished at the high value a Native American would place on such trinkets, but in that preindustrial world beadwork was limited to natural materials (such as shell, stone, bone, antler) that required considerable labor to fashion. The smooth and durable seed of the Texas mountain laurel did not have to be shaped; it was ready to be used as is. Red and shiny, the bean had few equals among natural objects for decoration. Ritualized and considered hallucinogenic, it was even more attractive.

Modern investigation into the chem-

istry of *Sophora* beans has not revealed strong evidence for hallucinogenic compounds. Seven quinolizidine alkaloids have been identified in the beans, the major ones being cytisine (once aptly named sophorine), N-methylcytisine, and sparteine, but other plants high in cytisine and related alkaloids are not generally considered hallucinogenic. Cytisine produces effects similar to nicotine's, such as "nausea, vomiting, pallor, drowsiness, dizziness, incoordination, muscle twitching, with delirium and coma occurring in severe cases" (Hatfield et al. 1977). These symptoms seem to be in line with much of what we have seen in previous descriptions. In fact, the only known case report of human intoxication by a *Sophora* seed (in 1878) describes an adult subject who "experienced headache, several bowel movements, great difficulty in walking, and sleep which lasted several hours when one-fourth of a seed (approximately 150 mg) was consumed" (Hatfield et al. 1977). This description echoes perfectly that of Havard, who mentions in his *Report on the Flora of Western and Southern Texas*, which has been repeatedly cited in much of the subsequent literature: "The Indians near San Antonio used this bean as an intoxicant, half a bean producing delirious exhilaration followed by a sleep which lasts 2 or 3 days, and it is asserted that a whole bean would kill a man" (Havard 1885).

The veterinary literature is replete with examples of *Sophora* poisoning from both the foliage and the seeds. Sheep and goats are primarily affected, though cattle are also susceptible. Nervous (rather than fatal) symptoms have been noted in sheep which, when forced to move, tremble violently, fall, and then lie somnolent for several minutes before regaining their feet to graze again. Cattle are not usually affected under range conditions, but when a calf was fed *Sophora* foliage (in the amount of 1% of body weight), it died within two hours (Radeleff 1970). Recently a case of *Sophora* bean toxicity in a dog was reported that matched the symptoms in sheep: "[The dog] would stiffen in his joints, tremble and then go sternal with splayed legs or full in lateral recumbency. He appeared exhausted after each episode and would sleep or doze for a few minutes, then fully recover and appear normal" (Knauer et al. 1995). There is even one rarely cited report of the bean's use to stun chickens: "A resident of Shumla [now a ghost town just east of Langtry] who had lived for a long time in Mexico states that the natives there crushed this bean and fed it to the chickens of neighbors. The chickens became stupefied and then unconscious, and were easily captured without commotion, thus acquiring new owners" (Martin 1933). The Comanche also ground the beans into a powder, which was used to kill vermin and lice.

Sophora beans are, then, best viewed as a poison, perhaps (and only secondarily) as a deliriant. This view accounts for the purgative and emetic effects described here. Within a given cultural context, the dreams, divinations, and visions attributed to the beans stem less from psychotropic compounds per se and more from the ceremonial setting and the participant's psychological state of mind. The alkaloids

and other toxic elements may start the somatic effects, but it is more the "ceremonial contexts in which [the beans] were consumed, and the vision seeker's belief and expectation that visions were . . . likely to occur in such contexts" that bring about the bean's reputation (Merrill 1977). Of course, if the *Sophora* bean was consumed with liquor, mescal, or peyote, many other compounds and agents were responsible for the symptoms.

A note about names is needed here. *Sophora* beans are called mescal beans throughout recent literature. Although *mescal* is the name commonly used in Mexico for a distilled spirit made from the fleshy leaf bases and trunks of various species of *Agave*, in the United States the term came to be applied indiscriminately to other intoxicants, or perceived intoxicants. Thus, one of the early names for peyote in the States was *mescal buttons*. Since there was some connection between peyote and *Sophora* already, *mescal bean* was also used to describe peyote. To this day the most active alkaloid in peyote is called mescaline, even though peyote has nothing in common with mescal except that both are used as intoxicants. Botanically they are members of separate families (Cactaceae and Agavaceae, respectively). "Until 1907 mescalbean was used *only* to mean the dried product of [peyote], since then called the Peyote button" (Stewart 1980). Following a famous court case in Oklahoma wherein the prosecution failed to win a case about the use of peyote because the law mentioned only "mescal beans," *peyote* came into its own use as a name for the little cactus, while

Sophora almost immediately became the sole proprietor of the name *mescal bean*. So the term *mescal* has been historically applied to three different (unrelated) genera: *Lophophora* (peyote), *Agave*, and *Sophora*. Throughout most of the twentieth century, however, the term *mescal bean* seems to have solidified around the seeds of *S. secundiflora*.

While we are on the topic of names: Texas mountain laurel is not the mountain laurel of the eastern United States (*Kalmia latifolia*), nor is it related to the laurel of Asia and the Mediterranean (*Laurus nobilis*).

SOURCES: Berlandier 1969; Boyd and Dering 1996; Cabeza de Vaca 1993; Campbell 1958; Dorsey 1904; Furst 1986; Garrett 2002; Gray 1850; Hatfield et al. 1977; Havard 1885; Howard 1957; James 1823; Knauer et al. 1995; La Vere 1998; Martin 1933; Merrill 1977; Mielke 1993; Newkumet and Meredith 1988; Opler 1940; Parsons 1941; Radeleff 1970; Schultes 1976; Schulz 1928; Sjoberg 1953; Stewart 1980; Troike 1962; Tull 1999; Turpin 1986; Wasowski and Wasowski 1997; Wellmann 1978; Wrede 1997

Mexican Buckeye

Ungnadia speciosa Endl.

If you take an early springtime walk down a rocky ravine in central Texas, you can, at a distance, easily mistake the Mexican buckeye for a redbud tree. Both are similar in height, inhabit much of the same region, and sport clusters of fragrant purple-pink flowers that spring forth before the leaves appear. On closer inspection, Mexican buckeye is a shrub with wandlike branches arising from its base. Although it has been reported to reach 30 feet, it rarely does so, usually retaining a shrubby habit, rather than that of a single-trunk tree. Mexican buckeye also is more particular in its habitat and narrower in its range than redbud, having a strong preference for moist canyons and rocky bluffs bordering streambeds. Of particular note are its conspicuous, reddish-brown, leathery, three-lobed, inflated fruits, which begin to crack open in fall and cling to the branches through winter and early spring. Mature fruits contain three beautiful, lustrous, brownish-black seeds, which rattle when the branches are shaken. These lovely seeds are at the center of an intriguing story.

Mexican buckeye is one of a dozen or so plants in Texas with a venerable archaeological past. In the Trans-Pecos, archaeological digs have uncovered seeds and pod fragments of the plant at many sites and across many mil-

ORIGIN OF SCIENTIFIC NAME

Ungnadia honors David Ungnad, the ambassador of Holy Roman Emperor Rudolph II to the Ottoman Empire. In 1576 Ungnad introduced the common horse chestnut to western Europe from Istanbul (though it was actually native to northern Greece). *Speciosa* means showy or pretty, referring to the flowers.

OTHER COMMON NAMES

Texas buckeye, Spanish buckeye, New Mexican buckeye, false buckeye, canyon buckeye, monilla

FAMILY

Sapindaceae (Soapberry Family)

DESCRIPTION

Large, many-branched shrub or small, shrubby tree, ca. 8–12', with pink flowers and distinctive three-lobed fruit.

HABITAT AND DISTRIBUTION

Mostly in limestone soils along rocky ravines, streambeds, and bluffs of central and western Texas; southernmost New Mexico; northern Mexico.

The early spring blossoms of Mexican buckeye.

Mexican buckeye's unusual three-lobed seedpods (opened) with black seeds.

lennia. In Val Verde County alone, at least two sites, the Fate Bell Shelter and Eagle Cave, yielded *Ungnadia speciosa* seeds in every stratum spanning the period from 7000 BCE to 1000 CE, with several other Val Verde sites showing similar dates. Even older seeds, dated to 7500 BCE, were uncovered in Frightful Cave in the Cuatro Ciénegas Basin of Coahuila, Mexico.

That the plant has been utilized by early Native Americans is well established; exactly how it was utilized remains a mystery. The seeds are known to contain high quantities of cyanogenetic lipids and are generally assumed to be toxic, and yet the sheer quantities of seeds found and the context in which they are found seem to suggest uses broader than mere poison. Poisons can, of course, be useful. One scholarly paper finds preliminary evidence that "Mexican buckeye will probably kill fish, and if applied to projectile points, will disable mammals or birds" (Adovasio and Fry 1976), but as the authors admit, the absence of fish remains at many of the sites casts doubt on the fish poison theory. The same authors promote what they believe is a more likely hypothesis, that Mexican buckeye is a possible psychotropic drug, based on the frequency with which the seeds are found together with mescal beans (the seeds of Texas mountain laurel); mescal beans have long been considered psychotropic, or at least involved in vision-seeking contexts. Not only do most of the sites mentioned above contain seeds of both of the plants scattered throughout many archaeological strata, but they also contain large quantities of the buckeye seeds stored in plaited or twilled baskets.

Mexican buckeye as it appears in August with drying fruits.

The only other plant material so stored (at least in the Cuatro Ciénegas sites) is mescal beans. Perhaps the strongest evidence that the authors cite for the psychotropic theory comes from Horseshoe Cave in Val Verde County, where a cache was found containing a pint of both buckeye seeds and mescal beans mixed together, along with items that could suggest ritualistic use, including rodent mandibles, terrapin shell, red ocher, deer hide, pink clay, and lithic artifacts. Perhaps, they further suggest, a type of hunting cult may have used the two kinds of seeds.

The sheer quantity of the seeds found, however, suggests that something else may be at stake. Adovasio and Fry state that one twilled basket cache contained eleven *pounds* of buckeye seeds. An expedition to Shumla Caves in west Texas found a stor-

age basket containing several thousand of the seeds, causing the author to think that they were "evidently much eaten" (Martin 1933). In Baker's Cave (Val Verde County) the seeds and fruits of buckeye were found in a cooking pit together with those of many other (mostly edible) plants. With such evidence it is difficult to imagine that the seeds were not eaten for food. Any foodstuff that could be stored without spoiling would have been a boon, and perhaps this explains why such large quantities were stored.

The issue of the toxicity of the buckeye seed is crucial; unfortunately, we have conflicting evidence that only broadens the mystery. One of the earliest published comments on the matter comes from Viktor Bracht, who, having visited the German settlements of central Texas in 1848, remarked that "at least several German immigrants became ill as a result of eating [the seeds], and one even died" (Bracht 1931). The famed botanist Valery Havard, who influenced most future commentators on the matter, stated that an adult could eat one or two of the pleasant-tasting seeds with impunity, but that "three or four soon produce giddiness and a sensation of heat and discomfort at the pit of the stomach" (Havard 1885). He goes on to relate how a four-year-old boy became giddy and began to stagger within half an hour of ingesting two or three buckeye seeds (the boy fully recovered in a few hours after taking an emetic). Going one step beyond Havard, a scientist who studied the chemistry of the seeds is reported to have said that five or six seeds could be deadly (Tull 1999). Deer rarely browse the seeds, and there is no record, as far as is known, of the seeds being eaten among the Apache or Comanche tribes.

On the other hand, Scooter Cheatham, author of *The Useful Wild Plants of Texas,* has reportedly eaten the seeds without incident (Tull 1999). Dr. B. L. Turner, professor emeritus of the University of Texas Botany Department, after watching a fellow naturalist eat literally handfuls of buckeye seeds with no ill effects on a field trip to northern Mexico in 1948, himself tried a few and was none the worse for it. He reports that their taste is similar to macadamia nuts (pers. comm.).

Something is odd here. A possible solution to the mystery is that the seeds are toxic until they are fully ripe, at which point they are edible, and perhaps then only in limited amounts. This phenom-enon is not unknown among certain food plants, such as the almond. Or perhaps one can get by with eating just a few, but larger amounts bring on toxic side effects, the threshold no doubt varying from individual to individual. It is also conceivable that the seeds were cooked before eating. Hydrogen cyanide—naturally found in bitter almond, peach stones, and in the leaves of cherry and cherry laurel—is highly volatile; food containing this compound could be detoxified with an hour or so of heating (George Hocking, pers. comm.). Finally, there is the possibility that the attractive seeds were not consumed by archaic peoples but were simply collected for beadwork and decoration, as were mescal beans. Into the twentieth century, boys used buckeyes as marbles.

Mexican buckeye blossoms provide an excellent early source of nectar for honeybees, and the shrub itself is a larval host plant for Henry's elfin butterfly. The plant is an ornamental and has begun to appear in nurseries. Easily grown from seed, it is certainly an excellent choice for Xeriscaping.

Ungnadia is a monotypic genus; that is, no plant other than *U. speciosa* is a member of the genus. Although the flowers and inflated fruits superficially resemble those of true buckeyes, Mexican buckeye is not a member of the buckeye family (Hippocastanaceae).

SOURCES: Adovasio and Fry 1976; Bracht 1931; Damude and Bender 1999; Havard 1885; Hocking 1997; Martin 1933; Parks 1937; Seigler et al. 1971; Standley 1920–1926; Tull 1999; Vines 1984; Wrede 1997

Yucca

Yucca spp.

Yucca is one of the most important economic plants in the American Southwest. It is widely used as an ornamental, and one species, *Yucca elata*, serves as the state flower of New Mexico. Along with lechuguilla, prickly pear, and sotol, yucca was one of the most useful plants to early humans in our state. Literally every part of the plant yields something of value, whether a foodstuff, fiber, soap, tanning agent, medicine, building material, or fuel. Amid hundreds of representations of animals and humans, yucca is one of the few wild plants depicted in prehistoric petroglyphs.

Four different parts of the yucca are edible. The flower stalk when fully grown, but before the buds have expanded, is considered by the Apache the most delicious part of the plant. This tribe roasted the stalks on embers and removed the charred portions to reveal the tender, sweet interior. Alternatively, they peeled the raw stalks, chopped and boiled them, and then dried them for storage. The Kiowa, likewise, consumed the stalks, as did Hispanic and Anglo settlers. Yucca blossoms themselves offer another delectable treat. In Texas, ingestion of

ORIGIN OF SCIENTIFIC NAME

Yucca is a native Caribbean name for cassava or manioc (*Manihot esculenta*), from which we get tapioca. This name, usually spelled *yuca* when referring to cassava, was accidentally given to our unrelated genus in the sixteenth century.

OTHER COMMON NAMES

beargrass, Spanish bayonet, Spanish dagger, soapweed, palmilla, palma pita

FAMILY

Agavaceae (Agave Family)

DESCRIPTION

Trunked or trunkless, branched or unbranched evergreen shrubs composed of rosettes of long, narrow, often flexible leaves, usually sharp-pointed; bell-shaped flowers in terminal spikes, creamy to greenish white.

HABITAT AND DISTRIBUTION

Throughout the U.S., but predominantly in the more arid areas of

the Plains and Southwest; Mexico, possibly Caribbean.

NOTE

There are approximately fifteen species of *Yucca* in Texas, many of which are limited to specific areas of the state, none being sufficiently distributed to be considered the dominant species. Given that their ethnobotanical uses, with few exceptions, are very similar, this account will treat *Yucca* as a genus.

*Twist-leaf yucca (*Yucca rupicola*) in flower.*

*The fleshy fruits of Spanish dagger (*Yucca treculeana*) of south Texas. Their thin, outermost layers are edible, but the most delectable fruits are those of the banana yucca (*Y. baccata*) of the Trans-Pecos.*

yucca flowers is dated by archaeological evidence to at least 500 BCE, but it likely predates this by several millennia. The whitish blossoms, with their pistils and stamens removed, are generally sweet tasting and rich in vitamin C. They can be eaten raw, sautéed, or fried. The Apache used the blossoms of *Yucca elata*, which seems to have some of the tastiest flowers, as soup vegetables; they also boiled, dried, and stored them. Pioneers reportedly gathered yucca flowers in quantities, pickling them or cooking them like cabbage. The yucca crowns offer a third, more infrequent, food source. The crowns (and sometimes young leaves) could be pit-baked like sotol and then immediately consumed or pounded into a flour to be dried and preserved.

By far the most famous and delectable part of the yucca is the fruit pulp from the species with fleshy pods. The best known of these is *Yucca baccata*, known as the banana yucca or dátil, which is found in Texas only in the Trans-Pecos. When the brown outer pulp of the banana yucca fruit is completely ripe, it is said to have a peculiar taste that variously resembles apples, applesauce, or dates (*dátil* being Spanish for "date"). Roasted, the fruits are compared to sweet potatoes. The fruits were a major food item among the Mescalero Apache, Lipan Apache, Navajo, and Zuni. Immature yucca fruits were frequently allowed to ripen indoors, to prevent animal and insect predation. They could be eaten raw, or following Navajo fashion, they could be dried, ground, and kneaded into small cakes, which were then sun-dried. Long-lasting and easy to transport, these cakes made a favorite staple for the warpath. When rehydrated, they were eaten with breads, meats, and other dishes. The Apache imbued dátil fruits and cakes with religious overtones; gathering and preparing the fruit required prayer, and the food was particularly used in puberty ceremonies for girls. Curiously, the extensive use of yucca fruits among Native Americans of the Southwest was only rarely adopted by Hispanics and was practically ignored by Anglo settlers. Northern Mexicans occasionally made a liquid from fermented yucca fruits that was distilled into a rather indifferent rum-like aguardiente. The fruits of the dry-capsuled species of *Yucca*, which make up about half of our species, are much less palatable (actually, they are nearly inedible). This may help to explain why yucca fruit consumption in general failed to gain wide acceptance among nonnative peoples. The Zuni, however, managed to eat even the dry capsules by boiling them into a "sort of pickle" (Standley 1912).

Perhaps the most common and wide-spread use of *Yucca* as a genus was for fiber. Certainly in the prehistoric desert Southwest no material was more popular for cordage. Yucca fibers were removed by slicing the leaves lengthwise and stripping them, or by soaking and pounding. Although generally weaker and more brittle than lechuguilla fiber, yucca fiber is still eminently useful, resembling hemp. Yuccas are also more widespread throughout the Southwest, lechuguilla being mainly confined to the Chihuahuan Desert. Pre-

historic humans twisted yucca fibers into cords that were the foundation for twine and rope used in diverse items, from bow-strings, straps, belts, lashings, rope ladders, snares, and nets to more complicated woven and plaited items such as cloth, which could be interwoven with feathers and strips of rabbit fur to make elaborate robes, and the ties of sandals, hundreds of which have been found throughout the Southwest and west Texas. Historic native uses included hats, hairbrushes, mattresses, and horse blankets. Mexicans have long used the fiber, variously referred to as *palmilla fiber, palma pita,* and *ixtle,* for tying bundles of cornstalks and fodder, and plantations of the American South made thongs from yucca for hanging hams and bacon. Toward the latter part of the nineteenth century, the U.S. Department of Agriculture patented a machine for yucca fiber extraction. The fiber surged in popularity during World War I, when supplies of jute from India became scarce. Approximately 80 million pounds of fiber from *Y. glauca* and *Y. elata* were collected at this time in New Mexico and Texas for the bagging of cotton bales. During World War II, the U.S. Navy extensively harvested *Y. glauca* for rope, twine, and a special type of heavy paper. Many rural Mexicans still rely on yucca harvesting for income, though the quality of the fiber is generally considered inferior to commercial cordage fibers, which keeps economic prospects limited.

Strips of the fibrous leaves of yucca were utilized in basketry and sundry items. Mescalero Apache basket makers used the leaves of *Y. glauca* extensively for baskets and special drying trays for dátil fruits. Many other tribes employed the leaves in the manufacture of plates, bowls, masks, tablets, dolls, prayer sticks, and various mats. The Tohono O'odham of southern Arizona still use yucca leaves for trays, sewing baskets, and decorative containers. Yucca leaves, chewed until the tips are frayed, are the traditional paintbrushes used to decorate native southwestern pottery and are still employed by contemporary Pueblo artists.

As the name *soapweed* suggests, another main use of yucca is for soap. Again like lechuguilla, the roots of most species of yucca yield a very decent laundry detergent, body soap, and shampoo. The fresh roots are pounded to a pulp and mixed with water, or shaved and simmered until foamy, to produce an excellent cleanser, called *amole* among Spanish speakers, which lathers freely and is easy on the skin. Amole is particularly suitable for woolen goods, such as blankets and rugs, since lye soaps tend to mat woolen fibers. Native American tribes, both north and south of the border, still make frequent use of yucca soap for laundry, though they equally value it as a shampoo, especially in ceremonial contexts. Traditionally, shampooing the hair with yucca root was required before partaking in ceremonies of the Comanche and Pueblo tribes, and amole was believed to make the hair long, straight, strong, and especially glossy. The Kiowa maintained that it controlled dandruff and skin irritations. Other ceremonial connections include the Yavapai, whose warriors purified themselves with yucca baths after battle,

and the Hopi, who wash the head of a newborn with yucca soap on the twentieth day after birth. At least one American company advertised amole in the early twentieth century, and the product is still available in specialty markets in San Antonio.

Although the vast majority of yucca uses centered around food, fiber, and soap, the plants provided for a variety of minor applications. The Kiowa, for instance, tanned hides with a yucca root preparation. The Tarahumara of Mexico used the roots and leaves for fish stupefaction. Various native tribes, as well as Hispanic and Anglo settlers, used both roots and leaves to prepare salves and tinctures to treat rheumatism, bruises, and inflammation. Beams and timber from the larger-trunked *Yucca* species have been found as building materials in ancient cliff dwellings, and the spongy fibrous wood was utilized for surgeon splints during World War I, when large quantities were shipped to European hospitals. Similar to sotol, yucca holds a special connection to fuel and fire. Many Indians, such as the Apache, used the dried flower stalks as hearth boards for their fire drills. The Tonkawa even had a Prometheus-like myth in which a wolf steals fire from the sun and manages to light a yucca stalk, saying, "This shall have fire from now on, and the flint-rock too, and several plants" (Sjoberg 1953). Dried yucca leaves, like those of sotol, make excellent fuel for fires, as the lower, inner layers on the trunk remain dry even in rainy weather. Yucca seedpods, when ignited, are said to make excellent flares (Flores 1990).

Livestock, such as cattle, relish yucca flowers, and animals have been known to overturn plants to obtain them. Naturalists attribute the near absence of yucca seedpods on heavily grazed ranges to that preference. During severe droughts in the Southwest, such as that of 1916–1919, the chopped trunks and leaves of *Yucca elata* and *Y. glauca*, supplemented with cottonseed meal, were extensively used to feed cattle, and special shredding machines were developed for processing.

All ethnobotany aside, it is impossible to leave *Yucca* without mentioning its special relationship to yucca moths. In a mechanism that discourages self-pollination, the male (pollen-bearing) flower parts of *Yucca* are remote from the female (ovule-bearing) parts of the flower. The fertilized female yucca moth gathers a sticky mass of this pollen and carries it to another flower, where, having laid her eggs in one of the carpels of the fruit, she crawls up the style and smears her pollen on the stigma. This ensures pollination and the development of seeds, on some of which her developing larvae will depend for survival. This special relationship of mutual dependence has traditionally been seen as a textbook example of obligate mutualism (Bogler et al. 1995). Forty-odd species of *Yucca* are believed to be virtually dependent on several species of yucca moth for sexual reproduction. Asexual (vegetative) reproduction can occur in the absence of these moths, and large clonal populations are found in the field.

SOURCES: Basehart 1974; Bell and Castetter 1941; Bogler et al. 1995; Bryant 1974; Carlson and Jones 1939; Castetter 1935; Castetter and Opler 1936; Cornett 1995; Crosswhite 1980, 1981; Curtin 1965; Dewey 1943; Diggs et al. 1999; Dunmire and Tierney 1995; Fletcher 1928; Flores 1990; Greene 1972; Havard 1885, 1896; Joutel 1998; Moore 1990; Newcomb 1961; Palmer 1878; Pasztor 2003; Pennington 1958; Porcher 1869; Schulz 1928; Sjoberg 1953; Smithers 1964; Standley 1912; Tull 1999; Vestal and Schultes 1939; Warnock 1970; Webber 1953; Whitehouse 1936

HERBACEOUS PLANTS, CACTI, GRASSES, VINES, AND AQUATICS

Wild Onion

Allium canadense L.

Allium drummondii Regel

Allium is a large and complex genus (more than 750 species) of the Northern Hemisphere famous for its handful of species that are world food crops: onions, leeks, scallions, chives, and garlic. Texas has approximately thirteen species, about half of which inhabit only the far western portions of the state. *Allium drummondii* and *A. canadense* are by far the most abundant and widespread species in the state. *Allium canadense* comprises several varieties, together called an alliance, representing "the only important center of diversity and probably dispersal of this genus on the North American continent east of the Continental Divide" (Ownbey 1950). *Allium canadense* var. *canadense* is unusual in having both sexual and asexual populations. Sexual plants produce white blossoms; asexual ones

ORIGIN OF SCIENTIFIC NAME

Allium (also *alium*) is the Latin word for garlic and may derive from the Celtic *all*, meaning hot or pungent. *Canadense* refers to the Canadian origin of the type specimen, collected in 1749 along the Hudson in upstate New York; at the time, the area was generically called Canada, as opposed to Virginia to the south. Ironically, there is evidence that *A. canadense* was probably not native to Canada and was only brought in by explorers from what is now the U.S. (Dore 1971). *Drummondii* honors Thomas Drummond (1780–1835), a Scottish botanist and naturalist who collected in Canada and the U.S. Before his

mysterious death in Cuba in 1835, he was one of the earliest collectors of Texas plants (1833–1834); his specimens were distributed worldwide, placing our state on the botanical map. Many Texas species bear his name.

OTHER COMMON NAMES

For *Allium canadense*: Canada onion, meadow garlic. For *A. drummondii*: Drummond's onion. For both: prairie onion, spring onion, wild garlic, cebollita

FAMILY

Liliaceae (Lily Family). Some recent workers segregate *Allium* into a new family Alliaceae.

DESCRIPTION

Stemless, herbaceous perennials arising from small bulbs, the entire

plant onion-scented. The flower scape of *Allium canadense* is generally 6–20" tall, and the white flowers are usually replaced by bulbils. The scape of *A. drummondii* is usually shorter (4–12") and sports pink flowers that often fade to ashy white.

HABITAT AND DISTRIBUTION

Allium canadense prefers the moister soils of central and east Texas; widely distributed in meadows, woods, and fields throughout eastern North America from Texas to Canada and the Atlantic Coast. *Allium drummondii* is widespread across the entire state but prefers limestone soils; north to South Dakota, also New Mexico and Arkansas; northern Mexico.

Drummond's onion in flower.

predominantly form bulbils in place of flowers, creating a bizarre appearance. *Allium drummondii* is unique in its ability to produce a second and even third flowering scape from a single bulb. Of the 70 species of *Allium* indigenous to North America, all but two are closely related. The comments here could apply more or less to all Texas species (indeed, to many U.S. species), but this account focuses on *Allium drummondii* and *A. canadense* because they are the most likely candidates for wild onion use in our area.

The most obvious thing to do with a wild onion is eat it. Wild onions tend to be much stronger in taste than domesticated onions, and a few can go a long way. Historically, their value as food lay more in their abundance than in their quality, and they were likely eaten in large amounts only when little else was available, though cooking significantly reduces their pungen-

cy. New England colonists, following the lead of neighboring Indians, adopted *Allium canadense* into their diet and cuisine. In our region the archaeological record shows evidence of wild onion consumption for many millennia, and local tribes were well acquainted with the plants. The Comanche cooked the bulbs in ashes and ate them with salt and meat. The Apache gathered several western species to eat raw, flavor soups, or season foods. The Kickapoo used *A. drummondii* as a condiment. People of European descent followed suit. The La Salle expedition of the late 1600s found the Texas wild onions, though small, as good as the onions in France. A colonial Spanish friar inspecting the east Texas missions in the mid-eighteenth century noted that wild onions made a good addition to salad (Solís 1931). Among Texas colonists, John C. Duval, one of the few to escape the Goliad massacre of 1836, was delighted to encounter wild onions several times during his weeks of deprivation while hiding from the Mexican army. Contemporary naturalists find Drummond's onion "edible and quite tasty" (Ajilvsgi 1984), having a unique "nutty background taste" (Cheatham and Johnston 1995). Many authors recommend any of our native onions, including the green bulbils of *A. canadense* (which can be pickled), as good additions to casseroles, meat dishes, omelets, salads, soups, stews, stir-fries, and stuffing. Care should be taken with young children as there are reports of gastroenteritis and potential toxicity (Lampe and McCann 1985).

Wild onion had a few medicinal uses. During the Stephen Long expedition to the Rockies (1819–1820)—which, incidentally, resulted in the first known botanical collection made in what is now Texas—wild onion was eaten to cure what is thought to have been scurvy (a disease of vitamin C deficiency). In folk medicine, pneumonia and colds have been treated with onion poultices, and the juice of wild onions, boiled into a thick syrup, has been used to treat croup and throat irritations. Several Indian tribes used the juice of crushed *Allium canadense* to treat bee and wasp stings; the juice was said to take immediate effect. The Kickapoo used crushed bulbs of *A. drummondii* to eliminate pimples.

We now know that domesticated onion and garlic bulbs are naturally antiseptic and can be used to heal wounds. Soldiers in both world wars applied garlic juice to wounds to prevent infections. Garlic and onion bulbs also contain vitamins B-1 and B-2 and high levels of vitamin C. Current research suggests that the sulfur compounds present in garlic (and, to a lesser degree, onions) reduce hypertension. Garlic is also believed to lower cholesterol and to thin the blood by inhibiting clotting. Given the close relationship of many of the species of *Allium*, it would not be surprising to find that our wild onions share at least some of these attributes.

Because of their strong odor, wild onions are able to impart their scent and taste to anything coming into contact with them. Livestock relish their leaves and flowers, which are one of the first greens to appear in early spring, but ranchers and dairy owners curse the herbs since the onion odor is transmitted to meat, milk, and butter, rendering all unfit for market. Another concern for ranchers is that consumption of wild onion in large amounts has led to death in cattle. Farmers must take care when harvesting to remove wild onion growth, since wheat, oats, and other grain crops can easily acquire the onion flavor. In light of the odor, Apache hunting lore specifically warns against attempting to hunt deer after gathering or eating wild onions. On a more positive note, Ferdinand Roemer, the German scientist who explored Texas in 1845–1847 and wrote the first monograph on Texas geology, mentions that the meat of a turkey that had foraged on wild onions had an "agreeable onion-like taste" (Roemer 1935).

Domesticated onions were among the very first commercial vegetable crops to be grown in Texas at the end of the nineteenth century, and the state has a national reputation for good onions. The Texas 1015 SuperSweet, a large, tearless onion developed by researchers at Texas A&M University in 1986 and named for its planting date (October 15), has received international interest. In the early twentieth century, Texas was the leading producer of early-season onions in the United States, and by mid-century the state ranked first in the nation in total acreage planted with onions.

SOURCES: Ajilvsgi 1984; Balandrin 1996; Basehart 1974; Bryant 1974; Castetter and Opler 1936; Cheatham and Johnston 1995; Diggs et al. 1999; Dore 1971; Duval 1892; Fletcher 1928; Gregory et al. 1998; Hussey 1974; Joutel 1998; Kindscher 1992; Kirkpatrick 1992; Lampe and McCann 1985; Latorre and Latorre 1977; Ownbey 1950; Ownbey and Aase 1955; Roemer 1935; Shafer 1986; Silverthorne 1996; Solís 1931; Tveten and Tveten 1997; Warnock 1974; Wilke 2005

Amaranth

Amaranthus spp.

With an inauspicious name like *pigweed* and with several of its species considered some of the world's worst weeds, it is little wonder that the genus *Amaranthus* gets little respect. Its species grow easily and rapidly in a variety of soils, tolerate drought, and produce tens of thousands of seeds per plant, which can lie dormant for decades. Practically every cultivated field, corner lot, or sidewalk crack bears testimony to the fertility of *Amaranthus*; conversely, undisturbed areas tend to be pigweed-poor. Why include such a scrappy weed in a book extolling the virtues of native plants?

The same characteristics that make the plants weedy also make them useful; the genus *Amaranthus* comprises some of the oldest and most important food crops in the world. Both cultivated and uncultivated species produce thousands of tiny seeds the size of pepper grains; these specks are edible and make for a grainlike crop. Most amaranth seeds have a very high protein content, up to 16%, which is higher than that of conventional varieties of wheat (12–14%), rice (7–10%), and corn (9–10%). Moreover, amaranth protein is rich in lysine, an amino acid that is low in most cereal proteins; its lysine content is twice that of wheat and three times that of corn. Ama-

ORIGIN OF SCIENTIFIC NAME
The genus name is from a Greek word meaning unfading (*a*, "not"; *marain*, "to wither" or "to perish"), referring to the persistence of the dried flower heads, with their color, of many species.

OTHER COMMON NAMES
pigweed, careless weed, red-root, quelite

FAMILY
Amaranthaceae (Amaranth Family)

DESCRIPTION
In our area, erect, sometimes prostrate, weedy annual herbs, 1–6' high (max. 9'), with simple, entire, alternate leaves; tiny flowers in small, headlike clusters, or in dense spikes.

HABITAT AND DISTRIBUTION
In disturbed sites, cultivated and fallow fields, and weedy areas, with several species (such as *Amaranthus albus, A. blitoides, A. palmeri*, and *A. retroflexus*) nearly ubiquitous throughout Texas and the U.S.; many species native to Latin America spread worldwide (Europe, Africa, India).

Amaranthus palmeri *in leaf.*

Flowering stalk of the wild Amaranthus palmeri.

ranth also contains more fiber, calcium, and oil than most other grains. The grain yield of the main cultivated grain species, *A. hypochondriacus* (not a Texas native, though it has been found here), is higher than that of soybeans and only just below that of wheat. All considered, cultivated grain amaranth is an excellent cereal-like crop that needs to be exploited more. Currently, it is mainly popular in East Africa and India, though it has made some inroads in organic food stores in the United States in flours and cereal products; in the 1990s at least 33 products in the U.S. marketplace contained amaranth.

The Aztecs used amaranth extensively as a grain and considered the plant a symbol of immortality. When Hernán Cortés began his campaign of conquest of the Aztec empire, he found that 20,000 tons of amaranth fruits from seventeen provinces were paid in *annual* tribute to Moctezuma. Realizing its importance as a food crop and religious symbol, he had the amaranth fields destroyed and made it a crime to grow the crop, punishable by death. Although amaranth rivaled corn as the most important Aztec crop, its religious usage likely led to its postcolonial demise. Amaranth seed was ground into a dough, mixed with popped amaranth seeds (like miniature popcorn), dyed red (with dye derived from amaranth flowers), and then shaped into various animal figures that were consumed in ceremonies at points throughout the year. The festival honoring the Aztec war god Huitzilopochtli, which included human sacrifice, involved the creation of an enormous idol that was made of this dough. The idol

was paraded through the streets, consecrated by the priests "as the bones and flesh of the war god," and then consumed by the masses (Cole 1979). The Spaniards at the very least saw the sacred amaranth seed as an opportunity for control. Given the context of human sacrifice and of idol veneration and consumption, it likely seemed a shocking and barbaric substance, a sort of satanic mocking of the bread of the Holy Communion. Spanish attitudes toward amaranth kept the crop in disrepute well into post-Conquest times. "Almost overnight one of the most important crops of the Americas fell into disuse and obscurity" (Schnetzler and Breene 1994), and corn and beans became the dominant seed crops. Amaranth was relegated to small pockets of rural farming in mountainous areas of Mexico and the Andes. Ironically, the amaranth dough, mixed with honey, lives on as a candy called *alegría* (happiness) and is occasionally made into decorative items such as, of all things, rosary beads.

Native American use of amaranth seeds in what is now the United States has a long though relatively unknown history. The oldest amaranth seeds found in the States were discovered near Grants, New Mexico, and possibly date to 6500 years ago. Coprolites from Hinds Cave along the lower Pecos River in Texas contain amaranth material dating to 5800 years ago. In historic times we know from many different tribes that the seeds were usually ground into a meal, sometimes mixed with corn, and either consumed as a mush or steamed or baked into a kind of tasty bread. Indians consuming amaranth seeds in this fashion include the Paiute of Utah; the Tohono O'odham of Arizona; the Acoma, Zuni, and Puebloans of New Mexico; and various tribes of the Southeast. In Texas, seed flour was noted among the Chiricahua and Mescalero Apache, and likely among the Caddo. The Yuman, along the lower Colorado River in southwestern Arizona, also popped amaranth seeds like popcorn, a practice that is still common in parts of Mexico. It is thought that the big-headed grain amaranths, likely domesticated in Mexico, did not reach U.S. tribes until historic times; however, many of the seeds of our local wild species, such as *Amarathus blitoides*, *A. palmeri*, and *A. retroflexus*, were used into the twentieth century, and one can assume they had a long history of use. Although these weedy species have significantly fewer seeds, they are still tasty and nutritious. Current sources provide directions on how to make amaranth flour (Tull 1999) and recipes using it (Cole 1979). Since amaranth seeds contain little functional gluten, it is necessary to mix amaranth meal with other flours to make a bread that will rise.

Amaranth is one of a few double-duty plants; in addition to its grain, its leaves provide an excellent vegetable crop. Usually treated as a potherb (a green that is boiled or sautéed briefly), the plants have a pleasing taste that compares favorably to spinach and artichoke. The leaves are especially nutritious, containing significant amounts of protein and vitamins A and C, as well as calcium, phosphorus, iron, and potassium. Leaf amaranths are consumed by native peoples of Africa, Southeast Asia, China, India, and the Caribbean. Since they are easy to grow from seed, thrive in tropical heat, produce an abundant harvest within five weeks, and can be sown and harvested continually throughout the year (where there is no winter), they are an excellent crop for tropical climes. In parts of Africa, protein from amaranth leaves makes up as much as one-quarter of the daily protein intake during the harvest season, and amaranths may actually be "the most popularly grown vegetable crop in the tropics" (National Research Council 1984).

Native use of amaranth leaves is well known in our area. Practically all of the approximately two dozen species of *Amaranthus* growing in Texas are edible. The Apache used both prostrate pigweed (*A. blitoides*) and red-root pigweed (*A. retroflexus*) for greens, but we know that the O'odham of Arizona also harvested careless weed (*A. palmeri*), which, given its abundance in Texas, was doubtless harvested by the Apache and many other tribes as well. Studies of traditional native diets of the desert Southwest suggest that amaranth was a critical source of greens during the parched summers. Among the New Mexican pueblos, it was one of the big four summer greens, along with beeplant (*Cleome* spp.), goosefoot (*Chenopodium* spp.), and purslane (*Portulaca* spp.). Both Hispanic and Anglo folk traditions include the greens as a potherb, calling the plant "quelite" and "careless weed," respectively. Amaranth thrives in the same hot and dry conditions that prohibit the cultivation of lettuce, cabbage, and other leafy greens. This characteristic alone deserves attention.

The timing of the harvest of amaranth leaves is important. There is wide agreement that the plants should be collected only when young, or at least only young leaves should be taken from older plants. *Young* here means anything five or six weeks and under in age (when some species may be only several inches tall). This is both the time at which the leaf proteins peak and the time of the traditional harvest among native tribes. Older plants and leaves can be bitter, as amaranths tend to accumulate excess nitrates that can be poisonous in large quantities. Livestock poisoning has been reported from both red-root pigweed and careless weed, though it seems this may have been due in part to a herbicide application and to unusually high rates of ingestion (Kingsbury 1964).

Amaranths in our area will likely continue to be considered mere pigweeds. They are not the cultivated grain species and are apt to be viewed at best as deer and jackrabbit forage and as seed plants for quail, dove, and turkey. They and their kin are, however, exceptional plants, exceptionally underutilized on their home turf. We should look beyond the hegemony of wheat, corn, and rice, and the whims of history, to seek out and encourage these and other natural food crops.

SOURCES: Alloway 2000; Babb 1985; Castetter and Opler 1936; Cole 1979; Core 1967; Crosswhite 1981; Diggs et al. 1999; Dunmire and Tierney 1995; Kindscher 1987; Kingsbury 1964; National Research Council 1984; Palmer 1878; Perttula 2005; Rea 1991; Schnetzler and Breene 1994; Shafer 1986; Tull 1999; Williams-Dean 1978

White Prickly Poppy

Argemone albiflora Hornem. subsp. *texana* G. B. Ownbey

Argemone polyanthemos (Fedde) G. B. Ownbey

Argemone albiflora is the most abundant poppy in the state, sometimes covering 30 acres at a time in big, gorgeous, white tissue paper–like blossoms, even in years of drought. The showy blooms had already caught the attention of Europeans by the end of the eighteenth century, and in 1815 it was given its scientific name from specimens growing in the Royal Botanic Garden of Copenhagen. It was immensely popular in European gardens around 1827–1830, when Texas was still part of Mexico. On the home front, neither white prickly poppy nor any of the many other showy species of the genus has ever achieved any popularity in American garden circles. This is no doubt due in part to its natural, sheer profusion. An early naturalist remarked, "If this plant were not so common, it would be extensively grown" (Parks 1937). It is also due to its reputation as a weed, and a very prickly one at that. White prickly poppy

ORIGIN OF SCIENTIFIC NAME

Argemone is a genus, like *Opuntia*, that contains only New World plants but is named for its resemblance to a plant mentioned in ancient Old World writing. Pliny's *Natural History* describes argemonia as having divided leaves, a flower like that of a wild poppy (*Papaver* spp.), and a saffron-colored sap; it also grew in cultivated fields and was used, among other things, to treat warts. Although Pliny's plant is not related to our genus *Argemone*, these descriptions are surprisingly on target. The name may also allude to the Greek word *argema*, a small ulcer of the eye, which a spiny-leaved plant mentioned in Theophrastus allegedly cured. *Albiflora* is straightforward Latin for white-flowered; *polyanthemos*, likewise, comes directly from Greek for many-flowered.

OTHER COMMON NAMES

Texas prickly poppy, thistle poppy, cardo, cardo santo

FAMILY

Papaveraceae (Poppy Family)

DESCRIPTION

Annual or biennial to 4' tall (max. 6'); leaves with many spines or prickles on leaf margins; flowers up to 4" across, with six papery-thin, crinkled petals, usually white (sometimes lavender in *Argemone polyanthemos*).

HABITAT AND DISTRIBUTION

Rocky or sandy soils, especially disturbed and weedy areas (vacant lots, fields, railroads, fencerows). *Argemone albiflora* subsp. *texana* inhabits the eastern half of the state; it has spread to Arkansas and Missouri. *Argemone polyanthemos* is found in prairies, foothills, and mesas in northern two-thirds of the state, including northern Trans-Pecos; throughout the Plains to South Dakota, west to Rockies.

The tissuelike flowers of the white prickly poppy.

thrives in disturbed areas. Given that even drought-starved cattle will not eat it on account of its bitter sap and prickles, it is generally a good indicator of overgrazed land. When one sees acreage of bare gravel and rocks, void of all other plants, but covered with thick stands of white prickly poppy, it is usually a sign of poor land stewardship. Perhaps our familiarity with this connection keeps the poppy low in our esteem. That its flowers wilt quickly upon cutting does not help its case.

White prickly poppy is not particularly well known in the United States as a medicinal outside Hispanic folk tradition and historic Native American usage. Most chemical studies have examined other species, especially *Argemone mexicana*, the yellow-flowered prickly poppy of southern Texas and Mexico; however, many of the same chemical constituents are found throughout the genus, to one extent or another, and medicinal uses follow suit. One of the more consistent uses involves the sap of white prickly poppy. The Comanche used the sap to treat sore eyes, and (perhaps this bespeaks its effectiveness) they made offerings to the plant in the form of beads or other objects when collecting it. The Kickapoo used the sap of several species, including ours, in curing pinkeye. The Shoshone utilized the pulverized seeds of *A. polyanthemos* for an eyewash. Similar uses are reported for various *Argemone* species in Mexico and Central America. Many isoquinoline alkaloids are in the sap of *A. mexicana*, including berberine, which is a well-known antimicrobial and astringent once used in the United States in commercial eyedrops, so reported treatments with other species are likely efficacious. *Argemone* sap is also said to be effective in the elimination of warts (Kirkpatrick 1992).

The poppy family is famous for its sedative properties. The opium poppy, *Papaver somniferum*, yields the latex known as opium, which is packed with isoquinoline alkaloids, including codeine and morphine, the latter a powerful narcotic analgesic. Traditional herbalists of the Southwest employed whole dried plants of *Argemone* species to make a sedative and analgesic tea, applied externally and taken internally for sunburns, sprains, fractures, and migraine headaches (Moore 1990). The late desert naturalist David Alloway recommended the diluted sap of *Argemone* as a topical application for sunburns, pain relief, and to aid healing; he also noted that the seeds can be mixed with tobacco as a sedative and sleep aid, and that the leaf tea relieved PMS symptoms and menstrual cramps (Alloway 2000). Many Plains tribes applied pulverized seeds of *A. polyanthemos* to treat burns, cuts, and sores.

As with many medicinals, toxicity is frequently a concern. The many physiologically active alkaloids found in *Argemone mexicana*, including berberine and protopine in the whole plant and sanguinarine and dihydrosanguinarine in the seeds, are generally considered poisonous if ingested in sufficient doses. Reported toxicity is rare, probably because the plant is so prickly and so distasteful (to humans and livestock). As late as 1998, however, several reports from India involved human poisoning from the ingestion of mustard oil in which the oil of *A. mexicana*, whose seeds closely resemble mustard seeds, had been inadvertently intermixed; 2500 people fell ill and 60 died of dropsy and high tension glaucoma (Sharma et al. 2000). *Argemone mexicana* is native to the West Indies but has spread extensively to southern Texas, Mexico, Africa, and India. In India it is commonly used in homeopathic and Ayurvedic medicines as a demulcent, emetic, expectorant, and laxative, and the seed oil is used as an illuminant, lubricant, ingredient in soap making, and for the production of fabric and art materials, such as painter's oil. Seed ingestion (in very small doses) of *Argemone* species is also recognized among southwestern herbalists as a laxative. In Texas, the seeds of white prickly poppy are known more for luring mourning doves and whitewings to their thick stands, a trait of which hunters are not ignorant.

Random facts about prickly white poppy include: it is sometimes referred to as "fried egg" (on account of its mass of brilliant yellow stamens inside the white petals); the entire plant of *Argemone albiflora* makes a tan dye; the Lakota used *A. polyanthemos* to dye their arrows yellow; and the Kiowa used the prickles of *Argemone* species to insert the plant's leaf ashes under the skin for tattooing.

SOURCES: Ajilvsgi 1984; Alloway 2000; Altschul 1973; Carlson and Jones 1939; Kindscher 1992; Kingsbury 1964; Kirkpatrick 1992; Latorre and Latorre 1977; Loughmiller and Loughmiller 1996; Moerman 1998; Moore 1990; Ownbey 1958; Parks 1937; Ranson 1933; Sharma et al. 2000; Tull 1999; Vestal and Schultes 1939; Wasowski and Wasowski 1997; Wills and Irwin 1961

White Sagebrush

Artemisia ludoviciana Nutt.

In the Southwest one is likely to be familiar with the genus *Artemisia* either from the species *tridentata*, the famous sagebrush of the western states, or from various cultivated species and hybrids that offer silver-gray contrast to gardens and window boxes. The most widespread and abundant species in Texas, *A. ludoviciana*, has, until recently, been considered a ratty invasive weed. Its ability to withstand the full sun and heat of our summers without water and in practically any soil has caught the attention of native landscaping enthusiasts, who find suitable habitat for the aromatic herb in parking lots and medians, where its spreading rhizomes, root masses, and offshoots (reportedly clustering up to one acre in the wild) can easily be contained. Many have now forgotten the notable medicinal history of this plant and its famous and infamous relatives around the globe.

Artemisia ludoviciana, broadly understood to include many subspecies proposed by taxonomists trying to cope with its bewildering variety in plant characters, is "one

ORIGIN OF SCIENTIFIC NAME

From the time of Pliny (first century CE) onward, two possibilities for the origin of the generic name have been proposed. Either it honors Artemisia, who built in the mid-fourth century BCE the famed Mausoleum at Helicarnassus, one of the Seven Wonders of the World, as a tomb for her husband Mausolus, King of Caria; or it refers to Artemis, the Greek virgin goddess of the hunt, who was also worshiped for fertility and childbirth, especially in Asia Minor. The species name,

ludoviciana, is based on the Latin for Louis (Ludovicus), either referring to Saint Louis, near which the prolific English naturalist Thomas Nuttall collected the type specimen on the banks of the Mississippi in 1810–1811, or, more likely, referring to Louisiana (the territory, not the state)—a way of saying "out West."

OTHER COMMON NAMES

white sage, western mugwort, Mexican sagebrush, Louisiana artemisia, Louisiana wormwood, cudweed sagewort, estafiate, istafiate, ajenjo del país

FAMILY

Asteraceae (Aster Family)

DESCRIPTION

Aromatic, silver-gray, perennial herb, 8–35" tall (max. 60"), highly variable in habit, leaf shape, and degree of silver vestiture; tiny yellowish-white flowers in loose spikes.

HABITAT AND DISTRIBUTION

Prairies, dry open soils, disturbed habitats, throughout most of Texas; widespread across most of the U.S.; south through central Mexico to Guatemala.

White sagebrush.

of the most popular plants in Mexican phytotherapy" (Heinrich 2002). Taken internally, teas and infusions of the plant's leaves have been utilized in Mexico for centuries to treat gastrointestinal distress such as stomachache, indigestion, colic, diarrhea, dysentery, and vomiting. These uses were also well known among Hispanics of the American Southwest, as well as among indigenous tribes such as the Kiowa and Kickapoo. White sagebrush tea, which is also taken as a general tonic and stimulant, is quite bitter. In fact, the plant's name in Mexico, *estafiate*, is derived from the Nahuatl *iztauhyátl,* which means "bitter / salty is its water" (Heinrich 2002) and echoes the adage "as bitter as wormwood."

White sagebrush leaves and especially the dried and powdered flowers are taken internally for two other major reasons:

as an emmenagogue to strengthen menstrual flow and relieve cramps and as an anthelmintic to expel intestinal worms. Because of the menstrual effect, pregnant women are advised to avoid drinking the tea, despite reports that it helps to alleviate morning sickness (Hicks 1966). The plant's use as an anthelmintic, also called a vermifuge, is common in the genus (hence the name *worm*wood). White sagebrush has been used to treat roundworms in humans and has been employed as a drench to treat worms in horses. Other Mexican and indigenous southwestern uses for this herb include the treatment of bronchitis and chest congestion, *aire* (a folk illness common in Mexico that involves headache, dizziness, and vomiting), and colds. The Kiowa chewed the leaves, swallowing the juice in order to treat sore throats; southwestern herbalists recommend inhaling white sagebrush steam for mouth sores.

Externally, the plant is used to treat swellings, sores, and inflammations, and it is famous among Native American tribes as a purifying agent. Poultices, extractions, and bath soaks are recommended in folk traditions on both sides of the border to relieve rheumatism, arthritis, swollen feet, and water on the knee. Antibacterial and antiseptic uses abound; the Kiowa and Kickapoo, as well as Mexican herbalists, have applied chewed leaves or decoctions of the entire plant to heal sores and cleanse wounds. Other miscellaneous external uses include a Comanche application of chewed leaves for insect and spider bites and a Kickapoo preparation of salted, pounded leaves to treat poison ivy. White sagebrush was used extensively as an aromatic in the sweathouses of the Comanche and Kiowa. The plant was used for ritual cleansing among many Plains Indian tribes; contemporary Mexican *curanderos* continue to include the herb in medicine bundles for their *limpias* (cleansings). It was one of the only plants allowed in the peyote ceremony of the Kiowa.

White sage, as the name implies, has a sagelike aroma, and not surprisingly, several other uses for the plant revolve around its fragrant odor. With overtones of ritual cleansing, the burning of white sage as an incense was common among the Comanche and Kiowa-Apache. *Artemisia ludoviciana* and *A. filifolia* were used extensively on tepee floors and as cushions, likely on account of their sweet smell and their tendency to repel insects. White sage can also be used to season

meats and stews, a practice with which the Chiricahua and Mescalero Apache were familiar.

Chemically, *Artemisia ludoviciana* has been shown to contain many sesquiterpene lactones, at least nineteen flavonoids, as well as essential oils, though more detailed pharmacological studies are needed. Many of these components appear throughout the genus and are responsible for an abundance of remarkably similar uses among the plant's relatives in the Old World. *Artemisia dracunculus*, a herb native to southern Europe and Asia, is our common kitchen tarragon and is used medicinally as a *digestif*, for poor digestion, intestinal distension, and flatulence. Common mugwort, *A. vulgaris*, is known as an emmenagogue and appetite stimulant. Native to southern India, *A. pallens*, called davana, has an exquisite aroma; its essential oil is used in the manufacture of expensive perfumes. The wormwood of the Bible, *A. herba-alba*, common on the steppes of the Middle East, is used in folk medicine to treat respiratory diseases, intestinal disturbances, and diabetes mellitus. Used for thousands of years in China to treat colds and fever, qing hao, or sweet wormwood (*A. annua*), is a source of the antimalarial drug artemisinin, which has only recently attracted attention from the World Health Organization as an agent against drug-resistant strains of the disease. Artemisinin-based drugs are one of the first traditional Chinese pharmaceutical products to receive broad international distribution and attention. Since 2001, sweet wormwood's market value has nearly quadrupled, and rural Chinese farmers are currently harvesting approximately 20,000 tons annually.

Artemisia's most notorious connection lies, oddly, in alcohol. Common wormwood, *Artemisia absinthium*, a perennial herb native to Europe and naturalized in the northeastern United States, was used for centuries in Europe for many of the same reasons as white sage, as a carminative, stomachic and tonic, anthelmintic, antiseptic, and treatment for arthritis. In addition, it had been used to flavor beer before hops (hence, some believe, the name *mug*wort). The species became infamous when a green, licorice-tasting liqueur, called absinthe, was created in Switzerland from the plant (along with several other herbs). Inducing stupor, euphoria, and hallucinations, and being addictive, the so-called green fairy became the national drink in France in the 1890s where it possessed a cult status and is said to have inspired an entire culture among the art community, including the likes of Van Gogh, Verlaine, Rimbaud, Oscar Wilde, and Hemingway. The toxicity of wormwood's essential oil, which is high in thujone (a neurotoxin chemically similar to the tetrahydrocannabinol of marijuana), was believed responsible for epileptic fits, convulsions, and brain damage among heavy drinkers of absinthe. The drink came to be viewed as a major social problem and was banned in the first decades of the twentieth century. Recently, a revival of the liqueur in much less potent form has appeared on the market. The bitter taste of vermouth also comes, in part, from small quantities of *A. absinthium* or *A. pontica*.

SOURCES: Berlandier 1969, 1980; Carlson and Jones 1939; Castetter and Opler 1936; Deans and Kennedy 2002; Deans and Simpson 2002; French 2005; Grieve 1967; Heinrich 2002; Hicks 1966; Kindscher 1992; Latorre and Latorre 1977; Linares et al. 1999; Liu and Mabry 1982; Moerman 1998; Moore 1990; Parks 1937; Reiff 1984; Shemluck 1982; Tull 1999; Vestal and Schultes 1939; Wasowski and Wasowski 1997; Wright 2002

Blue Grama

Bouteloua gracilis (Willd. ex Kunth) Lag. ex Griffiths

Sideoats Grama

Bouteloua curtipendula (Michx.) Torr.

Few if any native pasture grasses are likely to surpass the grama grasses in economic importance. They are undoubtedly among the most valuable forage grasses in the western United States, especially in the central and southern Plains and Southwest. The many species of this genus are widely distributed, abundant, and superior in quality. In the arid Southwest, grama grasses furnish the greater part of native forage from elevations of 7000 feet down to the desert. There are about seventeen species of grama (a Spanish word for grass) in Texas; some, such as blue grama, hairy grama, six-weeks grama, Texas grama, red grama, and sideoats grama, are widespread and well known to ranchers across the state. Blue grama (*Bouteloua gracilis*) and sideoats grama (*B. curtipendula*) are the two most famous, for together they make up a very large share of the native forage consumed in Texas and

ORIGIN OF SCIENTIFIC NAME

The Spanish botanist Mariano Lagasca named the genus in 1805 for two Spanish gardeners, the Boutelou brothers Claudio (1774–1842) and Esteban (1776–1813). *Gracilis* is Latin for slender, thin, or graceful. *Curtipendula* (short-hanging) refers to the distinctive way in which the seed heads hang on the inflorescence.

OTHER COMMON NAMES

For *Bouteloua curtipendula*: tall grama

FAMILY

Poaceae (Grass Family)

DESCRIPTION

Perennial bunchgrass with erect culms and mainly basal, narrow ($^1/_8$") leaves. *Bouteloua gracilis* is low-growing (1.5' high by 10" wide) with 1–2"-long seed heads that tend to arch into semicircles when dry. *Bouteloua curtipendula* is larger (2' high by 1.5' wide), with straight seed stalks adorned with 20–50 seed heads, arranged bilaterally but appearing to hang

loosely along one side of the stalk.

HABITAT AND DISTRIBUTION

Bouteloua gracilis inhabits dry plains, rocky hillsides, mesas, and canyons, primarily in the northern two-thirds of the state, especially in the Trans-Pecos and Panhandle; western half of U.S.; Canada and Mexico. *Bouteloua curtipendula* is widespread across the entire state and almost all of the U.S.; southeast Canada, Mexico south to Argentina.

the Plains. Historically cut for hay, blue and sideoats grama are better utilized for grazing, since most of their nutrients are found in their relatively short basal leaves (6–8"); the short leaf length discourages their use for hay. Being perennial, the species withstand grazing well, as long as they are not grazed too closely, at which point they may take two to three years to recover. All grama grasses have C4 metabolism, a special adaptation for arid environments that allows for more effective capture of carbon dioxide and reduces water loss through transpiration.

Almost everyone agrees that the single most important economic species of the genus is blue grama. Of all the grama grasses, blue grama produces the highest quality of wildlife and livestock forage in the greatest amounts. Tens of millions of American buffalo or bison, the largest land animal in North America, once depended heavily on this shortgrass. From the rancher's perspective, blue grama, along with certain other species of *Bouteloua*, has the advantage of maturing quickly, in just 60–80 days, producing a high proportion of protein per unit of volume. It is also cured by droughts, rather than by frosts, and its dry leaves lose little of their nutritional value.

If thickly sown and well tended, blue grama can make a decent turf grass. Its curled seed heads, which have been compared to musical notes, are an attractive addition to gardens. The White Mountain Apache of Arizona are believed to have eaten blue grama seeds during prehistoric times, and although evidence is lacking, we can assume that this and other species

were exploited by other tribes for their grains. The Blackfoot of Montana used blue grama to forecast the severity of winter. If the culm had but one seed head, the winter would be mild; if two or more, the winter would be relatively severe. On one hand, scientifically minded people would attribute seed head growth to length of growing season and amount of rainfall, but it is at least possible to question whether these factors may sometimes correlate with winter severity. On the other hand, the brevity and unpredictability of Texas winters perhaps makes the exercise moot in our region.

Sideoats grama is almost as nutritious for forage as its cousin, and it also has the advantage of a wider tolerance for soil types and greater distribution across practically the whole state. The tallest of the grama grasses, sideoats is a vigorous grower and can be used to reseed depleted areas and to prevent erosion. Like blue grama, it is winter hardy and drought resistant. For all these reasons, and for the beauty of its graceful form, the 62nd Legislature of Texas chose sideoats grama as the official state grass of Texas in 1971. Its seed stalks are uniquely adorned, as the ripe, dangling seed heads are often aligned along only one side of the stalk, resembling a row of feathers hanging along the edge of an Indian lance, a comparison not lost on the Kiowa. Warriors of this tribe wore a sideoats grama stalk if they had slain a member of the enemy tribe by lance. The Apache consider this species and others in the genus to be important ceremonially. Some of their most notable myths revolve around the culture hero Child-

The arched seed heads of blue grama.

Sideoats grama, the official state grass of Texas.

of-the-Water, who used grama grass as an arrow to slay the giants who were making the earth inhospitable to humans. Various Puebloans in New Mexico and Arizona formerly employed sideoats grama for brooms and brushes. They gathered the dried stalks and tied them into bundles. The soft (seed head) ends would be used as a whisk broom, and the stiffer butt ends would supply a hairbrush or a spine-removal brush for prickly pear fruit.

Many names, both scientific and common, have been applied to sideoats grama over the years. Texas grass expert Frank Gould pointed out that eighteen different Latin binomials have been proposed for this species over the last two centuries, in addition to about ten common names

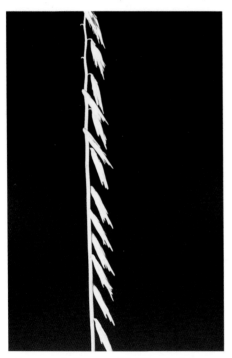

Close-up of sideoats seed heads, which have the appearance of feathers along a lance.

(Gould 1975). This is not really surprising given the extensive distributions of many grasses (hence, they have been available to more taxonomists to name), their economic importance (an incentive for yet more researchers to be involved), and the ease with which species can be confused without careful study. So it is that the names *muskit grass* and *mesquite grass* were applied to sideoats grama in at least some common references in the late nineteenth century, though the vast majority of instances refer to members of the genus *Hilaria*, which includes what is now known as common curly-mesquite (*H. berlangeri*). Given the ambiguity of *mesquite grass,* botanical historians must take care when examining historical records. That caveat aside, nineteenth-century records are rife with passages extolling the virtues of mesquite grass and encouraging livestock pasturing on the prairie. Unfortunately, it was only later understood that western grasses, which receive much less rainfall than their eastern relatives, cannot sustain as much livestock per acre. Overgrazing led to grass eradication and massive topsoil erosion. Today, careful land stewardship can take advantage of the native grasses without such losses.

SOURCES: Bartlett 1995; Castetter and Opler 1936; Diggs et al. 1999; Dunmire and Tierney 1995; Fletcher 1928; Gould 1975, 1979; Griffiths 1912; Havard 1885; Isenberg 2000; Johnston 1970; Kindscher 1987; Mielke 1993; Nelson 2000; Powell 1994; Texas Legislature 1971; Vestal and Schultes 1939; Warnock 1977

Chiltepín

Capsicum annuum L. var. *glabriusculum* (Dunal) Heiser & Pickersgill

Many in the South and Southwest know the chiltepín as an attractive, easy-to-grow, shade-tolerant ornamental that in the fall is covered with scores of pea-sized, bright red berries. The scarlet fruits against the dark green leaves attract birdlife (hence the name *bird* pepper) and are for many an early signal of the upcoming holiday season. It is easy to forget that this plant is actually a wild, native pepper, and not just any pepper but the reputed progenitor of all domesticated peppers classified as *Capsicum annuum,* the most important and widely cultivated pepper species in the world today, including such notables as the Anaheim, bell, cayenne, jalapeño, pimento, poblano, and serrano. Of all these cultivated varieties, and many more, our little chiltepín is "favored by the people . . . of Mexico over all other types of chillies" (Andrews 1995). Indeed, few Texans of Hispanic descent are unfamiliar with the piquant pepper as a condiment and spice.

Capsicum as a genus is native to the New World. There are approximately 27 species known, and 22 of these are endemic to an area in South America (including Bolivia, northern Argentina, and southern Brazil) believed to be

ORIGIN OF SCIENTIFIC NAME
Capsicum likely comes from the Greek *kapto* (to bite), in reference to the bitingly hot taste of its peppers. Others have suggested that it may derive from the Latin *capsa* (box), on account of the boxy shape of some of the fruits in the genus. The specific name means "annual." The variety name, "somewhat smooth," compares the stems and leaves with the hairier *C. hispidum.*

OTHER COMMON NAMES
chile pequín, chile petín, chili-pequín, chilipiquín, chilpequín (and other variations); bird pepper, bush pepper, bush redpepper

FAMILY
Solanaceae (Potato Family)

DESCRIPTION
Annual herb to short-lived perennial shrub, to 3' high (max. 5') with delicate, zigzagging branches and small, ovate leaves; ever-blooming with tiny white flowers; fruit 5/8"

long, round, oval, or conical in shape, yellowish or (usually) bright red when mature.

HABITAT AND DISTRIBUTION
Generally in moist soils of semi-shaded locations in southern half of state; believed to grow wild as far north as Waco, but widespread cultivation complicates the issue of native habitat; sporadic in southern parts of Southwest; throughout Mexico, south to Peru, widespread in Caribbean.

A particularly robust chiltepín, the official state native pepper of Texas. The species is the progenitor of almost all the cultivated peppers we know today.

the center of diversity for the genus. Of the 27 species, 5 have been independently domesticated over the past several millennia throughout Latin America. Several of these domesticates appear in Mexico, but the only one that was actually domesticated *in* Mexico is *C. annuum*, and its wild parent is believed to be the chiltepín. Archaeologists have found wild pepper remains in Mexico dating to 7200 BCE, which makes peppers one of the first documented spices used by humankind anywhere in the world. The domestication of *C. annuum* likely took place in eastern Mexico somewhere between 5200 and 3400 BCE, which allows pepper to be included among the ancient Mesoamerican domesticates of beans, maize, and squash. Domestication selected for larger and nondeciduous fruits, ones that would stay attached to the plants when ripe. Chiltepines detach readily from their stems when mature, which makes them difficult to harvest systematically.

Despite the domestication of peppers and the dozens of varieties produced, the wild chiltepín held its own as a spice. Francisco Hernández, physician and historian to King Felipe II of Spain, specifically mentioned it among the many Mexican peppers grown and consumed in the mid-sixteenth century. Mid-nineteenth-century visitors to Texas maintained, with some exaggeration, that cayenne pepper (likely the chiltepín) grew "exuberantly all over Texas" and that all people—Mexicans, Indians, and Anglos—"were extremely fond of it . . . no Mexican would willingly relinquish his chile for almost any other luxury" (Holley 1836). The little chiltepines pack a wallop of a bite, rating at the high end of the pungency scale (50,000–100,000 Scoville units), surpassed in heat only by the habaneros and Scotch bonnets. The tiny peppers also have a unique, recognizable flavor, however, and their heat, while very high, dissipates quickly, what is called *arrebatado* in Spanish. In Texas, as in Mexico, they have been used in a variety of ways, either crushed and added to soups and stews or soaked in vinegar for a pepper sauce, considerably hotter than regular Tabasco. They were also pounded into dried meats for seasoning and as a preservative. Native Americans in Texas and the Southwest, including the Apache, Comanche, Karankawa, Kickapoo, Tarahumara, Tonkawa, and Tohono O'odham, all included red pepper or chile in their cuisine during historic times. For about half of these tribes we know for certain that the chiltepín was involved, and for the other half this is an educated guess. What is known is that everyone who had access to chile pepper seemed to use it.

Peppers have recently acquired a handsome reputation in medicinal and health circles. Old-time Texas remedies include using chiltepines to make a cough syrup or simply swallowing the pill-like fruits for colds. Research has shown that all chile peppers are useful in raising metabolism, aiding digestion, reducing blood cholesterol, and preventing heart attacks. Chiles contain capsaicin, a volatile phenolic compound that is responsible for their pungency, as well as many of their medicinal properties. Capsaicin is renowned as a painkiller and is the most recommended topical medication for arthritis. The burn of pepper is what kills the pain, by wearing it out. A neurotransmitter called substance P, which is found at our nerve endings, informs the brain of pain sensations. Capsaicin causes more and more substance P to be released until, eventually, it is depleted and fewer pain messages are sent. Chile peppers are also an excellent source of vitamins and essential nutrients. Antioxidant vitamins A, C, and E are abundant, as are the B vitamins (thiamine, riboflavin, and niacin). For instance, our daily vitamin A requirement can be met by consuming half a teaspoon of red chile powder, and a medium-sized bell pepper contains about six times as much vitamin C as an orange (Bosland 1999). Ascorbic acid (pure vitamin C) was in fact first isolated in paprika peppers by the Hungarian scientist Albert Szent-Györgyi, who was awarded a Nobel Prize in Physiology or Medicine for this discovery in 1937.

The name *chiltepín* comes from Nahuatl, the language of the Aztecs. *Chil* or *chilli* was the generic Nahuatl name for the chile plant (and for the color red), to which could be added various prefixes and suffixes to designate specific kinds. *Tecpin*, for instance, meant flea, and *chiltecpin*, according to Dr. Hernández, indicated that the fruit had the size and bite of a flea (presumably, fleas bite hard). A bewildering number of modern approximations have evolved from this spelling, but none includes the "c" of tecpin. Jean Andrews, a.k.a. the Pepper Lady, prefers *chiltepín* for the plants with the tiny round fruits and *chilipiquín* for those with the slightly larger, conical fruits.

Thomas Jefferson planted Texas chiltepines in his garden as early as 1813. Mexicans and Texans have been planting the seeds as a dooryard herb for centuries, but certain growth requirements and a lack of machinery for harvesting have prevented large-scale cultivation. Recently, however, commercial growing of the pepper has begun in Sonora, Mexico. Chiltepín is economically profitable; an acre of the little pepper is worth ten times as much as an acre of bell pepper (Andrews 1998). The Texas Legislature, although it named the jalapeño the official state pepper in 1995, recognized the chiltepín as the official state *native* pepper only two years later.

SOURCES: Andrews 1995, 1998; Banta and Caldwell 1933; Basehart 1974; Bosland 1999; Bracht 1931; Crosswhite 1981; Gatschet 1891; Heiser 1969; Hernández-Verdugo et al. 1999; Holley 1836; Latorre and Latorre 1977; Loaiza-Figueroa et al. 1989; Rea 1991; Schulz 1928; Sjoberg 1953; Taylor 1936; Texas Legislature 1997; Tull 1999; Tyler 1993; Woodhull 1954

Goosefoot

Chenopodium spp.

The genus *Chenopodium* is one of the two great unsung heroes of Texas weeds. Like *Amaranthus*, which it resembles in many ways, *Chenopodium* contains numerous species of weedy, fairly unattractive herbs that are difficult to distinguish from one another. They appear in wastelands and disturbed areas, and they are considered major pests among our modern agricultural crops. The irony is that many *Chenopodium* species themselves are, or at least gave rise to, some of the world's great agricultural crops, crops that supply both vegetables and grains. Historically, several species were used extensively as food crops in both the Old and New Worlds, but the whims of fortune, taste, and fate have largely obscured these plants from the modern world, with one major exception in South America.

One of the most common and widespread members of *Chenopodium* in Texas and in much of the nation is *C. berlandieri*, commonly called pitseed goosefoot or lamb's-quarters. The boiled leaves of this plant make delicious greens but, unfortunately, have an unattractive odor, "reminiscent of the smell of dirty socks" (Tull 1999). Prehistoric peoples, who could not afford to be picky about such matters, apparently consumed the plant

ORIGIN OF SCIENTIFIC NAME

This genus presents a rare instance of a common name that is an exact anglicized equivalent of the scientific name. *Chen* in Greek means "goose," and *podion*, "a little foot." The resulting compound highlights the resemblance of the leaves of many of the species to the webbed feet of a goose.

OTHER COMMON NAME

lamb's-quarters

FAMILY

Chenopodiaceae (Goosefoot Family)

DESCRIPTION

Weedy herbs, erect, annual (occasionally perennial), some strongly aromatic, often with glandular foliage; flowers small, inconspicuous, crowded in small bunches, lacking petals.

HABITAT AND DISTRIBUTION

Chenopodium berlandieri is abundant and widely distributed across the state; *C. album* is also widely distributed but is somewhat less common; *C. ambrosioides* is primarily in the eastern half of the state. All three are found in almost every state in the union.

Goosefoot in bloom.

with relish. Pitseed goosefoot was one of the ancient food plants of the prairies. Seeds of this species have been found in archaeological sites in southwestern Illinois that were occupied from 6500 to 3000 BCE, and sites along the Pecos River of Texas contain seeds with unconfirmed dates from roughly this period. *Chenopodium* seeds have a long history of being ground into flour to make a bread or mush. Seeds recovered from dig sites do not prove that *C. berlandieri* served as a vegetable, but one can assume, from observing the use of the goosefoot plant in historic tribes, that such was the case. Both the Navajo and Akimel O'odham of Arizona collected young, tender plants of this species to boil for potherbs. Other tribes, such as the Tohono O'odham of Arizona as well as tribes of southern Appalachia, used other species of *Chenopodium* for this purpose. At least until recently, residents of all nineteen pueblos of New Mexico boiled or fried goosefoot greens, and we know that *Chenopodium* species were among the most important food sources for their Anasazi ancestors.

Chenopodium album, usually referred to simply as lamb's-quarters, is one of the most widely distributed plants in the world. It was once believed to be purely Eurasian in origin, but recently a native distribution that includes the United States has been discussed. Most people seem to agree that lamb's-quarters tastes better than other wild species north of Mexico. Its leaves, "one of the most delicious of wild vegetables" (Mitich 1988), can be consumed raw or boiled, added to salads, or cooked as potherbs. As is the case with many species of the genus, the leaves of lamb's-quarters are nutritionally rich. They contain more iron, protein, vitamins A, B-2, and C than cabbage or spinach. The cooked greens have more than three times as much calcium as spinach. Lamb's-quarters seeds are about equal to corn in calories but are higher in both protein and fat. Europeans, from Roman times to the sixteenth century, used lamb's-quarters extensively, both as a green and as a grain. The name *lamb's-quarters* may derive from a corruption of Lammas quarter, a harvest festival held on August 1 in the ninth-century English church, since *C. album* was one of the more readily available green vegetables at that time of year. In the Plains and desert Southwest, the Kiowa and the Apache used to eat the greens of lamb's-quarters (also called Indian spinach), and the Zuni mixed the ground seeds with cornmeal and formed the mixture into balls to be steamed. Pioneers added lamb's-quarters seeds, which taste like buckwheat, to breads, pancakes, muffins, and cookies.

A domesticated form of *Chenopodium berlandieri*, referred to as var. *nuttalliae*, was domesticated in Mexico and extensively cultivated among the Aztecs. Domesticated goosefoot was bred to have denser, more compact flower heads, like sorghum, and to flower and set fruit simultaneously. Pre-Columbian Aztecs were required to pay annual tributes of about 160,000 bushels of the seed grain to their government. Scholars have recently conjectured that this grain may have been mixed with, or even mistaken for, amaranth cultivars (Wilson 1990).

Regardless, it seems to have shared a fate similar to amaranth, for the conquistadores discouraged its use on account of connections to paganism and human sacrifice (see amaranth). Today, the crop survives mainly in the highlands of central Mexico in three cultivars: a vegetable crop similar to broccoli (huauzontle), a vegetable crop similar to spinach (quelite), and a grain crop with large fruits (chia). Oddly, the Mexican cultivar huauzontle appears in prehistoric sites in Arkansas and Kentucky. In Alabama, a basket of carbonized fruits of a domesticated *C. berlandieri*, dating to 2000 years ago, may indicate further evidence for Mexican introduction or possibly even an independent domestication (Smith 1984). Regardless, it is well established that domesticated forms of *Chenopodium* were cultivated in pre-Columbian North America.

South America has a particularly fine agricultural example of goosefoot. *Chenopodium quinoa*, which originated in the southern Andes, produces the grain crop known as quinua. Basically unknown beyond this continent, quinua currently is consumed by millions in Argentina, Chile, Bolivia, Peru, and Colombia. It is the living legacy of its indigenous domestication, for quinua, corn, and potatoes were the three major pre-Columbian crop plants of western South America. With a protein content as high as 19%, quinua seed is "one of the best sources of protein in the vegetable kingdom" (Wilson 1983). It is also rich in carbohydrates and contains twice as much lysine (an amino acid) as whole wheat. Quinua seeds, once processed and milled, are used in breads,

biscuits, tortillas, soups, and native beers. A great source of nourishment for the Inca, the ancient grain crop has survived all these years and is making a resurgence today.

In Texas at least one species of goosefoot is known more as a medicine and spice than as a food. *Chenopodium ambrosioides*, commonly called Mexican tea, is well established in Hispanic folk medicine. The tops of the plant, soaked in cold water, yield a tea that is given to treat chills and menstrual cramps and to stimulate milk production in nursing mothers. This goosefoot is also known as wormseed because it has been used to treat intestinal worms in both animals and humans. The plant contains the terpene ascaridol, so named for its toxicity to the worm genus *Ascaris*, which includes both human and pig roundworms. The plant is perhaps best known by the name *epazote*, which is the traditional seasoning used (in small quantities) in Mexico for cooking beans. The leaves tend to be used in beans and stews, and the seeds are employed to season meats. It is said to decrease flatulence. Along these lines, *C. album* was sometimes used to treat stomachache. One should be careful with epazote, since ascaridol in overdoses can be fatal.

SOURCES: Burlage 1968; Castetter and Opler 1936; Core 1967; Crosswhite 1981; Curtin 1965; Dunmire and Tierney 1995; Kindscher 1987; Kingsbury 1964; Mitich 1988; Moore 1990; Shafer 1986; Smith 1984; Tull 1999; Vestal and Schultes 1939; Williams-Dean 1978; Wilson 1981, 1983, 1990; Wilson and Heiser 1979

Plains Coreopsis

Coreopsis tinctoria Nutt.

Plains coreopsis is one of Texas' most popular wildflowers. It becomes a major attraction in the mass profusion of spring blooms in April and May, just as the bluebonnets and paintbrushes are going to seed. Coreopsis can be even more abundant than Indian blanket in wetter years or in low-lying areas, forming acres of magnificent bloom that earn it the moniker *goldenwave*. Long cultivated, it is listed among the top 20 favorite flowers among gardeners in every region of our state. This popularity was presaged a century and a half earlier by the species' author, Thomas Nuttall, who predicted, "It promises to be the favourite of every garden where it is introduced" (Nuttall 1821). As in Indian blanket, the proportion of yellow and red-brown varies greatly in the bicolored ray flowers, running the gamut from pure yellow to the more typical yellow with red-brown center dot (there are about six or seven degrees of variation here) to pure red-brown. Other color combinations are found in cultivated forms.

Early visitors to Texas were astounded by the spring bloom, and rhapsodic passages were penned in its praise from the very beginning. One of the best examples comes

ORIGIN OF SCIENTIFIC NAME

The genus is a straightforward combination of the Greek *koris*, "bug," and *opsis*, "appearance," rendering "looking like a bug." This refers to the fruits (achenes), which are flattened and in most species bear two short, forward-projecting awns at the end, recalling a small insect. *Tinctorius* is Latin, "pertaining to dyeing," in reference to the plant's use as a dye.

OTHER COMMON NAMES

golden tickseed, goldenwave, calliopsis, cardamine coreopsis, painted daisy, manzanilla silvestre

FAMILY

Asteraceae (Sunflower Family)

DESCRIPTION

Upright to sprawling, annual, aromatic forb; stems 1–2' tall (max. 3'); flower heads slightly over 1" diameter; petals (ray flowers) usually yellow with a reddish brown basal spot; centers (disk flowers) yellow or reddish brown.

HABITAT AND DISTRIBUTION

Low moist areas, often sandy soils, especially in eastern half of state; forms large patches in abandoned fields, around playa lakes of the Panhandle, and along bayou banks of southeast Texas; widespread across the U.S.; Canada and Mexico.

Plains coreopsis.

from Mary Austin Holley, cousin to Stephen F. Austin:

> It is impossible to imagine the beauty of a Texas prairie when, in the vernal season, its rich luxuriant herbage, adorned with its thousand flowers of every size and hue, seems to realize the vision of a terrestrial paradise. None but those who have seen, can form an adequate idea of its surpassing loveliness; and pen and pencil alike would fail in its delineation. The delicate, the gay and gaudy are intermingled with delightful confusion, and these fanciful *bouquets* of fairy Nature borrow tenfold charms when associated with the smooth verdant carpet of modest green which mantles around them. To say that admiration was excited in such a scene, would be but a faint transcript of the feelings. (Holley 1836)

Holley's text was intended, in part, to encourage immigration, but the passage is actually a fairly typical assessment of the genuine astonishment engendered by a first sight of real prairies in bloom—not just meadows of the eastern deciduous forest. Although plains coreopsis is not specifically mentioned, we know that it had to have been one of the most noticeable performers. When Ferdinand Roemer, the German geologist who traveled through Texas in the mid-nineteenth century, described the spring bloom, he managed to single out *Coreopsis*:

> Never had the prairie appeared to me more as a charming natural garden or park on a large scale. Countless blossoms—many of which had only recently been introduced in our gardens as ornamental plants, such as *Gaillardia picta* and several species of *Coreopsis*—formed

natural flower gardens miles in extent. (Roemer 1935)

The first improved hybrid of wild coreopsis, Goldfink (goldfinch), came from Germany. One wonders if Roemer had actually seen this hybrid; regardless, it is clear that he was already familiar with *Coreopsis* as a garden plant.

Unlike many wildflowers, *Coreopsis tinctoria*, as the Latin name suggests, had a specific and noted use, as a source of dye. The plant was well known to yield a red dye among the White Mountain Apache, Zuni, and Cherokee, and this knowledge was doubtless passed on to European colonists. Modern dye experts, by varying techniques and mordants, have produced a wide array of colors such as reddish brown, rusty red, orange-red, bright orange, gold, yellow, and even green. One dyer notes that after a hot summer, the resulting dyes will be generally stronger and more purple in color (Hasel 1973).

Odd as it may seem to us, who are accustomed to synthetic dyes that are unpalatable if not outright toxic, natural plant juices are often both sources of drink and dye (for example, grape juice). So it is with plains coreopsis. Both the Lakota and the Zuni made a red drink from the plant. One Lakota name for the plant translates as "boiled weed." This tribe boiled the flowers in water for a few minutes, until it turned red, and then used the liquid as a beverage. Plant tops were harvested and dried for later use as a tea to "strengthen the blood" (Kindscher 1992). The Zuni, likewise, made a hot beverage of the plant, until the introduction of coffee by traders. Fresh folded bundles of the plant once hung on Zuni walls to dry for this purpose.

Recent sources indicate that early pioneers added plains coreopsis to their mattress stuffing in order to repel fleas and bedbugs (Kirkpatrick 1992; Andrews 1992).

SOURCES: Ajilvsgi 1984; Andrews 1992; Dunmire and Tierney 1995; Hasel 1973; Holley 1836; Kindscher 1992; Kirkpatrick 1992; Moerman 1998; Nuttall 1821; Roemer 1935; Ryan 1998; Smith and Parker 1971; Tveten and Tveten 1997; Tull 1999; Wasowski and Wasowski 1997

With good rain, plains coreopsis truly earns the name goldenwave.

Buffalo Gourd

Cucurbita foetidissima Kunth

A conspicuous element of roadsides and rock piles in drier areas, buffalo gourd is Texas' most common native gourd. Capable of prodigious growth, even in poor soils and with little rain (as little as 6 inches), this tough survivor flourishes in hardscrabble places, dying back completely every winter and rebounding from its enormous taproot every spring. It can live up to 40 years, faithfully producing long, trailing vines of gray-green, foul-smelling leaves.

The leaves, as well as the fruit and roots, contain cucurbitacins, which are among the bitterest substances known to humans, detectable in dilutions as weak as one part per billion of water. Since attempts to eat the smelly, bitter fruit cause intense nausea, the gourds are more apt to be tossed by children as hand grenades, or used by grandmothers as darning eggs, than consumed. Many stories revolve around the plant's infamous bitterness. One source claims that mothers in northern Mexico rub the bitter pulp on their breasts to wean their babies, hence the name *chichicoyatas* (*chichi*, breast; *coyota*, trickster), which perhaps is etymologically related to the more commonly seen *chilicote* and *chilicoyote* (Tweit 1995). Another source mentions that cows that forage on the leaves impart a very disagreeable flavor to their milk and butter. An anonymous visitor to Texas in 1834, poking

---

ORIGIN OF SCIENTIFIC NAME
Straightforward Latin for "very stinky gourd" (*Cucurbita*, gourd; *foetidissima*, very fetid).

OTHER COMMON NAMES
stinking gourd, foetid gourd, Missouri gourd, calabazilla, calabacilla loca, chilicote, chilicoyote

FAMILY
Cucurbitaceae (Cucumber Family)

DESCRIPTION
Perennial trailing vine to 20'; yellow squashlike blossoms followed by small (4" diameter), round, variegated green fruits that ripen to yellow.

HABITAT AND DISTRIBUTION
Disturbed soils in prairies, low-lying areas, and along dry washes; nearly throughout state, more common in western half; desert Southwest, central Plains north to South Dakota; south to central Mexico.

Buffalo gourd.

fun at Texan misuse of English vocabulary, quotes two rustic locals: "If we could take this milk along with us in our gourd, and have it fresh on the Prairie, I tell you, it would be *nauceous*" (italics added, Goodrich and Wiley 1834). If the locals had buffalo gourd in mind, however, their word choice may have been more accurate than the visiting author realized.

Only two parts of the plant lack cucurbitacins, the seeds and flowers, and both are edible. The seeds, carefully removed from the bitter pulp, can be dried and roasted like pumpkin seeds or boiled into a kind of mush. Ground into meal, they compare favorably with cottonseed and soybean meal. The archaeological record shows buffalo gourd associated with humans for the past 9000 years, partly, one presumes, on account of its nutri-

tious seeds. They contain about 35% oil by weight, 60% of which is linoleic acid, a polyunsaturated fatty acid essential for humans and animals. Whole seeds contain approximately 31% crude protein, which is higher than that of most oil seeds, except for soybeans. They are also rich in both iron and zinc.

Odd as it may seem, given the plant's name, stinking gourd's primary use was for soap, based on the saponins contained in the gourd and root. Both Mexicans and Southwest Indian tribes mashed the gourds in water for hand and dish soap, laundry detergent, bleach, and shampoo; the Kiowa rubbed the dried fruit onto hides and clothes as a prewash stain remover. The huge starchy taproot (in just three or four years it can reach the size and shape of a small man, exceeding 150 pounds) was put to similar use, presumably when the gourds were not readily available. Buffalo gourd soap can be potentially strong and may cause skin irritation if particles cling to clothing.

As with other saponin-rich plants, medicinal and chemical uses abound. The root has been used by southwestern folk healers and native tribes for a powerful laxative and emetic, either finely ground and mixed in water or boiled in water and strained (the water being drunk). Several herbals warn that even moderate doses can be painful and possibly lethal, so one should probably not experiment with the root. Another oft-cited use of the plant is as a disinfectant and medicine to treat open sores on humans and horses; here again the root juice is used, but also poultices are made of mashed stems and leaves. Researchers have recently isolated from the roots a ribosome-inactivating protein, dubbed foetidissimin, which may have anticancer and antiviral properties (Zhang and Halaweish 2003). Various Pueblo tribes have used buffalo gourd as an insect repellent, crushing the gourds in water and sprinkling the liquid on crop plants, or placing gourd and leaf pieces in the corners of homes to ward off insects. A solution of root extract is thought to repel bedbugs. Oddly, luperinid beetles are wildly attracted to the plant's cucurbitacins, and it has been suggested that buffalo gourd could be used as a biological control, to divert beetle activity away from food crops (Tweit 1995).

On account of buffalo gourd's unsung attributes (such as a taproot that contains 50–65% starch of excellent quality, and seeds that are rich in unsaturated oils, high in protein, and capable of producing meal for animal feeds), the plant has been highly touted as a potential crop for semiarid lands since the mid-1980s. Yet, it apparently has not caught on in a major way, at least to judge from published literature.

Although *Cucurbita foetidissima* is our most common gourd, it is not likely the plant referred to as "gourd" in many Texan historical sources. Buffalo gourd is thin skinned, and when dried it does not stand up well to the abuse given the bottle gourd (*Lagenaria* sp.), which may or may not have been native to the New World. Since it is known that the Pueblo tribes of New Mexico cultivated bottle gourds at an early date, it has been proposed that these gourds occasionally washed down the Pecos and Rio Grande valleys where they were salvaged by various Indian groups and traded to other tribes farther east (Covey 1961). Cabeza de Vaca writes about the hollowed gourds filled with pebbles, used only in dances and healing ceremonies and treated with great respect, since the locals assumed they came from heaven when they found them after floods. There are numerous references to gourds as ceremonial rattles or tambourines among many native tribes across the state, including the Apache, Bidai, Caddo, Karankawa, Tawakoni, Tonkawa, and Waco. The Taovaya, a Wichita group that settled along the Red River, were cultivating gourds in the 1770s and trading them to the Comanche. There are many references to gourds as general containers, dippers, and bowls, used both by native groups and by early Anglo settlers. In the early nineteenth century, gourds were standard issue for carrying water on horseback. In most of these instances one can assume that the bottle gourd, not the buffalo gourd, was the likely candidate, but it was certainly not the exclusive one, given the ubiquity of the buffalo gourd and the ease with which it could have been applied to similar ends.

In light of a broader understanding of *gourd*, one which includes *Cucurbita foetidissima* at least in spirit, we should note that the durable fruit acquires iconic status in Texas as a symbol for rural life. A cowboy song, "The Texian Boys," dating from the days of the Republic, includes these verses: "And when you go to milk you'll milk into a gourd, / And set it in the corner and cover it with a board. / For that's the way with the Texians— / With the Texians" (Lomax and Lomax 1948). Many a Texas cattle brand is patterned after the gourd or its blossom, usually registered as "Spanish Gourd"; the design, via mestizo cattlemen, may hark back to rain and fertility symbols. James E. (Pa) Ferguson, a.k.a. Farmer Jim, governor of Texas from 1915 to 1917, when denouncing the evils of farm tenancy, used the gourd and wooden dipper as props to symbolize his rural allegiance. J. Frank Dobie, that prolific writer of Texana, subtitled a collection of folklore *Coffee in the Gourd*, and he was frank about his preference: "I keep a gourd to drink out of, and any liquid from it tastes better than from any other receptacle—except a horn" (Dobie 1935). Clearly the gourd as a make-do container, tinged with frontier virtues of self-reliance and simplicity, resonates throughout Texas history. We cannot be certain that *C. foetidissima* is implicated directly, but neither can we rule it out; as a gourd, it is drawn into the same historical consciousness.

SOURCES: Bartlett 1854; Basehart 1974; Bemis et al. 1978; Cabeza de Vaca 1993; Covey 1961; Curtin 1965; DeVeaux and Shultz 1985; Dobie 1935; Dunmire and Tierney 1995; Fair Publishing 1945; Fletcher 1928; Goodrich and Wiley 1834; Gould 2005; Havard 1885; Heiser 1979; Hinman 1984; Jelks 2005; Lancaster et al. 1983; Lomax and Lomax 1948; Moerman 1998; Moore 1990; Muir 1958; Richardson 1972; Schulz 1928; Tweit 1995; Vestal and Schultes 1939; Ward 1949; Whitehouse 1936; Zhang and Halaweish 2003

Jimsonweed

Datura spp.

Jimsonweed in flower is quite stunning. The large, trumpet-shaped, white blossoms, each opening in the early evening and lasting but one night, attract hawkmoths with their sweet scent. Tolerating full sun and partial shade and being fairly drought tolerant, jimsonweed increasingly appears in Xeriscapes. Though known today mainly as a garden ornamental, or as a flower prominent in Georgia O'Keeffe's paintings of the desert Southwest, it has a long and storied history as a narcotic drug, hallucinogen, medicine, and poison.

Many North American Indian tribes employed jimsonweed as an intoxicant, deliriant, and hallucinogenic in ecstatic dances, vision quests, shamanistic healings, and initiation rites. Many psychotropic plants, including jimsonweed, were known to central Mexican tribes, such as the Aztecs, but only a handful were used prehistorically in the American Southwest and areas bordering Mexico, and jimsonweed was one of them. In the United States, prehistoric *Datura* remains have appeared in archaeological sites in Arizona, New Mexico, Utah, and Texas. Recent investigators have proposed that the

ORIGIN OF SCIENTIFIC NAME

The genus name is a latinization of the Arabic *tatorah* or the Hindustani *dhatura*, both apparently common names for the species *Datura metel*, the Asiatic metel nut.

OTHER COMMON NAMES

Jamestown weed, Indian apple, thorn apple, stramonium, angel's trumpet, devil's trumpet, toloache

FAMILY

Solanaceae (Potato Family)

DESCRIPTION

Rank-smelling, widely branching, annual or perennial herb, 1–4' high, with large, showy, sweet-scented, funnel-shaped, white to lavender flowers, 2–9" long, 1 1/2–6" across.

HABITAT AND DISTRIBUTION

Wide-ranging weeds in disturbed soils across most of Texas and the U.S., especially in the South and Southwest; Mexico and northern South America; widely distributed in Europe, Africa, and Asia, possi-

bly through early introduction from the New World.

NOTE

Since the uses of the various species of *Datura* are very similar, the genus is here treated as a whole, with reference to species only as needed. In our area the smooth-leaved annual *D. stramonium* is generally found more to the east, and the fuzzy-leaved perennials *D. wrightii* and *D. inoxia* are more to the south and west.

Jimsonweed blossoms.

enlarged distal ends of the stafflike objects held by shamans depicted in ancient pictographs of the lower Pecos River area are, in fact, representations of *Datura* fruit (Boyd and Dering 1996).

Historically, each tribe that used the herb had its own specific formulations and rituals, but a common method of preparation was to bruise the roots, leaves, or seeds in water (sometimes in fermented beverages) in order to make a drink. Many southwestern tribes, such as the Mojave, Southern Paiute, and other southern Californian and Colorado River tribes, included the jimsonweed beverage in rituals and dances for its intoxicating and stupefying effects. Others, such as the Chumash, Yuman, and Yokut, employed jimsonweed to induce dreams, gain occult powers, predict the future, prepare for shamanhood, or acquire supernatural

help and insight from guardian spirits. Tarahumara medicine men drank the potion to help diagnose a patient's disease. Among the Zuni, jimsonweed belonged exclusively to the rain priests, who chewed jimsonweed root and sprinkled powdered root into their eyes when asking the spirits of the dead to intercede with the gods for rain. A decoction of the root is believed to have been a chief ingredient of wysoccan, utilized by the Algonquin of eastern North America as a deliriant in male initiation rites; the adolescents were kept drugged—"stark, staring mad"—for 18–20 days, until they were said to completely forget "all former things, even . . . their parents . . . and their language" (Safford 1922).

A group of British soldiers sent to Jamestown in the Virginia Colony to quell Bacon's Rebellion in 1676 were unaware (at least presumably) of the effects of *Datura stramonium*. In an oft-cited incident, the soldiers unwittingly gathered jimsonweed leaves among the greens that they boiled for potherbs. After consuming the meal, "they turned natural fools . . . : one would blow up a feather in the air; another would dart straws at it with much fury; and another stark naked was sitting up in a corner, like a monkey, grinning and making mows at them; a fourth would fondly kiss and paw his companions, and sneer in their faces." It took eleven days for the soldiers to return to normal, "not remembering anything that had passed" (Beverley 1855). Thereafter the plant became known as Jamestown weed; *jimsonweed* is a corruption of that name.

Another interesting incident, all but hidden in nineteenth-century medical literature, involved the case of a gentleman who smoked jimsonweed seeds in his pipe to alleviate a toothache.

> I . . . soon found that my misery was almost visibly abating. . . . I continued to smoke on, momentarily growing more ethereal . . . until finally I lost all terrestrial feelings and sympathies. . . . I was possessed of feelings whose incomparable happiness might have been envied by a houri. Visions, whose magnificent splendor surpassed the most vivid Oriental imagination, were mine; stars, the most brilliant yet discovered, within my sight; and music, the most delicious that ever syren sung . . . greeted my ears. My organs of sight were increased to such an extent that I could comprehend objects millions of miles distant. The machinery of the universe was laid open to my sight.

> . . . Rainbows of the most magnificent dyes were before me . . . and, amidst all the wild confusion of beauty and grandeur, came measuredly the sublimest harmony of sweet sounds that made my soul swell within me. (Porcher 1869)

Fortunately, the gentleman's wife, "seeing the deadly palor which was overspreading [his] countenance, sent immediately for a physician." It took days for him to recover fully, and he advised his readers "not to let their curiosity prompt them to try the experiment, as it is attended with unknown danger."

Unfortunately, those seeking visions and altered states of consciousness are usually ignorant of, or indifferent to, such trifles as chemical components, dosage, or side effects. All species of *Datura* have a similar chemical composition. They contain the extremely toxic tropane alkaloids hyoscyamine and scopolamine, as well as a number of chemically related alkaloids such as atropine, norscopolamine, and meteloidine. These alkaloids block acetylcholine at nerve synapses, resulting in anticholinergic poisoning. The symptoms of such poisoning are recognized by the mnemonic "hot as a hare, dry as a bone, blind as a bat, red as a beet, and mad as a hatter" (Diggs et al. 1999), referring to increased body temperature, lack of perspiration, dilated pupils, a flushed complexion, confusion, memory loss, illogical thinking, and visual hallucinations (such as flashes of light, warping or wavy surfaces, dancing lines). Convulsions, coma, and death can follow with sufficiently high doses of these alkaloids.

Jimsonweed is more common as a

source of poisoning than many other equally toxic plants because people purposely ingest it for hallucinogenic effects. The plant acquired cult status after the publication of Carlos Castaneda's *Teachings of Don Juan: A Yaqui Way of Knowledge* in 1968, and perhaps not surprisingly, its use tends to be more prevalent among the educated and middle class. In El Paso, Texas, alone, two to three dozen cases of jimsonweed poisoning were reported over a fifteen-year period; two students at an affluent high school were tragically killed there in 1994 when they each ingested a cupful of a highly concentrated jimsonweed root tea in order to get high (Rivas 1994). Native narcotic uses of jimsonweed likely involved the oversight of a shaman, medicine man, or other person who had previous experience with the plant, its preparation, and dosage. Jimsonweed is certainly not a good plant with which to experiment.

Jimsonweed was also employed medicinally, both by indigenous groups and colonists. The Zuni used the root as an analgesic, rendering patients unconscious while broken limbs were set, and south Texas cowboys smoked the leaves in small quantities to relieve asthma. Its use against asthma is believed to be effective since inhaled scopolamine would partially paralyze nerve endings in the lungs, relaxing the narrowed airways. Texas ranch remedies for asthma include a jimsonweed tea. Many folk traditions throughout the South and Southwest included leaf poultices to dress wounds, sores, and bruises, both on humans and pack animals, or to treat headache and high blood pressure. Nineteenth-century medical doctors took advantage of the plant's narcotic and antispasmodic properties to treat mania, epilepsy, tetanus, palsy, rheumatism, and anything involving acute pain. Perhaps the plant's most noted medicinal use was as a replacement for belladonna, the usual plant source of atropine, used to dilate the pupils for eye disorders. During both world wars, when atropine from belladonna was in short supply, jimsonweed was cultivated as a substitute source.

For all practical purposes, jimsonweed should be considered a poison. It is conspicuously absent from most of the ethnobotanical literature of the indigenous groups that once inhabited Texas (including the Apache, Caddo, Comanche, Karankawa, Kickapoo, Kiowa, and Tonkawa), even though other toxic and allegedly psychotropic plants, such as Texas mountain laurel, are discussed at length. This may reflect a realization that jimsonweed was simply too dangerous for practical application, or its sacred status may have discouraged its discussion when investigators made inquiries. In this light, an early researcher of the Zuni noted that the flower called "squash blossom" by other Zuni ethnographers was in fact a *Datura* blossom, and that the Zuni were only too happy to ignore the error since the flower is sacred to them (Stevenson 1915).

SOURCES: Beverley 1855; Boyd and Dering 1996; Cadwallader and Wilson 1965; Crosswhite 1980, 1980–1981; Curtin 1965; Diggs et al. 1999; Furst 1976; Furst and Furst 1982; Havard 1896; Heiser 1993; Palmer 1878; Porcher 1869; Reiff 1984; Rivas 1994; Safford 1922; Schultes 1976; Schultes and Hofmann 1973; Schulz 1928; Stevenson 1915; Tull 1999; Wills and Irwin 1961; Woodhull 1954

Purple Coneflower

Echinacea angustifolia DC.

Purple coneflower is one of our few native flowers that is as well known in gardening as in medicinal circles. An easily grown, dependable perennial with attractive, long-lasting, daisylike flowers, it has become a mainstay in landscaping, being equally suited to formal beds, native gardens, and wildscapes. In fact, the one place where it is increasingly unlikely to be seen is in its native habitat, the prairie. Not only is virgin prairie habitat rare, but, as one of the best-recognized and most touted of herbal remedies, the coneflower has also been heavily overharvested. Of the nine species of *Echinacea* (all of which occur in the eastern half of the United States), three have a history of clinical use: *E. angustifolia*, *E. purpurea*, and *E. pallida*. As *E. pallida* is considered less desirable medicinally than the first two, and as *E. purpurea* only barely enters Texas in the extreme northeastern corner, *E. angustifolia* is the primary medicinal species in Texas. Historically, however, all three have been used as herbal medicines, for better or worse, with little regard to species. The state of Missouri actually had to ban the harvest of the three species in 1987 to prevent their eradication.

The recent overharvesting of purple coneflower is the

ORIGIN OF SCIENTIFIC NAME

At maturity the center of the flower head becomes a rounded, spherical, or somewhat cone-shaped group of prickles, which are the stiff pales protruding beyond the obscured disk florets. The eighteenth-century German botanist Conrad Moench compared the spiky assemblage to a hedge-hog (Greek *echinos*). *Angustifolia* is Latin for narrow-leaved.

OTHER COMMON NAMES

narrow-leaved purple coneflower, echinacea, snakeroot, Kansas snakeroot, black sampson, scurvy root, Indian head, comb flower

FAMILY

Asteraceae (Sunflower Family)

DESCRIPTION

Perennial herbs to 3' tall with large terminal heads on long peduncles; striking flower heads composed of purple-pink (sometimes white)

ray florets and disks of dark, sharp-pointed bristles; roots thick and black, drying to grayish brown.

HABITAT AND DISTRIBUTION

In fields, open woods, and dry upland prairies of central and north Texas, including the Panhandle; throughout the Great Plains north to the Canadian border.

Purple coneflower.

end result of a storied history of its root as a medicine, first noted among indigenous peoples. Indeed, this plant "was the most widely used medicinal plant of the Plains Indians" (Kindscher 1989) and "seems to have been employed as a remedy for more ailments than any other plant" (Vestal and Schultes 1939). The Omaha, having noticed the tingling and slightly numbing sensation of macerated coneflower root, used it as a local anesthetic, and the Comanche employed the same specifically for toothache. Along similar lines, the Kiowa and Cheyenne chewed the ground root, swallowing the juice to treat sore throats and coughs; the Comanche boiled the root into a tea for the same maladies. The Cheyenne imbibed echinacea root tea to treat rheumatism and arthritis. Many tribes of the Missouri River, such as the Sioux, swore

that coneflower root was an excellent cure for snakebite (hence the name *snake-root*) and used it to treat various stings, bites, poisons, and burns. Other Plains tribes, such as the Crow, Meskwaki, Pawnee, Ponca, and Winnebago, used the herb as a general medicine, especially in healing wounds, skin diseases, and inflammations. The Sioux also thought the root helped to alleviate rabies, and Hidatsa warriors believed the root to be a stimulant and chewed it when traveling by night. Apart from the hegemony of medicinal uses, echinacea's bristly flower disks were employed as hair combs among the Omaha, Ponca, and Meskwaki, a practice continued into the twentieth century by Kiowa women (hence the name *comb flower*).

Aside from a few passing references to coneflower as a treatment for saddle sores or toothache, Anglo healers did not take much notice of the plant until the second half of the nineteenth century. During this time and well into the twentieth century, a school of physicians known as the Eclectics became active and influential in the United States. Eclectic doctors relied exclusively on botanical medicines. Although they later fell out of favor, their clinical knowledge of plants left a legacy for future herbalists and naturopathic healers. A certain German lay physician, H. C. F. Meyer of Pawnee City, Nebraska, became enamored of purple coneflower root, and around 1870 he formulated his own patent medicine containing echinacea called Meyer's Blood Purifier. He contacted two highly influential Eclectics of his day, Dr. John King and John Uri Lloyd, boasting that his tonic could cure snakebite and that he was willing to prove it personally. After much discussion and counterdiscussion, the doctors, who initially dismissed Meyer as a quack, agreed that echinacea was indeed a new type of wonder drug. By the turn of the century, coneflower was the most popular of all medicinal plants used among the Eclectic School. Dr. King's classic *American Dispensatory* of 1905 reported that the plant was useful for treating blood poisoning, gangrene, sores, ulcers, inflammation, and meningitis. At this time coneflower roots brought 20 to 30 cents to the pound and probably were a profitable side-harvest for some farmers. Early settlers of Oklahoma in 1914 were said to use the root for practically any sickness.

As one might expect, the American Medical Association had little respect for the Eclectics and never officially accepted these claims. In 1909 the AMA excluded *Echinacea* from its list of remedies because of a "lack of scientific scrutiny" (Upton 1997). Although there was a grudging respect for the herb among pharmacists (*Echinacea angustifolia* was listed in *The National Formulary* from 1916 to 1950), overall the plant fell out of favor from the 1930s onward. At the same time, interestingly, Europeans became excited about the herb, encouraging more than 50,000 pounds of the plant to be exported annually from the United States to their markets. Botanicals and natural remedies have enjoyed continued popularity in Europe, but it was not until the back-to-nature movement of the 1970s that purple coneflower once again became popular in the States. Today, practically every herbal company sells at least one product containing an *Echinacea* species, and purple coneflower is considered to be one of the "top-selling herbs of all time" (Hobbs 1990).

The culture wars between alternative and conventional medicine continue to this day, and *Echinacea* sits at the center. Those who support herbal remedies promote coneflower root primarily as a means to reduce the severity of colds, flu, or fever. Secondary modern uses for the substance continue to run a familiar gamut of applications: infections and wounds, upper respiratory and urinary tract infections, strep throat, whooping cough, burns, herpes, skin ulcers, psoriasis, boils, eczema, arthritis, and toothaches. Italian investigators have found some grounds for wound healing effects, which they attribute to echinacin B, a polysaccharide that temporarily increases hyaluronic acid, a cellular binding and protective agent. Other research uncovered highly active polysaccharide molecules that possess immuno-stimulating properties. German studies found the root to contain mild antibiotic activity against both *Streptococcus* and *Staphylococcus* bacteria. Other investigations discovered insecticidal compounds in the plant that were toxic to mosquitoes and houseflies.

Despite these findings, the debate continues, as research cannot unequivocally confirm even the modest, much less the extravagant, medicinal claims made for the plant. As recently as 2005 the *New England Journal of Medicine* published a study showing that echinacea was no better than a placebo in preventing colds or lessening their severity (Turner et al. 2005). Even more recently a meta-analytical survey of studies published in *The Lancet Infectious Diseases* reached the opposite conclusion (Shah et al. 2007). More moderate alternative healers take the middle path, agreeing that the herb does not prevent colds but does in fact reduce their duration and intensity. Part of the problem lies in dosage, the species used, and which part of the plant is employed (roots, stems, or leaves). Only recently, it seems, has anyone bothered to notice the difference in these factors, and many preparations available commercially do not make the distinctions.

SOURCES: Carlson and Jones 1939; Diggs et al. 1999; Henkel 1907; Hobbs 1990; Kindscher 1989, 1992; Moerman 1998; Shah et al. 2007; Turner et al. 2005; Upton 1997; Vestal and Schultes 1939

Horsetail

Equisetum spp.

Horsetail has one of the longest fossil records of any living genus of plants. *Equisetum* is the only representative of the family Equisetaceae, which in turn is the only family in the division (Equisetophyta). If any terrestrial vascular plant deserved the moniker *living fossil*, it would be a horsetail. If we could go back in time to the late Devonian (more than 350 million years), we would find their immediately recognizable ancestors (known as sphenophytes), not only in the form of understory plants but also as immense woody trees 60 feet high with bases 2 feet thick that formed some of Earth's first extensive forests. These forests and many other pteridophytes (non-seed-bearing plants) reached a peak in diversity and abundance during the Carboniferous Period (350–290 million years ago), in which 75% of the world's coal was formed. So we can indirectly thank horsetail's ancestors for a major source of modern energy. The Permian mass extinction of 248 million years ago (mya), also known as the Great Dying, was the greatest extinction on Earth. It saw the disappearance of 90–95% of known marine species and nearly three-fourths of terrestrial animals and plants, but the horsetails were survived by the genus *Eq-*

ORIGIN OF SCIENTIFIC NAME

The genus takes its name from the Latin *equi*, "of the horse," and *seta*, "bristle," presumably because the plants resemble horsehair, as is stated in Pliny's *Natural History*. Linnaeus, in officially naming the genus, may have also had in mind the coarse black roots of the purely aquatic *Equisetum fluviatile*.

OTHER COMMON NAMES

scouring rush, cola de caballo, cañuela, cañutillo del llano

FAMILY

Equisetaceae (Horsetail Family)

DESCRIPTION

Erect, rushlike herbs with extensively creeping rhizomes and hollow, jointed stems

HABITAT AND DISTRIBUTION

Along streams, lakes, irrigation ditches, seepage slopes, sloughs, marshy and swampy areas; widely distributed over Texas and the U.S.

NOTE

Since the genus *Equisetum* is ancient and very distinctive, and since many of its species readily hybridize and are difficult to distinguish, I am here discussing the genus as an entity in itself (unless otherwise noted). The two principal species in Texas are *E. hyemale* and *E. laevigatum*. *Equisetum arvense* is reported in the Panhandle.

uisetum, which thrived in the Cretaceous (65–144 mya), the Jurassic (144–206 mya), and possibly as far back as the Triassic (206–248 mya). The genus thus predates continental drift, having inhabited the supercontinent of Pangaea before it split into Gondwana and Laurasia (approximately 200 mya). It then lived on to dot the landscape of the dinosaurs. The genus is ancient and unique, having lost all close relatives several hundred million years ago. All species of *Equisetum* have a chromosome number in their sex cells of 108, which presumably has kept the genus from becoming unusually speciose over time. The two main species in Texas are known to intergrade and are difficult to distinguish.

Completely isolated taxonomically, *Equisetum* has a unique habit. Rigid, upright, cone-tipped canes seem to compose the entire plant. The canes, or stems, are markedly ridged, and the internodes are hollow, rather like bamboo. Strangely, one can pull the internodes apart at the nodes and reassemble them as if they were Tinkertoys; they don't grow back into place, but they temporarily give the impression of reconnection. In the two principal species in Texas, there is no branching and, seemingly, no leaves. Leaves are actually present, but they are radically reduced and fused into a sheath that encloses the base of each internode. It has been shown that the detached internodes can form new plants simply by floating on the water's surface, providing a meaningful method of vegetative reproduction. The stomata (tiny openings for air exchange) on the stems are "perhaps the most structurally complex stomata in the entire plant kingdom" and are so unusual that a single one "is all that is needed to identify the genus . . . from among all other living plants" (Dayanandan 1977). Finally, the rhizomes (underground stems, not roots) have been noted in some species to form multiple horizontal layers connected by vertical rhizomes; this tiered structure may also be unique in the plant kingdom. These deep subterranean stems (more than 6 feet below the surface) may well explain both how the genus survived the Permian extinction and why farmers and gardeners as far back as Pliny have considered various species to be obnoxious weeds. The plants are an excellent way to preserve water-soaked banks. One rancher in Bandera County, in order to save a stream bank from erosion, planted a single specimen of horsetail. In three years he had a colony of 100 square yards, reaching more than 30 feet from the stream up the bank (Reiff 1984).

As if all this were not enough to distinguish the genus, *Equisetum* has an unusual relationship to the element silicon. In fact, it is the only plant known to *require* silicon as a nutrient in order to grow. Silicon helps keep the stems erect and functions much like lignin does in woody plants (*Equisetum* is significantly low in lignin). Large quantities of the silicon compound silica appear as wartlike tubercles on the surface of the stems. These make the plant rough to the touch and perfect for a scouring agent or polisher. Both Native Americans and early settlers, who were familiar with European species, used horsetail stems for cleaning and polishing. Natives used them to pol-

Horsetail, a living fossil.

ish pipes, bows, arrows, bone tools, and fingernails, and Europeans utilized them in cleaning tinware, pots, and pans. Used to scour pewter, stems of *Equisetum* had even acquired the name *pewterwort.* In Japan a variety of *E. hyemale,* called *tokusa,* is used to polish fine wooden products. A careful study has shown that the silicon-laden stems are superior to commercial sandpaper in their ability to create higher glosses and smoother surfaces (Noguchi et al. 1981). Highly silicified species such as *E. hyemale* are reported to have a relative hardness of 4 on the Mohs scale. Silicon also protects the genus against pathogens and predators. When a solution is made from boiled *E. arvense,* research has shown that the potassium silicate will protect against damping off (in cucumbers) and powdery mildew.

A few other uses are worthy of mention. The vast majority of medicinal reports surrounding *Equisetum* center on diuretic uses and urinary and kidney problems. For food the swollen bases of *E. arvense* were eaten raw by the Kiowa, and tribes of the southern Appalachians used roots (technically, rhizomes and tubers) of at least some species for food and constructed mats from the stems. Several species have been shown to be good biological monitors for heavy-metal pollution present in the water, or for gold present in the soil. Finally, as an ironic endnote, members of the horsetail genus are reportedly poisonous to horses.

SOURCES: Brussell 1978; Burlage 1968; Core 1967; Dayanandan 1977; Diggs et al. 1999; Golub and Whetmore 1948; Hauke 1958, 1967, 1978; Hoffman and Hillson 1979; Kaufman et al. 1971; Lemus et al. 1996; Marshall 1984, 1986; Mitich 1992; Moerman 1998; Moore 1990; Noguchi et al. 1981; Quarles 1995; Ray and White 1979; Reiff 1984; Scagel et al. 1984; Vestal and Schultes 1939; Vikramaditya et al. 1993; Wagner and Hammitt 1970

Rattlesnake Master

Eryngium yuccifolium Michx.

Eryngium yuccifolium is an odd plant. Aptly named, this species, when young, can fool even a seasoned naturalist into thinking it is a yucca. But it is no yucca. In bloom, the compact, prickly flower heads resemble the buds of a thistle about to open, but they are not buds (they are flowers), and this is no thistle. It is, rather, an umbel, a member of the carrot family. Its common name, rattlesnake master, is outlandish, and meaningless for identifying the plant in the field. Yet the name of this native has a homegrown value and is crucial to its historical understanding.

Many Native American tribes of the Southeast and the eastern portion of the Great Plains valued this plant first and foremost as an antidote against poison in general and snake venom in particular. Three of the five so-called civilized tribes, the Cherokee, Choctaw, and Creek of the southern Appalachians and Deep South, are known to have treated snakebite victims with rattlesnake master, and tribes as far away as the Great Lakes (such as the Meskwaki) employed the plant for the same purpose. One Cherokee physician, who authored an influential medicobotanical book based on native cures, declared the herb "one of the most powerful and certain remedies

ORIGIN OF SCIENTIFIC NAME
Apparently known from the days of Hippocrates, the father of medicine (fifth century BCE), *Eryngion* is the Greek name for the Eurasian species *Eryngium campestre*. By the time of Pliny (first century CE), its root already had a reputation for counteracting poisons and venoms, treating wounds (especially those of snakes), and healing sores. The species name is Latin for "yuccalike leaves."

OTHER COMMON NAMES
button snakeroot, yucca-leaf snakeroot, bristle-leaf eryngo

FAMILY
Apiaceae (Carrot Family)

DESCRIPTION
Stout, upright perennial, 1–4' high (max. 6') with tuberous root; basal leaves long (to 3') and narrow (1 1/4"), armed with bristles along margins; round, buttonlike, terminal flower heads tightly packed with many small, greenish-white flowers.

HABITAT AND DISTRIBUTION
In sandy and clayey soils in prairies, open woods, thickets, and along roadsides in mainly the eastern third of the state; eastern half of U.S. (including Plains), minus New England.

for snake bite now known" (Foreman and Mahoney 1849). Almost invariably the root was the part used; it could be consumed raw, steeped in water as an infusion, boiled as a decoction, or chewed to make a poultice for external application. The Meskwaki also incorporated the plant's leaves and fruit in a traditional rattlesnake medicine song and dance.

The earliest Anglo settlers to Texas were reminded of the plant's alleged powers by Stephen F. Austin's cousin Mary Austin Holley, who noted in her famous book *Texas,* "A root called rattlesnake's master grows abundantly in the pine woods, and is said to be an efficient remedy" (Holley 1836). William Bollaert, the writer, chemist, geographer, and ethnologist who

Rattlesnake master in flower.

The yuccalike leaves of rattlesnake master.

traveled extensively through the Republic of Texas in 1842–1844 preparing a report for the British Admiralty, mentions that "there is no scarcity of snakes" in Texas, but that "rattle-snake master is in great abundance." He goes on to say that the root tastes like a "strong bitter carrot" (Hollon and Butler 1956). Special caution must be taken with common names of plants purported to treat snakebite. Indigenous peoples used many plants to this end, and settlers began applying English common names such as *snakeroot* and *snakeweed* indiscriminately to many plants. For instance, both *Eryngium yuccifolium* and *Liatris punctata* (gayfeather, a member of the aster family) were both called at various times "button snakeroot" and "rattlesnake master."

Native Americans and folk healers employed *Eryngium yuccifolium* for nu-merous other medicinal purposes. The Meskwaki, Choctaw, and natives living along the Arkansas River used the root as a powerful diuretic (increases urine). Apparently, if used in larger doses, the root can act as an emetic (incites vomiting). The Alabama and Cherokee, in fact, used an infusion of the plant for its emetic properties, either to treat illness or, as in the case of the Seminole, for ceremonial purification. Southeastern tribes may have added rattlesnake master to their black drink (a tea made from yaupon) to impart strong emetic properties to the drink for ritualistic purposes. The Cherokee used a decoction of the plant to protect children against whooping cough, and an infusion was held in the mouth to treat toothaches. Antebellum African American healers soothed the coughing of tuberculosis with a root tincture. From 1820 to 1873 the *U.S. Pharmacopoeia* listed the rattlesnake master's properties as a diaphoretic (increases sweating), expectorant (controls coughing), and emetic; late-nineteenth-century treatises of medicinal botany add to this list the properties of stimulant, febrifuge (reduces fever), caustic antifungal, and gangrene preventive.

Many of these uses are unlikely to stand up to the rigor or potency of modern synthetic drugs, and the number and variety of uses begins to smack of panacea; but the one specific treatment for snakebite should, perhaps, give us pause. Many American tribes were aware of this precise use, across thousands of miles, and identified the same part of the plant for treatment. In the Old World, the Romans utilized the root of another species of *Eryngium* for exactly the same purpose. Rural Jordanians employ yet another species to treat scorpion bites, for which there is scientific evidence of the plant's effectiveness (Kindscher 1992). Despite all this, there is an absence of research on the effectiveness of rattlesnake master in treating snakebites. Given that the Apiaceae contains many species with reported medicinal uses, this absence is surprising.

All but forgotten in historic times is the prehistoric use of rattlesnake master as a fiber plant. Footwear constructed from its fibers are arguably among the oldest in North America. Sandals and slip-ons, found in cave deposits in central Missouri, have been radiocarbon-dated to 8300 calendar years before the present. Cords, bags, braided work, and even burial cloth composed of the fibers appear in abundance in prehistoric sites in Arkansas, Kentucky, Tennessee, and Ohio. Rattlesnake master leaves, similar to those of yucca, can be shredded or used in their entirety; the stems also contain a strong bast fiber. Oddly, the use of this plant for fiber seems to have disappeared in historic times, as researchers have noted (Whitford 1941). Not a single entry for this plant as a source of fiber, or any other species of *Eryngium* for that matter, appears in the exhaustive scholarly work *Native American Ethnobotany* (Moerman 1998). One has to assume that native peoples found better substitutes or that somehow ancient knowledge was lost.

Eryngium yuccifolium is a prairie plant, often considered an indicator for the tallgrass prairie. With the rich soils of the prairie having long ago been plowed for cultivation, rattlesnake master has doubtless diminished in numbers and is less commonly recognized. It is easily grown in gardens, where it makes an interesting and historically rich specimen plant.

SOURCES: Core 1967; Foreman and Mahoney 1849; French 1971; Hamby 2004; Havard 1896; Holley 1836; Hollon and Butler 1956; Kindscher 1992; Kuttruff et al. 1998; Mathias 1994; Millspaugh 1974; Moerman 1998; Parks 1937; Smith 1928; Whitford 1941

Indian Blanket

Gaillardia pulchella Foug.

One of the best known of native Texas wildflowers aside from the bluebonnet, Indian blanket, the most showy of the gaillardias, is a "pride of Texas prairies" (Whitehouse 1936). Coming into bloom just as the bluebonnets are fading, Indian blankets replace the bluebonnets' azure with "veritable sheets of glowing reddish brown and gold" (Ranson 1933) and rival their ability to cover vast acreage. Among gardeners who are native plant beginners, Indian blanket is an easy sell. It thrives in unconditioned, poor (but well-drained) soils, can be easily sown in large swaths, and makes long-lasting cut flowers. *Gaillardia pulchella* is widespread and weedy, and there is considerable variety within the species (size, leaf shape, flower color) that has led to the distinction of several varieties and forms.

This variability is especially true in the color of the ray flowers, which can sometimes lead to confusion and premature cries of "new species." Some of the departures from the species' norm include "cream with yellow scallops, coral with peach scallops, peach with yellow scallops,

ORIGIN OF SCIENTIFIC NAME
Unlike many of the genera in our area, which were named predominately by British and American botanists in the nineteenth century, *Gaillardia* was named by a Frenchman, Auguste Denis Fougeroux de Bondaroy (1732–1789), based on plants collected in Louisiana and sent to France about 1786. The name honors M. Gaillard de Charentoneau, an eighteenth-century French magistrate and patron of botany.

Pulchella is the diminutive of the Latin *pulcher*, "beautiful."

OTHER COMMON NAMES
firewheel, blanket flower, beautiful gaillardia, rose-ring gaillardia, Indian sunburst, bandana daisy

FAMILY
Asteraceae (Sunflower Family)

DESCRIPTION
Annual, 1–2 ¹/₂' tall, with wide-spreading branches; flower heads 1–2" across; petals (ray flowers) usually reddish and tipped with variously sized orange-yellow

bands, rarely all yellow or all red; centers (disk flowers) reddish brown with yellowish centers.

HABITAT AND DISTRIBUTION
In a variety of soils (sand, clay, gravel, marl, and limestone) in prairies, disturbed areas, and coastal sands, nearly throughout Texas; north to Nebraska, west to Arizona, south to Mexico. The coastal variety has been spread east along the coast throughout practically the entire eastern seaboard.

Indian blanket.

and red with white scallops" (Wasowski and Wasowski 1997). The point is that flower color is often quite variable even within a single population and is not necessarily indicative of distinct species. In the case of *Gaillardia pulchella*, there is wide variety in ray coloration. Careful study has shown that the color of the ray tips results from the presence of a yellow carotenoid and the relative absence of a magenta anthocyanin. The two pigments combine in the rest of the ray, resulting in a brick red. The degree to which the anthocyanin extends toward the tips varies strikingly among individuals (Heywood 1986). This study further demonstrates that there are at least two ecotypes (populations adapted to a given climate and substrate) in central Texas. One, which has a larger tip of yellow at the end of the ray, tends to grow on limestone soils; another, which has shorter tips, prefers noncalcareous soils.

Wildflowers are rarely mentioned by name in early literature. Early explorers were more interested in plants with immediate economic benefit, such as timber trees and edible fruits. Most wildflowers were broadly described as part of a background tapestry of bloom that astonished early visitors. In the case of Indian blanket, we actually see it peeping out amid the floral bouquet in this description of an April prairie just north of Galveston Bay, from an early anonymous book, *A Visit to Texas* (emphasis added):

> I had never been at all prepared for the indescribable beauty of a Texas Prairie at this season of the year. . . . The

wild flowers had greatly multiplied, so that they were often spread around us in the utmost profusion, and in wonderful variety. *Some of those which are most cultivated in our northern gardens* were here in full bloom and perfection, intermingled with many which I had never before seen, of different forms and colors. I should despair of giving my reader any adequate idea of the scenes which were thus so richly adorned. . . . Among the flowers were the largest and most delicate I had ever seen, with others the most gaudy. Among them were conspicuous different species about six inches in diameter, presenting *concentric zones of the brightest yellow, red,* and blue in striking contrasts. In more than one instance these fields of flowers were not only so gay and luxuriant as to seem like a vast garden richly stocked with the finest plants and abandoned to a congenial soil, but extensive almost beyond limitation: for it was sometimes difficult to discover whether they stopped short of the horizon. (Goodrich and Wiley 1834)

No native wildflower other than the Indian blanket has concentric zones of yellow and red, at least so far as this author is aware. Adding blue to the mixture is pure fancy, unless perhaps a deep reddish purple is meant, and the six-inch diameter is a bit of a stretch; but this is implicitly *Gaillardia pulchella*, and a rare mention of a specific wildflower in a popular publication. Interesting also is the note that some of the flowers were familiar already as garden plants in the north. Shortly after its early French debut in the late eighteenth century, *G. pulchella* was taken into cultivation in England. At the time of *A Visit to Texas,* Thomas Drummond, a Scottish naturalist who collected in Texas in 1833–1834, was introducing Texas forms of *G. pulchella* to English gardens. So it is certainly possible that this visitor had seen at least cultivated varieties of a native Texas wildflower before arrival. Ferdinand Roemer, a German scientist who explored Texas in 1845–1847, was more explicit:

> Never had the prairie appeared to me more as a charming natural garden or park on a large scale. Countless blossoms—many of which had only recently been introduced in our gardens as ornamental plants, such as *Gaillardia picta* and several species of *Coreopsis*—formed natural flower gardens miles in extent. (Roemer 1935)

Roemer may have read *A Visit to Texas* before his travels; early travelogs often borrowed heavily from each other. Regardless, a species of *Gaillardia* (*G. picta* is now considered a coastal variety of *G. pulchella*) already had an international reputation as a garden ornamental by the mid-1800s.

As with the bluebonnet, there are several legends about the origin of the Indian blanket; unlike the bluebonnet, none seems to predominate. Perhaps the earliest was noted by Eliza G. Johnston in the mid-nineteenth century in her hand-illustrated compendium of Texas wildflowers (Johnston 1972). This legend is reportedly Mexican in origin and relates how the Indian blanket, beloved among the Aztecs, was once entirely yellow. After the invasion by Cortés, the flowers were permanently stained by the blood of the slain. Another legend, perhaps better known, was mentioned in one of Texas' earliest published floral guides (Schulz 1928). In this account a little Indian girl becomes lost in the woods and, with night coming on, asks the Great Spirit to cover her with the beautiful orange and red good-luck blanket that her mother had woven for her warrior father. When she awoke the next morning, she found herself covered with *Gaillardia*, which her people called "Indian blanket" from that day forward. A third version, appearing in a recent flora (Kirkpatrick 1992), tells the story of a talented Indian weaver, renowned throughout the region for his exquisite blankets. Approaching the end of this life, he decided to weave his own burial blanket, a magnificent work that would surpass his other weavings. Upon his death, the Great Spirit was so taken by the colorful blanket that the following spring he covered the man's grave with flowers of the same color and design. Although it is doubtful that the three legends actually stem from Native American oral narrative, we do know that the Kiowa consider the flowers of *G. pulchella* to bring luck, and they pick the flowers for ornament in their homes.

There is relatively little mention of *Gaillardia pulchella* or many other wildflowers among Native American sources, or other medicinal or economic botany treatises. Yellow gaillardia (*G. pinnatifida*),

a perennial of the Trans-Pecos, Panhandle, and southern Plains, receives some attention among Hispanics of the Southwest. Called "coronilla," it is used to treat sinus headaches, bladder pain, anemia, and female infertility. *Gaillardia aristata*, of the mountain west, was employed among the Blackfoot to treat a number of conditions, among which was the sore nipples of nursing mothers. The mother was given a tea made from the plant, which finds an echo in the only medicinal report of *G. pulchella* (known to this author): the plant was rubbed on mothers' breasts to wean infants, noted for the Acoma and Laguna of New Mexico (Moerman 1998). Delena Tull, in her very thorough research of native dye plants, has coaxed both a pale green and bright yellow dye from the flower heads (Tull 1999).

Our Indian blanket is highly regarded as a honey plant. Its extensive coverage of many acres is the source of large quantities of a good-quality yellow honey.

Gaillardia pulchella has just recently been named the state wildflower of Oklahoma, where it, rather oddly, competes with the state floral emblem (mistletoe) and the state flower (Oklahoma rose).

SOURCES: Andrews 1992; Goodrich and Wiley 1834; Heywood 1986; Johnston 1972; Kirkpatrick 1992; Moerman 1998; Parks 1937; Pellett 1976; Ranson 1933; Roemer 1935; Ryan 1998; Schulz 1928; Silverthorne 1996; Stoutamire 1977; Tull 1999; Vestal and Schultes 1939; Wasowski and Wasowski 1997; Whitehouse 1936

Sunflower

Helianthus annuus L.

Helianthus annuus is one of the most readily recognized wildflowers in North America. Weedy by nature, it is widely distributed across most of the continental United States. Drought tolerant and long blooming (May through October), the sunflower sports its conspicuous yellow heads in masses along roadside fences, seemingly ubiquitous and ever cheery, even in the hottest and driest of summer months. Of the sixteen or more species of sunflower in the state of Texas, *Helianthus annuus* is the most abundant. For many people, its familiar bloom is practically the paradigm for a typical flower. This so-called flower, however, is actually a collection of flowers, consisting of a tightly packed cluster of yellow petaloid ray flowers around the periphery with many brown tubular flowers in the center. The entire cluster is surrounded by leafy bracts that mimic the calyx around typical flowers.

It is well noted among both domesticated and wild forms of *Helianthus annuus* that the sunflower is phototropic or heliotropic; that is, its flowering stalks grow toward the light, or sun. Before the flowers open, the terminal buds and upper leaf surfaces follow the course of the sun, facing toward the east in the morning, straight up at noon, and sharply toward the west in the

ORIGIN OF SCIENTIFIC NAME

A straightforward combination of the Greek *helios*, "sun," and *anthos*, "flower," the genus name presumably refers either to the flower's sunlike appearance or to the turning of the inflorescences toward the sun. *Annuus* is Latin for "annual."

OTHER COMMON NAMES

common sunflower, mirasol, girasol

FAMILY

Asteraceae (Sunflower Family)

DESCRIPTION

Annual with extreme variation in size, from 4" to 12', though usually 3–6'; bright yellow flower heads usually 4" across (in wild forms).

HABITAT AND DISTRIBUTION

Widely distributed across Texas and North America in abandoned fields and disturbed areas, along stream bottoms, roadsides, and railroad tracks.

The wild sunflower.

responses to it. One of the first trained botanists to collect in Texas, Jean L. Berlandier, on a horseback ride from San Antonio to the Rio Grande in 1834, remarked on the sunflower's prodigious height by pointing out that it grew over one's head "even when on horseback." A curious comment on the sunflower's weedy nature is made in connection to the little-used and overgrown roads between Houston and the fledgling capital of Austin during the difficult years of the Texas Republic. William Bollaert, the English scientist who visited the Republic between 1842–1844 to prepare a report for the British Admiralty, had this intriguing observation:

> The lands [around La Grange] are very rich, but at present there are but few plantations and farms worked; the roads are choked up with the wild sun-flower and weeds, so much so that other roads are made by the side of the old ones, for the little transit there is in this direction: viz.—a very few travellers and the "mail rider." . . . The sun-flower roads are called "Sam Houstons" and the comparative desolation of this and the western part of Texas is attributed to his removal of the seat of Government from Austin, thus suspending in a great measure the former trade and traffic. (Hollon and Butler 1956)

late afternoon. At night, the leaves point downward, while the terminal buds face toward the sky, gradually leaning eastward again as dawn approaches. Once the flowers start to open and the first ray florets unfurl, the stems below the flower heads harden, and the flowers freeze in a position tilted toward the east or northeast. The Kiowa Indian name for the sunflower, *ho-soṅ-a*, literally translated means "looking at you"; according to their plant lore, the heliotropic turning makes it a traveler's companion. Although many flowers exhibit heliotropism, perhaps none does so as remarkably, and throughout such a wide distribution, as the common sunflower. Indeed, this trait is likely what gives the plant its common name.

A few historical passages germane to Texas illustrate both the natural growth habits of the sunflower as well as human

Anyone who dwells next to an abandoned field or whose house backs up to an alley is likely to know the weedy nature of sunflowers and can well imagine that an unused road would quickly become overrun with them. One wonders if Sam Houston, who very much wanted the capital returned to the city named in his honor, and who partly used Austin's remote, defenseless location to bolster its return, would have been privately pleased that the sunflower-choked roads bore his name. All weeds and politics aside, these sunflower roads would have been cheerful, for especially when blooming in masses, the flowers seem happy. People often relate the head of the flower to a human face, one that is always smiling. The frontier ballad "The Santa Fe Trail" contains the following stanza (emphasis added):

> I seen her ride down the arroyo,
> Way back on the Arkansaw sands;
> *She had smiles like an acre of sunflowers*
> And a quirt in her little brown hand.
> (Lomax and Lomax 1948)

If you have ever beheld a field of sunflowers, you'll know that the metaphor is not far stretched.

Both current and historical uses for the sunflower are manifold. The seeds are the most obvious part used, not only for eating (raw or roasted) but also for obtaining oil. Sunflowers provide one of the world's most important vegetable oils, used in cooking, salad dressing, soap, and candles. Some Native American tribes obtained the oil by boiling the seeds and skimming off the oil, which was later used for cooking and as a base in ceremonial paints. The Caddo added ground sunflower seeds to cornmeal in the preparation of cakes or tamales. They also added sunflower seed meal to porridge or rolled it with roasted corn into small balls called bogan. The

Apache often made a kind of bread from sunflower dough baked on hot rocks. The fine and long fibers from sunflower stems have been used for thread, cordage, paper, and as an adulterant of silk in China. The coagulated sap provided a thirst-quenching chewing gum for the Kiowa.

The flowers provided their own myriad uses. They adorned participants in rituals and ceremonies among various Puebloans and Apache. Small unopened flower heads can be eaten whole; they taste similar to artichokes, which are also members of the aster family. Actually, the flowers in Texas have been found in coprolites in the Lower Pecos dating back to 6000 BCE. The ray flowers (petals) yield a yellow dye used among several tribes, and the Hopi still grow a variety of *Helianthus annuus*, "perhaps the most distinct variety in the world," with purple-black seeds, which they use to make a black dye for basketry, cotton, and wool (Nabhan 1979). Mexican *curanderos* brewed the flowers and stems into a shampoo to treat sunstroke victims. The most common medicinal use of the plant worldwide is for pulmonary affections.

Like many wild plants, the sunflower was taken into domestication. What is remarkable is that *Helianthus annuus* is, so far as is known, the only undisputed food plant completely domesticated in what is now the United States. Practically all New World food plants (corn, beans, squash, potatoes, etc.) were domesticated in Mexico or South America. It has been proposed that the sunflower's center of diversity is the southwestern or western United States, where it became a camp-following weed and extended its distribution. In the eastern United States, a slightly larger-seeded variety evolved, from which a mutation for a single-headed, unbranched form likely arose, which Native Americans then helped to cultivate and secure (Heiser 1976). Domesticated sunflowers were already being cultivated by many tribes in what is now the United States when Europeans first came into contact with them. Although there is some argument that the sunflower may also have been separately domesticated in Mexico (Lentz et al. 2001), the most recent DNA evidence confirms that extant domesticated sunflowers derive from a genetic bottleneck occurring in eastern North America (Harter et al. 2004). Russia, of all countries, gets the credit for popularizing and mass cultivating the sunflower. Introduced there only around the nineteenth century, the sunflower was not on the list of oil-rich foods prohibited during Lent by the Russian Orthodox Church. It thus became immensely popular and widely cultivated in Russia, and the best-known variety, Mammoth Russian, or Russian Giant, was exported back to the United States in the late nineteenth century before, ironically, the nation took any real notice of its own native son.

Since domesticated *Helianthus annuus* can thrive in hot and dry climes, it is often cultivated on the plains. It is the state flower of Kansas, which is known as the sunflower state and where the highest point is Mount Sunflower. In Texas, sunflower production is strong on the southern High Plains of the Panhandle, especially in the counties near Lubbock. Aspermont, the county seat of Stonewall County, 60 miles north of Abilene, was once called Sunflower Flat by early residents.

The sunflower is held in special esteem at the University of Texas School of Law, where each graduate is pinned with the flower at the annual graduation ceremony. This tradition started around the turn of the twentieth century, when law students, who had been overlooked as participants in the committee selecting graduation regalia, chose the sunflower as their distinctive insignia, in lieu of cap and gown, and as a sign of their dissent. The official reasons advanced to justify their choice, however, were that sunflowers belong to a family with worldwide distribution and that they always keep their face to the sun, just as lawyers must always face the light of justice.

SOURCES: Berlandier 1980; Bolton 1987; Bryant 1986; Castetter and Opler 1936; Dunmire and Tierney 1995; Griffith 1954; Harter et al. 2004; Heiser 1976, 1993; Hollon and Butler 1956; Joutel 1998; Lentz et al. 2001; Lomax and Lomax 1948; Nabhan 1979; Schaffner 1898, 1900; Schulz 1928; Smithers 1964; Tull 1999; Vestal and Schultes 1939

Indian Rush-Pea

Hoffmannseggia glauca (Ortega) Eifert

Indian rush-pea is a plant of the underground in more ways than one. The irregularly shaped, yellowish flowers are individually charming, but their delicate appearance on often short flower stalks does not produce a particularly eye-catching effect. Beneath the soil, however, lies unseen wealth, in a deep, extensive, underground network of stems and small tuberlike root swellings. The plant's connection to humans lies underground, too, for outside of Native American circles, Indian rush-pea is practically unknown. The plant was not included in early Texas floras, either because its range in Texas is largely away from areas of dense population or because it was not deemed sufficiently attractive. As late as 1937, it did not have an English common name in Texas (Parks 1937). Recent literature on the plant sometimes treats it as a pesky weed of cotton fields or as a food for hogs. But there is a little underground story here, almost forgotten, that needs to be brought to the surface.

ORIGIN OF SCIENTIFIC NAME

The genus honors Johann Centurius, Count Von Hoffmannsegg (1766–1849), a German botanist, entomologist, and ornithologist who explored Hungary, France, Portugal, and Spain and coauthored a flora of Portugal, *Flore Portugaise* . . . (1809). The Greek word *glaukos* means blue- or gray-green; in botanical usage it tends to imply this color when obtained by a light-colored overlay or whitish coating, such as that found on cabbage. Here it likely references the leaves.

OTHER COMMON NAMES

hog potato, sickle-pod rush-pea, Indian potato, camote de ratón, mesquite weed

FAMILY

Fabaceae (Legume or Bean Family)

DESCRIPTION

Perennial herb, 2–12" tall (max. 20"); deep taproot with extensive underground stems (6–40" beneath the soil surface) bearing small ($3/4$–1") tuberlike root swellings; small leaves twice compound; small, 5-petaled flowers, yellow with red markings, along short (2–9") flower stalk.

HABITAT AND DISTRIBUTION

Various soils of roadsides, disturbed areas, slopes, plains, and rangelands in a rather odd semicircle around the western half of Texas (including Rolling Plains, Panhandle, Trans-Pecos, Rio Grande plains, and some coastal plains), but largely absent from central and eastern parts of the state; desert Southwest, southwestern Oklahoma, and Kansas; Mexico south to Puebla, with disjunct populations in Peru, Argentina, and Chile.

The earliest common names from west Texas and New Mexico are *camote de ratón* (Spanish, "mouse's sweet potato") and *Indian potato*. Both reflect the plant's renown among Hispanics and Native Americans for its small (mouse-sized), edible roots. John Cremony, who lived among the Apache, wrote what is probably one of the earliest notes on the plant's use. Having befriended an elderly tribal member, Sons-in-jah, who informed him about many aspects of Apache life, Cremony asks how the Apache were able to survive in areas without game or plunder. Sons-in-jah replied:

> "There is food everywhere if one only knows how to find it. Let us go down to the field below and I will show you."
>
> There appeared to be no herbage whatever on the spot. The earth was completely bare, and my inexperienced eyes could detect nothing. Stooping down he dug w/ his knife, about 6" deep, and soon unearthed a small root about the size of a large gooseberry. "Taste that," said he; I did and found it excellent, somewhat resembling in flavor a raw sweet potato, but more palatable. He then pointed out to me a small dry stalk, not larger than an ordinary match, and about half as long: "Wherever you find these," he added, "you will find potatoes." This was in October, and a few days afterward the field was covered with Indians digging these roots, of which they obtained large quantities. (Cremony 1868)

This passage almost certainly describes *Hoffmannseggia*. Indians who lived

The blossom of the Indian rush-pea.

within the plant's distribution, such as the Akimel O'odham, Chiricahua and Mescalero Apache, Cocopah, Comanche, and the various Pueblo tribes of the Rio Grande in New Mexico, all consumed these tuberlike roots raw or variously prepared by boiling or roasting. As Cremony did, some compare the taste to a sweet potato, saying the roots are "sweet, tough, not unpleasant" (Fletcher 1928); others suggest something more akin to the Irish potato (Castetter 1935). Castetter reports that the roots, once commonly consumed, had by 1935 waned in popularity among the Apache and Puebloans. This follows a general pattern in which native plants were supplanted by nonnative cultivated plants for various uses in the early twentieth century (often through forced acculturation), after which many native plant uses were neglected, forgotten, or relegated to the status of a curiosity. The Akimel O'odham once considered the Indian rush-pea a major, though occasional, food. Women of this tribe dug for the tubers, which, it was noted, grew "at considerable depths" (Rea 1991). The root and subterranean stem system are known to reach a depth of slightly over 3 feet.

Anglo settlers, supplied with the much larger Irish potato, probably saw no reason to trouble themselves with the tiny root swellings of the Indian rush-pea. If they bothered to dig up the plant, they fed it to hogs, hence the common name *hog potato,* still prevalent in agricultural circles. Although not considered a major problem, rush-pea does usually grow in extensive colonies, and severe infestations of the plant pose problems for irrigated cotton fields, especially in the Rolling Plains and occasionally in the Panhandle of Texas, as well as in southwestern Oklahoma.

The genus *Hoffmannseggia* is one of a number of genera that have an amphitropical distribution, that is, a disjunct distribution on both sides of the tropics. Eleven species occur in the southwestern United States and adjacent Mexico, and eleven occur in west-central South America, for a total of 21 separate species; one of the species, our *H. glauca,* is actually found in both areas. This distribution is exciting for evolutionary biologists who must account for how populations of this genus (and our specific species) managed to be separated by almost 6000 miles. DNA research has shown that *Hoffmannseggia* arose in South America and was dispersed to North America four separate times. There is speculation that humans may have acted as dispersal agents, but the familiarity of many North American Indian tribes with the plant as a food source suggests that Indian rush-pea was present in their lands for many centuries, likely into pre-Columbian times. Hence, it is argued that bird dispersal is the most likely explanation (Simpson et al. 2005).

On account of its ability to bloom in dry summers without rain, Indian rush-pea has been recommended as a roadside plant, especially in the plains country, and even as a bed or border plant, provided it has plenty of room. Given that the roots are edible and pleasant-tasting, it would be interesting to see if this all-but-forgotten food could not, at the very least, be introduced to farmer's markets as a native curiosity.

SOURCES: Carlson and Jones 1939; Castetter 1935; Castetter and Opler 1936; Castner et al. 1989; Cremony 1868; Everitt et al. 1999; Fletcher 1928; Havard 1885; Moerman 1998; Parks 1937; Rea 1991; Simpson 1999; Simpson et al. 2004, 2005; Standley 1912; Warnock 1974

Peyote

Lophophora williamsii (Lem. in Salm-Dyck) J. M. Coult.

Small and difficult to locate beneath thorny shrubs, sometimes shrunken below the soil's surface, and inhabiting only a handful of Texas counties, peyote would seem an unlikely candidate for a work such as this. Yet the unassuming cactus has one of the richest ethnobotanical legacies of any plant in our state. With an established connection to archaic humans in Texas six millennia ago, peyote was one of the first psychoactive plants of the New World to be known to Europeans and certainly the most renowned. Despite centuries of attempts to eradicate its usage among the native peoples of Mexico and the United States, peyote continues to be revered as a medicinal and vision-altering plant, so much so that it is perhaps the most intensely investigated species of native North American psychoactive plants. As if that were not enough, peyote sparked the foundation of a church, which has become "the most widespread and popular intertribal religious movement of the American Indian" (Anderson 1980). Moreover, given that Texas is the only state in the country where peyote grows naturally, and

ORIGIN OF SCIENTIFIC NAME

The generic name is a straightforward Greek compound for crest-bearing (*lophos*, crest; *phoreus*, a bearer), referring to the tufts of hairs borne in each areole. The identity of the Williams honored in the specific epithet has, unfortunately, been lost in time.

OTHER COMMON NAMES

mescal buttons, dry whiskey, divine cactus, devil's root, dumpling cactus, piote, piotl, peyotl, raíz diabólica, tuna de tierra

FAMILY

Cactaceae (Cactus Family)

DESCRIPTION

Small, spineless cactus, rarely more than 3" high (often barely protruding above the ground), 1 1/2–4" in diameter, chalky blue-green in color, bearing wartlike tufts of hairs; ribs and furrows, 4–14 in number, highly variable in shape; long, carrot-shaped underground stem and roots.

HABITAT AND DISTRIBUTION

Shallow, rocky, limestone soils of hills and plains, often in the partial shade of mesquite, acacia, and creosote shrubs. In Texas, largely confined to two areas: the Rio Grande drainage between Laredo and McAllen (Hidalgo, Starr, Jim Hogg, Webb, and Zapata counties) and, to a lesser extent, the Trans-Pecos (southern Presidio, Brewster, and Val Verde counties). Outside Texas, in the Chihuahuan Desert of Mexico, as far south as San Luis Potosí, with a disjunct population near Querétaro.

A potful of peyote.

given that peyote use has spread as far north as Canada, this small cactus is one of the most widely exported native Texas plants in current use.

Both historically and currently, peyote has two main uses, as a medicine and as a psychoactive drug. Among many native groups the medicinal use is just as important as the psychoactive use, if not more so, despite popular opinion. Francisco Hernández, physician to Felipe II of Spain, extensively researched the medicinal plants of Mexico in the mid-sixteenth century, and he mentioned that peyote, applied as a poultice, relieved painful joints. To this day, northern Mexican tribes mix macerated peyote with alcohol as a topical application for muscle aches, arthritis, and rheumatism. Chewed bits of peyote are also applied externally to treat sunstroke, headache, burns, bruises, wounds, fractures, and snakebite. Sometimes a decoction of dried or powdered peyote is taken internally for many of these ailments. As a stimulant and tonic, peyote alleviates hunger, thirst, and fatigue and is said to assure health and longevity. Spiritual and psychic associations with peyote include the notion that consuming the cactus assures tribal and community welfare, that it protects against evil (such as witchcraft), that it allows one to foretell the future, find lost objects, and most important, contact supernaturals for assistance. There is a long-held belief among many U.S. tribes that peyote use reduces alcoholism, a huge problem on many reservations, though it is unclear whether there is a medical basis, or a more psychological one, for the claim.

Peyote's psychoactive effects have propelled the cactus to fame. The green tops of the cactus, removed just below the soil, resemble large buttons, which are usually consumed dried. Consuming just a few of these buttons produces only a sense of wakefulness, hypersensitivity, and contentment, but four to twelve buttons will bring on a "shimmering intensification of colour and texture, frequent geometric imagery, and distortions in body image and depth perception" (Boyd and Dering 1996). Rarely are these brilliant colors and kaleidoscopic patterns (called form constants) considered actual hallucinations (à la LSD), and seldom do consumers of peyote speak of a "high," as that word is usually understood in drug culture. In short, it is somewhat misleading to speak of peyote as a true hallucinogen, despite the rather loose application of this term in the literature. Visualizing something that is not actually present is rare, though expectations of peyote users may certainly influence what is perceived. Many peyotists describe their experience in purely spiritual terms, of awe, respect, and profound inward reflection. When present, distortions in sound, taste, feeling (such as weightlessness), and vision (such as macropsia, in which objects appear enlarged) are more often understood as by-products of an intense religious experience and not as goals in themselves.

The chemical composition of peyote is complex, with at least 57 alkaloids and related compounds identified to date. Peyote has the distinction of being the source for the first naturally occurring, chemically pure, psychoactive compound ever isolated. Called mescaline (rather inappropriately named, since the liquor mescal comes from the genus *Agave*, which is not even a cactus), this phenylethylamine compound is the alkaloid responsible for the visual imagery. Mescaline was identified at the end of the nineteenth century by the German pharmacologist Arthur Heffter. Heffter's classic studies on peyote, some of the best pharmacological work of its time, paved the way for subsequent synthesis of the drug, which permitted clinical trials. Mescaline, like LSD, is known to increase the random discharge of neurons in the visual cortex, as well as to modulate neurotransmitters that are critical in the regulation of pleasure. That being said, mescaline intoxication is not the same as peyote intoxication, given that the former is the effect of a clinically pure substance acting in isolation, and the latter involves the cactus's entire array of alkaloids and their physiological interactions.

The earliest prehistoric evidence of peyote's connection to humankind is currently found in Texas. Ancient peyote samples have been excavated from the Shumla Caves at the confluence of the Pecos River and the Rio Grande with radiocarbon dates to roughly 5200 BP. Since peyote provides no known food source or material (such as fiber), it is assumed that archaic humans utilized the cactus as a physical and spiritual medicine, much as historic tribes did and contemporary indigenous peoples continue to do. Peyote samples from the Shumla Caves still contain mescaline today, making *Lophophora williamsii* the "oldest plant drug ever to yield a major bioactive compound" (El-Seedi et al., 2005). Archaeologists have also proposed that the stunning pictographs of the caves of the Lower Pecos, dating from 2950–4200 BP, provide the earliest known record of peyotism, the consumption of peyote in a religious or ritualized context (Boyd and Dering 1996).

Between prehistory and the eighteenth century, most of the evidence of peyotism is from Mexico, where the Spaniards, as early as the 1560s, noted widespread and entrenched use of the cactus. The word *peyote* derives from the Nahuatl *peyotl*, a name for the cactus as well as a term applied to several other plants with medicinal properties. The Chichimeca believed that peyote gave them the courage to fight without fear. The major Mexican tribes that continue to use peyote are the Cora, the Tarahumara (who consider the plant a vegetal incarnation of a deity left behind by Father Sun to cure humanity's ills), and the Huichol, the renowned peyote tribe of Mexico, who hold peyote in a special relationship to deer and corn. Despite many attempts, the Spaniards were incapable of stamping out the "devil's root," and the Church in some cases quietly resigned itself to the plant's persistent use. In Coahuila a mission was actually named El Santo de Jesús Peyotes, and a calendar saint, Santa Niña de Peyotes, was attributed with miraculous powers that locals otherwise accorded the plant. The Huichol and Tarahumara still make annual, 300-mile pilgrimages to the peyote fields. These journeys contain much ritual and symbolism. The stunning, multicolored yarn paintings of the Huichol, known as "nearikas," depict visions seen by the pilgrims and are a traditional part of their religious paraphernalia.

Although peyotism was probably practiced north of what is now the Mexican border for centuries before European contact, the first historical records appear toward the beginning of the eighteenth century. One of the earliest reports of peyote use among unspecified tribes in Texas dates from 1716 (Slotkin 1951), and the Caddo of east Texas used peyote in the eighteenth century as well. But the real legacy of peyotism in Texas begins with the Lipan Apache, who acquired peyote from the Carrizo Indians of northeastern Mexico during that century. By the 1770s, as the Lipan became increasingly missionized, they began incorporating Christian elements into traditional peyote rituals. Over time, a ritual involving several days of tribal dancing was transformed into a shorter, quieter, more solemn ceremony for a small group of people. By the 1830s, the Tonkawa of central Texas had also acquired the cactus. Together with the Lipan, the two tribes were the main practitioners of peyotism north of the Rio Grande through most of the nineteenth century. The Lipan introduced peyotism to the Mescalero Apache around 1870. Other Texas tribes known to be familiar with peyote include the Jumano, Karankawa, and Kickapoo.

The watershed for peyotism began in the 1880s when the Kiowa and Comanche, who may have acquired the peyote ritual from raids into Mescalero lands, began to practice and actively spread the religion. At a time when most of the Plains tribes were being extirpated and forced onto reservations, peyotism provided solace and hope. The Comanche and Kiowa added elements of Plains culture and, to some extent, additional Christian components; they made long journeys to the Pecos River and the Rio Grande to collect the plant. The great Comanche chief Quanah Parker himself came into the Big Bend seeking the "gift-of-god" cactus. Many Plains tribes, such as the Oto, Arapaho, and Cheyenne, began to participate in peyote rituals as the cult spread farther northward and grew in prestige. The Caddo, who had been familiar with the cactus for several centuries, saw a renewed interest in peyote through the efforts of the so-called peyote prophet John Wilson. He created a variant ritual known as Big Moon Peyotism which was highly influential among the Delaware, Osage, Quapaw, Wichita, Shawnee, Seminole, and others.

The first half of the twentieth century saw phenomenal growth in the peyote religion. In 1918 several peyote groups collaborated to form the Native American Church, especially to avoid religious persecution. The NAC, an intertribal religion now counting 250,000–500,000 members among 40 tribes stretching from Texas to Canada, uses peyote as a sacrament. The Navajo have been major participants since the 1960s. Building on the ideas of early peyote prophets, members of the NAC promote "right living," self-respect, and brotherly love. Peyote meetings are called for many reasons, but usually to cure a sick person, to give thanks, to pray for loved ones away from home, or to help someone with a particular problem. Rituals are usually small, meditative, and highly disciplined affairs in which worshipers typically consume only small amounts of peyote (less than 100 mg of mescaline), which amplifies emotions but does not necessarily induce full-fledged psychotropic experiences.

Texas is the major supplier of peyote for the Native American Church. Although 90% of all *Lophophora williamsii* grows in Mexico, providing ample supplies for the comparatively small Mexican tribes, the remaining 10% that grows in Texas furnishes the entire commercial crop for the NAC. As Martin Terry, a botanist at Sul Ross State University, notes, "In effect, you have a whole continent grazing on little pieces of South Texas" (Moreno 2005). Because of a variety of factors, the Texas peyote supply is dwindling. The cactus grows in viable numbers in only four counties in south Texas (Starr, Jim Hogg, Webb, and Zapata), and it is more lucrative for ranchers in these areas to lease their lands to hunters and petroleum companies than to peyote gatherers, known as peyoteros. Certain land-management practices, such as root plowing, destroy peyote populations. Cultivation of peyote is illegal, and overharvesting of native populations has made for fewer viable populations and smaller cacti. The Texas Department of Public Safety licenses peyoteros; there were seven in 1999, but currently there are only four. Mexican laws prohibit harvesting south of the border, though the NAC has considered pursuing importation from Mexico.

Peyote is currently left in an odd and precarious position. It has likely been consumed for 6000 years in our area, it commands a sacred status among millennia-old traditions in Mexico, and it is the sacrament for a modern, grass-roots church with more than a quarter of a million worshipers, yet it is an illegal substance. Federal law prohibits non-Indians (including cactus collectors, horticulturists, and scientists without permits) from possessing or using peyote. Peyote, along with LSD, is considered a Schedule I substance, defined as having a high potential for abuse and no accepted medical use in the United States, even though studies indicate that peyote is not addictive, causes no withdrawal syndrome, and shows no marked tolerance (Anderson 1980, Halpern et al. 2005). There are no confirmed deaths resulting from peyote consumption. Furthermore, there would appear to be a long history of medical use of the plant that merits further study. It would appear that our disdain for peyote is probably cultural and largely unsubstantiated. A final irony is that peyote is completely legal (essentially since 1918, but formally since 1994) for members of the NAC, who must show federally recognized tribal affiliation. So the law allows it for some but not for others. Perhaps this is a good thing, for under current harvesting practices on the lands open to peyoteros, the little cactus is becoming increasingly scarce.

SOURCES: Anderson 1969, 1980; Babb 1985; Berlandier 1969; Bolton 1987; Boyd and Dering 1996; De Cordoba 2004; *Economist* 1999; El-Seedi et al. 2005; Furst 1972, 1976; Halpern et al. 2005; Horgan 2003; La Barre 1989; Latorre and Latorre 1977; Moreno 2005; Morgan 1983; Powell and Weedin 2004; Schultes 1938; Schultes and Hofmann 1973; Slotkin 1951; Swan 1999; Terry et al. 2006; Vestal and Schultes 1939; Warnock 1970

Texas Bluebonnet

Lupinus texensis Hook.

For a Texan, it is daunting to write about a flower so well known, well loved, and imbued with state pride as the Texas bluebonnet. If, as one writer has claimed, the "bluebonnet is to Texas what the shamrock is to Ireland, the cherry blossom to Japan, the lily to France, the rose to England and the tulip to Holland" (Maguire 1975), then its iconic status will overshadow attempts to account for its fame. We can point to facts and historical tidbits, but like all symbols, the flower still remains somewhat elusive.

One would think a flower of such emblematic weight would have deep historical roots in early narratives of Texas natural history. Oddly, this is not the case. There is little description of the bluebonnet *per se* among the scores of the better-known travelogs and notes of nineteenth-century naturalists who traversed the state. One of the possible exceptions is Frederick Law Olmsted, the famous landscape architect who visited Texas in 1853–1854: "The prairies were laughing with flowers in ravishing luxuriance, whole acres of green being often entirely lost under their decoration of blue and purple" (Olmsted 1857). Bluebonnets were a player in the spectacular spring show of prairie flowers. Swept up in a kaleidoscope of colors, they were part and parcel of the spring bloom that writers commented on as a whole, rather than individually. Unlike trees, shrubs, and grasses, many of which had imme-

ORIGIN OF SCIENTIFIC NAME	OTHER COMMON NAMES	HABITAT AND DISTRIBUTION
The Latin word *lupinus* ("relating to a wolf") was applied to the genus based on an incorrect assumption that the plants robbed soils of their nutrients. *Texensis* needs no comment.	Texas lupine, buffalo clover, blue lupine, wolf flower, el conejo **FAMILY** Fabaceae (Legume Family) **DESCRIPTION** Winter annual to 2' tall with striking blue and white flowers.	Rocky, limestone soils and clay; endemic to central Texas prairies and Edwards Plateau; native distribution expanded through highway plantings to include most of south- and north-central Texas and a small portion of southern Oklahoma.

A magnificent carpet of Lupinus texensis. *Any of the state's six bluebonnet species count as the official state flower.*

diate economic benefits, the bluebonnets and most annual forbs tended to be given little written attention.

At the beginning of the twentieth century that changed, and what had been part of a floral tapestry was singled out, individualized, and placed on a pedestal. This moment came when the bluebonnet, having defeated the cotton boll ("the white rose of commerce") and the prickly pear cactus blossom (promoted by Cactus Jack Garner, who would serve as U.S. vice president under Franklin D. Roosevelt), was declared the state flower of Texas on March 7, 1901. By the time Theodore Roosevelt visited Austin four years later, thousands of schoolchildren,

singing "America," were tossing the flowers in his path. The bluebonnet was off to an auspicious start, but then came the unsettling realization that the species designated as the official flower, *Lupinus subcarnosus*, was not the deep-blue and white-tipped species of central Texas (*L. texensis*) but its less common and slightly less showy sister of the sand belts. This oversight nagged people (sometimes more, sometimes less) over the next 70 years until the Legislature decided to set the matter straight. Can one simply dethrone a monarch that ruled for seven decades and replace her with her sister, especially given that there are other equally deserving contenders to the throne (*L. havardii* of the Trans-Pecos, for instance), and given that botanical legitimacy is predicated on ever-changing taxonomic nomenclature? Apparently not, for the Legislature decided in 1971 to include not only *L. texensis* but also "any other variety of Bluebonnet not heretofore recorded" (Andrews 1993). Hence, Texas currently can claim six bluebonnet species that all equally reign as state flower. Should subsequent new species be discovered in the state, they too will reign.

The disparate common names deserve comment. The term *bluebonnet* undoubtedly refers to the flower's resemblance to old-fashioned pioneer bonnets. *El conejo* (Spanish for "rabbit") alludes to the tops of the flower stalks, dense with silver hairs, that appear white from a distance, resembling the tails of cottontail rabbits. *Buffalo clover* refers to the early settlers' belief that buffalo liked to graze on the plants. *Wolf flower,* applied more to the genus than to our species, comes from a mistaken belief that the plants greedily wolfed nutrients from soils, impoverishing them. It turns out just the opposite is true. Lupines do not cause impoverished soils; they simply thrive in them. This is because, like most legumes, they are capable of forming their own nitrogen-rich fertilizer via root nodules containing the nitrogen-fixing bacterium *Rhizobium*. Lupines are great fertilizers; when plowed under, they release their nitrogen back into the soil for other plants to use. Lupine soil enrichment was known as far back as the first century CE with Pliny, but it was not fully understood until the end of the nineteenth century.

Bluebonnet with reddened banner spot on lower blossoms.

Bluebonnet enthusiasts have long noted that a reddish color appears toward the bottom of the flower stalk on older flowers. More precisely, the white spot on an individual flower's banner, aptly called the banner spot, turns red-purple. There is a widely held belief that the color change indicates that the flower has been fertilized. Not quite. Careful study has shown that the banner spot becomes ruddy simply through age, starting on the fifth day after opening, whether fertilized or not. The gist, though, is similar. The color change coincides with a sharp decline in both the flower's fertility and its pollen content. It behooves the bluebonnet to direct the pollinating bee to its most fertile (white-spotted) flowers, and it behooves the bee to spend its labor where the pollen is (Schaal and Leverich 1980).

The bluebonnet is one of our few native flowers that has a legend directly related to it. First published in 1924 by the Texas Folklore Society (Reid 1964), given further renown in J. Frank Dobie's *Tales of Old Time Texas* (Dobie 1928), and eventually made into a beautifully illustrated children's book (DePaola 1996), the legend is best read from these sources. Briefly, though, it is the tale of a Comanche tribe who, having weathered severe flooding, drought, and a bitter winter, were suffering pestilence and starvation. The Great Spirit informed the medicine men that in penance for its wrongdoings, the tribe would have to make a burnt sacrifice of its most valued possession. Having overheard these ominous words, a little girl decided that she must sacrifice her only and most prized possession, a warrior doll made from deer skin and adorned with a headdress made of blue-jay feathers. Sneaking out at night, she burned her doll and scattered its ashes to the four winds as directed by the Great Spirit. In the morning, the surrounding hillsides were blanketed in blue. The tribe agreed it must be a sign that the sacrifice was accepted, and at once nature seemed

to rebound. The little girl was given a new name, which translates as "she who dearly loves her people." Whether or not this is a legitimate Comanche legend, it has already taken firm root in Texan folklore. Rich in archetypal themes of hardship, sacrifice, love, and renewal, it is hard not to like it. The fragrant fields of blue are our annual harbingers of spring, announcing the advent of one of the nation's best native floral displays.

Horticulturists are playing with the time-honored color of blue. In the late 1980s a pink variety was developed, the first seed-propagated cultivar of *L. texensis*, called "Abbott Pink" after the late Carroll Abbott, a native plant enthusiast, founding member of the Native Plant Society of Texas, and editor and publisher of the *Texas Wild Flower Newsletter*. A lavender cultivar was named "Barbara Bush," for the former First Lady, in the 1990s. Finally, a maroon-colored bluebonnet was announced in 2000. Other color lines, such as white and light blue, are available and are continuing to be refined. For most folks, the natural azure is unsurpassed, for it reflects when "the sky falls on Texas" (Morgan 1941).

SOURCES: Andrews 1993; Davis et al. 1994; DePaola 1996; Dobie 1928; Mackay et al. 2000; Maguire 1975; Morgan 1941; Olmsted 1857; Parsons et al. 1994; Reid 1964; Schaal and Leverich 1980; Schulz 1928; Whitehouse 1936; Wills and Irwin 1961

Horsemint

Monarda spp.

As with so many members of the mint family, *Monarda*'s claim to fame lies in its pungent fragrance, due to its abundant volatile oils; many of its species offer variations on a scented theme, with fragrances redolent of lemon, orange, mint, basil, and oregano. If this weren't reason enough to admire the genus, several species are also a wildscape gardener's delight, given their easy growth, prolific and long-lasting blooms, and ability to reseed generously. *Monarda citriodora*, an annual lavender-white to purple flower with a strong lemon odor, is touted as the ideal candidate for those needing an instant wild-flower patch.

The many pungent scents of the genus are used for fragrance and spice. The Kiowa soaked the flowers of both the lemon beebalm and plains beebalm in water to make a perfume for the hair. Legend has it that Native American braves chewed the leaves of lemon beebalm to sweeten their breath for courtship. *Monarda fistulosa*, a perennial with a pleasant minty smell, has been frequent-

ORIGIN OF SCIENTIFIC NAME

The genus name honors Nicolás Monardes (1493–1588), the Spanish physician and botanist who in 1574 authored a seminal work on plants and their medicinal properties, later translated into English with the title *Joyful Newes out of the Newe Founde Worlde*. Living in Seville, Spain's chief port at the time, Monardes had firsthand access to the many new plants arriving from the Americas and West Indies. He introduced Europe to such oddities as tobacco and the peanut.

OTHER COMMON NAMES

For *Monarda citriodora*: lemon beebalm, lemon horsemint, purple horsemint. For *M. punctata*: spotted horsemint, yellow horsemint, sandy-land horsemint. For *M. clinopodioides*: basil beebalm. For *M. fistulosa*: wild bergamot, long-flowered horsemint. For *M. pectinata*: plains beebalm

FAMILY

Lamiaceae (Mint Family)

DESCRIPTION

Annual and perennial herbs to 3', with flowers whorled, often at

regular intervals along the stem, resembling multitiered pagodas.

HABITAT AND DISTRIBUTION

Open pastures, roadside ditches, prairies, and meadows in variety of soils. *Monarda citriodora* (3 varieties) and *M. punctata* (5 varieties) are scattered over most of the state; *M. clinopodioides* and *M. fistulosa* inhabit eastern two-thirds and one-third of state, respectively; *M. pectinata* is in Panhandle and Trans-Pecos.

ly added to sachets and potpourris. Its leaves, both fresh and dried, are also used to flavor foods. New Mexicans of Spanish ancestry as well as many of the Pueblo and Apache tribes still employ *M. pectinata* and a non-Texan species (both locally called orégano) for seasoning cabrito, frijoles, and various stews.

The strong scents of horsemints can also be used to repel as well as entice. The volatile oils of lemon beebalm yield citronellol, the active ingredient of citronella oil, long used as an insect repellent and well known as an ingredient in insect sprays and patio candles. In the absence of a chemical lab, you can simply crush the dried leaves of the plant and rub them directly on the body. A source from the early twentieth century reports that lemon beebalm was placed in chicken nests to drive off mites and fleas, and more recently, the leaves of *M. fistulosa* were shown to be potentially useful in deterring weevil infestation in stored foodstuffs (Schulz 1928; Weaver et al. 1995).

Like other mints, *Monarda* can be enjoyed as a tea, but many of our local species are so strongly flavored that they tend to be reserved for occasional or medicinal use. A hot leaf tea of the lavender-pink *M. fistulosa* was used by the Cherokee to check fevers and assist in a good night's sleep, and by southern Appalachian tribes in treating respiratory and bronchial infections. *Wild bergamot,* the common name of *M. fistulosa,* comes from the resemblance of its scent to the Italian bergamot citrus orange (*Citrus aurantium* subsp. *bergamia*), which yields the bergamot oil used in perfumes and cosmetics and is

Basil beebalm, Monarda clinopodioides.

renowned for scenting Earl Gray tea. Our wild bergamot is in no way related to the bergamot orange, but you can create a mock Earl Gray tea by steeping the dried horsemint flowers or leaves in your favorite black tea, or simply enjoy them alone as an herbal tea. The Shakers drank wild bergamot tea to soothe sore throats, and they employed a tea made from *M. punctata* as a diuretic, tonic, and carminative.

A species of horsemint that does not grow in our area has a unique place in American history. A tea from the leaves of *Monarda didyma,* a scarlet-flowered species long used by the tribes of upstate New York for colds and coughs, became popular with American colonists after the Boston Tea Party. In a display of patriotic fervor, revolutionaries began to drink

"Oswego tea" during their boycott of British tea, and growing this horsemint in the dooryard was a symbol of their burgeoning democratic pride (Albert 2000).

Spotted or yellow horsemint, *Monarda punctata*, which grows throughout our area, was briefly famous in medical circles. Thymol, an antiseptic and fungicide once used extensively in the treatment of wounds, skin irritations, eczema, and burns, was originally derived from common thyme (*Thymus vulgaris*). It so happens that yellow horsemint contains twice as much thymol (a.k.a. monardin) in its leaves as thyme. When European thyme fields were destroyed in World War I, yellow horsemint temporarily gained economic importance as a substitute source. Thymol is now produced synthetically, but *Monarda* hybrids are still investigated as potentially viable commercial crops, and their natural oils are still economically viable. Thymol is one of the main active ingredients of Listerine and is still extensively used in lip balms, toothpaste, cough syrups, and various antiseptics.

We cannot leave *Monarda* without noting its special relationship to bees. Horsemint flowers attract moths, butterflies, and hummingbirds, but bees are particularly fond of them. In fact, Texas beekeepers consider *M. punctata* in particular, but also *M. clinopodioides* and *M. citriodora*, their most important sources of honey in the state, as they provide approximately 20% of the total honey crop. Horsemint honey has a decidedly minty flavor, which many people find to be overpowering, like the tea, compared with milder, white-clover honey. There is one more bee connection. If you are stung by a bee or other insect, the fresh leaves of horsemint, crushed and applied as a poultice, reportedly soothe the sting (hence the name *beebalm*).

SOURCES: Ajilvsgi 1984; Albert 2000; Castetter and Opler 1936; Core 1967; Curtin 1965; Dalby 2004; Dunmire and Tierney 1995; Hocking 1997; Kirkpatrick 1992; Mazza et al. 1993; Pellett 1976; Reiff 1984; Schulz 1928; Tull 1999; Turner 1994; Tveten and Tveten 1997; Vestal and Schultes 1939; Wasowski and Wasowski 1997; Weaver et al. 1995

Yellow Lotus

Nelumbo lutea (Willd.) Pers.

Many Texans are understandably reluctant to venture into marshy backwaters to acquaint themselves with aquatic flora. They don't know what they are missing. The yellow lotus is an ancient taxon, intriguing in habit, stunning in flower, generous in its provision of food, and inspirational in its close relation to one of the world's most storied flowers.

Nelumbo lutea has many distinctive and unusual features. Unlike the leaves of the water lily (*Nymphaea* sp.), which float on the water and usually have a pie-shaped gap in the blade, the blades of yellow lotus are large (up to 3 feet across), perfectly round, and mostly held several feet above the water's surface on stiff petioles that attach at the center of the blade. In our area no other aquatic plant of similar size has leaves like this. The above-water surface of the leaves has a waxy coating that repels liquid so thoroughly that water spilled on them beads into what looks like small drops of mercury. The rhizomes grow so densely that one acre of yellow lotus can contain 45 miles of them (stretched out), and the plant can extend itself outward 45 feet in one growing season at a rate of over 2 inches per day. Obviously, the plant can be difficult to eradicate once established, and owners of small ponds will likely want to place them in submerged containers.

The flowers and fruit attract the most attention. Ap-

ORIGIN OF SCIENTIFIC NAME

Nelumbo is a Sri Lankan name for the sacred lotus (*N. nucifera*). *Lutea* is Latin for yellow.

OTHER COMMON NAMES

American lotus, yellow nelumbo, water chinquapin, yonquepin, pond nut

FAMILY

Nelumbonaceae (Lotus-lily Family)

DESCRIPTION

Robust, perennial aquatic herb with large round leaves sometimes floating on the water, but usually emergent.

HABITAT AND DISTRIBUTION

Primarily eastern half of the state in shallow lakes, ponds, slow-moving streams, marshes, swamps, and backwaters of reservoirs where water depth does not exceed 6'; outside our borders in eastern half of U.S.

Yellow lotus on the shores of Caddo Lake.

pearing in late summer, the blossoms are cream-colored to pale yellow, lightly scented, and large, reaching a diameter of 10 inches. Opening in the morning, closing in late afternoon, the erect showy flowers usually last only two days after the initial opening of the bud. The combination of lofty flower and leaf can be striking; one writer calls the yonquepin "the crowning glory of Caddo Lake," and adds it to the ranks of cypress trees and Spanish moss as a distinguishing feature of the east Texas lakescape (Dahmer 1989). In the center of these compelling flowers lies the receptacle, a strange-looking inverted cone, which has been compared to a shower-head or the nozzle of a watering can. Each hole is a small cavity that contains a pistil. After pollination the seeds grow within these cavities, and the yellow receptacle turns green before drying to a chocolate brown, acquiring a rather alien appearance described variously as a moonscape with craters or a wasp's nest. Before completely

The bizarre (dried) seed receptacle of yellow lotus.

drying, the receptacles usually face east and tend to bend about 45 degrees, which allows the seeds to drop. Gathered at this stage, the pods are an exotic addition to dried flower arrangements and command high prices at market. Left to their own devices, the pods break off and fall to the water where, floating about, they distribute any remaining seeds. Although the yellow lotus mainly reproduces vegetatively through its many rhizomes, the seeds offer a backup system. They sink into the mud, where they can remain viable for hundreds of years, even after periods of complete drought. At more than 1000 years old, the "oldest demonstrably viable and directly dated seed" to be germinated belongs to the sacred lotus, *Nelumbo nucifera* (Shen-Miller et al. 1995).

Few would now suspect that the yellow lotus harbored foodstuff, yet, as with so many native food sources that have been overlooked in the mass market, earlier folks were well acquainted with its dietary potential. The immature seeds, which contain up to 19% protein, can be eaten raw, boiled, or roasted. When ripe, they resemble the small nuts of the Allegheny chinquapin, a member of the chestnut genus *Castanea* (hence the term *water chinquapin*). Some claim they taste like chestnuts as well. Native Americans and Anglo pioneers alike gathered them by the sackful. Within the mud, yellow lotus holds another prize, its tubers, shaped vaguely like bananas and reaching 10 inches in length. When baked, the tubers taste somewhat like a starchy sweet potato. In southeast Texas and along the coast the Bidai Indians consumed the tuber, and it seems likely that their neighbors, the Karankawa and Akokisa, did as well. Inland, the Comanche enjoyed them boiled, baked, or fried, and an early botanist noted that the Tonkawa made "cakes" from a flour that is likely derived from this tuber, though possibly it was from the rhizomes of a *Nymphaea* water lily (Berlandier 1980). At least one modern source mentions their preparation in a casserole (Dahmer 1989).

One cannot discuss *Nelumbo lutea* without a passing reference to its relative, the sacred lotus of Asia, *N. nucifera*. Together, these plants represent the only two species of the genus *Nelumbo*, which is the only genus in the family. This type of taxonomic exclusivity is not common and often points to an ancient lineage. Chinese and Indians alike recognized the uniqueness of the eastern lotus blossom, relating it to divinity and pureness. The pink-red flowers are sacred in India, Tibet, and China, where the lotus is the flower of the Buddha. Both he and Brahma spring from the lotus's creative power and purity, and both gods employ the flower as their divine throne. The iconic status of the lotus in the East centers on the discrepancy between the lowliness of its origins (mud) and the purity of its high-reaching blossoms. It becomes a metaphor for the heart's ability to remain pure when surrounded by worldly temptations, or humankind's ability to gain wisdom and enlightenment despite poverty in upbringing. The sacred lotus may, in fact, be the plant called soma, the famous psychotropic of the ancient Aryans, which receives rich attention in the Hindu Vedas, one of the world's most ancient religious texts (McDonald 2004).

SOURCES: Berlandier 1980; Canonge 1958; Carlson and Jones 1939; Dahmer 1989; Hall and Penfound 1944; Havard 1895; Kirkpatrick 1992; McDonald 2004; Newcomb 1961; Schulz 1928; Shen-Miller et al. 1995; Silverthorne 1996; Sjoberg 1951; Stuzenbaker 1999; Tull 1999; Wasowski and Wasowski 1997; Wiersema 1997

Prickly Pear

Opuntia engelmannii Salm-Dyck ex Engelm.

Opuntia phaeacantha Engelm.

When in 1995 the Texas Legislature passed a resolution naming the prickly pear cactus the official state plant, those outside the Southwest might well have remarked on the mounting evidence for the inherent insanity of Texans. After all, the prickly pear is associated with dry and barren places, wastelands in the eyes of many. With its sprawling habit and assemblage of nasty thorns, it is not exactly photogenic. Many early visitors to the state

---

ORIGIN OF SCIENTIFIC NAME

The genus name refers to a passage in Theophrastus (371–287 BCE), regarded by many as the first botanist, in which a plant capable of putting forth roots from its leaves is mentioned growing near the ancient Greek town of Opus (hence, *Opuntia*). Given that all cacti are native to the New World, the Greek plant alluded to is not related to prickly pear. George Engelmann (1809–1884) of Saint Louis was a German-born physician and botanist who was an early authority on many western U.S. species, especially cacti. His legacy helped to found the Missouri Botanical Garden, one of the oldest botanical institutions in the nation. *Phaeacantha* is Greek for dark-thorned (*phaios*, "dusky," "dark"; *acantha*, "thorn," "spine"), although many of this species' spines are light-colored.

OTHER COMMON NAMES

For *Opuntia engelmannii*: Engel-mann's prickly pear, Texas prickly pear, nopal. For *Opuntia phaeacantha*: brown-spined prickly pear, New Mexico prickly pear

FAMILY

Cactaceae (Cactus Family)

DESCRIPTION

Semierect or sprawling shrubs, 1–10' tall, with jointed, flattened stems, forming mats or thickets to 20' across (max. 30'); flowers bright yellow (with red centers in *Opuntia phaeacantha*), fading to orange or red; dark, reddish-purple fruits.

HABITAT AND DISTRIBUTION

Opuntia engelmannii grows predominantly in the southern two-thirds of the state and, including varieties, stretches west to California, east to Louisiana, north to Oklahoma, and south to Mexico. *Opuntia phaeacantha* prefers the northern two-thirds of the state, including the Panhandle; north to northern Colorado and Utah, west to Arizona and California.

NOTE

"*Opuntia* is notorious for its taxonomic complexity" (Powell and Weedin 2004), because of the many interspecific hybrids, the difficulty of making and using dried herbarium specimens, differences between immature and mature specimens, and, frankly, a paucity of dedicated taxonomic studies. Many names have been applied to the same plants over the past decades. Included in this account is the name *Opuntia lindheimeri* (often considered a variety of *O. engelmannii*). No distinction is made here between the varieties of *O. engelmannii* or those proposed for *O. phaeacantha*. For that matter, most of the comments here would be germane to many *Opuntia* in the state, but the two species listed here are likely our most widespread and best known. Throughout this account *prickly pear* will refer to both of these species.

Prickly pear in full bloom.

Prickly pear fruits, or tunas, quickly replace faded blossoms.

spoke of the plant's "impenetrable thickets" (Holley 1836), and there were some very unflattering portrayals, such as this one published in 1877:

> In the crevices of these stones, that fierce ugliness, the prickly pear, has struck its roots. . . . Its ferocious aspect and the strangeness of its situation add to the grimness of the scene. This thing living on stones in the most desolate spots of earth, reminds me of the infernal fiends who are said to disport themselves and play games of hell in hissing flames and lakes of liquid fire. It may appropriately be called the Floral Fiend; for surely it is hideous enough, bristling with deadly spines, sharper than needles, and set off with flame-red plumes, suggestive of the flames below. I dare say that if anyone should run against one of these fiends at night, he would smell an odor of brimstone. (Taylor 1936)

Even famed author Stephen E. Ambrose betrayed a common sentiment toward the plant, when depicting Captain Meriwether Lewis's unusually good mood: "he even found something good to say about the prickly pear" (Ambrose 1997). Moreover, one might ask, is not the prickly pear part of the national emblem of *Mexico*?

In this case, at least, the Legislature knew what it was doing, for prickly pear is one of the most historically important plants in the state. Practically every part of this widely distributed cactus, including stems, flowers, fruit, seeds, thorns, and even sap, has been variously used from prehistoric to contemporary times, by every culture from Native Americans and Spanish colonials to Hispanic and Anglo Texians, cowboys, and even current connoisseurs of southwestern cuisine. It is also an immense food source for native wildlife and livestock. One could argue that the prickly pear, of all our native plants, has been most responsible for keeping humans and beasts from starving during times of deprivation. Wonderfully adapted to the extremes of the Texas climate, prickly pear is seen as a survivalist. Tough and ornery, but generously giving, it is viewed symbolically as "indomitable and proud" (Texas Legislature 1995) and takes a place of honor in the pantheon of Texas icons.

Unless in flower, the prickly pear's most obvious feature is its flat, oval pads. Sometimes erroneously referred to as leaves, the pads are actually the plant's stems, often called joints or cladodes in cactus circles. The flattened stems are one of the plant's many adaptations to arid environments where water is scarce. Precious moisture is lost through leaves, which transpire freely, and the prickly pear has over time largely done away with them. Instead, as is the case with practically all cacti, the stems themselves evolved into the prime energy-gathering devices. The prickly pear still has vestigial leaves that appear only on young pads and resemble green, swollen rice grains, but these soon fall off, leaving only the spines behind, which anatomists believe are also highly modified leaves. Other moisture-retaining adaptations common in the cactus family include a thick, waxy impermeable cuticle; stems that can store large quantities of water; shallow, horizontal roots that can collect the most insignificant of rainfall; and a photosynthetic pathway known as Crassulacean acid metabolism (CAM). CAM, which 98% of all cacti use, is a special adaptation in which plants gather carbon dioxide at night (unlike almost all other plants) and process it during the day, though on cloudy or wet days they may also collect CO_2 during the day, and in extreme drought they may refuse to collect it at all. In this way they minimize water loss, which is inevitable during gas exchange.

What may be the real surprise about prickly pear pads is their historic importance as a food source, item of material culture, and healing agent. As a food staple, the pads have been consumed for millennia in at least the western portion of the state, and unlike those other staples, lechuguilla and sotol, prickly pear was widely distributed and did not have to be baked for two days in a pit oven. After the spines are removed by scraping or singeing, the pads are ready to be eaten boiled, steamed, roasted, or simply raw; they are less likely to be eaten raw unless the pads are young. Archaeological evidence suggests that prickly pear remained a staple for 8000 years, and we know from current Native American tribes such as the Tohono O'odham in Arizona and the Kickapoo in northern Mexico that the pads were likely consumed wherever they could be obtained. The real legacy of prickly pear stem consumption appears in Hispanic cuisine as nopalitos, in which *Opuntia* pads, with their spines removed, are thinly sliced, boiled, and sautéed with

eggs or added to various dishes such as stews. Rich in vitamin A and calcium, they are a healthy addition to Tex-Mex fare, and some studies suggest that eating nopalitos before meals can help to control diabetes mellitus (Pimienta-Barrios et al. 1993). As Hispanic culture spread into cowboy lore, various cattle songs began to boast of eating cactus as part of a tough southwestern image: "Now we'll fill you up on prickly pear and cholla / Till you are ready for the trail to Idaho" (Lomax and Lomax 1948). In the past few decades nopalitos have slowly made the transition from a purely ethnic specialty to a frequent item in restaurants specializing in southwestern cuisine and even in more mainstream venues.

Although prickly pear pads were likely not part of ancient material culture to the same extent as fiber plants (lechuguilla and sotol), they still played a role. Remains of pads split laterally and then sewn together again along the edges have been found in archaeological sites in the Trans-Pecos. These have variously been interpreted as water bags or carrying pouches, which may seem less unlikely when we consider that some Coahuiltecan groups of south Texas were thought to have lacked pottery until its introduction by the Spanish. Many of the polychrome shaman figures that adorn rockshelters of west Texas have, dangling from outstretched arms, what appear to be fringed bags or prickly pear pouches (Kirkland and Newcomb 1967), though it is possible, too, that these pictorial items simply represent the pads themselves (as food), or even the fruit of jimsonweed, another plant altogether. Unaltered *Opuntia* pads have been found in prehistoric sites, separately tied and knotted with lechuguilla strips, presumably to facilitate their transport. Regardless, a pad pouch was found that contained a "tobacco" of juniper twigs and foliage, still aromatic. Small fish have even been found inside split pads, which perhaps were used as a way to steam them. Along these lines, a desert survival expert recommends steaming meat in pad pouches placed directly on coals (Alloway 2000).

Prickly pear pads have also been employed as a topical healing agent to treat a variety of ailments such as wounds, sores, swellings, and insect bites. This use seems to be well ingrained in traditional medicine, and reports of its effectiveness seem to be reliable (Havard 1885). The usual method of application involves heating or toasting the pad (removing the thorns), splitting it laterally, and using the inner mucilaginous side as a poultice. The Mescalero Apache used this to reduce infection or heal a cut, and the Kiowa employed the same to stop bleeding. The poultice is used with the idea of drawing out heat or poison, and so has been applied as a ranch remedy on both sides of the border to treat inflammations, minor burns, sunburn, bruises, ulcers, boils, tarantula bites, snakebites, and thorn removal. Other uses include placing peeled pieces of pad on mouth sores, aching teeth, or infected gums.

The mucilaginous gel has an odd assortment of historic and current applications. The Kiowa used the gel to varnish buckskin moccasins, and Appalachian tribes used it as a sizing to fix colors painted on hides. Boiled with tallow, the gel has been utilized to harden candles; mixed with charcoal, it can serve as an emergency sun block. A particularly odd use for the gel to clarify water was noted as early as 1885 by the botanist Havard; it appears in Hispanic traditions along the entire Rio Grande and is even reported for the Blackfoot tribe of the Northwest. The pulp and gel from a few pads are stirred into muddy water. A scum of the gel forms on the surface, which after about half an hour settles to the bottom, like egg albumin, dragging sediment with it and leaving the water remarkably clear. This technique is still recommended among desert survivalists. In Algeria as late as the 1960s, the same procedure was used to control mosquitoes by preventing larval development in infested pools.

Prickly pear flowers, which tend to appear from April to June, are brilliantly colored and short-lived. In our species the tepals (undifferentiated petals and sepals) are bright yellow upon opening but usually fade to pale or reddish orange. Many do not realize that a single flower usually blooms for only one day, especially if it opens before noon; flowers opening in the afternoon may reopen the second day. Large amounts of pollen found in coprolites dating from 500 BCE to 800 CE indicate human ingestion of the flowers. This may seem eccentric to us today, but the flowers are perfectly edible, as are those of many squash, yuccas, and agaves.

Prickly pear fruit, usually called pears or tunas, constitute yet another boon from this cactus. Usually maturing in mid- to late summer to a dusky red-purple, these fruits can be very sweet and juicy when fully ripe. Some pears are 70-80% sugar by dry weight, and before the European introduction of sugarcane and the honeybee, they were one of the few abundant sweets available to American Indians of the Southwest. Approximately one-third of the sugar content is fructose, which is better tolerated by diabetics than glucose and sucrose. Tunas are also rich in vitamin C, calcium, and phosphorus. That could be why, in a 9000-year-old cooking pit in the Devils River tributary of Val Verde County, the seeds and fruit of *Opuntia* were the second most abundant plant remains found (only after walnuts). At another site along the Pecos River, 74% of the 6000-year-old coprolites contained prickly pear seeds and seed fragments. Clearly, when in season, tunas were a valued, if not critical, source of nutrition to those who could acquire them.

Millennia later, in the early sixteenth century, when Cabeza de Vaca was living among our coastal Indians, he mentioned that one of the major highlights of the year was tuna season, when tribes would travel many miles to prickly pear thickets (believed to be south of San Antonio), where they would gorge on tunas for three months, eating practically nothing else. Later sources report that tribal agreements and alliances were often made at this time. During winter months, when there was nothing to eat for days and spirits were down, Cabeza de Vaca wryly added that the Indians "tried to cheer us up by telling us that we should not be sad, because soon there would be prickly

pears," even though tuna season was five to six months away (Cabeza de Vaca 1993). He also recorded that the natives dried the tunas, which were stored in baskets like figs, ground the peelings into a powder, and squeezed the juice into holes in the ground for drinking (he maintains they did this because they lacked vessels). Lest we think the importance placed on tunas is exaggerated, consider that in historic times more than half of the food supply of the Tohono O'odham of Arizona came from the annual saguaro harvest and the trade that resulted from the saguaro and its by-products (saguaro syrup, jam, seed meal, etc.).

Tuna consumption was noted in historic times among many Texas tribes. The

A ripening tuna atop its pad, a flattened stem.

fruit was a very important food for the Mescalero Apache, who ate them fresh and sun-dried them for future use, when they were usually boiled before eating. Some informants considered the fruit more tasty after it had been frost-bitten twice. The Lipan Apache also rated tunas highly and even have a myth involving the tuna as a fruit connected to the underworld, vaguely reminiscent of Persephone and the pomegranate (Opler 1940). The Kickapoo, Karankawa, Jumano, Comanche, Tonkawa, and Kiowa all consumed the fruit. The Kiowa also made jam and candy from them, which, if it involved sugar, would have to have been only in postcolonial times.

Caution is required when harvesting tuna. *Opuntia*s are the only cacti that produce tiny, hairlike deciduous spines, called glochids, which are easily dislodged and readily penetrate human skin. On account of their harpoonlike barbs, they are difficult to remove. An unfortunate soldier of the La Salle expedition to Texas in the 1680s actually died from suffocation when, having eaten a tuna without scraping it, his throat swelled shut with inflammation. Various techniques have been employed to ensure glochid removal before consumption. The Apache used a stiff brush of sacaton grass (*Sporobolus* spp.) for this purpose, the Tonkawa used pincers made from deer antler, and the Karankawa rolled them about on the sand with their feet (presumably well callused). Ground squirrels have been reported rolling the tunas around in the gravel for the same purpose.

In the past century, various products have been made from tunas, primarily in Mexico from the spineless species *Opuntia ficus-indica*, but north of the border from whatever tunas were handy. With boiling, tuna pulp yields a couple of products, a thin syrup (sometimes sold as is) and a sweet paste. When cooled, the syrup forms a popular taffy known as "miel de tuna," and after much processing the paste is cut into bricklike cakes called "queso de tuna," which is a specialty in San Luis Potosí made from *O. streptacantha*. Tuna juice yields melcocha, a thick jelly, and an alcoholic drink called colonche is prepared from fermented juice. Jellies and jams are commonly made from tuna (see Kirkpatrick 1992 and Tull 1999 for instructions). Nineteenth-century Anglo settlers reportedly made pies from tunas, and a tuna tea was thought to treat gallstones.

A couple of brief comments about spines and seeds are worthy of note. The Kiowa actually used the spines for arrow points on small arrows to kill birds. The Apache used the spines as tattoo needles, and both tribes used them for minor surgical procedures (such as lancing boils). The seeds of the tuna, which are exceedingly numerous and quite hard, could be ground into a flour and baked, but apparently this was rarely done. High in oil and protein, the flour is still recommended as an addition to soup (Tull 1999). On a bizarre note, it is thought that certain Coahuiltecan tribes may have practiced the custom of defecating in the same area, facilitating the collection of tuna seeds from their dried feces (Newcomb 1961). The seeds could then be ground up, roasted, and eaten again. This so-called second harvest is documented among natives of the Sonoran Desert with organ pipe cactus seeds; however, the custom in Texas is rather speculative, as far as the author is aware, being based on the single phrase "deer excrement and other things I will not talk about" in Cabeza de Vaca's *Account* (Cabeza de Vaca 1993).

In the southern and southwestern portions of the state where three to four out of every seven years may be said to be in drought in terms of obtaining an adequate grass crop, ranchers quickly learned the value of prickly pear pads in feeding livestock. Thanks to the CAM pathway, *Opuntia* are four to five times more efficient in converting water to dry matter than most plants. Prickly pear pads thus have a high moisture content (80–90%) and are used to feed cattle and sheep. They also contain 7–8% protein (compare 10% for corn). Special propane burners were developed to burn the spines off the pads, and the cattle, once accustomed to this feed, "would come running" when they heard the burners ignite (Hicks 1966). Cattle will also eat the pads, spines and all, if they are hungry, developing "*pear mouth*—lots of embedded spines and slobber" (Ted Gray, pers. comm.). During prolonged drought, when the pads become thin through water loss, naturally occurring oxalic acids may become too highly concentrated and cause sickness if consumed. Although too much prickly pear is often a sign of overgrazed land, at least some pear (as it is called among Texas ranchers) is encouraged as a possible permanent foodstuff in cattle operations. The U.S. Department of Ag-

riculture has variously promoted and discouraged prickly pear fodder over the past century.

As one can imagine, prickly pear is a boon to our native wildlife. White-tailed deer, javelina, coyotes, foxes, as well as rabbits, raccoons, packrats, mice, squirrels, tortoises, and many birds (turkey, doves, and quail, just to name a few), are known to eat the fruits. Javelina, packrats, and jackrabbits will also eat the pads, but usually only during drought. In a ranking of the top 40 plant species eaten by white-tailed deer in south Texas, prickly pear was found to have the highest percent volume and frequency of any species (Arnold and Drawe 1979). The plants also provide precious desert shelter and protection to quail, skunks, wood rats and other rodents, and reptiles. Cactus wrens, roadrunners, and thrashers frequently nest in the plants.

It is impossible to leave these plants, already so rich in human connections, without mentioning cochineal. What often appear to be splotches of cottony fungus on prickly pear pads are actually the soft, waxy webs of the females of the scale insect *Dactylopius* sp. that feed on the plants. These tiny insects produce carminic acid, presumably to protect themselves against their own predators, which makes for a noncarcinogenic, brilliant red dye known as cochineal. If one rubs any of the white cottony material between one's fingers, the striking dye is immediately evident. Cochineal dye was used by the Aztecs, whose vibrant red imperial robes dazzled the Spanish conquistadores. The Spaniards began to export the dye

White splotches are the webs of the cochineal insect.

to Europe and from about 1520 to 1850 cochineal dye was behind only gold and silver as the most valuable export from New Spain. Before synthetic aniline dyes of the mid-nineteenth century, cochineal was one of the surest and brightest of red coloring agents. It gained renown in the robes of European royalty, the redcoats of the British Regulars, and the jackets of the Canadian Mounties. Carminic acid from cochineal insects is still used for coloring in foods, soft drinks, and many cosmetics, especially given that some aniline dyes have been linked to cancer.

The last decade of the twentieth century saw a resurgence of interest in *Opuntia* with the creation of the International Cactus Pear Network in 1992. There is increasing interest in *Opuntia* as an economic crop (for fodder, fruit, cosmetics, and dyes), especially in arid and semiarid lands. Various species (but most com-

monly *O. ficus-indica*) are cultivated in Africa, Italy, Israel, Spain, the United States, Mexico, Colombia, Brazil, Peru, Bolivia, Chile and Argentina.

SOURCES: Alexander 1970; Alloway 2000; Ambrose 1997; Arnold and Drawe 1979; Babb 1985; Basehart 1974; Bement 1989; Bryant 1986; Cabeza de Vaca 1993; Core 1967; Crosswhite 1981; Curtin 1965; Fletcher 1928; Gatschet 1891; Gonzalez 1989; González 1998; Hatfield 1954; Havard 1885, 1896; Hester 1980; Hicks 1966; Holley 1836; Joutel 1998; Keasey 1981; Kirkland and Newcomb 1967; Kirkpatrick 1992; Lomax and Lomax 1948; Meyer and McLaughlin 1981; Newcomb 1961; Nobel 1994; Opler 1940; Pimienta-Barrios et al. 1993; Powell and Weedin 2004; Reiff 1984; Russell and Felker 1987; Shafer 1986; Sjoberg 1953; Taylor 1936; Taylor et al. 1997; Texas Legislature 1995; Tull 1999; Vestal and Schultes 1939; Wade 2003; Williams-Dean 1978; Woodhull 1954

Tasajillo

Opuntia leptocaulis DC.

Tasajillo, in the words of a prominent west Texas rancher, is "one of the worst cactuses we have" (Ted Gray, pers. comm.). The plant is usually a bizarre mess of thin, spiny branches. On account of its exceedingly slender, cylindrical stems (the most slender of all southwestern chollas, if not of all cacti), tasajillo seems rather inconsequential, more air than mass. It is well armed with spines up to 2 inches long, in effect turning its pencil-thin stems into something six times their diameter. Add to this the tendency of the stems to break off at the slightest touch (giving the impression that they jump, hence the name *jumping cactus*) and the way that the plants often ramble through bushes and grasses where they are hidden from sight, and it is easy to see how tasajillo has marred many a hike. Given its propensity to form thickets over large areas, the scrappy cactus is not undeserving of such epithets as "troublesome" (Warnock 1974) and "prolific pest" (Enquist 1987). In west Texas, tasajillo seems to have a special association with creosote bush and mesquite (also a scrubby bush in this area), which act as protection for tasajillo seedlings and provide support for their spindly growth. Tasajillo flowers from as early as April to as late as September, depending on rain and locality. The blos-

ORIGIN OF SCIENTIFIC NAME

For the genus name, see the preceding account (prickly pear). The specific epithet is a combination of the Greek *leptos* (slender, thin, delicate) and *kaulos* (stalk, stem) in reference to the pencillike stems of this species.

OTHER COMMON NAMES

desert Christmas cactus, pencil cactus, pencil cholla, Christmas cholla, tesajo, rat-tail cactus, slender-stem cactus, jumping cactus, aguijilla, garambullo

FAMILY

Cactaceae (Cactus Family)

DESCRIPTION

Low to erect shrubs, 2–3' tall (max. 5'), with irregular, widely spreading, spiny branches consisting of thin joints, 2–12" long, $^1/_4$–$^1/_2$" diameter; small, greenish-yellow flowers followed by red (occasionally yellow) fruit, 1" long.

HABITAT AND DISTRIBUTION

In clay and alluvial soils, mainly western two-thirds of state; southern Oklahoma, New Mexico, and Arizona; Mexico, south to Puebla.

The pale yellow flowers (center), red fruits, and green, pencil-like stems of tasajillo.

soms are pretty in themselves, but their greenish-yellow color does not make them eye-catching. The little pear-shaped, scarlet fruits, which ripen in late fall and last through the winter months, are quite attractive; their bright red color against the green stems gave rise to the name *Christmas cactus*.

In tasajillo's defense, humans are at least partly responsible for its spread, and its brambles, flowers, and red fruits are useful to wildlife. The ease with which the stems detach is a good method of re-production, common among cacti, since passing animals will carry the stems some distance before they are dislodged, leaving them to sprout again in the right condi-tions. Unlike the roaming of wild animals, livestock tend to be high in number and

penned in a relatively small area; the likeli-hood that they will encounter and spread tasajillo is considerable. Tasajillo is also quite sensitive to fire, more so than several other cactus species. Human suppression of natural fires no doubt has increased its spread, especially in grassland areas. Con-trolled burns would help to decrease its density, and cattle will eat tasajillo stems if the spines are singed off (as they do prickly pear cactus). Tasajillo flowers are frequently visited by bees for both nec-tar and pollen. The slender cactus seems to have a special relationship with quail, which roost under its protective branches and relish the bright fruits. In west Texas, "anywhere you find tasajillo, you'll find quail" (Ted Gray, pers. comm.).

The fruits of tasajillo, like prickly pear

tunas, are edible by humans. Given their small size and the difficulty of collecting them, the fruits are apt to offer little more than a curious nibble. They are also covered with tiny, hairlike spines called glochids (peculiar to the genus *Opuntia*), which must be removed before eating. There is some concern in the literature that tasajillo fruits may be mildly hallucinogenic. Delena Tull says, "Scooter Cheatham (interview, Sept. 1984) reports that the fruits have a reputation for being slightly hallucinogenic, so use them sparingly" (Tull 1999). The late desert survivalist expert David Alloway wryly remarked that the "fruit . . . are hallucinogenic in large amounts. While they may not be toxic, do you really need to have an Elvis sighting in a survival context?" (Alloway 2000). So far as is known, the only source for these concerns is an early ethnobotanic study of the Chiricahua and Mescalero Apache, in which the authors state:

> The small, red fruits . . . are still used by being crushed and mixed with *tulbai*. They are reported as having such pronounced narcotic effects that the Indians

will not walk close to plants which bear them, and they claim that eating a single fruit will make one "drunk and dizzy." (Castetter and Opler 1936)

It is important to note that the fruit was being added to tulbai, which, as the authors carefully elucidate, is a fermented beverage prepared from mashed corn sprouts. It is possible that the alleged psychoactive effects derive more from the alcohol than from the tasajillo fruit itself, which is being tainted by association. The Akimel O'odham of northern Jalisco and southern Arizona have for many years eaten tasajillo fruits raw as a minor food item in their traditional diet, with no special side effects noted. That being said, one should proceed with caution in the absence of chemical studies; plant components, even in the same species, may vary according to conditions and locale.

SOURCES: Alloway 2000; Anthony 1954; Bunting et al. 1980; Castetter and Opler 1936; Enquist 1987; Griffiths and Hare 1906; Hrdlick 1908; Kirkpatrick 1992; Pellett 1976; Powell and Weedin 2004; Rea 1991; Tull 1999; Warnock 1970, 1974; Wills and Irwin 1961

Mistletoe

Phoradendron tomentosum (DC.) Engelm. ex A. Gray

It is usually easy to ignore mistletoe altogether until late autumn. Then, as deciduous trees begin to shed their leaves, one notices what appear to be large clumps, sometimes whole sections of a tree, that tenaciously refuse to turn brown. As it turns out, these leafy branches are not part of the tree at all but rather are evergreen parasites that have established themselves on their host. The dioecious plants bloom from December through March, though the inconspicuous yellowish-green male flowers have been observed as early as October. Mistletoe provides the year's first source of pollen and nectar for Texas beekeepers. The white pearly fruit on the female plants is the mistletoe's most distinguishing feature, well known through Christmas lore.

The term *mistletoe* can be broadly applied to any number of species of shrubby, parasitic plants across three families (Viscaceae, Loranthaceae, and Eremolepidaceae), but undoubtedly the most common understanding of the word in the Western world is reserved for two genera of the Viscaceae, *Viscum* and *Phoradendron*. *Viscum* contains the European mistletoe *Viscum album*; *Phoraden-*

ORIGIN OF SCIENTIFIC NAME

The genus name is a combination of two Greek words, *phor*, "thief," and *dendron*, "tree" ("tree-thief"), which refers to the parasitic nature of mistletoe. The specific name derives from the Latin *tomentum*, the stuffing of a mattress or pillow, and in botanical usage means closely covered with down or matted hairs.

OTHER COMMON NAMES

Christmas mistletoe, hairy mistletoe, injerto

FAMILY

Viscaceae (Mistletoe Family)

DESCRIPTION

Evergreen parasite, forming a globose mass up to 3' in diameter on the branches of many species of trees and sometimes shrubs. Plants are often yellowish green in color; female plants are well known for their translucent white berries in winter.

HABITAT AND DISTRIBUTION

Common throughout the state, except the Panhandle. Including several varieties, *Phoradendron tomentosum* stretches from the East Coast through the Southeast and portions of the Southwest to California and Oregon; entire northern half of Mexico. *Phoradendron* spp. inhabit every country of South America except Chile.

Mistletoe in fruit.

dron contains our American species, being the largest genus of mistletoe in the Western Hemisphere and, arguably, the world. The species most common in Texas displays great variety in leaf size and shape, pubescence, inflorescence size, and host species. Some workers recognize several subspecies in Texas, admitting that in our state distinctions between them represent a "taxonomic nightmare" (Kuijt 2003).

Phoradendron tomentosum in Texas is very abundant and is known to grow especially on hackberry, mesquite, cedar elm, Osage orange, and *Acacia* species, perhaps less so on ash, oak, willow, sycamore, and walnut. Given its abundance, it is surprisingly slow growing. The first year after germination is spent simply attaching itself to its host; the second year sees only a single pair of leaves produced

on a $^3/_4$-inch plantlet; and the third year brings on only a second pair of leaves. Although growth tends to accelerate after the initial years, a hand-sized sprig may still be only 5 to 7 years old, and bushy bundles could easily reach 20 years of age. Once established, mistletoe can grow to a very ripe age. There is a report of a 409-year-old mistletoe (probably not our species) growing on a 425-year-old cedar (Haller 1978). Mistletoe's growth and overall habit depends on the position and location within the host tree, where conditions of light, temperature, and moisture will vary. Environmental conditions in Texas and neighboring Oklahoma are apparently propitious. Mistletoe's abundance in southern Oklahoma led to its adoption as the territory's floral emblem as early as 1893, in time for its use in the

An example of a yellow-hued mistletoe in winter; a.k.a. the golden bough, an icon of Western mythology.

Chicago World Fair. When Oklahoma received statehood fourteen years later, mistletoe became the only state floral emblem that is a parasite (Oklahoma later added the Indian blanket as state wildflower and the Oklahoma rose as its state flower).

The term *parasite,* as used here, is not completely accurate. Technically, mistletoe is a hemiparasite or semiparasite, which is to say that it only partially feeds off its host. On the one hand, it does indeed invade the tissue of its host. Its rootlike haustorium grows into the cambium layer of the host tree and then sends out so-called sinkers that grow until contacting the tree's xylem vessels, from which it can obtain substantial amounts of water and minerals. On the other hand, mistletoe contains chlorophyll (the plant is green, after all) and carries out photosynthesis to make its own foodstuffs. Unlike a complete parasite, it does not feed on the primary products of photosynthesis contained in the host's phloem. *Phoradendron* affects its host by robbing it of a portion of its water and minerals, thereby stunting its growth. Branches often become swollen and distorted, forming burls and making the tree more susceptible to insect attack. Sometimes the portion beyond the mistletoe's attachment will wither and die. Contrary to popular belief, *Phoradendron* does not outright kill its host on most occasions; doing so would be suicidal. It may keep its host in a stressed situation, but it can do so almost indefinitely without causing serious harm. When mistletoe growth does get out of hand, gardeners traditionally remove the plants by hand. Regrowth is common unless the tree branch is removed well below the point of the plant's attachment. There is at least one report of a chemical control agent, a dimethylamine salt, that appears promising for pecans (Wood and Reilly 2004).

Mistletoe's growth habits are responsible for the plant's mystique and adoration. Like other, more conventional evergreens such as holly, ivy, and fir, mistletoe survives winter's apparent death; in fact, by flowering and fruiting in the darkest months of the year (in the Northern Hemisphere), it thrives when most of nature sleeps. Add to this the plant's ability to flourish seemingly without roots or contact with soil, and it is not hard to imagine why prescientific people would imbue the plant with supernatural powers. The European mistletoe, and to a lesser extent our own, often acquires a yellowish hue, which is rhetorically viewed as golden. Mistletoe poeticized is a golden bough, appearing suddenly in autumn in random places, mysteriously lacking terrestrial connections, and fruiting in the dead of winter. It is little wonder that the classical world could find Jupiter residing in a mistletoe bush, or know that Medea, the sorceress, gathered its stems for potions, or accept the notion that its branches assured safe passage through the underworld. Mistletoe is so richly endowed in archetypal lore that James Frazer entitled his monumental work on myths *The Golden Bough* in its honor (Frazer 1940).

The Druids of pre-Roman Britain seemed to have adored mistletoe the most, especially when it grew on their sacred oaks, which in northern Europe was rare. They held an elaborate annual ceremony at the beginning of the New Year in which the priests cut the mistletoe with a golden hook, catching it before it touched the ground. They then made a potion made from the plant that allegedly prevented sterility, an idea doubtless connected to mistletoe's fertility in winter. Mistletoe was gathered during medieval agricultural festivals at the solstices, which survives in our current custom of decorating with the plant at Christmas time. The custom of kissing under the mistletoe, which became part of the English Christmas tradition around the turn of the seventeenth century, apparently harks back to the carnal excess of the Roman Saturnalia celebrated near the winter solstice (a rite that the Christian Church overcame with its emphasis on the Nativity). The tradition became popularized with the publication of *The Pickwick Papers,* by Charles Dickens, which contained a scene with a mistletoe kissing spree. The fertility theme finds a distant echo in a Texas folk tradition, which holds that sleeping with mistletoe under the pillow allows one to dream of his or her future spouse (Turner 1954).

Phoradendron tomentosum has few medicinal applications, partially, perhaps, because of its alleged toxicity. A long history of folk tradition revolves around its use as an abortifacient and its ability to both lower and raise blood pressure, but the general consensus until recently was that the plant is simply too toxic to fool with. Assertions that ingestion of the plant (especially the berries) causes slow pulse and diarrhea, complete cardiovascular collapse, and acute gastroenteritis, or even death, have understandably raised great concern.

Recent studies that carefully document incidents of mistletoe ingestion from emergency rooms and poison control centers, however, find that many of these claims for toxicity are exaggerated. In a review of 1754 cases of exposure to the plant (most of which were pediatric cases), 99.2% had an outcome associated with no morbidity, and not a single fatality was reported. The authors state, "It is apparent that accidental exposures, especially by children, are associated with little or no toxicity" (Krenzelok et al. 1997). One possible explanation for the discrepancy is that the polypeptide phoratoxin may break down considerably in the stomach's digestive enzymes. Other reasons are that the known toxicity of European mistletoe (*Viscum album*) has created a prejudice against its American cousin. In addition, most toxicity reports of *Phoradendron* are small, accidental doses. One study suggests that medical evaluation is not necessary for the ingestion of fewer than 20 berries or five leaves (Spiller et al. 1996). Given the maxim that the only difference between a drug and a poison is its dose, it is possible that ingestion of larger amounts could cause very different results. All in all, it is probably wise to be cautious with mistletoe. On a positive note, it is reassuring to find that proteins isolated from *P. tomentosum* showed initial promise of antitumor activity in vitro (Johansson et al. 2003). A southwestern

species of the same genus also showed evidence of anti-HIV activity (Kashiwada et al. 1998).

A few other uses for mistletoe are intriguing. The berries of several southwestern species of *Phoradendron* were consumed by both American Indians and non-Indians, though mainly at times of deprivation or only in small numbers. A Texas ranch remedy for headache is to chew on mistletoe leaves. The Tonkawa supposedly poisoned their arrows with the juice of the leaves, and after switching to firearms, they continued putting the juice in the barrels of their guns. Less mystical but perhaps more bizarre is mistletoe's use to catch birds. Mistletoe berries are notoriously sticky once their outer coating is broken. The semitransparent, gelatinous viscin surrounding the seed is what adheres the seed to its branch before germination. This same substance was once taken from *Viscum album* to manufacture a glue (birdlime) that was spread on branches to ensnare small birds. Although the philology is not entirely clear, the *mist* of *mistletoe* may derive from an Old Dutch word for birdlime. *Viscum*, the Latin word for both mistletoe and birdlime, after which the Old World genus is named, is likely related to *viscos*, sticky. Even the honey produced from mistletoe is of a sticky and gluey texture, difficult to extract from the comb.

Birds have a strong connection to mistletoe even apart from birdlime. Practically all mistletoe genera depend on birds to disperse their seeds, contained within tasty berries. The viscin tissue that surrounds the seeds is sweetish in taste, likely adding to the fruit's appeal, but its stickiness ensures that the seeds adhere to beaks and feet to be dislodged later on other plants. More important, viscin is a highly specialized material that, once devoured, speeds the seed through the bird's digestive tract and remains sticky enough to attach the expelled seed to a host branch, preventing rain from washing it off for the many weeks required for germination. In the desert Southwest, the silky flycatcher relies so heavily on the berries of *Phoradendron californicum* that it may not breed if berry production is poor. Mistletoe fruit is such a mainstay of the flycatcher's diet that football-sized mounds of defecated seeds appear on the branches beneath highly coveted perches. This strange phenomenon recalls the more commonly accepted history of the name *mistletoe*. In this view, the Anglo-Saxon *misteltan* is a combination of *mistel* (Old German *mist*, "dung") and *tan* ("twig"), for *dung-twig* graphically describes the plant's origins in bird droppings. In our area, mockingbirds, sparrows, cardinals, and cedar waxwings are the top candidates for the dissemination of the fruit.

If supplying birds with a food source at a critical time of year were not reason enough to be less cavalier about mistletoe eradication, we might consider that at least twelve species of insect herbivores depend exclusively on *Phoradendron tomentosum* for larval food. The larvae of the lovely great purple hairstreak butterfly, the largest widely distributed lycaenid butterfly in the country, feed exclusively on its leaves in our area in the spring.

In November and December the gathering of mistletoe for Christmas decorations provides a small but thriving business for a handful of family-owned companies in Texas, Oklahoma, and California who wholesale to florists across the continent and even overseas.

SOURCES CITED: Calder 1983; Castetter 1935; Cowles 1972; Curtin 1965; Frazer 1940; Haller 1978; Hardin and Arena 1974; Hocking 1997; Johansson et al. 2003; Kashiwada et al. 1998; Krenzelok et al. 1997; Kuijt 2003; Lampe and Fagerström 1968; McPherson 1987; Moore 1990; Newcomb 1961; Paine and Harrison 1992; Pellett 1976; Prior 1939; Samuelsson 1973; Silverthorne 1996; Sjoberg 1953; Spiller et al. 1996; Turner 1954; U.S. Geological Survey Online 2004; Whittaker 1984a, 1984b; Wood and Reilly 2004; Woodhull 1954; Wyeth Laboratories 1966; York 1909

Pokeweed

Phytolacca americana L.

Phytolacca americana, perhaps more than any other plant in common use, treads a thin line between nutritious foodstuff and noxious weed, between utility and obsolescence, between rich history and modern obscurity, between medicine and poison.

Calling it pokeweed, or simply poke, early settlers throughout the eastern third of the United States gathered the spring shoots to prepare what was commonly known as poke salet, a dish similar to cooked spinach. This meal, apparently common in the nineteenth and early twentieth century, has slowly disappeared from the common palate, remaining a foodstuff only in rural areas or among those who still live in close connection to the land. Even our parents have usually heard of poke salet only from their elders. Although it once may have joined the ranks of the better-known cooked greens (such as turnip greens, mustard greens, and kale) and may have found a more enduring popularity among southern African Americans, poke has quietly passed into obscurity, the stuff of old times, folk tales, and a song sung by Elvis ("Poke Salet Annie").

ORIGIN OF SCIENTIFIC NAME
The genus name is a combination of two languages. *Phyton* is Greek for plant. *Lacca* is either a latinization of the Hindi *lākh*, for the resinous substance excreted by the south Asian lac insect used in the manufacture of varnishes (hence, shel*lac* and *lac*quer) and in the production of a red coloring matter, or a latinization of the French *lac*, referring to a crimson color. The intent is to refer to the red berries of many of the species in the genus. The specific name *americana* is self-evident.

OTHER COMMON NAMES
pokeberry, poke, scoke, inkberry, garget, pigeonberry, shoe-button plant

FAMILY
Phytolaccaceae (Pokeweed Family)

DESCRIPTION
Perennial plant 4–9' (max. 12') with reddish stems and oblong leaves up to 1' long; tiny ($1/4$") pinkish-white flowers in racemes, followed by dark purple fruits, $1/3$" across.

HABITAT AND DISTRIBUTION
Scattered colonies in stream-bottom woods and thickets throughout much of the eastern two-thirds of the state; eastern half of the U.S.; southern Quebec, Ontario. Appears near cultivated fields, recent clearings and roads, and in disturbed soils near rivers; thanks to bird dispersal, thrives along fencerows.

Perhaps for good reason, for the entire plant is largely poisonous and can cause cramps, nausea with persistent vomiting, slowness of breath, spasms, convulsions, and death. Two parts of the plant can be salvaged with care. The first leaves of early spring, if cut not too close to the stem, can be gathered into what is colorfully called "a mess of poke." This is brought home to the stove, boiled at least twice (pouring off the water each time), and then simmered in a skillet for half an hour. In the South one adds fatback pork, salt, sugar, and a dab of bacon grease, and sometimes a scrambled egg; the goal is a delicious dish that tastes something like a cross between spinach and asparagus. Poke, like spinach, contains iron, and in folk usage the plant gained a reputation for cleaning the liver. The other part of the plant that is edible is the fruit, poke-berries, which are palatable *when cooked* and are used in pies. If the berries are not cooked, one might get away with eating a few, but in the literature one finds that a five-year-old girl died after ingesting pokeberry juice prepared from a large number of crushed berries, sugar, and water (Hardin and Arena 1974), and there is a report of Boy Scouts in Kentucky who suffered from cramps and diarrhea after eating pokeberry pancakes (Edwards and Rodgers 1982). Actually, human fatalities from the ingestion of pokeberries are rare; more common is gastrointestinal distress.

The purple berries, which hang in lovely racemes and resemble old-fashioned shoe buttons, have a storied past. Crush one and you will find your fingers stained a bright crimson from the anthocyanins,

Close-up of pokeweed berries.

which are also responsible for the purple-red coloring of the stems. The name *poke* is thought to come from *pocan* or *puccoon*, an Algonquian term for a plant that contains dye, which may derive from *pak*, meaning "blood." The berries yield a red dyebath, or lake, which is one of the few bright red dyes obtained from plants; indeed, "pokeberries and prickly pear fruits are probably the only wild Texas plants that produce bright reds [in dyeing]" (Tull 1999). Unfortunately, the red fades quickly with exposure to light and apparently does not hold up well to washing, so it has not succeeded in the textile industry despite many attempts from 1800 to the present. The juice did make

Pokeweed in fruit.

a decent substitute for ink, and this use was apparently prevalent in the Civil War. Internet rumors that the U.S. Constitution was written in pokeberry ink are false (actually, it was oak gall ink), but there is evidence that the first bear flag of California may have proclaimed the "California Republic" in pokeberry juice (De Voto 1942). Pokeberries have also been used to color cake frostings, and the Caddo Indians included them in a dark dye used in basketry. Kiowa girls strung the dried fruits in necklaces.

In even earlier times the berries were put to such good use that laws had to be passed against them. In the middle of the seventeenth century, pokeweed was introduced into the Mediterranean region, where the berries were used to improve the color of low-grade wines and liquors.

Louis XVI and other contemporary monarchs tried in vain to put an end to this practice on account of the potential toxicity, but pokeweed continued to be cultivated for wine enhancement in Portugal, Spain, France, and Italy. It has been conjectured that the appearance of *Phytolacca americana* in California's wine district was the result of its introduction from southern European vintners, rather than directly from the eastern United States by either birds or humans. Birds, incidentally, are the plant's main dispersal agent; the seeds remain viable after passage through the bird's digestive system.

Pokeweed root is perhaps the most potent part of the plant. Capable of reaching up to one foot in diameter, the taproot contains bioactive compounds and at least eight triterpenoid saponins. Treated carefully as medicine, the root can be used as a purgative and emetic; Native Americans of the Southeast employed the root in this regard. Colonial New Englanders were already appropriating this and other uses from local tribes as early as 1650, and in the nineteenth century poke was used for a variety of ailments from syphilis, cancer, rheumatic joints, and ulcers to ringworm, scabies, and other skin irritations. Noah Smithwick, who wrote perhaps the single best book about early settler life in Texas, mentions the effective use of the root (boiled and mashed to a pulp) to treat horse fistulas. Even into the twentieth century the U.S. Department of Agriculture encouraged farmers to gather poke as a profitable sideline, as the berries and roots were listed in the official *U.S. Pharmacopoeia* until 1916. Considered as a poison, the root can have dire, if not lethal, consequences for foraging pigs, to say nothing of naturalists who think they have found a wild parsnip or horseradish. In a particularly striking case, 25 occupants on six floors of a lab building where pokeroot was being milled became quite ill (some bedridden for days) apparently from inhaling root particles floating in the air (Sauer 1950).

Current reports of poke continue to show the close relationship between medicine and poison. On the one hand, the plant is now known to contain antiviral proteins that are unusually potent. Pokeweed antiviral peptide (PAP) blocks the reproductive cycle of a large variety of viruses in a diverse number of hosts. PAP not only inhibits the replication of herpes simplex virus, poliovirus, and influenza virus but also has been shown to inhibit HIV replication. On the other hand, researchers studying pokeweed have themselves experienced hematological changes, and it is thought that the plant's highly potent mitogens (which stimulate mitotic proliferation in cells) can possibly be absorbed through breaks in the skin. Some have advised that gloves be worn when collecting the berries or roots.

On a completely different note, supporters of James Knox Polk, eleventh president of the United States (1845–1849), wore sprigs of poke during his campaign as a party emblem, presumably playing off the homophones "Polk" and "poke."

SOURCES: Armesto et al. 1983; Babb 1985; Core 1967; De Voto 1942; Edwards and Rodgers 1982; Foreman and Mahoney 1849; Hardin and Arena 1974; Hatfield 1954; La Vere 1998; Peacock 1982; Rogers 1985; Sauer 1950, 1952; Schulz 1928; Smithwick 1983; Tull 1999; Tveten and Tveten 1997; Vestal and Schultes 1939; Zarling 1990

Greenbrier

Smilax spp.

Anyone who has ruined clothes in a firsthand encounter with greenbrier will wonder at the plant's inclusion in this work, for its relationship to humans seems purely adversarial. Tellingly called blaspheme-vine, greenbrier is often a mess of brambles and an impediment to travel. The Kiowa, in fact, used the vine to block the path of pursuers. Even native-plant enthusiasts are unlikely to champion the plant's cause. This is all the more reason to tell the greenbrier's all-but-forgotten history, for many species of the genus provided sources of food, drink, drug, and material culture for centuries.

Our ignorance of greenbrier as a food source is understandable, given that the most important part of the plant for this purpose is entirely hidden underground. Almost all species of the genus have either extensive networks of long, looping, underground stems called stolons, or large tubers, or both. Those species with large tubers (in Texas these include *Smilax bona-nox, S. glauca, S. lanceolata,* and *S. laurifolia*) provide a starch that southeastern indigenous tribes once used in their cuisine. William Bartram, America's first native-born naturalist, best described the

ORIGIN OF SCIENTIFIC NAME
The genus has a classical Greek name applied, as early as Theophrastus (third and fourth centuries BCE), to a variety of plants, such as the holm oak, yew tree, and several vines including bindweed and a species of greenbrier.

OTHER COMMON NAMES
catbrier, stretchberry, zarzaparilla, blaspheme-vine

FAMILY
Smilacaceae (Greenbrier Family)

DESCRIPTION
Woody, trailing, and climbing vines, deciduous, semievergreen, and evergreen, armed to varying degrees with thorns or prickles, arising from rhizomes or woody tubers; leaves generally tough and shiny; flowers inconspicuous, greenish, followed by small, round, blackish berries in clusters.

HABITAT AND DISTRIBUTION
Rocky and sandy soils of open woods, pastures, shaded thickets, bottomlands, creekbeds, and fencerows of eastern third of Texas (*Smilax bona-nox* in eastern two-thirds); predominately southeastern U.S.

NOTE
The dozen or so species of *Smilax* in the southeastern U.S., most of which are represented in Texas, are difficult to distinguish, and their ethnobotanical uses generally include several species at once, if not all the species in our area.

Greenbrier with fruit.

preparation of greenbrier root at an Indian feast that he attended. (Bartram explored the Southeast at the time of the Revolution, making many botanical discoveries as well as anthropological notes on the Cherokee and Creek Indians.) The tubers were pounded in a mortar and mixed with water; the solid bits were strained off, and the sediment allowed to settle. Left to dry, the sediment became a fine reddish flour or meal, which the natives used in two different ways. Mixed with water and sweetened with honey, the mixture made a "very agreeable cooling sort of jelly" called conte, which was "beautiful, delicious . . . very nourishing and wholesome" (Coker 1944). The tuber meal was also mixed with fine corn flour and fried in bear oil to make hotcakes or fritters; the meal was also used to thicken soups. The Cherokee, Florida Seminole, Chocktaw, and Houma

were known to use the meal, but doubtless many other southeastern tribes did as well.

Perhaps acquiring the tubers was too taxing (digging beneath brambles being what it is), or the labor and time involved in preparation was simply too great. Perhaps the final product was not worth the effort, since the meal was said to be used especially in times of hardship. Perhaps, too, as native plant lore waned, knowledge of the correct plant species, time of gathering, and preparation techniques was lost. Several species, such as *Smilax rotundifolia* and *S. tamnoides*, lack tubers altogether, and *S. bona-nox* and *S. glauca* tend to have tubers that are smaller, harder, and woodier, generally less useful for meal. By the early twentieth century, use of greenbrier root among the Alabama Indians of Polk County, Texas, had already passed into legend; once upon a time the bear was their hog, the turkey their chicken, and the ka'nta (*Smilax* root) their flour (Swanton 1929). Recent attempts to prepare the jelly proved rather disappointing (Tull 1999). Rural folk were still eating the raw tuber ("kind'a stingy") in South Carolina as late as the 1940s (Coker 1944), but recent nature guides ignore the roots in favor of discussing the gastronomical merits of the vine's new shoots and growing tips. Offering little more than a nibble, these shoots are consumed raw or steamed like asparagus; they are known throughout the South and were once offered for sale at markets in Charleston, South Carolina.

Greenbrier root was historically the basis of a drink. The root, mixed with molasses and water and allowed to ferment lightly in open tubs, was seasoned with sassafras and drunk as an "extemporaneously prepared beer" among southern Civil War soldiers (Porcher 1869). The soldiers' attempts alluded to sarsaparilla, an old-fashioned soft drink made from the roots of several tropical species of *Smilax*. Many species of *Smilax*, even in the States, are still referred to as sarsaparilla, though in Texas usually with the Spanish spelling, *zarzaparilla*. The word actually derives from the Spanish *zarza* (bush) and *parra* (vine), meaning approximately "little vine bush." Sarsaparilla was historically and continues to be one of the many herbal components of root beer.

Though largely ignored now, the medicinal properties of greenbrier also centered heavily on the roots. A root tea, sometimes referred to as China ale (since greenbrier was also called China-brier),

was used extensively in the eighteenth and nineteenth centuries as a general tonic, something that stimulates metabolism, produces sweating, removes impurities and waste, and purifies the blood. The tea was prescribed to treat fever, sores, chronic rheumatism, and, fancifully, venereal diseases. Probably on account of its stimulant properties, the root is used today among bodybuilders for a "safe anabolic push" during training (Moore 1990), and others maintain that it enhances sexual performance. Various species of *Smilax* are known to contain steroidal saponins, though these have not been proven to have anabolic effects in humans. Current uses of greenbrier species in Mexico center on weight loss.

Rumor has it that greenbrier root once was used in the manufacture of tobacco pipes. Some maintain that the starchy rootstocks, being light and porous, made good pipe bowls (Porcher 1869) and that in the late nineteenth century nearly three million of these pipes were made per year in the United States (Mueller 1884). There seems to have been occasional use of greenbrier root in the rural South for this purpose, but production on a large scale is unlikely. The more likely explanation is a confusion of vocabulary. The famous brierwood of brier pipes comes from the roots of a small tree in the heather family, *Erica arborea*, found mainly along the Mediterranean. A French pipe maker in the mid-nineteenth century discovered that the tight, hard-grained wood of the tree's lower stem made excellent pipe bowls, and the wood soon replaced clay and meerschaum as the premier pipe material. *Heather* in French is *bruyère*, which was anglicized to *bruyer*, then *brier*, and later often spelled *briar*. This word was often confused with *brier* (also *briar*), meaning a prickly plant, or bramble. The term "brierwood burl" could be easily misconstrued. In light of the near absence of commentary on greenbrier pipes, both in botanical literature or in books on pipe history, the case for large-scale manufacture of these pipes appears slim. We do know that the Comanche used the leaves of our common *Smilax bona-nox* for cigarette paper, as it were, a leaf pipe.

Greenbrier vines afford superb protection and food for wildlife. Greenbrier fruit, which can linger long on the vine, is consumed by at least 38 species of birds, including grouse and wild turkey, making the bramble a favorite winter haunt. The leaves, which contain respectable amounts of protein, are also an important deer browse, especially in the southern Appalachians. Because many species stay green into winter and their leaves are slow to wither, they have been used in decorations. The berries contain an elastic tissue that can stretch up to four or more times its length and contract back to near its original size, hence the name *stretchberry*. Children used to add them to chewing gum to make it stretch like rubber. Both the berries and root yield a beautiful array of dye colors, including rusty red, tan, gray, olive- and forest-green, blue-gray, and yellow.

SOURCES: Balandrin 1996; Burlage 1968; Cadwallader and Wilson 1965; Carlson and Jones 1939; Coker 1944; Duncan 1974; Hacker 1984; Hocking 1997; Linares et al. 1999; Moerman 1998; Moore 1990; Mueller 1884; Porcher 1869; Schulz 1928; Smith 1974; Sterns 1888; Swanton 1929; Tull 1999; Weber 1962

Silverleaf Nightshade

Solanum elaeagnifolium Cav.

Silverleaf nightshade is one of our most common wild-flowers. The hues of its star-shaped blossoms, which vary in intensity from faded blues to vibrant violets, decorate the roadsides and fields in profusion, even in the driest and hottest months of summer. A deep-rooted perennial that propagates freely from rhizomes, silverleaf nightshade is tolerant of, if not stimulated by, frequent roadside grading; it is recommended for any area where such activity is frequent. Beyond its native range, especially eastward, the plant was once considered a garden plant.

The idea of intentionally planting silverleaf nightshade will shock any farmer, as the same traits that make the plant a hardy survivor also make it, in the context of crop harvesting, a pernicious weed. Heavy growth of *Solanum elaeagnifolium* has reduced cotton yields by as much as 75% in the United States. Tillage tends to spread the plant, and soil herbicides perform poorly, since they are designed primarily to control annuals. In the twentieth century, silverleaf nightshade has managed to invade agricultural fields as far away as Australia and South Africa, possibly via commercial seed and feedstuffs harvested from fields heavily populated with the plant.

ORIGIN OF SCIENTIFIC NAME

Solanum is the Latin name for a species of nightshade. It may possibly be related to the word *solatium* ("solace," "comfort"), on account of the sedative properties found in many species of the family. The specific epithet means "with leaves like *Elaeagnus*," the silver-berry oleaster.

OTHER COMMON NAMES

trompillo, bull nettle, white horse nettle, purple nightshade, meloncillo del campo, tomatillo del campo

FAMILY

Solanaceae (Potato Family)

DESCRIPTION

Pale, silvery perennial, 1–3' high, covered throughout by tiny stellate hairs; stems unarmed to densely prickly; flowers 5-pointed, blue-purple (rarely white), with pronounced, bright yellow, banana-shaped stamens; berries round, about 1/2" in diameter, ripening to yellow, purple, and black.

HABITAT AND DISTRIBUTION

Prairies, roadsides, old fields, disturbed areas, and waste places throughout Texas; southern half of U.S.; invasive, introduced weed in southern Europe, Middle East, South Africa, and Australia.

The common name for silverleaf nightshade in South Africa, *satansbos* (Satan's
bush), bespeaks the level of regard in
which it is held in agricultural circles, and
there is much literature on how to control
the weed on a global basis.

Ranchers are also likely to have a dim
view of this nightshade, since consumption of the ripe berries can produce mod-
erate to severe poisoning (and death) in
cattle. Silverleaf nightshade berries contain the toxic glycoalkaloids solanine and
solasonine, which are gastrointestinal ir-
ritants. All parts of the plant are considered poisonous, but the ripe berries are
especially toxic (unlike most plants, where
unripe berries tend to be more toxic) and
the leaves less so. Sheep seem less affected
than cattle, and goats appear to be relatively unharmed by the plant. Human fatalities are rare, probably because the taste
of the berries is so unappealing.

How odd it is that folk tradition
throughout the Southwest employs these
poisonous fruits in the manufacture of a
food product. Peoples of Hispanic and
Native American descent on both sides
of the U.S.-Mexico border have used silverleaf nightshade berries to curdle goat
milk, making either an allegedly delicious beverage, like the Zuni, or, more
commonly, a type of cheese. This cheese,
which is noted among native tribes of
Arizona and New Mexico, such as the
Akimel O'odham, Navajo, and Cochiti,
is known among Spanish- and Mexican-
Americans as asadero cheese. Modern ren-
ditions likely use rennet or synthetic substitutes, but the traditional asadero cheese
often relied on silverleaf nightshade

Silverleaf nightshade in fruit.

berries (dried or fresh) for curdling, 5–8
berries per gallon of milk (Moore 1990).
Sometimes the powdered berries were suspended in the milk in a bag, and at other
times they were simply crushed directly
into the milk. Whether nightshade berries were preferred for this process or were
simply more easily obtained than rennet (or cheaper) is unclear. Asadero, also
called Oaxaca cheese, is considered one
of the best cheeses of Mexico. The name
roughly translates as "that which is fit for
roasting," and it is often made into the
popular melted dip chile con queso. Giv-
en that livestock (goats, sheep, and cows)
and the milk they provide were all introduced to the New World by the Spanish,
one can safely assume that Native Americans adopted cheese-making from them.

Silverleaf nightshade in bloom.

It is unclear, however, whether silverleaf nightshade berries had an indigenous, precolonial use (chemically transforming some other substance), or whether the Spanish possibly employed berries from European species of nightshade for rennet substitutes. Two things we do know: cheese-making came to the area from the Old World, and *Solanum elaeagnifolium* is native only to the New.

Certainly Native Americans were aware that silverleaf nightshade was useful in other contexts. For instance, the Kiowa added the pounded leaves to brain tissue in the tanning of their buckskins. Medicinally, traditional peoples of the Southwest had a plethora of uses for the plant. The fruits (sometimes the plant itself) were used to bring on sweating, increase nasal secretions, and treat colds and eye inflammations among the Akimel O'odham, Navajo, San Diego Indians, and Mexican folk healers. The Zuni used the chewed root to treat toothache and as a poultice for snakebites. The Isleta ate the seedpods or boiled them into a syrup for use as a laxative. The Keresan gave an infusion of the plant to nursing mothers to sustain milk flow. Hispanic uses include treating tonsillitis by making a poultice of the unripe, green berries to be bound to the throat, or by blowing the dried, powdered, ripe berries directly into the mouth. The Comanche are said to have used a decoction of the boiled roots as a general sedative. Given the potential for poisoning, and the absence of precise directions, all these uses are discouraged. Presumably, human consumption of the plant is in much smaller amounts than that found in livestock. As with most medicinal plants, dosage and application make all the difference between cure and poison. In the 1960s researchers found the fruits to be rich in solasodine, a chemical used in the manufacture of steroidal hormones.

As a member of the genus *Solanum*, silverleaf nightshade has an unusual relationship with bees. The bright yellow, outward-jutting anthers, typical of the genus, are specially adapted for exclusive use by certain solitary and social bees (such as *Ptiloglossa* and *Bombus*). The large anthers do not open to shed their pollen, as they do in most flowering plants; instead, a bee must literally shake the anthers in order to propel the pollen through minute pores at their tips. For this to work, the bee must vibrate at a specific frequency, by rapidly contracting its pterothoracic flight muscles for one to several seconds. This is known as sonicating, and *Solanum*, with its pollen exceedingly rich in nitrogen and protein, has evolved such that its pollen can be efficiently harvested only by sonicating bees. Approximately 544 plant genera (or about 8% of the world's species of flowering plants) have these types of anthers, and roughly 50 genera of bees routinely use floral sonication to harvest their pollen (Buchmann and Cane 1989).

SOURCES: Boyd et al. 1984; Buchmann and Cane 1989; Curtin 1965; Fletcher 1928; Flores 1990; Havard 1885; Kindscher 1992; Kingsbury 1964; Moerman 1998; Moore 1990; Parks 1937; Schulz 1928; Vestal and Schultes 1939; Wills and Irwin 1961

Spanish Moss

Tillandsia usneoides (L.) L.

Ball Moss

Tillandsia recurvata (L.) L.

Bearding with pendulous swags the stately oaks of plantation lanes, garlanding the cypress swamps with their gothic traceries, or festooning the lonely grove in gray-green filigree, no other plant so readily identifies the Deep South as Spanish moss. This stringy plant has a venerable history that would surprise even old Southerners.

Alvar Núñez Cabeza de Vaca noted the plant in the fall of 1528 on what was probably Galveston Island (or

ORIGIN OF SCIENTIFIC NAME

The genus name honors Elias Tillands, professor in Åbo, Finland (1640–1693), and memorializes an amazing event of his youth. Having become so seasick while crossing the Gulf of Bothnia from Sweden to Finland as a student, Mr. Tillands would only consent to return to Sweden by land, walking on foot for more than 1000 miles. Linnaeus, who mistakenly believed that the surface hairs of *Tillandsia* shed water, named the genus after his water-averse colleague. *Till land* in Swedish also roughly translates as "by land," a play on words that Linnaeus likely had in mind. *Usneoides* means "like *Usnea*," which is an epiphytic lichen that superficially resembles a moss. *Recurvata* refers to the recurved (bending backward) leaves.

OTHER COMMON NAMES

For *Tillandsia usneoides*: hair moss, long moss, black moss, Florida moss, New Orleans moss, southern moss, old man's beard, treebeard, vegetable wool, crape moss, wool crape. For *T. recurvata*: bunch moss, gallitos, heno pequeño

FAMILY

Bromeliaceae (Bromeliad Family)

DESCRIPTION

Tillandsia usneoides is an elongate twining bromeliad, usually under 25' in length (extremes over 60' reported) but rarely more than 18" actually alive at any one time. Apparent length results from overlap of several shorter plants. *Tillandsia recurvata* is a small, slow-growing bromeliad (individual plants rarely larger than 6" across) forming dense clusters or balls.

HABITAT AND DISTRIBUTION

Tillandsia usneoides is usually found draped in tree branches in warm, humid, and sunny conditions. In Texas, mainly in south and southeastern parts of the state, but extending northward along riverbeds as conditions allow; throughout the Coastal Plain of the southeastern U.S. to Virginia; Mexico, Central America, south to Argentina and Chile, a range of some 5000 miles and the greatest distribution of any bromeliad. *Tillandsia recurvata* usually clings to the underside of tree branches in the southern half of Texas, including the Trans-Pecos; southern Florida, southern Arizona, and Baja California, with recent introduction in Louisiana; Mexico, Central and South America. Second only to Spanish moss in greatest distribution among bromeliads.

Dense clumps of Spanish moss.

Follet's Island just to the west), giving Spanish moss the distinction of being one of the first plants mentioned in writing from what is now the United States, a full century before the pilgrims landed. Speaking of the Capoque and the Han, two bands of Karankawa (or possibly Atakapa) Indians among whom he was held captive, Cabeza de Vaca says, "All the people of this land walk around naked. Only the women wear on their bodies something covered with a wool that grows on the trees" (Cabeza de Vaca 1984; my translation). Indeed, skirts of Spanish moss worn by Native American women were noted in other accounts in Louisiana and Florida. The common names *vegetable wool* and *wool crape* are well deserved.

Most of the reported Native American uses of Spanish moss in Texas center on padding and general absorption. The early nineteenth-century botanist Berlandier noted in the huts of the Tonkawa, camped along the Colorado in 1828, that the Indians placed the moss (called pastle) under furs to form their sleeping pallets. He reported the same use among the Tejas, who enjoyed slightly more sophisticated cots: "Beds are arranged around the room and were made of branches supported on four legs and covered with *tapetsle*, or Spanish moss . . . which grows everywhere in this country. This formed a mattress beneath sundry skins and furs, as I have seen it used among several other nations" (Berlandier 1969). The Atakapa of southeast Texas used the moss as a sort of diaper, placed between the papoose's legs to absorb the discharges, and as wicks in their alligator-oil lamps. Other Native Americans used the moss for menstrual pads, for covering patients during sweat baths, and for combustible material for torches. French and Spanish colonials who noted these uses also took pleasure in naming the plant at each other's expense. The French called the moss *barbe espagnole* ("Spanish beard"), while the Spanish, in retort, referred to the epiphyte as *perruque française* ("French wig").

In nineteenth-century Texas narratives, the moss is seen both as a stunning inhabitant of the live oak and as an indicator of pestilence. Although *Tillandsia usneoides* will grow on almost any tree, it seems particularly fond of live oaks, or perhaps people are simply more apt to notice its dramatic display draped on their branches. Frederick Law Olmsted, the founder of American landscape architecture, speaks of this connection: "As far West as beyond the Guadalupe, [the live oaks] are thickly hung with the grey Spanish moss, whose weird color, and slow, pendulous motions, harmonize peculiarly with the tone of the tree itself" (Olmsted 1857). As for illness, it was well known that malarial fevers, chills, and agues were prevalent in low-lying, moist places along coasts and waterways (the preferred habitat of the moss), and the plant was astutely seen as a warning to prospective settlers. William

Bollaert's comments are fairly typical of the mid-nineteenth-century traveler to Texas:

> I could not help remarking the peculiar and melancholy appearance the Spanish moss . . . in some places gives to the "timbers" or "bottoms." Its long, shaggy and hungry grey appearance, contrasting strangely with the deep green foliage. When much of this moss is seen growing, the locality does not sustain a good character for healthiness—"chills and fever" being common. (Hollon and Butler 1956)

The mosquito's role as a vector for malaria and yellow fever was not understood until the very end of the century. The early colonists, not understanding the cause but recognizing some connection between the air of the region and disease, chose a fairly reliable indicator of the humidity necessary for the mosquito's survival.

Tillandsia usneoides has been used as an all-purpose stuffing and packing material for centuries. Inside the living plant are wiry fibers that are strong, insect resistant, and especially resilient. It had long been noted that the green (living) moss would decay on the forest floor and turn black; that is, the cortex would fall away and leave behind the fibers. This process could be sped up by retting the moss (soaking in water, followed by two to three months of composting), which, after cleaning or ginning, provided an end-product that could be used as an inexpensive substitute for horsehair in mattresses, upholstery, car seats, horse collars, bridles, saddle blankets, and even as wadding in rifle and revolver shells. Henry Ford is said to have used it in the cushions of his first Model T's. Cured moss appeared in the earliest New Orleans markets (ca. 1718), but it probably reached its heyday in the 1920s–1950s. Since there was a 75% reduction in total weight (from raw product to fiber), and since the curing process took up to four months, the discovery of cheap and easily manufactured foam rubber, around World War II, brought about the quick demise of the industry.

Spanish moss was largely a folk industry of Louisiana and Florida. Texas probably never had sufficient supplies of the plant to make its harvest widespread; however, it is said that several prominent Texas families made their first money in moss mattresses (Schulz 1928). There are reports from east Texas of its use in pliable mud bricks, or mud-cats, used in stick-and-mud chimney construction, which echoes the more extensive use of moss as a binding material in plastering homes. The famous Absinthe House of Bourbon Street, New Orleans, erected in 1806, still has moss embedded in its plaster that has lost none of its original resiliency, almost 200 years later and post-Katrina.

Spanish moss tea has long been used in south Louisiana for the treatment of diabetes mellitus; at least one scientific paper found that it reduced blood glucose levels in rats (Keller et al. 1981). Contemporary African American folk healers employ decoctions to treat high blood pressure. In Brazil it has been employed popularly for analgesic properties, which, likewise, at least one academic paper supports (Costa et al. 1989).

From a botanical perspective *Tillandsia usneoides* is unusual for a number of reasons. First, one should remember that *Tillandsia* belongs to the pineapple or bromeliad family, though even the ardent collector of bromeliads might not immediately recognize its relationship. Having at maturity only four to five leaves, these plants are thought to represent the most extreme case of reduction found in the family. Usually rootless, or having only adventitious roots for securing the seedlings, the inconspicuous bromeliad sends out renewal shoots from the axil of one of the lower leaves, which elongates into an internode until the next plantlet comes along. The photosynthetic tissue (cortex) of the internode eventually dies, leaving the plants connected by a fibrous tissue. Eventually, too, the older plantlets die but stay connected to the growing portion of the plant, which is rarely more than 18 inches in length (and frequently only 6–8 inches). The apparent great length of the festoons is really due to numerous short strings of plants overlapping each other.

In contrast to Spanish moss, which expands in great wiry lengths, ball moss holds itself tightly, as its name suggests, in little balls. Sometimes dotting tree limbs as if artfully arranged, at other times growing so densely that it appears as if the trees themselves are sprouting the growth, these small hairy globes are diminutive and slow-growing. Few fully appreciate their unhurried pace. After one full year, a ball moss seedling is usually only half an inch high with barely three leaves.

Ball moss.

The second year adds another leaf or two and doubles the height. By the end of the third year, a small ball of two to three individual plants has formed. A four-year-old ball claims eight to twelve small plants, few of which exceed 2 ¹/₂ inches. Thereafter, the mature plant will produce four or five leaves in a season. Taking this growth rate into account, the average ball moss we see might be 10–15 years old, and many of the more venerable ones reach 20–25 years.

Both Spanish moss and ball moss are true epiphytes; that is, they draw their entire nourishment from airborne water and nutrients, which they absorb through dense layers of large, multicellular hairs, or trichomes, that cover every part of their stems and leaves. They are not parasites, taking no nourishment whatsoever from the trees that they cling to, which they use merely for attachment. Spanish moss is frequently found in completely dead trees, and ball moss exhibits an extraordinary diversity of substrates, such as board fences, oak posts, concrete beams,

cliffs, lava flows, rocks, even telephone wires and barbed-wire fences. The propensity for both of these bromeliads to thrive on the dead or dying branches of living trees gives the mistaken impression that they are responsible for the tree's demise. Actually, naturally dying branches simply provide good habitat for the bromeliads, because they are bare and generally offer the best conditions of light and relative humidity. Both of these so-called mosses (neither is botanically a moss) can potentially endanger trees only insofar as their density may block sunlight, and as their weight, especially after a rain, can break weak branches. There is some evidence that bromeliads may indirectly parasitize their hosts by absorbing the lion's share of atmospheric nutrients (such as nitrogen, phosphorus, and potassium) before these reach the ground where the tree's roots can absorb them. This action has been called nutritional piracy (Benzing 2000).

Because epiphytes absorb multiple airborne trace substances that can be extracted and quantified, and because of their high ratio between surface area and mass, both of these species of *Tillandsia* are excellent biofilters, that is, they provide a cheap and easy way to assess air contamination in a given locale. Both effectively bioaccumulate heavy metals (such as cadmium, copper, lead, manganese, mercury, nickel, and zinc), which makes them good candidates for air monitors, especially in urban areas where pollution is of high concern. Spanish moss has been employed successfully in Brazil to monitor atmospheric mercury in and around gold workshops, and ball moss has been utilized in two industrialized cities in Colombia to ascertain the degree of pollution from heavy metals, pesticides, and polycyclic aromatic hydrocarbons.

Spanish moss produces seeds, but it is most successful at reproducing itself vegetatively by windblown strands. Many birds, especially the Parula warbler, will take the plant into their nests, and the occasional bat will take refuge in its dense fibers. Perhaps unique to this species is alligator dispersal. Female alligators in south Florida have been reported to use the moss occasionally to construct nests.

Ball moss replicates primarily by seeds, which germinate at the end of winter where wind and rain have lodged them in rough bark, often on the underside of branches. More drought tolerant than Spanish moss, ball moss even flourishes in desert conditions in Baja California (where it attaches to cacti, desert shrubs, and yuccas), so long as it can receive moisture from ocean winds and night fogs. It is the only bromeliad found in the state of Arizona.

Both mosses have been utilized in floral wreaths and holiday decorations. Austin's first public Christmas lights in 1924 were festooned with Spanish moss over downtown streets.

SOURCES: Bennett 1986; Benzing 1980, 2000; Berlandier 1969; Birge 1911; Cabeza de Vaca 1984; Costa et al. 1989; Diggs et al. 1999; Dyer 1917; Garth 1964; Guard and Henry 1968; Hamby 2004; Harvey 1996; Hollon and Butler 1956; Humphrey 1971; Keller et al. 1981; Kirtley 1954; Kniffen and Comeaux 1979; Malm et al. 1998; Martin et al. 1985; Martínez 1968; Olmsted 1857; Penfound and Deiler 1947; Pénicaut 1953; Pyatt et al. 1999; Record 1916; Schrimpff 1984; Schulz 1928; Schwartz 1986; Smith and Wood 1975; Stanford 1990

Cattail

Typha domingensis Pers.

Typha latifolia L.

If you find yourself in any temperate or tropical wetland habitat around the world, there is likely to be a species of cattail nearby. If you are stranded and without food, this is a good thing, for the cattail, called "the supermarket of the swamps" by the early native-food promoter Euell Gibbons, has something edible to offer in virtually its every part. Cattail is equally generous in its ability to provide all-purpose matting and building materials, used in shelter and transport. The plants are amazingly prolific. In one experiment, a single seedling produced 98 shoots in one season (Morton 1975). This has given cattail a reputation as a pest in areas where it is unwanted, such as earthen stock tanks and farm ponds, rice paddies, recreational lakes, and drainage canals. In addition to its multitudinous uses, cattail is excellent at preserving and improving wetlands. Its abundance, at least in the right places, is nothing but a boon.

ORIGIN OF SCIENTIFIC NAME

Typhe is the classical Greek name for cattail. The name may possibly be related to the Greek *typhos* (swamp, marsh), on account of its habitat, or *typhos* (smoke, mist), on account of the light, airy floss of its ripe seed heads. *Domingensis* is a latinization of *Santo Domingo*, the place where the species was collected; *latifolia* means broad-leaved.

OTHER COMMON NAMES

For *Typha domingensis*: narrow-leaf cattail, southern cattail, lesser reed mace, tule. For *Typha latifolia*:
common cattail, broad-leaf cattail, great cattail, great reed mace, tule espadilla

FAMILY

Typhaceae (Cattail Family)

DESCRIPTION

Erect, perennial, aquatic herbs to 9' tall, with long, flat, strap-like leaves and thick, branching rhizomes; flowers in dense, felty, pokerlike spikes, the male (staminate) flowers arranged above the female (pistillate) flowers. *Typha domingensis* has narrower leaves (1/4–3/4" wide) and a small gap between male and female flowers;
T. latifolia has wider leaves (to 1") and lacks the gap (male and female sections usually touching).

HABITAT AND DISTRIBUTION

Both species abundant throughout Texas in similar habitat, wet ground to shallow water, ditches, bogs, ponds, and lake margins; throughout the U.S. (*Typha domingensis* mainly in southern two-thirds); Canada, Mexico, Central America, and Europe. In addition, *Typha latifolia* is represented in Asia and Japan, and *T. domingensis* occurs in the West Indies, South America, and Australia.

As a foodstuff, cattail is best known for its rootstock. As early as the third century BCE, Theophrastus noted that children ate the "part next to the roots" (Theophrastus 1916). Most do not realize that the main edible subterranean part is the rhizome (an underground stem), and usually only its innermost core. The rhizomes should be roasted or boiled, for depending on the species, place, and time of year, the raw parts are apt to be disappointingly fibrous and may cause nausea. The rhizomes are filled with starch (45% by dry weight), especially in early winter after a full season of storing nutrients.

In China and Europe these were pickled and served in salads, while many North American Indians cooked them, to be consumed either as a staple or as a famine food. American tribes also made a flour from the rhizome starch, used in preparing various breads. Modern authorities recommend washing the starch out of the rhizomes in water and then adding it, wet, to pancake, bread, and biscuit flours (Tull 1999); it can also be used as a substitute for cornstarch in puddings. Some Native American tribes, such as the Iroquois, produced cattail flour by pulverizing the dried rhizomes. This method was repeated at the Cattail Research Center of Syracuse University in 1947. Investigators found that the rhizomes yielded 50–60% flour with a starch content of 40–60%, and that the flour contained as much protein as corn or rice and more carbohydrate than the potato. The flour is slightly sweet-tasting, and cookies made from it were considered "highly acceptable" (Morton 1975). By macerating and

A ripening spike of female flowers on cattail.

boiling cattail rhizomes, the Iroquois also prepared a syrup, which they used as a sweetener on cornmeal pudding and other tribal dishes.

Young cattail plants, or shoots, are also edible. They must be collected early in the spring, their outer leaves removed, and only the inner heart saved. If gathered early before turning bitter, the sprouts can be added raw to salads, or they can be boiled. Cossacks of the Don Valley in Russia consumed the cooked sprouts, called Cossack asparagus, and closer to home, the Mescalero Apache did as well. Tender white buds, which are usually pulled up with the rhizomes and roots, are also edible, raw or boiled, and resemble cabbage in taste.

Contemporary Americans may find it strange that cattail flower heads are edible. When they first appear in late spring, the immature flowers (both male and female) are green. These can be consumed raw, or they can be boiled and eaten like corn on the cob, coated with butter, leaving the stalk itself alone. Cattail on the cob, which is said to be delightful and to taste just like corn (Crider 2001), was considered a special delicacy among the Paiute when added to soups. The flowers can also be removed from the immature spikes and mixed with flour for baked goods.

An edible part of the cattail that is even more bizarre to people today is the pollen. For most plants, pollen in quantities sufficient for human consumption would be out of the question, but cattail produces copious amounts of the protein-rich, bright yellow substance. Pollen gathered from a mere two dozen flower stalks (the preferred method is to shake the pollen into a paper bag) is enough to make a boiled porridge or to be sifted into bread and muffin dough. One native-plant culinary expert recommends making pancakes with one part cattail pollen and two parts Bisquick (Crider 2001). The cooked pollen must be tasty, for cultures far removed from one another have managed to make startlingly similar recipes. The Swamp Arabs of southern Iraq and Iran, whose marshy habitat almost disappeared under Saddam Hussein, mix the pollen of *Typha domingensis* with sugar and steam

the mixture (called kharet) in a bag. Thousands of miles away in New Zealand, the Maori created the delicacy pua by mixing cattail pollen with water, wrapping the mixture in leaves, and steaming it in an earth oven. The yellow-brown cake was said to have a "biscuity" aroma, tasting a bit like gingerbread (Prendergast et al. 2000). In the archaeological record of Texas, cattail pollen has been found in large amounts in human coprolites along the Pecos River dating to 500 BCE, suggesting pollen (or flower) ingestion. Many southwestern tribes in the past century, however, have considered the pollen important purely for ceremonial reasons. The Akimel O'odham, Apache, and many Pueblo tribes, who likely see a connection between the cattail and water (a sacred commodity in arid communities), all use cattail pollen for face and body paint in dances and rituals.

When the female flowers of the cattail ripen, the familiar brown, velvety, cigar-shaped spikes burst open, releasing up to 200,000 minute seeds (per spike), each attached to tufts of fine, fluffy, whitish hairs. The seeds are yet another edible item, but acquiring them in quantity and detaching them from their silky floss is a daunting task. A report from the 1930s tells of a fascinating Paiute solution. One removes enough floss and seed to cover an area 5–6 feet across to a depth of half an inch; then one ignites the floss. The fire almost instantly consumes the fluff, leaving the roasted seeds behind, which have a nutty flavor (Curtin 1965). The speed with which cattail floss ignites was once exploited in theatricals to simulate lightning. Needless to say, the floss makes good tender for starting campfires. The entire, intact flower spike, soaked in kerosene, also makes a decent torch.

The soft floss from ripe cattail heads has provided stuffing for a variety of articles. Native Americans utilized the silky fibers to pad cradleboards and to make baby diapers and comforters. The Caddo mixed the floss with cottonwood fluff and wild goose feathers to stuff pillows. Cattail silk has been used around the globe in mattresses, carriage seats, sleeping bags, vests, and even baseballs. During World War II, when supplies were difficult to acquire and substitutions were needed, the Germans used cattail floss for heat and sound insulation in buildings, while the U.S. Navy replaced several million pounds of kapok used in life vests with cattail and milkweed floss, both very buoyant.

Cattail leaves are the real gift to material culture. Since they resist decay, absorb water, and swell, the dried leaves (especially the lower, butt ends) are handy for caulking casks, barrels, boats, canoes, and even log cabins. Cattail leaves also float, a trait exploited by many American Indians to make durable, unsinkable watercraft. In our area the leaves were more apt to be used for roof thatching, flooring, and mats. Cattail thatching was widespread. The Jumano along the Pecos River made huts of tule in which to entertain Spanish explorers as early as 1684. Traditional houses of southern and southwestern tribes, such as the Akimel O'odham, Caddo, Isleta, and Zuni, employed cattail thatching, said to be wind- and water-

proof, on wooden and adobe structures. Puebloans and Hispanics of the Southwest placed the roof thatch on top of the vigas and then applied a liberal coating of mud. Mid-nineteenth-century visitors to San Antonio remarked on the windowless, wooden cabins, or jacales, with roofs of thatched tule, that surrounded the Alamo square.

Perhaps most common of all was the use of cattail leaves as a weaving material. The upper parts of the leaves are especially suited for this purpose, and all sorts of floor and sleeping mats were woven wherever cattail was available. Mats more than 10,000 years old have been discovered in Nevada caves. Cattails can be woven, twisted, or plaited into any number of everyday practical items such as baskets, slippers, sandals, sacks, fans, rope, and twine. Caning, or the weaving of chair seats, called flag bottoms, was practiced with cattails with some renown in central New York State. Other uses for the leaves include the making of paper and cloth. In the mid-1800s a fair amount of cattail paper was manufactured in the eastern United States, though it was difficult to bleach. Soft fibers extracted from the leaves were used to make cloth and rugs in Germany and Romania during World War I, and in Russia as late as the early 1950s.

Aside from the usual array of alleged medicinal properties commonly ascribed to many natural plants, such as use as an astringent and febrifuge, one medicinal treatment is repeatedly ascribed to cattail, the dressing of wounds and burns. Dioscorides, a Greek medical doctor and botanist from the first century, noted that cattail floss was mixed with hog grease to treat burns. In 1809, the supplies of an Arikara medicine man in South Dakota included a considerable quantity of cattail down to treat cases of burns and scalds. As late as the 1940s, cattail floss was used to dress serious burns in a Paris hospital. Cattail root jelly, probably a mashed poultice, is also reported as a treatment for burns.

More recently the amazingly useful cattail has been touted for its role in wetland ecosystems. Like many aquatic plants, cattail naturally filters water, stabilizes soil, and helps to prevent bank erosion. The roots help to fix nitrogen in the soil and reduce soil salinity. Egyptians have planted a species of cattail along the Nile to reduce salinity; when the plants are mature, they are removed, so that rice can then be grown successfully. Much of the recent literature on cattail centers on its use in wastewater treatment. The plants are shown to be quite successful in removing suspended solids, nitrogen, ammonia, phosphate, and fecal coliforms from small-scale constructed wetlands, offering a viable and economic sewage treat-ment for small villages. Floating mats of cattails (and other aquatics) can be used to remove nutrients from swine lagoons, the vegetative cover being more attractive and reducing odors as well. Finally, cattails provide habitat for a host of bird species, attracting red-winged blackbirds, marsh wrens, coots, bitterns, rails, and grebes, among others. Muskrats thrive in cattail patches, feeding heavily on their rhizomes, leaves, and stems; feral pigs and deer also feed on the plants. Given the diversity of uses for this plant, and its ability to offer "more usable food per acre than most grain crops" (Tull 1999), the cattail deserves much more respect than it usually receives.

SOURCES: Basehart 1974; Bolton 1908; Breeden 1994; Bryant 1974; Burlage 1968; Castetter and Opler 1936; Coleman et al. 2001; Crider 2001; Crosswhite 1981; Curtin 1965; Dioscorides 1959; Dunmire and Tierney 1995; Everitt et al. 1999; Hubbard et al. 2004; Kausch et al. 1981; Kindscher 1992; La Vere 1998; Mitich 2000; Morton 1975; Muenscher 1944; Olmsted 1857; Palmer 1878; Prendergast et al. 2000; Solano et al. 2004; Theophrastus 1916; Tull 1999

Frostweed

Verbesina virginica L.

Many a casual stroller has been surprised on a chill autumn or winter morning to find what appear from a distance to be balls of cotton or strips of Styrofoam clinging to the lower stems of dead plants. Closer inspection reveals that the white masses are ice, bursting forth along the longitudinal axes of the stems. Some of these formations appear as long, pencil-shaped swellings along the margin of the stems, as if a seam on an upholstered corner had split and the stuffing was beginning to bulge out. Others, from smaller cracks in the bark, take on fantastic shapes, resembling flowers, bows, potato chips, and clams. Frequently, as if squeezed through a cake-decorating tube, the ice appears in delicate ribbons, with wavy or fluted edges, which sometimes turn back in on themselves like Christmas ribbon candy. These frozen whimsies give the frostweed, or iceplant, its name.

The phenomenon, well known among rural folk, first appeared in the scientific literature in the early nineteenth century and then resurfaced every few dozen years, each time catching a new generation of naturalists by surprise. A short note in Stephen Elliott's *A Sketch of the Botany of South-Carolina and Georgia,* published in 1824, seems to be the earliest published account of the

ORIGIN OF SCIENTIFIC NAME
The generic name is said to be derived from the genus *Verbena,* because of some resemblance in the foliage. *Virginica* ("of Virginia") is in reference to the location of the type species, collected in 1753.

OTHER COMMON NAMES
iceplant, white crownbeard, Virginia crownbeard, richweed, squaw weed, Indian tobacco, tickweed

FAMILY
Asteraceae (Aster Family)

DESCRIPTION
Stiff, upright perennial to 9' tall; single-stemmed, branching only when flowering; flowers white, usually with 3–7 petals (actually ray florets), arranged in clusters, several clusters forming a flat to rounded head.

HABITAT AND DISTRIBUTION
Often growing in dense stands in partial to heavy shade along stream banks and slopes, and under tree canopies; eastern two-thirds of Texas minus the southernmost portion; southeastern U.S., as far north as Virginia, west to Kansas.

Frostweed in winter with ice appearing along length of lower stem.

ice formations. The plant in question was what is now called stinking camphorweed (*Pluchea foetida*), a member, like frostweed, of the aster family. Only four years later, the second scientific record of plant frost appeared in our own backyard. Jean Louis Berlandier, the Swiss-educated botanist who made some of the earliest collections in Texas, noted the ice on our frostweed on November 30, 1828, just northwest of San Antonio. Unfortunately, his observation was not published until well over a century later. The frost phenomenon has been noted for several other plant species over the ensuing years, including common dittany (*Cunila origanoides*) in the mint family, other species of *Verbesina* and *Pluchea*, and another flower that bears the common name *frostweed, Helianthemum canadense* in the

sun-rose family. European reports include thistle and heliotrope. By the 1920s, the unusual frosts were attributed to approximately 30 different plant species, including herbaceous annuals and perennials, as well as trees such as walnut and papaw (Missouri Botanical Garden 1924).

The general consensus on how the ice crystals form seems to be the following. The earth must be moist and above freezing in temperature, and the roots of the plant alive and functioning, although the stems and leaves may be completely withered. The temperature of the air drops suddenly below freezing. The roots, still absorbing water and transporting it through the xylem, are able to push the liquids up only so far before they freeze, usually within a foot from the ground. The plant stems must be brittle, and as the water turns to ice and expands, they split along their longitudinal axes. The ice that is first formed is forced outward by more water, which freezes, in turn, as it hits the surface. The process keeps repeating, forming a ribbon that can become 4–5 inches long. One of the best conditions in which to see these ice menageries is when a good rain with above-freezing temperatures is followed by a hard freeze. The requirement of unfrozen earth explains why the phenomenon is observed more frequently in the late fall, with winter occurrences confined to southern states.

Frostweed's purported medicinal values were noted mainly among Native American tribes and have largely been ignored or forgotten over time. The roots and occasionally the leaves, variously prepared as

Crystalline flowers and curled ribbons, some of the many whimsies of frostweed ice.

Frostweed in true flower.

teas and infusions, are said to be diuretic (increasing the flow of urine), diaphoretic (causing perspiration), and depurient (removing impurities, cleansing sores, and purifying the blood, as in a blood tonic). Southeastern tribes, such as the Chickasaw, Choctaw, and Seminole, used the teas to treat chills and fevers. One of the plant's many common names, *squaw weed,* alludes to this Indian connection, but it may also refer specifically to applications for women. The Chickasaw used the whole plant as an abortifacient and gynecological aid, and the Kickapoo as late as the 1970s were still using hot decoctions of the plant for near-term and postpartum issues, such as cleansing the womb and stanching excessive bleeding. Berlandier, who first noted the ice crystals in Texas, mentioned that frostweed roots were employed successfully to treat syphilis, a use echoed by the Choctaw of the same time; however, the on-off nature of this disease caused many treatments to be touted, erroneously, as cures. In Texas folk medicine, frostweed root tea, mixed with whiskey to keep it from souring, was used as a blood thinner and to clear muddy complexions.

Explanations for the plant's many common names range from the fairly straightforward to the obscure. *Richweed* calls attention to frostweed's fondness for rich soil, though *shadeweed* would be more precise. *Indian tobacco* underscores that Indians used the dried leaves for tobacco, though there appears to be scant evidence for this claim. *Tickweed* alerts the unwary passerby to the many seedticks that are said to inhabit dense frostweed colonies. *Crownbeard* presumably refers to the white flowers that appear in crown-sized clusters and at the crowns of the stems—pick your metaphor. Berlandier reported two Spanish names used for the plant in the early nineteenth century: *lengua de vaca* ("cow's tongue"), possibly for the tongue-shaped leaves, and *yerba de la capitana* ("captain's herb"), for unknown reasons. The common name *capitana* is still used today for *Verbesina microptera*, a species from south Texas.

Frostweed is a good honey plant for bees, and although it is not deer resistant, it is not frequently browsed. It delights native gardeners by remaining green through hot Texas summers without supplementary water.

SOURCES: Ajilvsgi 1984; Berlandier 1980; Burlage 1968; Campbell 1951; Darlington 1837; Elliott 1824; Hatfield 1954; Hocking 1997; Jennison 1931; Latorre and Latorre 1977; MacDougal 1893, 1894; Missouri Botanical Garden 1924; Moerman 1998; Parks 1937; Schulz 1928; Torrey 1931; Wasowski and Wasowski 1997

Wild Grape

Vitis spp.

The United States, but Texas in particular, has a unique relationship to grapes. Of the several score of *Vitis* species worldwide, the majority (some say three-fourths) are native to this country. Texas, with roughly a dozen species and several varieties, has more than half the U.S. total. Despite this abundance, the grape that we all know as a fruit, the source of raisins and wine, comes overwhelmingly from just one species, *Vitis vinifera*, which is not American. This species, native to Asia Minor and the Caucasus, was domesticated in the fourth millennium BCE and has been propagated worldwide in thousands of horticultural varieties. As is so often the case with edible plants, the economic importance of the dominant agricultural species completely overshadows its undomesticated relatives. In the story of *Vitis*, however, the wild species, and the Texan ones in particular, have played a critical, literally supporting role in the maintenance of the world crop. Few people have enjoyed our native grapes in their unadulterated form, but practically all have tasted them in spirit.

Wild grapes grow everywhere in Texas. Stephen F. Austin observed that "nature seems to have intended Texas for a vineyard" (English 1986). Nineteenth-century explorers noted that in river bottoms, such as that of the Brazos, grapevines wove such dense networks that

ORIGIN OF SCIENTIFIC NAME	DESCRIPTION	HABITAT AND DISTRIBUTION
Vitis is the classical Latin name for the grape. **OTHER COMMON NAMES** Grapes, uvas. Common names for individual species are given in the text. **FAMILY** Vitaceae (Grape Family)	Woody-stemmed, perennial vines (high-climbing or clump-forming), some to 40' or more in length, or vinelike shrubs; panicles of small fragrant flowers followed by pulpy, 2- to 4-seeded berries, often arranged in dense clusters.	In a variety of soils, often along stream and river bottoms, hillsides, rocky slopes, and thickets, but also frequent along fencerows and in disturbed areas; throughout Texas, the U.S., and many parts of the world, mainly Northern Hemisphere (not counting cultivars).

The well-known mustang grape.

"it seemed . . . one could climb and walk at ease from tree to tree" (Taylor 1936). Reports of grapevine trunks as thick as a man's body were not uncommon. Some of the better-known wild Texas grapes include the larger-fruited mustang and muscadine, the more modest-sized summer and sweet mountain grapes, and the tiny gray-bark grapes.

The mustang grape (*Vitis mustangensis*) is perhaps the best known, as it is abundant in the eastern half of the state and produces vigorous, drought-resistant vines with small bunches of large grapes ($^1/_2$–$^3/_4$ inches in diameter). The skin of the fruit and the juice lying just beneath it are so acrid that the grapes both irritate the hands when harvested and burn the throat when tasted, earning them the moniker *cut-throat grapes.* Yet with copious amounts of sugar, the fruits

The variety of gray-bark grape that helped save the French wine industry.

make excellent pies, tarts, preserves, jellies, and wines. The muscadine or scuppernong grape (*V. rotundifolia*) of east Texas, which is distinct in having small (2–4 inches), rounded, unlobed leaves, is known for its sweet, musky-tasting fruit. The purple-black to bronze grapes, reaching 1 inch in diameter, are arranged not in true bunches but rather in clusters of seldom more than four. The fruits' arrangement, plus the habit of individual grapes maturing at different times and dropping when ripe, has discouraged the commercial propagation of this grape in large numbers throughout the Southeast. Summer or pigeon grape (*V. aestivalis*), a clump-forming vine of the eastern half of Texas, produces many bunches of modest-sized (roughly half-inch) fruit, which remain on the vine long after frost, wrinkled and shrunken, having become, in effect, raisins. Sweet mountain or champin grape (*V. monticola*), a Texas endemic, inhabits the Edwards Plateau. Its large clusters of dark blue (sometimes red) grapes are much sought after in the area and adorn trellises and fences. The gray-bark grape (*V. cinerea*), with bunches of tiny fruits ($^1/_8$–$^3/_8$ inch in diameter), grows throughout the eastern two-thirds of the state. A variety of this species (var. *helleri*), once known as *V. berlandieri*, is native to the limestone regions of central Texas and has had immense importance to the French wine industry.

Native American tribes and the majority of early (pre-1850) Anglo settlers in Texas saw wild grapes primarily as a source of food. The Mescalero Apache, like many southwestern tribes, consumed the fresh fruits of canyon grape (*Vitis arizonica*), which inhabits Texas in the Trans-Pecos. Indeed, prehistoric evidence from the Devils River area confirms that canyon grape was consumed as early as 7000 BCE. Other historic Texan tribes, such as the Caddo and Comanche, in addition to eating grapes fresh, would sun-dry them into raisins for storage. The Co-

manche historically made balls of raisins by pounding grapes with a pestle, forming balls of the mashed material, and then allowing these to dry on arbor roofs to be stored for winter. Early American settlers to our region, before cultivated fruits were available, used wild grapes to make pies and jellies.

The most interesting story that our wild Texas grapes have to tell, however, begins with wine making, which is peculiar for a state notorious for dry counties, long-neck beers, and whiskey. The Spanish get the credit for being the first wine makers in the state. In 1659 Franciscan priests had established the first permanent Spanish settlement in the El Paso area (at Ciudad Juárez) and began to plant Spanish vines for their sacramental wines. The grapes came to be known as mission or El Paso grapes and were praised by many visitors to the area over the ensuing centuries. Several subsequent missions in the area, such as Corpus Christi de la Isleta (now Ysleta), which is the oldest permanent settlement in Texas (est. 1682), were partly the result of the success of agriculture in this region.

To understand the subsequent wine history of Texas requires a quick detour to the East Coast. Early colonial American attempts at cultivating European grapes (*Vitis vinifera*) met with poor results. This was partly attributable to weather and soils, but mainly the problem was a phylloxera insect. Now called *Dactylasphaera vitifoliae*, the louse was native to America, and many of our grapes were partly, if not completely, immune to it. The sap-sucking, aphidlike insect generally produced only small galls on the underside of our native grape leaves, but it wreaked havoc on the thin-barked *vinifera* grapes, girdling the rootstocks and wilting the vines. As early as the eighteenth century, settlers had already started to domesticate varieties of wild American grapes, such as the fox grape of the eastern United States (*V. labrusca*), and to cross them with *vinifera* vines. Native fox grape refinements and crosses, such as Catawba and the immensely popular Concord, became commercially important in the East, while Southerners relied more on the muscadine. In Texas, glowing (and likely exaggerated) accounts of wines of "exquisite quality" appear during the earliest days of Anglo settlement (Holley 1836). Mid-nineteenth-century accounts of a Hill Country "fiery Texas wine" may refer to the use of our abundant mustang grape, which was also used to make a decent white wine of this period (English 1986). The town of Boerne and its surrounding vicinity produced at least 50,000 gallons of wine in one season toward the last quarter of the 1800s.

Texas' historic claim to viticulture fame came not from its own wine industry but rather from its rescue of another country's vines. Europeans, in their pursuit of new grape varieties and crosses, had unwittingly brought phylloxera to the Old World, where it first appeared in southern France in the mid-1860s. Over the next two decades, two-thirds of Europe's vineyards were destroyed, including practically all of those in southern France, where arguably many of the world's best wines were produced. Many

small vintners lost their livelihood; at least one-third of France's vineyards were never replaced. The French were desperate for a solution. They sent viticulturists to the United States in search of resistant rootstocks on which they could graft their many *vinifera* varieties. Originally, the disease-resistant fox grapes and our own native mustang grapes seemed to offer a solution, until it was realized that these did not flourish in the chalky soils of southern France. Most developed chlorosis, withered, and died.

Texas still saved the day. Thomas Volney Munson, a denizen of Denison, was a renowned grapevine expert. He was intimately familiar with our many native species, their growth habits, and commercial potential. In 1887 Mr. Munson accompanied the preeminent French scientist and viticulturist Pierre Viala on horseback on a collecting expedition along the Red River, directing him to the calcareous areas of the Hill Country where rootstocks of limestone-growing species could be obtained. Mr. Viala decided that two varieties of the gray-bark grape of central Texas (*Vitis cinerea* var. *cinerea*, and *V. c.* var. *helleri*) and the frost grape of northeast Texas (*V. vulpina*) would be the best candidates to save the French vines. Although many of the rootstocks did not do the trick directly, the cross-breeding of the Texan *V. berlandieri* (as *V. cinerea* var. *helleri* was then known) with various French vines was a smashing success. The resulting rootstocks yielded high-quality fruit and were resistant to both phylloxera and chlorosis. They were used to replant the entire Champagne, Charente, and

Cognac regions. T. V. Munson became known as "the man who saved the French vineyards" (McLeRoy and Renfro 2004). Practically all French and Italian (indeed, most European) grapevines are grown on grafted rootstocks of American (often Texan) heritage.

In 1889 Munson was only the second American to be awarded the prestigious French Legion of Honor for his efforts in helping France (the first was Thomas Edison, the third was Dwight Eisenhower). He is not only credited with saving the French wine industry but also was known as America's foremost grape authority, both botanically and agriculturally. He authored seminal works on grapes and viticulture, such as the landmark *Foundations of American Grape Culture* (1908), the standard reference on viticulture in the United States to this day. He also developed 300 new hybrid grape varieties (many of Texas natives), which is more than any other individual or agency. In his efforts to match grape varieties to particular climates and soils, and to imbue them with resistance to specific diseases and pathogens, he was said to be a century ahead of his time. He developed a strain of summer grape that allowed southern states to grow true bunch grapes for the first time. The T. V. Munson Memorial Vineyard and Viticulture and Enology Center at Grayson County College commemorates this man's work and still grows 65 of his original varieties.

Texas currently ranks fifth among American producers of wine, boasting nearly 150 commercial vineyards and 50 wineries scattered among six designated regions. The Hill Country, at 15,000 square miles, is the country's largest official American Viticultural Area. In 2004, the state produced well over a million gallons of wine, up from a paltry 14,000 gallons merely 25 years ago. The overwhelming majority of these grapes come from *vinifera* crosses, but Munson's hybrid rootstocks are some of the most widely used in the world today, and many contain our native heritage. Some Texas wineries are still experimenting with old Spanish crosses with our native grapes, and with native grapes themselves.

Approximately fifteen place names in Texas, including six towns and seven creeks, use the word *grape*. Grapevine in Tarrant County hosts the annual Grape Fest, touted as the largest wine festival in the Southwest.

SOURCES: Basehart 1974; Canonge 1958; English 1986; Foster 1995; Goodrich and Wiley 1834; Griffith 1954; Hester 1980; Holley 1836; Krochmal and Grierson 1961; La Vere 1998; Lipe 1979; Massey 1945; Maverick 1921; McLeRoy and Renfro 2004; Parks 1937; Rice 2004; Schulz 1928; Smithwick 1983; Sperry 1994; Taylor 1936; Tull 1999; Walters et al. 1990; Winkler 1949

Glossary

Given that a minimum of botanical, chemical, and medicinal terminology is unavoidable in a work such as this, a glossary of terms is necessary. In addition to the technical terms listed here, thumbnail sketches of just over 100 Native American tribes are provided. Very brief geographic and demographic information is given for tribes whose historic ranges remained largely outside Texas, while more inclusive information is provided for tribes that inhabited Texas (even briefly). A few biographical sketches of classical botanical authors are also included.

Abortifacient. A substance that produces the abortion of a fetus through uterine contractions.

Acetylation. A chemical reaction in which an acetyl functional group is introduced into an organic compound.

Acoma Indians. A Pueblo tribe numbering about 5000 living in west-central New Mexico.

Adventitious. Appearing in an unusual or unexpected place, such as buds or roots developing directly on the stem.

Aflatoxin. A toxin produced by many species of the fungus genus *Aspergillus* that infect certain foods and animal feeds, especially during harvesting and storage.

Aglycone. An organic compound, usually an alcohol or phenol, that combines with a sugar to form a glycoside.

Ague. An old medical term for malaria.

Akimel O'odham. The "people of the river," historically called the Pima, an indigenous tribe along the Gila and Salt rivers of southern Arizona, and also Sonora, Mexico; the largest group on the U.S. side, together with the Piipaash (Maricopa), number 16,000 and currently live just south of Phoenix.

Akokisa Indians. A subgroup of the Atakapa, once living west of the lower Neches River to the Trinity River in southeastern Texas. Some maintain that the Han Indians, among whom Alvar Núñez Cabeza de Vaca lived, were likely a tribe of Akokisa.

Alabama Indians. A tribe from central Alabama, after which the state is named, forced to relocate to Texas and Oklahoma by the early 1800s. See Alabama-Coushatta Indians.

Alabama-Coushatta Indians. Two closely allied and highly intermarried tribes that emigrated from Alabama, eventually arriving in the Big Thicket in southeast Texas in the 1780s; in the 1850s they were granted a reservation near Livingston in Polk County, where currently approximately 550 tribe members live.

Algonquin Indians. In the strictest sense, a Native American tribe historically inhabiting the Ottawa River valley of Quebec and Ontario, and the northern tributaries of the Saint Lawrence River; currently, about 11,000 still live in Quebec and Ontario. Broadly speaking, any tribe speaking an Algonquian language in the eastern half of North America, from Canada south to the Carolinas, from the Atlantic coast west as far as the Rockies.

Alkaloid. A naturally occurring organic compound, often bitter in taste, produced in plants; frequently has a pharmacological effect on humans and animals.

Allelopathy. The inhibition of development of a plant species through the chemical compounds released by another (usually in the soil).

Alternate. With respect to leaves, an arrangement in which a single leaf appears at a node, the direction of the leaves alternating from side to side along the stem.

Amphitropical. Existing on both sides of the tropics, but not in the area between the tropics.

Anabolic. Stimulates constructive metabolism, building up organs and tissues.

Analgesic. Relieving pain by quieting nerve sensory centers; any substance that produces this effect.

Anasazi Indians. An older term for the ancestral Puebloans, a prehistoric Native American culture, which reached a zenith between the tenth and twelfth centuries CE, centered in the Four Corners region of the American Southwest; renowned for cliff dwellings and stone houses.

Anemia. Deficiency in hemoglobin, usually accompanied by reduced number of red blood cells, causing pallor and weakness.

Angiosperm. A plant that has a true flower with a fruit that encloses its seed.

Aniline dyes. Dyes synthesized from coal tar; starting in the mid-nineteenth century, these replaced traditional natural dyes on account of their price, greater range of colors, and superior properties.

Annual. A plant that completes its growth cycle (from seed to flower) in one year.

Anthelmintic. A substance that kills or expels intestinal worms.

Anther. The pollen-bearing portion of the flower at the tip of the stamen.

Anthocyanin. Red, purple, or blue water-soluble pigment found in many roots, stems, flowers, and fruits.

Apache Indians. A collective name for several southwestern U.S. tribes divided into two main groups, the Western (Navajo, San Carlos, Chiricahua, and Mescalero) and the Eastern (Jicarilla, Lipan, and Kiowa). The term *Apache* is used in this work only when more specific designations were lacking in references.

Arapaho Indians. In historic times, a tribe inhabiting the eastern plains of Colorado and Wyoming that had adopted the Plains culture of hunting buffalo on horseback.

Areole. On a cactus, a small area, raised or depressed, where spines appear.

Arikara Indians. An agricultural tribe, speaking a Caddoan language, that cultivated corn on the South Dakota plains for centuries; currently living with the Mandan and Hidatsa on reservation land in North Dakota.

Aryans. An ancient (ca. 2500 BCE) Indo-European culture.

Astringent. Contracting and hardening tissues, reducing secretions and inflammation; any substance that produces this effect.

Atakapa Indians. A native tribe occupying coastal territory from southwestern Louisiana west as far as the Trinity River until the early 1800s; hunted game, fish, roots, and berries, but also planted crops; decimated by 1850s largely from disease; by 1908 only nine known descendants in Louisiana.

Banner. The largest upper petal of the pealike flowers of the Fabaceae (bean family).

BCE. In dates, Before Common Era (equivalent to BC).

Bidai Indians. A tribe, possibly kin to the Atakapa, that inhabited the area between the Brazos and Trinity rivers in southeastern Texas; epidemics had decimated the population by the early nineteenth century; survivors were absorbed into the Akokisa or ended up in Indian Territory (Oklahoma), where their identity was lost.

Blackfoot Indians. A tribe (currently 25,000 large) that adopted the Plains Indians culture in the early 1800s, inhabiting the eastern slopes of the Rockies from northern Wyoming to southern Canada; reservation in northwestern Montana.

Blackland Prairie. In Texas the vegetational area running north-south from the Red River to approximately San Antonio, characterized by rich, black, heavy clay soils, once dominated by tallgrass prairie. Ideally suited to agriculture, practically all of the grassland has been plowed under for cultivation; less than 1% remains, making the tallgrass prairie one of the most endangered large ecosystems in North America.

Bract. A modified or reduced leaf, usually just below the flower and sepals; some bracts cluster around the flower base, as in sunflowers; others are so showy that they are mistaken for the petals themselves, as in dogwood and poinsettia.

Bromeliad. A member of the bromeliad family, native to the tropical and subtropical areas of the New World, which includes pineapple; roughly half the species are epiphytes.

Caddo Indians. The term *Caddo* now refers generically to a group of 25 tribes that originally inhabited much of east Texas and western Louisiana; historically these tribes were characterized by intense agriculture, sedentary living, sophisticated technology, long-distance trading, and complex social, religious, and political structures. By 1859 the tribes had been forcibly removed to a reservation in western Oklahoma, where they number about 4000 today.

Cahuilla Indians. A desert tribe from southern California, now Riverside and San Diego counties, numbering about 2400 spread across nine reservations.

Calyx. The outermost envelope of the flower, usually meaning the sepals, taken collectively; when present, often cup-shaped and green.

Cambium. The thin layer of rapidly dividing cells that form wood and bark.

Capoque. One of two bands of Karankawa Indians along the Texas coast identified by Alvar Núñez Cabeza de Vaca as his captors; usually spelled "Coaque" in reference works.

Carboniferous. The geologic period from 350 million to 290 million years ago, when bark-bearing trees made their first appearance; named for its extensive coal beds.

Carminative. A substance that reduces formation of gas in, or expels it from, stomach and intestines.

Carpel. Broadly speaking, a division of a fruit.

Carrizo Indians. One of the many Coahuiltecan groups of northeastern Mexico and adjacent southern Texas; a 1789 census of Laredo included 111 Carrizos.

Catawba Indians. A tribe historically along the banks of the Catawba River in North and South Carolina; currently living near Rock Hill, South Carolina.

Catkin. A slim, flexible, usually drooping, cylindrical cluster of small, inconspicuous flowers that lack petals.

Caustic. Destructive of tissue to which the substance is applied.

CE. Common Era (equivalent to AD).

Cenozoic. The geologic era in which we are currently living, having started approximately 65 million years ago with the extinction of the dinosaurs.

Central Mineral Region. An area of central Texas (primarily in Llano and Mason counties) having granitic outcrops, which weather into sandy soils.

Charruco Indians. An unidentified tribe, possibly Karankawan, among whom Alvar Núñez Cabeza de Vaca lived; believed to have been located near Matagorda Bay.

Cherokee Indians. A tribe whose original homeland comprised much of what is now Kentucky, Tennessee, northern Alabama and Georgia, and western portions of Virginia and the Carolinas; reservations in eastern Oklahoma and western North Carolina; currently considered the largest tribe in the United States, with more than 700,000 who claim at least partial affiliation.

Cheyenne Indians. A Plains tribe that historically inhabited lands from southern Colorado to South Dakota; reservations in southeastern Montana and central Oklahoma.

Chichimeca Indians. A generic term that the Aztecs and colonial Spaniards used to denote any number of various seminomadic hunter-gatherers of northern Mexico.

Chickasaw Indians. A tribe originally inhabiting northern Mississippi and western Tennessee, forcibly removed to south-central Oklahoma in the mid-1800s, where their reservation is today.

Chihuahuan Desert. The largest desert in North America, covering a vast portion of north-central Mexico; in the United States it includes the Trans-Pecos of Texas, southern New Mexico, and a tiny portion of southeastern Arizona; characterized by yuccas, agaves, cacti, and creosote bushes.

Chippewa Indians. A popular name for the Ojibwa Indians; originally from the Lake Superior area, they now stretch from Michigan to Montana, and in Canada from western Quebec to eastern British Columbia.

Chiricahua Apache. Several bands of Apache in historic times inhabiting southeastern Arizona, southwestern New Mexico, and northern Mexico; some of the last Native Americans to resist U.S. government control; currently living in Oklahoma, Arizona, and New Mexico.

Chlorosis. An abnormal condition in which plants turn yellowish through insufficient chlorophyll production, usually brought on by nutrient deficiency.

Choctaw Indians. An indigenous people historically inhabiting what is now Alabama, Louisiana, and Mississippi; current descendants number around 175,000 on lands in Alabama, Mississippi, and especially Oklahoma.

Cholla. Any of several species of *Opuntia* having cylindrical, instead of flattened, stems.

Chumash Indians. A tribe historically inhabiting southern coastal California and several Channel Islands; current reservation in area.

Cladode. A stem or branch having the general form or function of a leaf, as in the flattened green stems (pads) of prickly pear.

Clone. A plant or group of plants that are the vegetatively produced progeny (as in offshoots) of a single individual; clones are genetically identical to the parent.

Coahuiltecan Indians. The term *Coahuiltecan* includes hundreds of individually named, small bands of autonomous hunter-gatherers of southern Texas and northeastern Mexico, who were displaced by Spaniards from the south and by Apache from the north. The impoverished state of these groups in the historical record (largely from the Spanish explorers and friars of the seventeenth and eighteenth centuries) does not necessarily reflect accurately their original lifestyles, though it is generally agreed that the region is one of the poorest of indigenous North America. It is even unclear whether the term describes a uniform culture or language. By 1800, epidemics, warfare, slavery, and intermarriage had caused these groups to die out, or at least their tribal names (more than 1000 have been recorded) disappeared from the record; however, descendants of these groups doubtless live on in scattered communities throughout the area.

Cochiti Indians. One of the Pueblo

tribes of northern New Mexico, currently numbering about 1000.

Cocopah Indians. A Yuman tribe historically from Baja California, Mexico, that settled at the mouth of the Colorado River; currently, three reservations near Yuma, Arizona, number 1000 members.

Colic. In humans, an affliction in which babies cry incessantly, variously attributed to abdominal gas, acid reflux, or immature nervous systems; in horses, any abdominal pain or gastrointestinal distress (from various causes) that may require surgery and frequently leads to premature death.

Comanche Indians. A collection of Native American bands emerging as a distinct people just before 1700, when they acquired the horse and split from the Shoshone people in Wyoming. Their mastery of horsemanship and buffalo-hunting took them to the southern Plains of western Kansas and Oklahoma, northern and central Texas (from the Panhandle south to San Antonio), and northeastern New Mexico, pushing the eastern Apache who were living there at the time farther southward. Once numbering 20,000 in the mid-nineteenth century, they were reduced within 25 years to one-tenth that number by disease and the eradication of the buffalo before they were placed on a reservation in Oklahoma, which was later dissolved through white encroachment. Many Comanche (15,000–20,000) still live in Oklahoma, Texas, and California.

Compound leaf. A leaf that is composed of two or more leaflets. *Pinnately compound* describes leaflets that are distributed along both sides of a long axis, featherlike. *Twice compound* (or bipinnate) indicates that the leaflets are again subdivided along a secondary axis.

Coprolite. Petrified animal or human fecal material.

Cora Indians. A Native American tribe, numbering around 16,000, currently inhabiting west-central Mexico; considered one of the Chichimecan tribes.

Cortex. Generally, the outer portion of a stem, such as the rind or bark.

Cossacks. A community of mainly Slavic peoples inhabiting the southern steppes of Eastern Europe and Russia from the fifteenth century onward.

Crassulacean acid metabolism (CAM). The particular pathway of photosynthesis used by only about 6% of all plant species, but by 98% of all cacti, characterized by the gathering of carbon dioxide at night to be processed during the day.

Cree Indians. A Native American tribe that ranges from the Rockies to the Atlantic Ocean in both the United States and Canada; currently the largest First Nations tribe in Canada, with more than 200,000 members.

Creek Indians (Confederacy). An older name for the Muscogee, a loose confederacy of indigenous peoples historically inhabiting what is now Georgia, Alabama, and Tennessee; currently numbering 50,000–60,000 in Oklahoma and Alabama.

Cretaceous. The geologic period from 144 million to 65 million years ago, when flowering plants began to flourish; the period ends in the famous Cretaceous-Tertiary extinction event, in which the dinosaurs became extinct.

Croup. A respiratory disease of young children characterized by a hoarse, barking cough and difficult breathing.

Crow Indians. A tribe of Native Americans who historically dwelled on the upper Plains; current reservation is in Montana; tribal enrollment includes approximately 10,000 members.

Cucurbitacins. A class of extremely bitter secondary compounds common in the cucumber family, believed to have evolved to deter insect predation.

Culm. The hollow or pithy stem (the straw) found in grasses.

Cyanogenetic lipids. Fats that are capable of producing toxic cyanide.

Cyanogenic glycoside. The often-toxic chemical compound cyanide, as it

is usually found in plants, bound to a sugar molecule; presumably a defense against herbivores.

Dakota Sioux. See Sioux Indians.

Decoction. An extract usually obtained by adding vegetable matter to water, bringing the mixture to a boil for 10–15 minutes, then allowing it to cool before straining out the vegetable matter.

Delaware Indians. Also known as Lenape Indians, loosely organized bands of Native Americans historically, and currently, inhabiting lands around the Delaware and Hudson rivers in New Jersey and New York.

Deliriant. A substance that excites cerebral functions, confusing the mentality.

Demulcent. A substance that soothes, relaxes, and protects irritated or inflamed mucosal linings (such as sore throat).

Dendroclimatology. The science of analyzing trees to extract data about climate, especially the reconstruction of historical climate conditions by examining tree rings.

Depurient. A substance said to remove impurities, cleanse sores, or purify the blood, as in a tonic.

Devonian. The geologic period from approximately 415 million to 350 million years ago, in which the first seed-bearing plants appeared.

Diaphoretic. A substance that brings on sweating or perspiration.

Dioecious. Having male flowers on one plant and female flowers on a different plant.

Dioscorides, Pedanius (ca. 40–90 CE). A Greek medical doctor and botanist who traveled extensively, servicing the armies of the Emperor Nero. His five-volume De Materia Medica is considered one of the most influential pharmacological books in Western history, emphasizing the medicinal uses of plants; it remained in use through the sixteenth century.

Disk flower/floret. In the sunflower family, the small, tubular flowers lacking

rays that compose the center part of the flower head.

Distichous. In leaves, occurring in two rows on opposite sides of the stem.

Diuretic. A substance that stimulates the flow of urine.

Drench. A veterinary term for administering a draft of medicine by force.

Dripline. With trees, the circle formed on the ground just beneath the outermost branches, the entire area of which demarcates where the majority of the tree's fine feeder roots lie.

Dropsy. An older term for edema, the swelling of organs or tissue due to an accumulation of excess lymph fluid.

Drupe. A one-seeded fruit with a stony seed, fleshy middle part, and outer skin, such as a cherry or plum.

Dysentery. An infectious disease marked by inflammation of the lower intestines and severe, hemorrhagic diarrhea.

Ecotone. The transitional zone where two large plant communities meet, such as grasslands and forest.

Ecotype. A population within one widespread species adapted to a given habitat, usually that of climate or soil.

Edwards Plateau. The region of west-central Texas, roughly between the Pecos and Colorado rivers, consisting primarily of limestone and shallow soils with elevations to 3000 feet; considered the southernmost unit of the Great Plains.

Emesis. Vomiting.

Emetic. Causing or producing vomiting; any substance that produces this effect.

Emmenagogue. A medicine that stimulates, strengthens, or restores menstrual discharge.

Endemic. Confined to, or native to, a given region or area.

Entire. With regard to leaves, indicates smooth margins, lacking teeth.

Epiphyte. A nonparasitic organism that grows on or is attached to a living plant, which it depends on for support.

Expectorant. Controls coughing usually

by increasing and expelling bronchial secretions; any substance that produces this effect.

Febrifuge. A substance that reduces fever.

Fistula. With regard to horses, any of various pus-filled inflammations characterized by the formation of passages through the tissues to the skin's surface.

Flavonoid. Any of a number of water-soluble plant pigments beneficial to health.

Forb. Any herb that is not a grass or sedge.

Gallinaceous birds. Birds found in the order Galliformes, which contains chickens, grouse, quail, pheasants, and turkeys.

Gastroenteritis. A general term for inflammation or infection of the stomach and intestines.

Genus. The taxonomic category between family and species that comprises one or more (sometimes hundreds) of species.

Glochids. Tiny hairlike, deciduous, barbed spines or bristles.

Glycoalkaloid. One of many bitter-tasting poisons found in species of the potato or nightshade family (Solanaceae).

Glycoside. Any of a group of organic compounds in which a sugar part is bound to one or more nonsugar substances (aglycones); many plants store important chemicals as inactive glycosides.

Guaraní Indians. An indigenous tribe historically found in what is now Paraguay and northern Argentina; contemporary populations still in Paraguay.

Gum arabic. A natural gum exuded from the bark of sub-Saharan species of *Acacia* trees; used in the food industry as a thickener and stabilizer, but also utilized in pharmaceuticals, pigments, and inks.

Gymnosperm. A plant that lacks a true flower and has exposed seeds (such as a pine or yew tree).

Hallucinogen. A substance that produces hallucinations, a sensory experience of something that does not exist in reality, but appears entirely realistic to the observer.

Han Indians. One of two bands of Karankawa (some claim Atakapa or Akokisa) Indians along the Texas coast identified by Alvar Núñez Cabeza de Vaca as his captors.

Hasinai Caddo. One of the three confederacies of the Caddo, inhabiting east Texas in the area from Nacogdoches (originally a Caddo settlement) southwest to the Neches River; given the name *Tejas* by the Spaniards, based on the Caddo word for "friend," after which Texas is named.

Haustorium. A suckerlike attachment organ that parasitic plants use to draw nutrients from their host plants.

Havasupai Indians. A Yuman tribe of more than 600 people currently living along the southern side of the Grand Canyon, just east of the Hualapai Reservation, in northern Arizona.

Heliotropic. In botany, growing toward the sun, or tracking the sun's motion from east to west; largely replaced now by *phototropic*.

Hematological. Having to do with blood or blood-forming organs.

Hidatsa Indians. An indigenous tribe primarily inhabiting North Dakota; allied and intermarried with the Mandans, both tribes living together with the Arikara (known as the Three Affiliated Tribes) on a reservation in North Dakota.

Hippocrates (ca. 460–370 BCE). Known as the father of medicine; through careful observation, first separated the art of healing from pure superstition and mysticism, in ancient Greece.

Holocene. The current geologic epoch, dating from approximately 9500 BCE (when most of the Pleistocene glaciers had retreated) to the present.

Hopi Indians. A Pueblo tribe in northeastern Arizona, famous for their stone houses atop mesas, which they have inhabited continuously for over a millennium; currently number more than 11,000.

Houma Indians. An indigenous tribe historically located around the mouth of the Mississippi River; the Houma peoples, not yet federally recognized, currently live in south-central Louisiana.

Hualapai Indians. A Yuman tribe of more than 1300 people currently living along the southern side of the Grand Canyon in northern Arizona.

Huichol Indians. An indigenous tribe of approximately 25,000 living in west-central Mexico in the Sierra Madre Occidental, where they have retained much of their original culture through deliberate isolation; considered one of the Chichimecan tribes.

Hydrolyze. To undergo hydrolysis, the process in which a chemical compound is broken down into two or more simpler compounds by reacting with water.

Hydrophilic. Highly attracted to or dwelling in water.

Hypoglycemic. An agent that lowers levels of glucose in the blood.

Impetigo. A contagious skin disease, common among young children, characterized by pimplelike, pustular eruptions.

Inflorescence. Commonly used to describe an arrangement of flowers along the plant stem.

Infusion. The steeping or soaking of vegetable matter in water, using boiling water (for hot infusions) or room-temperature water (for cold infusions, usually allowed to steep overnight).

Internode. The space on the stem between two nodes.

Interspecific. Between different species.

Intoxicant. A substance (usually a liquor or drug) that temporarily reduces physical and mental control, causing stupefaction, stimulation, or excitement.

Iroquois Indians. A confederacy of

(currently) six indigenous nations historically based in upstate New York, Ontario, and Quebec; numbering about 75,000.

Isleta Indians. One of the Pueblo tribes of northern New Mexico, just south of Albuquerque, currently numbering around 3000.

Isoquinoline. A heterocyclic, aromatic, organic compound that appears in many naturally occurring alkaloids, such as morphine; isoquinoline derivatives are frequently used in medicines.

Jumano Indians. A poorly understood group of Native Americans that may have comprised several separate and distinct peoples, including both sedentary Puebloan-like farming peoples (along the Rio Grande and Rio Conchos valleys in west Texas and Mexico), as well as nomadic, trading, buffalo-hunting Plains groups who may have engaged in seasonal farming on the southern Plains as far east as the Colorado River. What little is known of the Jumano comes from Spanish sources in the sixteenth and seventeenth centuries. The term *Jumano* virtually disappears by the middle of the eighteenth century; various theories propose that the peoples were absorbed into other groups, such as the Apache (their traditional enemies) or the Kiowa.

Jurassic. The geologic period extending from 206 million to 144 million years ago, in which conifers were dominant.

Karankawa Indians. A term applied to several nomadic groups of now-extinct indigenous people along the Texas coast who shared a common language and culture, including, among others, the Capoque. Strikingly tall (over 6 feet) and powerful warriors, they primarily inhabited barrier islands and the neighboring mainland between Galveston Bay and Corpus Christi Bay, where they depended on hunting, gathering, and fishing. Spanish attempts to Christianize the Karankawa in missions were largely unsuccessful, as were attempts by Mexican authorities to make peace with them. Anglo pioneers, including Stephen F. Austin, largely believed extermination was the answer. Encroachment and warfare with both settlers and other tribes led to their eventual annihilation around 1860.

Keresan Indians. Seven of the Pueblo tribes in northern New Mexico that speak various dialects of the same (Keresan) language. Divided into two main groups, the Western Keresan (Acoma and Laguna) and the Eastern Keresan (Cochiti, San Felipe, Santo Domingo, Zia-Santa, Zia Pueblo).

Kickapoo Indians. Originally an indigenous tribe of the Michigan area of the Great Lakes; migrated southwestward, splintering many times into separate tribes. Currently, the officially recognized tribes in the United States are in Kansas, Oklahoma, and Texas, while other groups exist in Arizona and Coahuila, Mexico. Total tribal membership is about 3500. The Texas tribe resides just south of Eagle Pass, numbering more than 400 people, but did not become federally recognized until 1983. In effect, the Texas land is a summer home for the seminomadic Mexican tribe that considers El Nacimiento, Mexico (130 miles southwest of Eagle Pass), their primary residence. The Oklahoman, Texan, and Mexican Kickapoo are considered to have some of the most traditional lifestyles of extant Indians, largely shunning contemporary lifestyles and government schools.

Kiowa Indians. An indigenous tribe originally from the north (Montana, South Dakota) that progressively pushed or was forced southward, adopting a nomadic Plains Indian lifestyle. During Texas pioneer times, they inhabited lands from eastern New Mexico through the plains of the Panhandle to Oklahoma, but they were famous for their long-distance raids well beyond this region, from Mexico to Canada. After 1790 they were allied with the Comanche. Currently 12,000 members live in southwestern Oklahoma.

Kiowa-Apache Indians. A small group of indigenous peoples speaking an Apachean language, from the earliest historical records allied with and functioning as a band of the Kiowa. Apart from their language, they were virtually indistinguishable from the Kiowa, inhabiting the Texas Panhandle and southwestern Oklahoma in the nineteenth century.

Lactones. See Sesquiterpene lactones.

Laguna Indians. One of the Pueblo tribes of northern New Mexico, west of Albuquerque, currently numbering more than 7000.

Lakota. See Sioux Indians.

Lignan. A group of chemical compounds found in plants and one of two major classes of phytoestrogens, which are antioxidants found in a variety of well-known foods, such as flax seeds, soybeans, and broccoli.

Lignin. A chemical compound that strengthens the cell walls of plants; one of the most abundant organic compounds on Earth; accounts for up to one-third the dry mass of wood.

Linnaeus, Carolus (1707–1778). Swedish botanist, physician, and zoologist, known as the father of modern taxonomy; established the convention, now universally accepted, of binomial nomenclature, in which all living organisms have a generic and a specific name.

Lipan Apache. The only Apache tribe whose lands were primarily within Texas, the Lipan inhabited the region between the Colorado River and the Rio Grande by the mid-eighteenth century, where they posed a constant threat to Spanish colonists at towns like San Antonio, before the Comanche and others pushed them farther southward, eventually into Mexico. They had adopted a Plains, buffalo-hunting lifestyle, but retained some seasonal farming. Currently, a small number of Lipan live on the Mescalero Apache Reservation in New Mexico.

Lobature. With leaves, the degree to which they have lobed margins.

Lobed. Having rounded divisions or indentations that do not break completely with the continuity of the structure.

Luperinid beetles. Beetles in the Luperini tribe; some, such as cucumber beetles, also known as corn rootworms, are highly destructive to agricultural crops such as beans, corn, cotton, and cucumbers.

Lycaenid butterfly. Any butterfly in the family Lycaenidae, which contains more than 6000 species worldwide (commonly called gossamer-winged butterflies).

Macropsia. A condition affecting vision in which objects appear larger than normal.

Mandan Indians. A sedentary indigenous tribe historically inhabiting the banks of the Missouri River in North and South Dakota; joined the Hidatsa and Arikara on a reservation in North Dakota; the last full-blooded Mandan is said to have died in 1971, but several thousand of mixed ancestry are still alive.

Maricopa Indians. See Piipaash Indians.

Mast. In botanical and horticultural contexts, refers to the seeds and fruits produced by trees and shrubs that are consumed by animals (but especially acorns by hogs).

Mescalero Apache Indians. Several bands of Apache in historic times inhabiting southeastern New Mexico and the northern edge of the Trans-Pecos in Texas, especially the Guadalupe Mountains; current reservation, numbering more than 3100 people, is in south-central New Mexico.

Meskwaki. An indigenous tribe known as the Fox by the French and Anglos; historically inhabiting lands in Michigan and Wisconsin, they merged with the closely related Sac (Sauk) Indians; today about 4000 live in Oklahoma, Kansas, and Iowa.

Mesocarp. The middle layer of the fruit wall, generally anything between the seed and the skin.

Mitogen. A chemical that stimulates cells to divide.

Mohs scale. Developed in the early nineteenth century by Friedrich Mohs, a rating scale that determines mineral hardness by measuring the hardest material a mineral can scratch (talc rates 1, diamond rates 10). The silica appearing on the surface of horsetail rates 4, equivalent in hardness to fluorite.

Mojave Desert. Comprises southeastern California, southern Nevada, and parts of western Arizona and Utah; the tree-sized yucca known as Joshua tree is considered characteristic, but it occurs only at certain elevations; some do not consider the Mojave a distinct desert.

Monotypic. A taxonomic group that has only one type; in botany, a monotypic genus contains only one species, and a monotypic family is composed of only one genus.

Mountain Pima. An indigenous tribe of the Sierra Madre Occidental, on the border of the states of Chihuahua and Sonora, Mexico; linguistically and culturally related to the O'odham of Arizona and Sonora.

Mycorrhizal fungi. Fungi that have a mutually beneficial relationship with a plant, in which tiny filaments from the fungi colonize the roots of the host plant, assisting the plant with mineral and water absorption, while providing the fungi access to the plant's nutrients.

Narcotic. A substance that tends to paralyze the nervous system and, in various doses, numbs the senses, relieves pain, induces sleep, or causes death; in legal contexts the term may refer to opium, cocaine, marijuana, or any illegal drug, whether or not a narcotic in the medical sense.

Natchez Indians. An indigenous agricultural, mound-building tribe living along the banks of the Mississippi River in Louisiana near the town that bears the same name; eventually decimated by French settlers and absorbed into neighboring tribes.

Navajo Indians. The second-largest Native American tribe in North America, approaching 300,000 members, currently living in the Four Corners region of the Southwest.

Neurotoxin. Any toxin that specifically affects nerve cells; many venoms (from snakes, bees, scorpions, etc.) contain neurotoxins.

Node. The joint of a stem, where branches, leaves, thorns, or flowers may attach.

Obovate. Of leaves, shaped like an egg, with the narrow end at the base.

Omaha Indians. An indigenous tribe that historically lived in Missouri, Iowa, and Nebraska; about 3000 still live on a reservation in Nebraska.

O'odham Indians. A term that includes both the Akimel O'odham (Pima) and Tohono O'odham (Papago) tribes.

Osage Indians. An indigenous tribe that historically inhabited the southern half of Missouri and northern half of Arkansas, including eastern parts of Kansas and Oklahoma; currently the Osage Nation, numbering 10,000, is centered in north-central Oklahoma.

Oto Indians. A tribe of Native Americans that split off from the Winnebago of the Great Lakes region and moved southwestward to eastern Nebraska, where they were the first native tribe encountered by the Lewis and Clark expedition; together with the Missouri Indians, with whom they share a reservation in north-central Oklahoma, they number more than 1400.

Otomí Indians. An indigenous people of central Mexico, scattered among the states of Hidalgo, México, Puebla, Querétaro, Tlaxcala, and Veracruz.

Ovate. Of leaves, shaped like an egg, with the wider end at the base.

Paiute Indians. Paiutes are indigenous Americans divided into two large cultural groups, the Northern Paiute (California, Nevada, and Oregon) and the Southern Paiute (Arizona, California, Nevada, and Utah). The two groups are actually more closely related to other tribes (Shoshone and Ute, respectively) than they are to each other. Several reservations are scattered across several of these states.

Pale. A chafflike scale or bract common on the flower heads of many members of the sunflower family.

Palsy. Any of several muscular conditions characterized by partial paralysis, loss of feeling, and uncontrolled body movements (such as tremors or shaking), commonly seen in hands, arms, and legs.

Panicle. An elongate, many branched, loose clustering of flowers (or fruit).

Pawnee Indians. Historically a tribe, largely sedentary and agricultural, that lived along the Platte River in present-day Nebraska; currently 2500 live in Oklahoma.

Payaya Indians. One of the Coahuiltecan tribes that ranged from San Antonio, Texas, southwestward to the Frio River and beyond; most records are from the San Antonio area of the eighteenth century.

Pedicel. A stalk that supports a single flower within a flower cluster.

Peduncle. The general term for the stem or stalk that supports a single flower or a flower cluster.

Pemmican. A foodstuff, capable of long storage, widely used across many tribes of North America, consisting of dried, pulverized meat, rendered fat, and usually dried fruits or nuts.

Perennial. A plant that lives several growing seasons (years) and that does not perish after blooming and fruiting.

Petiole. The stalk of a leaf or base of the blade.

Phenolic. A substance derived from or containing phenol, an aromatic, water-soluble, crystalline solid usually derived from coal tar or benzene. Phenol, formerly known as carbolic acid, is toxic and has a long history of use as a disinfectant or antiseptic.

Phloem. The food-conducting tissue in a plant.

Phototropic. Growing in a particular direction in relation to light; most plant shoots grow toward the light (positive phototropism) while roots grow away from the light (negative phototropism).

Phytobezoar. A bezoar is a rounded gastric concretion or stone commonly found in the stomach or intestines of most ruminant animals, but it can also appear in humans; the prefix *phyto* indicates a plant origin (from leaves, vegetables, seeds, or fibers).

Piipaash Indians. Indigenous peoples, until recently called Maricopa, historically inhabiting the Colorado River in Arizona; currently living with the Akimel O'odham, with whom they have been allied since the nineteenth century, along the Gila and Salt rivers of southern Arizona.

Pima Indians. See Mountain Pima and Akimel O'odham.

Pinnately compound. See Compound leaf.

Pistil. The female reproductive part of a flower, consisting of an ovary, a stalklike style, and a stigma, where the pollen is received.

Playa lakes. Small, round depressions that temporarily fill with rain, common on the southern High Plains of the Texas Panhandle and eastern New Mexico.

Pleistocene. The geologic epoch from 1.8 million to approximately 11,500 years before the present, characterized by repeated glaciation.

Pliny the Elder (23–79 CE). Roman general and natural philosopher who completed his encyclopedic, 37-volume *Historia Naturalis* in 77 CE, just before he died investigating the eruption of Mount Vesuvius; the monumental work covered anthropology, astronomy, botany, gardening, geography, horticulture, medicinals, metals, stones, and zoology.

Polycyclic aromatic hydrocarbons. Chemical compounds primarily formed through the incomplete combustion of carbon; widespread organic pollutants, many of which are suspected of causing cancer.

Polypeptide. A long series of molecules, or peptides, formed from defined linkages of amino acids.

Polysaccharide. A relatively complex carbohydrate composed of simple sugars; e.g., starch, cellulose.

Pome. A fleshy, nonsplitting fruit that develops from a compound inferior ovary, such as an apple or pear.

Ponca Indians. Historically a tribe, largely sedentary and agricultural, that lived along the Niobrara River in northern Nebraska; currently more than 4000 have at least partial tribal affiliation, with many living in Nebraska and Oklahoma.

Post Oak Savannah. A belt of vegetation stretching from the northeast corner of Texas southwestward to south-central portions of the state, characterized by post oak-hickory forests interspersed with grasses; essentially the ecotone, or transitional zone, between the deciduous forests to the east and the prairie grasslands to the west.

Potherb. A green, often leafy vegetable used in cooking, usually boiled or sautéed, like spinach.

Poultice. An external application of organic material, usually soft, moist, and often heated; often held in place by cloth or bandage.

Psychotropic. Any substance that acts on the central nervous system that affects mental processes, such as changes in perception, consciousness, mood, and behavior.

Pteridophyte. A vascular plant that neither flowers nor bears seeds, but reproduces from spores, such as mosses, horsetails, and ferns.

Pubescence. In botany, the state of being covered with fine hairs.

Pueblo Indians. An inclusive term for any of the more than two dozen tribes, now mainly in New Mexico and Arizona, who traditionally built stone houses and subsisted on agriculture; famous examples include the Acoma, Hopi, Taos, and Zuni.

Purgative. A laxative; a substance that causes evacuation of the bowels.

Quapaw Indians. A tribe historically from eastern Arkansas along the Mississippi River; other tribes referred to the Quapaw as "Akansea" whence Arkansas derives its name; currently approximately 1400 live in northeastern Oklahoma.

Quinolizidine alkaloids. A specific class of alkaloids based on a quinolizide structure; usually bitter tasting and toxic to animals, these alkaloids may be present as a defense mechanism for the plant.

Raceme. An elongated inflorescence, each flower being attached to the stem with pedicels.

Ray flowers/florets. In the sunflower family, the flowers with rays (petals) that usually occupy the outer perimeter of the flower head.

Rhizomatous. Bearing a rhizome.

Rhizome. An underground stem capable of producing leaf shoots on the upper surface and roots on the lower.

Ringworm. Any of several contagious skin diseases, characterized by ring-shaped eruptions, brought on by parasitic fungi.

Rosette. As used here, a cluster or whorl of leaves at the base of a plant, especially when a clearly defined stem or trunk is absent, or hidden, as in cabbage and many agaves.

San Diego Indians. Any of numerous tribes across three main divisions (and three languages) now referred to as Kumeyaay, who historically inhabited southern California, Baja California, and Sonora; currently there are thirteen Kumeyaay reservations in southern San Diego County and four more in Baja.

Sapogenin. A nonsugar portion of a saponin usually obtained through hydrolysis; can be used as a starting point in the synthesis of steroid hormones.

Saponin. Any of various amorphous glucosidal compounds of steroid structure, frequently found in plants, characterized by an ability to form emulsions and soapy froth in water.

Savannah. A grassland with occasional, widely spaced trees, or with trees and shrubs in small clumps.

Scape. A naked flowering stalk arising from the ground, common in the lily family.

Screwworm. The larvae of certain flies that infest the open cuts or wounds of domestic livestock (and humans) and feed on the living flesh; can be fatal without treatment.

Seminole Indians. Originally a tribe of Creek Indians who, at the encouragement of the English, attacked native tribes inhabiting Spanish lands in Florida and occupied their lands. These Creeks absorbed remnants of other indigenous peoples of the area, as well as runaway slaves, and gradually became regarded as a separate tribe. Most of the Seminole were forcibly removed to Oklahoma in the 1800s, but a small contingent remained behind in Florida.

Seri Indians. An indigenous group inhabiting the mainland coast of the Gulf of California in the Mexican state of Sonora.

Sericulture. The raising of silkworms for the production of raw silk.

Sesquiterpene lactones. Lactones are any of various organic esters derived from organic acids by removal of water. Terpenes are any of various hydrocarbons found in the essential oils and resins of plants; *sesqui* ("one and a half") refers to the specific chemical structure of a type of terpene.

Shawnee Indians. A Native American tribe originally inhabiting areas of Kentucky, Ohio, Pennsylvania, and West Virginia, later migrating to Maryland, South Carolina, and Florida, as well as Illinois and Kansas; the majority of Shawnee today live in Oklahoma.

Shoshone Indians. An indigenous tribe historically divided into three large divisions inhabiting portions of Colorado, Idaho, Montana, Nevada, Utah, and Wyoming; the Shoshone also merged with other tribes, and currently many live on reservations across these states.

Simple leaf. A leaf that is single, of one piece; not divided into parts, such as a compound leaf.

Sioux Indians. A relatively large group of indigenous peoples of the northern Plains, frequently referred to as the Sioux Nation, often divided into three main groups based on dialect and subculture: (1) Lakota or Teton; (2) Dakota, also called Isanti or Santee; (3) Nakota or Yankton. Approximately 150,000 Sioux maintain many separate tribal governments across communities in Canada, North and South Dakota, Minnesota, and Nebraska.

Sonoran Desert. The hottest North American desert, covering all of southwestern Arizona, southeastern California, and, in Mexico, large portions of Baja California and Sonora; famous for its succulent shrubs such as the saguaro cactus.

Southern Paiute. See Paiute Indians.

Species. The taxonomic rank below genus, given to a group or population of plants that are actually or potentially capable of interbreeding in nature.

Spike. An elongated inflorescence in which the flowers lack pedicels, attaching directly to the stem.

Stamen. The male reproductive part of a flower, consisting of a filament (or stalk) and an anther, which bears the pollen.

Staminal. Pertaining to a stamen.

Stellate. Star-shaped; in plant hairs, those having many arms radiating from a central stalk at one point.

Steroid. Any of various fat-soluble,

organic compounds from animals, plants, and fungi, most of which have specific physiological actions.

Stigma. The tip (usually sticky or rough) of the pistil that receives the pollen.

Stolon. A creeping horizontal or looping stem (or runner) that extends along the surface of the ground, rooting at the nodes; sometimes applied generically to an underground stem, technically known as a rhizome.

Stomachic. A substance that stimulates appetite and increases the secretion of gastric juices, promoting digestion.

Style. The stalked portion of the pistil that connects the ovary to the pollen-receptive stigma.

Styptic. A substance that stops external bleeding by causing blood vessels to contract at the wound.

Suma Indians. A poorly known group of Native Americans that some researchers identify as a western division of the Jumano; in the seventeenth and eighteenth centuries, ranging from northern Sonora and Chihuahua, Mexico, east as far as the El Paso area.

Surfactant. From "surface-active agent"; any substance that reduces surface tension in water or lowers the interfacial tension between two liquids; common in detergents, fabric softeners, emulsifiers, and paints.

Tannin. Any of various bitter, astringent, phenolic plant compounds that precipitate proteins; used extensively in tanning hides and in making dyes; also employed medicinally.

Taovaya Indians. A Wichita band probably from Kansas and Nebraska, forced south by other tribes to southern Oklahoma and northern Texas in the eighteenth century; semipermanent, farming settlements on both sides of the Red River near Spanish Fort; descendants currently live in Oklahoma.

Tarahumara Indians. An indigenous people of the state of Chihuahua in northern Mexico, currently concentrated in the Copper Canyon area,

who practice a traditional way of life; current numbers are 50,000–70,000.

Tawehash Indians. Apparently a synonym for Taovaya, one of the Wichita bands. In the 1850s Tawehash villages were located on the Wichita and Brazos rivers in Texas.

Tawakoni Indians. A Wichita band probably originally from Kansas, pushed into Texas by other tribes and inhabited the lands between Waco and Palestine in the late 1700s; merged into the Wichita tribe on reservation in Oklahoma; only a single individual reported this tribal name in 1910.

Tepal. A term for "petal," when indistinguishable from the sepal, although occupying different whorls; common in cacti and lilies.

Terpene. A major component of resin (and turpentine, whence the name), any one of a large and varied group of hydrocarbons produced mainly in plants, especially conifers (such as pine trees); the main constituents of the essential oils of many plants and flowers.

Terpenoid. Any one of a large and diverse class of organic chemicals similar to terpenes; naturally occurring in plants; extensively used for their aromatic qualities (e.g., eucalyptus, cinnamon, cloves, menthol). Terpenoids can be classified according to the number of isoprene units that compose them.

Theophrastus (ca. 371–287 BCE). Ancient Greek philosopher known as the father of botany; his works *De causis plantarum* ("The Causes of Plants") and *De historia plantarum* ("The History of Plants") begin the science of botany by classifying 500 plants, developing a terminology for describing their structures and growth forms, and describing plant sexual reproduction, as well as germination and propagation.

Thompson Indians. Also known as Thompson River Indians or Thompson Salish, an indigenous tribe now in southern British Columbia, Canada;

once also in northern Washington State.

Timucuan Indians. A Native American tribe historically inhabiting northeast and north-central Florida and parts of Georgia; largely exterminated by the mid-eighteenth century; now extinct.

Tincture. In herbal medicine, an extract obtained by adding vegetable matter to grain alcohol and allowing the mixture to steep for one to two weeks before straining.

Tohono O'odham. The "people of the desert," historically called the Papago, an indigenous tribe of south-central Arizona and also Sonora, Mexico; including both sides of the border, they number more than 25,000; closely related to the Akimel O'odham.

Tonic. A broadly used, poorly defined, old-fashioned term for any substance that increases general body tone, restoring strength, vitality, and energy. Eighteenth- and nineteenth-century uses of the word might encompass other meanings, such as a nerve tonic that calms (rather than excites) the nerves, or a blood tonic that purifies the blood by inducing sweating and increased metabolism. The basic idea seems to be that a tonic restores one to a healthy normal state.

Tonkawa Indians. The Tonkawa are a group of independent bands that apparently united in the early eighteenth century in central Texas. They were pushed out of the Edwards Plateau by the Apache, and later Comanche, inhabiting lands along the edge of the plateau and to the south and east. Traditionally they were believed to be native to Texas, but new evidence suggests they might have immigrated to the area from the High Plains in the seventeenth century. They had a Plains Indian culture (buffalo, tepees, etc.), but supplemented their diet with items that were not part of that culture, such as fish and oysters. From the mid-eighteenth century to the mid-nineteenth, they were largely enemies of the Spanish and allies of the Anglo colonists. After many attacks on them, both by colonists and other Indian tribes, by the late nineteenth century there were fewer than 100 Tonkawa; these merged and intermarried with Lipan Apache bands and settled on reservations in north-central Oklahoma. Current tribal numbers are over 300.

Trans-Pecos. The area of Texas west of the Pecos River, a boundary approximating the eastern limit of the Chihuahuan Desert in the United States.

Triassic. The geologic period extending from 248 million to 206 million years ago, in which the first flowering plants may have evolved.

Trichome. A hair or hairlike outgrowth from the surface of a plant.

Triterpenoid. A terpenoid consisting of six isoprene units.

Tropane alkaloids. A group of alkaloids derived from the nitrogenous organic compound tropane; known especially in the plants of the potato family (e.g., henbane, deadly nightshade, and jimsonweed) and in the family containing the coca plant, whence cocaine is derived.

Tuber. A modified, usually enlarged, underground stem (not a root); e.g., potato.

Twice compound. See Compound leaf.

Vascular plant. A plant that contains conducting cells or vessels; this term includes practically all common plants, with the exception of algae, slime molds, liverworts, and a few others.

Vermifuge. A substance that expels intestinal worms often by paralysis.

Vestiture. Any covering (such as hair or scales) on the surface.

Viscin. In mistletoe, a highly specialized, sticky tissue surrounding the seed just beneath the fruit's outer skin.

Viticulture. The cultivation of grapes.

Volatile oil. A distilled oil, especially one obtained from plant tissues.

Waco Indians. A subdivision of the Tawakoni, one of the Wichita bands; joined the Tawakoni proper, as well as Wichita, on a reservation in Oklahoma in the nineteenth century. The city of Waco, Texas, not surprisingly, was located on the site of a former Waco village.

White Mountain Apache. One of the bands of Western Apache living on historic lands in eastern Arizona.

Whorled. With flowers, with three or more attaching at a node, forming a circle or ring around the stem.

Wichita Indians. A loose confederacy of Caddoan-speaking tribes of the southern Plains, ranging from central Texas to Kansas, but represented in Texas history primarily by a settlement in north-central Texas along the Red River in the latter half of the eighteenth century. A semisedentary tribe, the Wichita lived in fixed villages of dome-shaped, grass-covered dwellings and engaged in agriculture during the summer, hunting buffalo in the winter. By 1858, they were relocated, together with the Tawakoni and Waco, to a reservation in west-central Oklahoma; recent (2000) census records show their numbers around 1400. In Texas a river, county, and city bear the Wichita name.

Winnebago Indians. A tribe of Native Americans native to Wisconsin and Illinois; currently about 8000 members inhabit lands primarily in Wisconsin (where they are now called the Ho-Chunk) and Nebraska.

Xylem. The water-conducting tissue in a plant.

Yaqui Indians. An indigenous agricultural tribe originally from the lands along the Río Yaqui of Sonora, Mexico, later with populations in southern Arizona; currently living in Sonora and on a reservation near Tucson.

Yavapai Indians. A Yuman tribe originally inhabiting the Verde River in west-central Arizona, closely allied to the Apache; small reservations near Phoenix and Prescott.

Yokut Indians. Any of several indigenous subtribes in the San Joaquin Valley of central California, where scattered reservations exist today.

Yuchi Indians. A Native American tribe (not recognized at the federal level) originally inhabiting the Tennessee River valley of Tennessee, Alabama, and Georgia; removed to Oklahoma; current descendants often enrolled in the Creek (Muscogee) tribe.

Yuman Indians. A collective name for a group of southwestern U.S. tribes who speak languages in the Yuman family, including, in this work, Cocopah, Havasupai, Hualapai, and Yavapai. The Yuma proper, now called Quechan, inhabit historic lands on the lower Colorado River in southwestern Arizona.

Zuni Indians. One of the Pueblo peoples of New Mexico, currently living in western New Mexico on their historic lands south of Gallup, numbering more than 9000.

Bibliography

Adair, A. Garland, and Ben B. Hunt. 1940. *The Amusing Legend of the Dogwood Tree.* Austin, TX: Adair & Hunt.

Adams, Robert P. 1987. "Investigation of *Juniperus* Species of the United States for New Sources of Cedarwood Oil." *Economic Botany* 41(1):48–54.

———. 1991. "Cedarwood Oil: Analysis and Properties." In *Modern Methods of Plant Analysis, New Series, Vol. 12: Oil and Waxes,* ed. H. F. Linskens and J. F. Jackson, 159–173. Berlin: Springer Verlag.

———. 2004. *Junipers of the World: The Genus Juniperus.* Vancouver: Trafford Publishing.

Adams, Robert P., and B. L. Turner. 1970. "Chemosystematic and Numerical Studies of Natural Populations of *Juniperus ashei* Buch." *Taxon* 19:728–751.

Adovasio, J. M., and G. F. Fry. 1976. "Prehistoric Psychotropic Drug Use in Northeastern Mexico and Trans-Pecos Texas." *Economic Botany* 30(1):94–96.

Ajilvsgi, Geyata. 1984. *Wildflowers of Texas.* Fredericksburg, TX: Shearer.

Al-Rabab'ah, Mohammad, and Claire G. Williams. 2004. "An Ancient Bottleneck in the Lost Pines of Central Texas." *Molecular Ecology* 13:1075–1084.

Albert, Susan Wittig. 2000. I Can Garden.Com s.v. "*Monarda,*" http://www.icangarden.com/document.cfm?task=viewdetail&itemid=1454 (accessed Jan. 6, 2005).

Albiero, Adriana L. M., Jayme Antonio Aboin Sertié, and Elfriede Marianne Bacchi. 2002. "Antiulcer Activity of *Sapindus saponaria* L. in the Rat." *Journal of Ethnopharmacology* 82(1):41–44.

Alexander, Robert K. 1970. *Archaeological Excavations at Parida Cave, Val Verde County, Texas.* Papers of the Texas Archeological Salvage Project, no. 19. Austin: Texas Archeological Salvage Project.

Alloway, David. 2000. *Desert Survival Skills.* Austin: Univ. of Texas Press.

Altschul, Siri von Reis. 1973. *Drugs and Foods from Little-Known Plants: Notes in Harvard University Herbaria.* Cambridge, MA: Harvard Univ. Press.

Ambrose, Stephen E. 1997. *Undaunted Courage: Meriwether Lewis, Thomas Jefferson, and the Opening of the American West.* New York: Simon & Schuster. First Touchstone Ed.

Anderson, Arthur B. 1955. "Recovery and Utilization of Tree Extractions." *Economic Botany* 9(2):108–140.

Anderson, Edward F. 1969. "The Biogeography, Ecology, and Taxonomy of *Lophophora* (Cactaceae)." *Brittonia* 21:299–310.

———. 1980. *Peyote: The Divine Cactus.* Tucson: Univ. of Arizona Press.

Anderson, Kit. 2003. *Nature, Culture, and Big Old Trees: Live Oaks and Ceibas in the Landscapes of Louisiana and Guatemala.* Austin: Univ. of Texas Press.

Andrews, Jean. 1992. *American Wildflower Florilegium.* Denton: Univ. of North Texas Press.

———. 1993. *The Texas Bluebonnet.* Austin: Univ. of Texas Press.

———. 1995. *Peppers: The Domesticated Capsicums.* New ed. Austin: Univ. of Texas Press.

———. 1998. *The Pepper Lady's Pocket Pepper Primer.* Austin: Univ. of Texas Press.

Anthony, Margery. 1954. "Ecology of the Opuntiae in the Big Bend Region of Texas." *Ecology* 35(3):334–347.

Armesto, J. J., G. P. Cheplick, and M. J. McDonnell. 1983. "Observations on the Reproductive Biology of *Phytolacca americana* (Phytolaccaceae)." *Bulletin of the Torrey Botanical Club* 110(3):380–383.

Arnold, Leroy A., and D. Lynn Drawe. 1979. "Seasonal Food Habits of White-tailed Deer in the South Texas Plains." *Journal of Range Management* 32(3):175–178.

Arteaga, Silvia, Adolfo Andrade-Cetto, and René Cárdenas. 2005. "*Larrea tridentata* (Creosote Bush), An Abundant Plant of Mexican and U.S.-American Deserts and Its Metabolite Nordihydroguaiaretic Acid." *Journal of Ethnopharmacology* 98(3):231–239.

Babb, Jewel. 1985. *Border Healing Woman: The Story of Jewel Babb as Told to Pat LittleDog.* Austin: Univ. of Texas Press.

Baker, James B., and O. Gordon Langdon. 1990. "Loblolly Pine (*Pinus taeda*)." In Burns and Honkala, 1990, s.v. "*Pinus taeda.*"

Balandrin, Manuel F. 1984. "Whole-Plant Nonpolar Lipids and Hydrocarbons as Industrial Raw Materials." Annual Meeting of the Botanical Society of America, Fort Collins, CO, Aug. 5–9. *American Journal of Botany* 71(5 Part 2):129.

———. 1996. "Commercial Utilization of Plant-Derived Saponins: An Overview of Medicinal, Pharmaceutical, and Industrial Applications." In *Sapo-*

nins Used in Traditional and Modern Medicine, ed. George R. Waller and Kazuo Yamasaki. Advances in Experimental Medicine and Biology, vol. 404, 1–14. New York: Plenum.

Ball, Carleton R. 1949. "The Willows: Helpers of Man." Scientific Monthly 69(1):48–55.

Ball, Jeff. 2000. "The Versatile Osage-Orange." American Forests 106(3):60–62.

Banks, Larry. 2004. Handbook of Texas Online, s.v. "Lewisville Site," http://www.tsha.utexas.edu/handbook/online/articles/view/LL/bbl4.html (accessed December 8, 2004).

Banta, Capt. William, and J. W. Caldwell, Jr. 1933. Twenty-Seven Years on the Texas Frontier. Rewritten from an original copy and revised by L. G. Park. First pub. 1893. Council Hill, OK.

Barkley, Fred A. 1937. "A Monographic Study of Rhus and Its Immediate Allies in North and Central America, Including the West Indies." Annals of the Missouri Botanical Garden 24(3):265–460.

Barkley, Fred A., and Elizabeth Ducker Barkley. 1938. "A Short History of Rhus to the Time of Linnaeus." American Midland Naturalist 19(2):265–333.

Barlow, Connie. 2001. "Anachronistic Fruits and the Ghosts Who Haunt Them." Arnoldia 61(2):14–21.

Barrows, David Prescott. 1967. The Ethnobotany of the Coahuilla Indians of Southern California. Banning, CA: Malki Museum Press.

Bartlett, John Russell. 1854. Personal Narrative of Explorations and Incidents . . . Boundary Commission, During the Years 1850, '51, '52, and '53. 2 vols. New York: Appleton.

Bartlett, Richard C. 1995. Saving the Best of Texas: A Partnership Approach to Conservation. Photographs by Leroy Williamson. Austin: Univ. of Texas Press.

Basehart, Harry W. 1974. Mescalero Apache Subsistence Patterns and

Socio-Political Organization: Commission Findings on the Apache. Vol. 12 of American Indian Ethnohistory: Indians of the Southwest. New York: Garland.

Battey, Thomas C. 1876. The Life and Adventures of a Quaker Among the Indians. Boston: Lee & Shepard.

Bedichek, Roy. 1950. Karánkaway Country. Garden City, NY: Doubleday.

———. 1994. Adventures with a Texas Naturalist. Austin: Univ. of Texas Press.

Bell, Willis H., and Edward R. Castetter. 1941. The Utilization of Yucca, Sotol, and Beargrass by the Aborigines in the American Southwest. Univ. of New Mexico Bulletin: Ethnobiological Studies in the American Southwest, no. 7. Albuquerque: Univ. of New Mexico Press.

Belmares, Hector, J. Ernesto Castillo, and Arnoldo Barrera. 1979. "Natural Hard Fibers of the North American Continent: Statistical Correlations of Physical and Mechanical Properties of Lechuguilla (Agave lechuguilla) Fibers." Textile Research Journal 49(11):619–622.

Bement, Leland C. 1989. "Lower Pecos Canyonlands." In Hester et al. 1989, 63–76.

Bemis, W. P., L. D. Curtis, C. W. Weber, and J. Berry. 1978. "The Feral Buffalo Gourd, Cucurbita foetidissima." Economic Botany 32(1):87–95.

Bennett, Bradley C. 1986. "The Florida Bromeliads: Tillandsia usneoides." Journal of the Bromeliad Society 36(4):149–151, 159–160.

Benzing, David. H. 1980. The Biology of the Bromeliads. Eureka, CA: Mad River.

———. 2000. Bromeliaceae: Profile of an Adaptive Radiation. Cambridge: Cambridge Univ. Press.

Berlandier, Jean Louis. 1969. The Indians of Texas in 1830. Ed. John C. Ewers. Trans. Patricia Reading Leclercq. Washington, DC: Smithsonian Institution Press.

———. 1980. Journey to Mexico

During the Years 1826 to 1834. Trans. Sheila M. Ohlendorf, Josette M. Bigelow, and Mary M. Standifer. 2 vols. Austin: Texas State Historical Assoc.

Berry, James Berthold. 1964. Western Forest Trees: A Guide to the Identification of Trees and Woods for Students, Teachers, Farmers and Woodsmen. New York: Dover.

Betts, H. S. 1943. Cottonwood. American Woods Series. U.S. Dept. of Agriculture, Forest Service. Washington, DC: U.S. Government Printing Office.

———. 1954. Black Walnut (Juglans nigra). American Woods Series. U.S. Dept. of Agriculture, Forest Service. Washington, DC: U.S. Government Printing Office.

Beverley, Robert. 1855. The History of Virginia, in Four Parts. Richmond, VA: J. W. Randolph.

Biffle, Kent. 2000. "Kent Biffle's Texana." Dallas Morning News. November 5.

Birge, Willie I. 1911. "The Anatomy and Some Biological Aspects of the 'Ball Moss,' Tillandsia recurvata L." Bulletin of the University of Texas, no. 194. Scientific Series, no. 20.

Black, Stephen L., and A. Joachim McGraw. 1985. The Panther Springs Creek Site: Cultural Change and Continuity Within the Upper Salado Creek Watershed, South-Central Texas. Archaeological Survey Report, no. 100. San Antonio: Center for Archaeological Research, Univ. of Texas.

Boatright, Mody C., ed. 1949. The Sky Is My Tipi. Publications of the Texas Folklore Society, No. 22. Austin: Texas Folklore Society. Distributed by University Press, Dallas.

Boatright, Mody C., Wilson M. Hudson, and Allen Maxwell, eds. 1954. Texas Folk and Folklore. Publications of the Texas Folklore Society, No. 26. Dallas: Southern Methodist Univ. Press.

Bogler, D. J., J. L. Neff, and B. B. Simpson. 1995. "Multiple Origins of the Yucca–Yucca Moth Association." Proceedings of the National Academy of Science 92:6864–6867.

Bohrer, Vorsil L. 1983. "New Life from Ashes: The Tale of the Burnt Bush (*Rhus trilobata*)." *Desert Plants* 5(3):122–124.

Bolton, Herbert Eugene. 1987. *The Hasinais: Southern Caddoans as Seen by the Earliest Europeans*. Ed. Russell M. Magnaghi. Norman: Univ. of Oklahoma Press.

———, ed. 1908. *Spanish Exploration in the Southwest: 1542–1706*. Reprint, New York: Barnes & Noble, 1959.

Bosland, Paul. 1999. "The History of the Chile Pepper." In *Chile Peppers: Hot Tips and Tasty Picks for Gardeners and Gourmets*, ed. Beth Hanson, 6–16. 21st-Century Gardening Series, Handbook no. 161. New York: Brooklyn Botanic Garden Publications.

Boyd, Carolyn E., and J. Philip Dering. 1996. "Medicinal and Hallucinogenic Plants Identified in the Sediments and Pictographs of the Lower Pecos, Texas Archaic." *Antiquity* 70 (268):256–275.

Boyd, J. W., D. S. Murray, and R. J. Tyrl. 1984. "Silverleaf Nightshade, *Solanum elaeagnifolium*, Origin, Distribution, and Relation to Man." *Economic Botany* 38(2):210–217.

Boyer, W. D. 1990. "Longleaf Pine (*Pinus palustris*)." In Burns and Honkala, 1990, s.v. "*Pinus palustris.*"

Bracht, Viktor. 1931. *Texas in 1848*. Trans. Charles Frank Schmidt. San Antonio: Naylor Printing.

Bray, William L. 1904. *Forest Resources of Texas*. U.S. Dept. of Agriculture, Bureau of Forestry, Bulletin no. 47. Washington, DC: U.S. Dept. of Agriculture, Bureau of Forestry.

Breeden, James O., ed. 1994. *A Long Ride in Texas: The Explorations of John Leonard Riddell*. College Station: Texas A&M Univ. Press.

Brisson, Jacques, and James F. Reynolds. 1994. "The Effect of Neighbors on Root Distribution in a Creosote-

bush (*Larrea tridentata*) Population." *Ecology* 75(6):1693–1702.

Brown, Clair A. 1984. "Morphology and Biology of Cypress Tress." In *Cypress Swamps*, ed. Katherine C. Ewel and Howard T. Odum, 16–24. Gainesville: Univ. of Florida Press.

Brown, G. I. 1998. *The Big Bang: A History of Explosives*. Stroud, Gloucestershire, UK: Sutton Pub.

Brussell, David. 1978. "*Equisetum* Stores Gold." *Phytologia* 38(6):469–473.

Bryant, Vaughn M., Jr. 1974. "Prehistoric Diet in Southwest Texas: The Coprolite Evidence." *American Antiquity* 39(3):407–420.

———. 1986. "Prehistoric Diet: A Case for Coprolite Analysis." In Shafer 1986, 132–135.

Buchmann, Stephen L., and James H. Cane. 1989. "Bees Assess Pollen Returns While Sonicating *Solanum* flowers." *Oecologia* 81(3):289–294.

Bunting, Stephen C., Henry A. Wright, and Leon F. Neuenschwander. 1980. "Long-term Effects of Fire on Cactus in the Southern Mixed Prairie of Texas." *Journal of Range Management* 33(2):85–88.

Burlage, Henry M. 1968. *Index of Plants of Texas with Reputed Medicinal and Poisonous Properties*. [Austin].

Burns, Russell M., and Barbara H. Honkala, eds. 1990. *Silvics of North America*. 2 vols. Agriculture Handbook, no. 654. Washington, DC: U.S. Dept. of Agriculture. Forest Service, http://www.na.fs.fed.us/spfo/pubs/silvics_manual/table_of_contents.htm.

Burton, J. D. 1990. "Osage Orange (*Maclura pomifera*)." In Burns and Honkala, 1990, s.v. "*Maclura pomifera.*"

Bush, Ava. 1973. "Bride of the Forest." *East Texas Historical Journal* 11(1):28–32.

Cabeza de Vaca, Alvar Núñez. 1984. *Naufragios y Comentarios*. Ed. Roberto Ferrando. Madrid: Historia 16.

———. 1993. *The Account: Alvar Núñez Cabeza de Vaca's* Relación. Trans. Martin Favata and José Fernández. Houston: Arte Público Press.

Cadwallader, D. E., and F. J. Wilson. 1965. "Folklore Medicine Among Georgia's Piedmont Negroes After the Civil War." *The Georgia Historical Quarterly* 49(2):217–227.

Calder, D. M. 1983. "Mistletoes in Focus: An Introduction." In *The Biology of Mistletoes*, ed. Malcolm Calder and Peter Bernhardt, 1–18. Sydney: Academic Press.

Campbell, T. N. 1951. "Medicinal Plants Used by Choctaw, Chickasaw, and Creek Indians in the Early Nineteenth Century." *Journal of the Washington Academy of Sciences* 41(9):285–290.

———. 1958. "Origin of the Mescal Bean Cult." *American Anthropologist* 60:156–160.

Canonge, Elliott. 1958. *Comanche Texts*. Norman: Summer Institute of Linguistics of the Univ. of Oklahoma.

Carlson, Gustav G., and Volney H. Jones. 1939. "Some Notes on Uses of Plants by the Comanche Indians." *Michigan Academy of Science, Arts, and Letters* 25:517–542.

Carr, David E., and Lauren E. Banas. 2000. "Dogwood Anthracnose (*Discula destructiva*): Effects of and Consequences for Host (*Cornus florida*) Demography." *American Midland Naturalist* 143(1):169–177.

Carter, Maureen, and Paul Feeny. 1999. "Host-Plant Chemistry Influences Oviposition Choice of the Spicebush Swallowtail Butterfly." *Journal of Chemical Ecology* 25(9):1999–2009.

Castetter, Edward. 1935. "Uncultivated Native Plants Used as Sources of Food." Univ. of New Mexico Bulletin, no. 266. *Ethnobiological Studies in the American Southwest*. Vol. 4, no. 1. Albuquerque: Univ. of New Mexico.

Castetter, Edward, and M. E. Opler. 1936. "The Ethnobiology of the Chiricahua and Mescalero Apache: The Use of Plants for Food, Beverages and

Narcotics." Univ. of New Mexico Bulletin, no. 297. *Ethnobiological Studies in the American Southwest*. Vol. 4, no. 5. Albuquerque: Univ. of New Mexico Press.

Castner, E. P., D. S. Murray, N. M. Hackett, L. M. Verhalen, D. L. Weeks, and J. F. Stone. 1989. "Interference of Hogpotato (*Hoffmanseggia glauca*) with Cotton (*Gossypium hirsutum*)." *Weed Science* 37(5):688–694.

Chakraborty, A., and A. H. Brantner. 2000. "Evaluation of Biological Activities of *Rhus aromaticae* Extracts." *Pharmaceutical and Pharmacological Letters* 10(2):76–81.

Chávez-Ramírez, Felipe, and R. Douglas Slack. 1993. "Carnivore Fruit-Use and Seed Dispersal of Two Selected Plant Species of the Edwards Plateau, Texas." *Southwestern Naturalist* 38(2):141–145.

Cheatham, Scooter, and Marshall C. Johnston. 1995. *The Useful Wild Plants of Texas, the Southeastern and Southwestern United States, the Southern Plains, and Northern Mexico*. Vol. 1. Austin, TX: Useful Wild Plants.

———. 2000. *The Useful Wild Plants of Texas, the Southeastern and Southwestern United States, the Southern Plains, and Northern Mexico*. Vol. 2. Austin, TX: Useful Wild Plants.

Clarke, H. David, David S. Seigler, and John E. Ebinger. 1989. "*Acacia farnesiana* (Fabaceae: Mimosoideae) and Related Species from Mexico, the Southwestern U.S., and the Caribbean." *Systematic Botany* 14(4):549–564.

Coker, W. C. 1944. "The Woody Smilaxes of the United States." *Journal of the Elisha Mitchell Scientific Society* 60:27–69.

Cole, John N. 1979. *Amaranth: From the Past, for the Future*. Emmaus, PA: Rodale Press.

Coleman, Jerry, Keith Hench, Keith Garbutt, Alan Sexstone, Gary Bissonnette, and Jeff Skousen. 2001. "Treatment of Domestic Wastewater

by Three Plant Species in Constructed Wetlands." *Water, Air and Soil Pollution* 128(3/4):283–295.

Cooper, D. T. 1990. "Eastern Cottonwood (*Populus deltoides*)." In Burns and Honkala, 1990, s.v. "*Populus deltoides*."

Coppen, J. J. W., and G. A. Hone. 1995. *Gum Naval Stores: Turpentine and Rosin from Pine Resin*. Non-Wood Forest Products, 2. Rome: Food and Agriculture Organization of the United States.

Core, Earl L. 1967. "Ethnobotany of the Southern Appalachian Aborigines." *Economic Botany* 21:199–214.

Cornett, James W. 1995. *Indian Uses of Desert Plants*. Palm Springs, CA: Palm Springs Desert Museum.

Costa, M., L. C. Di Stasi, M. Kirizawa, S. L. J. Mendacolli, C. Gomes, and G. Trolin. 1989. "Screening in Mice of Some Medicinal Plants Used for Analgesic Purposes in the State of São Paulo, Brazil, Part II." *Journal of Ethnopharmacology* 27(1–2):25–34.

Covey, Cyclone, trans. 1961. *Cabeza de Vaca's Adventures in the Unknown Interior of America*. Albuquerque: Univ. of New Mexico Press.

Cowles, Raymond B. 1972. "Mesquite and Mistletoe." *Pacific Discovery* 25(3):19–24.

Cox, Paul W., and Patty Leslie. 1999. *Texas Trees: A Friendly Guide*. San Antonio: Corona.

Cremony, John C. 1868. *Life Among the Apaches*. San Francisco: A. Roman & Co.

Crider, Kitty. 2001. "Survivor Cuisine, Texas-Style." *Austin American-Statesman*, May 2. Life and Food Section, E8.

Crosswhite, Frank S. 1980. "Dry Country Plants of the South Texas Plains." *Desert Plants* 2(3):141–179.

———. 1980–1981. "The Story of Jimson Weed." *Desert Plants* 2(4):245.

———. 1981. "Desert Plants, Habitat and Agriculture in Relation to the Major Pattern of Cultural Differentiation

in the O'odham People of the Sonoran Desert." *Desert Plants* 3(2):47–76.

Cuno, John B. 1926. "Utilization of Dogwood and Persimmon." U.S. Dept. of Agriculture Bulletin, No. 1436.

Curtin, Lenora Scott Muse. 1965. *Healing Herbs of the Upper Rio Grande*. Los Angeles: Southwest Museum.

Dahmer, Fred. 1989. *Caddo Was—: A Short History of Caddo Lake*. Austin: Univ. of Texas Press.

Dalby, Richard. 2004. "Dogbane and Horsemint: Two Interesting Honey Sources." *American Bee Journal* 144(1):46–48.

Damude, Noreen, and Kelly Conrad Bender. 1999. *Texas Wildscapes: Gardening for Wildlife*. Austin: Texas Parks and Wildlife Press.

Darlington, William. 1837. *Flora Cestrica: An Attempt to Enumerate and Describe the Flowering and Filidoid Plants of Chester County . . . Pennsylvania*. West-Chester, PA: S. Siegfried. p. 350.

Dart, Bob. 2007. "A Symbol of Endurance Along Gulf Coast." *Austin American-Statesman*, Sunday, March 18, Section A.

Davis, Tim D., Steven W. George, Wayne A. Mackay, and Jerry M. Parsons. 1994. "Development of Texas Bluebonnets into Floricultural Crops." *HortScience* 29(10):1110, 1211.

Dayanandan, P. 1977. "Stomata in *Equisetum*: A Structural and Functional Study." Ph.D. diss. Univ. of Michigan.

De Cordoba, José. 2004. "Down in Texas Scrub: 'Peyoteros' Stalk Their Elusive Prey." *Wall Street Journal*, May 12.

De Voto, Bernard. 1942. *The Year of Decision, 1846*. Boston: Houghton Mifflin.

Deans, Stanley G., and Alan I. Kennedy. 2002. "*Artemisia absinthium*." In Wright 2002, 79–89.

Deans, Stanley G., and Elisabeth J. M. Simpson. 2002. "*Artemisia dracunculus*." In Wright 2002, 91–97.

Dennis, T. S., and Mrs. T. S. Dennis. 1925. *Life of F. M. Buckelew the Indian*

Captive, As Related by Himself. Bandera, TX: Hunter's Printing House.

DePaola, Tomie. 1996. *The Legend of the Bluebonnet: An Old Tale of Texas.* New York: Penguin.

Dering, Philip. 1982. "Analysis of Carbonized Botanical Remains from the Choke Canyon Reservoir Area." Appendix 3 in *Archaeological Investigations at Choke Canyon Reservoir, South Texas: The Phase I Findings,* by G. D. Hall, S. L. Black, and C. Graves, pp. 518–530. Choke Canyon Series 5. Center for Archaeological Research, University of Texas at San Antonio.

Desmond, Charles. 1919. *Wooden Ship-Building.* New York: Rudder.

DeVeaux, Jennie S., and Eugene B. Shultz, Jr. 1985. "Development of Buffalo Gourd (*Cucurbita foetidissima*) as a Semiaridland Starch and Oil Crop." *Economic Botany* 39(4):454–472.

Dewey, Lyster H. 1943. *Fiber Production in the Western Hemisphere.* U.S. Dept. of Agriculture Miscellaneous Publication, no. 518. Washington, DC: U.S. Government Printing Office.

Diggs, George M., Jr., Barney L. Lipscomb, and Robert J. O'Kennon. 1999. *Shinners and Mahler's Illustrated Flora of North Central Texas.* Fort Worth: Botanical Research Institute of Texas.

Dioscorides, Pedanius, of Anazarbos. 1959. *The Greek Herbal of Dioscorides, Illustrated by a Byzantine, AD 512; Englished by John Goodyer; Edited and First Printed AD 1933.* Ed. Robert T. Gunther. New York: Hafner.

Dobie, J. Frank. 1928. *Tales of Old-Time Texas.* Austin: Univ. of Texas Press.

———. 1967. *Some Part of Myself.* Boston: Little, Brown.

———, ed. 1935. *Coffee in the Gourd.* Publications of the Texas Folk-Lore Society, no. 2. Reprint of 1923. Austin: Texas Folk-Lore Society.

Doorenbos, Norman J. 2004. "Development of Natural Products Research at University of Mississippi." *Economic Botany* 58(2):172–178.

Dorado, Oscar, Gerardo Avila, Dule M. Arias, Rolando Ramírez, David Salinas, and Guadalupe Valladares. 1996. "The Arbol del Tule (*Taxodium mucronatum* Ten.) Is a Single Genetic Individual." *Madroño* 43(4):445–452.

Dore, William G. 1971. "Canada Onion: Its Method of Spread into Canada." *Le Naturaliste Canadien* 98(3):385–400.

Dorsey, George A. 1904. *The Mythology of the Wichita.* Washington, DC: Carnegie Institute of Washington.

———. 1905. *Traditions of the Caddo.* Washington, DC: Carnegie Institute of Washington.

Duke, James A. 1981. *Handbook of Legumes of World Economic Importance.* New York: Plenum.

Duncan, Wilbur H. 1974. *Woody Vines of the Southeastern United States.* Athens: Univ. of Georgia Press.

Dunmire, William W., and Gail D. Tierney. 1995. *Wild Plants of the Pueblo Province: Exploring Ancient and Enduring Uses.* Santa Fe: Museum of New Mexico Press.

Durand, Herbert K. 1973. "Texas *Mahonia:* A Neglected Economic Plant." *Economic Botany* 20(4):319–325.

Duval, John C. 1892. *Early Times in Texas, or The Adventures of Jack Dobell.* Ed. Mabel Major and Rebecca W. Smith. Dallas, TX: Tardy, 1936.

Dyer, Joseph O. 1916. *Historical Sketch: Comparison of Customs of Wild Tribes Near Galveston a Century Ago, with Ancient Semitic Customs.* Galveston, TX: Oscar Springer.

———. 1917. *The Lake Charles Atakapas Cannibals, Period of 1817–1820.* Eight-page pamphlet, not numbered. Galveston, TX: Dyer.

Economist (U.S.). 1999. "Semi-Legal Drugs: Peyote Grows Naturally in Only Four Texas Counties, and Is Used by Members of the Pan-Tribal Native American Church." April 3, p. 27.

Edwards, N., and G. C. Rodgers. 1982. "Pokeberry Pancake Breakfast, or, It's Gonna Be a Great Day!" *Veterinary and Human Toxicology* 24(Suppl.):135–137.

El-Seedi, Hesham R., Peter A. G. M. De Smet, Olof Beck, Göran Possnert, and Jan G. Bruhn. 2005. "Prehistoric Peyote Use: Alkaloid Analysis and Radiocarbon Dating of Archaeological Specimens of *Lophophora* from Texas." *Journal of Ethnopharmacology* 101(1–3):238–242.

Elkavoich, Stella D., and Kenneth L. Stevens. 1985. "Phytotoxic Properties of Nordihydroguaiaretic Acid, A Lignan from *Larrea tridentata* (Creosote Bush)." *Journal of Chemical Ecology* 11(1):27–33.

Elliott, Stephen. 1824. *A Sketch of the Botany of South-Carolina and Georgia.* 2 vols. Charleston: J. R. Schenck.

Ellis, Clyde. 1990. "'Truly Dancing Their Own Way': Modern Revival and Diffusion of the Gourd Dance." *American Indian Quarterly* 14:19–33.

English, Sarah Jane. 1986. *The Wines of Texas: A Guide and History.* Austin: Eakin Press.

Enquist, Marshall. 1987. *Wildflowers of the Texas Hill Country.* Austin: Lone Star Botanical.

Eusman, Elmer. 2005. "The Ink Corrosion Website," http://www.knaw.nl/ecpa/ink/index.html (accessed May 21, 2005).

Everitt, James. H., D. Lynn Drawe, and Robert I. Lonard. 1999. *Field Guide to the Broad-Leaved Herbaceous Plants of South Texas Used by Livestock and Wildlife.* Lubbock: Texas Tech Univ. Press.

Eyde, Richard H. 1987. "The Case for Keeping *Cornus* in the Broad Linnean Sense." *Systematic Botany* 12(4):505–518.

Fair Publishing (Fort Worth). 1945. *A Century of Texas Cattle Brands.* Amarillo: Russell Stationery.

Fairbanks, Charles H. 1979. "The Function of Black Drink Among the Creeks." In Hudson 1979, 40–82.

Fernald, Merritt Lyndon. 1950. *Gray's Manual of Botany: A Handbook of the Flowering Plants and Ferns of the Central and Northeastern United States and Adjacent Canada*. 8th (Centennial) ed. Portland, OR: Dioscorides Press.

Fletcher, Henry T. 1928. *Notes on the Vegetation of the Green Valley Region*. West Texas Historical and Scientific Society Publications, no. 2. Alpine, TX: Sul Ross State Teachers College.

Flores, Dan. 1990. *Caprock Canyonlands: Journeys into the Heart of the Southern Plains*. Austin: Univ. of Texas Press.

Foreman, Richard, and James W. Mahoney. 1849. *The Cherokee Physician, or Indian Guide to Health*. Asheville, NC: Edney & Dedman.

Foster, J. H. 1917. "The Spread of Timbered Areas in Central Texas." *Journal of Forestry* 15:442–445.

Foster, William C. 1995. *Spanish Expeditions into Texas 1689–1768*. Austin: Univ. of Texas Press.

Fowler, Gene. 1993. "The Texas Pecan: Munching for Health Along the River of Nuts." *Texas Highways* 40(12):12–21.

Francaviglia, Richard V. 2000. *The Cast Iron Forest: A Natural and Cultural History of the North American Cross Timbers*. Austin: Univ. of Texas Press.

Frazer, James George. 1940. *The Golden Bough: A Study in Magic and Religion*. New York: Macmillan.

Freeman, C. Edward, and William H. Reid. 1985. "Aspects of the Reproductive Biology of *Agave lechuguilla* Torr." *Desert Plants* 7(2):75–80.

French, David H. 1971. "Ethnobotany of the Umbelliferae." In *The Biology and Chemistry of the Umbelliferae*, ed. V. H. Heywood, 385–412. New York: Academic Press.

French, Howard W. 2005. "Malaria Drug Drives Village's Development." *Dallas Morning News,* Sept. 4.

Friedman, William E. 1990. "Double Fertilization in *Ephedra*, a Nonflower-

ing Seed Plant: Its Bearing on the Origin of Angiosperms." *Science* 247(4945):951–954.

Furst, Peter T. 1976. *Hallucinogens and Culture*. San Francisco: Chandler & Sharp.

———. 1986. "Shamanism, the Ecstatic Experience, and Lower Pecos Art: Reflections on Some Transcultural Phenomena." In Shafer 1986, 210–225.

———, ed. 1972. *Flesh of the Gods: The Ritual Use of Hallucinogens*. New York: Praeger.

Furst, Peter T., and Jill L. Furst. 1982. *North American Indian Art*. New York: Rizzoli.

Garrett, Howard. 2002. *Howard Garrett's Texas Trees*. Lanham, MD: Lone Star Books.

Garth, R. E. 1964. "The Ecology of Spanish Moss (*Tillandsia usneoides*): Its Growth and Distribution." *Ecology* 45(3):470–481.

Gatschet, Albert S. 1891. "The Karankawa Indians, the Coast People of Texas." *Papers of the Peabody Museum of Archaeology and Ethnology, Harvard Univ.* 1(2):1–103.

Gehlbach, Frederick R. 2002. *Messages from the Wild: An Almanac of Suburban Natural and Unnatural History*. Austin: Univ. of Texas Press.

Gentry, Howard Scott. 1982. *Agaves of Continental North America*. Tucson: Univ. of Arizona Press.

Golub, S. J., and Whetmore, R. H. 1948. "Studies of Development in the Vegetative Shoot of *Equisetum arvense* L. I. The shoot apex." *American Journal of Botany* 35:755–767.

Gonzalez, C. L. 1989. "Potential of Fertilization to Improve Nutritive Value of Pricklypear Cactus (*Opuntia lindheimeri* Engelm.)." *Journal of Arid Environments* 16:87–94.

González, Esther Peña. 1998. *Little Known History of the South Texas Hill Country*. Rio Grande City, TX: González.

Goodrich & Wiley [publ.]. 1834. *A Visit to Texas: Being the Journal of a Trav-

eller*. Facsimile of the 1st ed. Austin: Steck, 1952.

Gould, Frank W. 1975. "What's in a Plant Name?" *Journal of Range Management* 28(4): 330.

———. 1979. "The Genus *Bouteloua* (Poaceae)." *Annals of the Missouri Botanical Garden* 66(3): 348–416.

Gould, Lewis L. 2005. *Handbook of Texas Online*, s.v. "Progressive Era." http://www.tsha.utexas.edu/handbook/online/articles/view/PP/npp1.html (accessed January 24, 2005).

Graham, Joe S. 1975. "Tradition and the Candelilla Wax Industry." In *Some Still Do: Essays on Texas Customs,* ed. Francis Edward Abernathy, 39–54. Austin, TX: Encino Press.

Grande, Gregory A., and Stephen R. Dannewitz. 1987. "Symptomatic Sassafras Oil Ingestion." *Veterinary and Human Toxicology* 29(6):447.

Gray, Asa. 1850. "*Plantae Lindheimerianae,* Part II: An Account of a Collection of Plants Made by F. Lindheimer in the Western Part of Texas, in the Years 1845–6, and 1847–8." *Boston Journal of Natural History* 6(2):141–240.

Greene, A. C. 1972. *The Last Captive: The Lives of Herman Lehmann, Who Was Taken by the Indians as a Boy . . .* Austin, TX: Encino Press.

Gregory, M., R. M. Fritsch, N. W. Friesen, F. O. Khassanov, and D. W. McNeal. 1998. *Nomenclator Alliorum: Allium Names and Synonyms, A World Guide*. Kew: Royal Botanic Gardens.

Grieve, Maud. 1967. *A Modern Herbal: The Medicinal, Culinary, Cosmetic and Economic Properties, Cultivation and Folk-Lore of Herbs, Grasses, Fungi, Shrubs and Trees*. New York: Hafner.

Griffith, William Joyce. 1954. *The Hasinai Indians of East Texas as Seen by Europeans, 1687–1772*. Philological and Documentary Studies, vol. 2, no. 3. New Orleans: Middle American Research Institute, Tulane Univ.

Griffiths, David. 1912. "The Grama

Grasses: *Bouteloua* and Related Genera." *Contributions from the U.S. National Herbarium* 14(3):343–428.

Griffiths, David, and R. F. Hare. 1906. "Prickly Pear and Other Cacti as Food for Stock II." *New Mexico College of Agriculture and Mechanic Arts,* Bulletin No. 60.

Grimé, William Ed. 1976. *Botany of the Black Americans.* St. Clair Shores, MI: Scholarly Press.

Groom, Nigel. 1992. *The Perfume Handbook.* London: Chapman & Hall.

Guard, Arthur T., and Marilee Henry. 1968. "Reproduction of Spanish Moss, *Tillandsia usneoides* L., by Seeds." *Bulletin of the Torrey Botanical Club* 95(4):327–330.

Guenther, Ernest. 1973. *The Essential Oils,* Vol. 6. New York: Van Nostrand.

Hacker, Richard Carleton. 1984. *The Ultimate Pipe Book.* Beverly Hills, CA: Autumngold Publishing.

Haislet, John A., ed. 1971. *Famous Trees of Texas.* 2nd ed. College Station: Texas Forest Service.

Hall, Grant D. 2000. "Pecan Food Potential in Prehistoric North America." *Economic Botany* 54(1):103–112.

Hall, Marian D. 1948. "Essential Oil" (Abstract). *Economic Botany* 2(2):227–228.

Hall, Marion Trufant. 1952. "Variation and Hybridization in *Juniperus.*" *Annals of the Missouri Botanical Garden* 39:1–64.

Hall, Thomas F., and William T. Penfound. 1944. "The Biology of the American Lotus, *Nelumbo lutea* (Willd.) Pers." *American Midland Naturalist* 31:744–758.

Haller, John M. 1978. "Tree Thief." *American Forests* 84(12):11–13, 30–31.

Halls, Lowell K. 1990. "Common Persimmon (*Diospyros virginiana*)." In Burns and Honkala, 1990, s.v. "*Diospyros virginiana.*"

Halpern, J. H., A. R. Sherwood, J. I. Hudson, D. Yurgelun-Todd, and H. G. Pope, Jr. 2005. "Psychological and Cognitive Effects of Long-Term Pey-

ote Use Among Native Americans." *Biological Psychiatry* 58(8):624–631.

Hamby, Erin Brooke. 2004. "The Roots of Healing: Archaeological and Historical Investigations of African-American Herbal Medicine." Ph.D. diss. Univ. of Tennessee.

Hardin, James W., and Jay M. Arena. 1974. *Human Poisoning from Native and Cultivated Plants.* Durham, NC: Duke Univ. Press.

Harms, Robert T. 2007. "A Field Study of Hybridization Between *Berberis swaseyi* and *B. trifoliolata* (Berberidaceae) in Hays County, Texas." *Lundellia* 10:18–31.

Harrar, Ellwood S., and J. George Harrar. 1962. *Guide to Southern Trees.* New York: Dover.

Hart, Katherine, and Elizabeth Kemp, eds. 1974. *Lucadia Pease and the Governor: Letters, 1850–1857.* Waterloo Book, no. 5. Austin, TX: Encino Press.

Harter, Abigail V., Keith A. Gardner, Daniel Falush, David L. Lentz, Robert A. Bye, and Loren H. Rieseberg. 2004. "Origins of Extant Domesticated Sunflowers in Eastern North America." *Nature* 430:201–204.

Harvey, Celia A. 1996. "Patterns of Seed Colonization and Seedling Establishment of Ball Moss (*Tillandsia recurvata*) on Sand Live Oak Trees (*Quercus geminata*) in Central Florida." *Florida Scientist* 59(2):76–81.

Hasel, Esther K. 1973. "*Coreopsis* for Reds on Cotton and Wool." *Plants and Gardens* (new ser.) 29(2):33.

Hatch, Charles E., Jr. 1957. "Mulberry Trees and Silkworms." *Virginia Magazine of History and Biography* 65(1):3–61.

Hatfield, G. M., L. J. J. Valdes, W. J. Keller, W. L. Merrill, and V. H. Jones. 1977. "An Investigation of *Sophora secundiflora* Seeds (Mescalbeans)." *Lloydia* 40(4):374–383.

Hatfield, Sadie. 1954. "Folklore of Texas Plants." In Boatright et al. 1954, 273–278.

Hauke, Richard L. 1958. "Is *Equisetum*

laevigatum a Hybrid?" *American Fern Journal* 48(2):68–72.

———. 1967. "Stalking the Giant Horsetail." *Ward's Bulletin* (Ward's Natural Science Est.) 6(44):1–2.

———. 1978. "A Taxonomic Monograph of *Equisetum* Subgenus *Equisetum.*" *Nova Hedwigia* 30:385–456.

Havard, Valery. 1885. *Report on the Flora of Western and Southern Texas.* Proceedings of U.S. National Museum 8:449–533. Washington, DC: Government Printing Office.

———. 1895. "Food Plants of the North American Indians." *Bulletin of the Torrey Botanical Club* 22:98–123.

———. 1896. "Drink Plants of the North American Indians." *Bulletin of the Torrey Botanical Club* 23:33–46.

Heald, F. D., and F. A. Wolf. 1910. "The Whitening of the Mountain Cedar, *Sabina sabinoides* (H.B.K.) Small." *Mycologia* 2(5):205–213.

Heinrich, Michael. 2002. "Ethnobotany, Phytochemistry and Biological/Pharmacological Activities of *Artemisia ludoviciana* ssp. *mexicana* (Estafiate)." In Wright 2002, 107–117.

Heiser, Charles B., Jr. 1969. *Nightshades: The Paradoxical Plants.* San Francisco: W. H. Freeman.

———. 1976. *The Sunflower.* Norman: Univ. of Oklahoma Press.

———. 1979. *The Gourd Book.* Norman: Univ. of Oklahoma Press.

———. 1993. "Ethnobotany and Economic Botany." In *Flora of North America: North of Mexico,* ed. Flora of North America Editorial Committee, vol. 1, 199–206. New York: Oxford Univ. Press.

Henderson, Andrew. 1982. "Strawberry Trees." *Garden: Journal of the Royal Horticultural Society* 107(5):191–194.

Henkel, Alice. 1907. *American Root Drugs.* U.S. Dept. of Agriculture, Bureau of Plant Industry, Bulletin no. 107. Washington, DC: Government Printing Office.

Henrickson, James. 1972. "A Taxonomic Revision of the Fouquieriaceae." *Aliso* 7(4):439–537.

Hernández-Verdugo, Sergio, Patricia Dávila Aranda, and Ken Oyama. 1999. "Síntesis del Conocimiento Taxonómico, Origen y Domesticación del Género *Capsicum*." *Boletín de la Sociedad Botánica de México* 64:65–84.

Hester, Thomas R. 1980. *Digging into South Texas Prehistory.* San Antonio: Corona.

Hester, Thomas R., Stephen L. Black, D. Gentry Steele, Ben W. Olive, Anne A. Fox, Karl J. Reinhard, and Leland C. Bement. 1989. *From the Gulf to the Rio Grande: Human Adaptation in Central, South, and Lower Pecos Texas.* Arkansas Archeological Survey Research Series, no. 33. Fayetteville, AR: Arkansas Archeological Survey.

Heywood, John S. 1986. "Edaphic Races of *Gaillardia pulchella* in Central Texas." *Journal of Heredity* 77(3):146–150.

Hicks, Sam. 1966. *Desert Plants and People.* San Antonio: Naylor.

Hinman, C. Wiley. 1984. "New Crops for Arid Lands." *Science* 225 (4669):1445–1448.

Hobbs, Christopher. 1990. *Echinacea: The Immune Herb!* Santa Cruz, CA: Botanica Press.

Hocking, George Macdonald. 1997. *A Dictionary of Natural Products: Terms in the Field of Pharmacognosy.* Medford, NJ: Plexus.

Hodge, W. H., and H. H. Sineath. 1956. "The Mexican Candelilla Plant and Its Wax." *Economic Botany* 10(2):134–154.

Hoffman, Frank M., and Charles J. Hillson. 1979. "Effects of Silicon on the Life Cycle of *Equisetum hymale* L." *Botanical Gazette* 140(2):127–132.

Holley, Mary Austin. 1836. *Texas.* Reprint. Austin: Texas State Historical Assoc., 1985.

Hollon, Eugene W., and Ruth Lapham Butler, eds. 1956. *William Bollaert's Texas.* Norman: Univ. of Oklahoma Press.

Horgan, John. 2003. "Peyote on the Brain." *Discover* 24(2):69–74.

Howard, James H. 1957. "The Mescal Bean Cult of the Central and Southern Plains: An Ancestor of the Peyote Cult?" *American Anthropologist* 59:75–87.

Hrdlick, Ales. 1908. "Physiological and Medical Observations Among the Indians of the Southwestern United States and Northern Mexico." *Smithsonian Institution Bureau of American Ethnology,* Bulletin 34:1–427.

Hu, Shiu-Ying. 1969. "*Ephedra* (Ma-Huang) in the New Chinese Materia Medica." *Economic Botany* 23(4):346–351.

Hubbard, R. K., G. J. Gascho, and G. L. Newton. 2004. "Use of Floating Vegetation to Remove Nutrients from Swinelagoon Wastewater." *Transactions of the American Society of Agricultural Engineers* 47(6):1963–1972.

Hudson, Charles M., ed. 1979. *Black Drink: A Native American Tea.* Athens: Univ. of Georgia Press.

Humphrey, Robert. 1971. "Comments on an Epiphyte, a Parasite and Four Independent Spermatophytes of the Central Desert of Baja California." *Cactus and Succulent Journal* 43(3):99–104.

Hunziker, J. H., R. A. Palacios, Amalia G. de Valesi, and Lidia Poggio. 1972. "Species Disjunctions in *Larrea*: Evidence from Morphology, Cytogenetics, Phenolic Compounds, and Seed Albumins." *Annals of the Missouri Botanical Garden* 59:224–233.

Hussey, Jane Strickland. 1974. "Some Useful Plants of Early New England." *Economic Botany* 28(3):311–337.

Hyder, Paul W., E. L. Fredrickson, Rick E. Estell, Mario Tellez, Robert P. Gibbens. 2002. "Distribution and Concentration of Total Phenolics, Condensed Tannins, and Nordihydroguaiaretic Acid (NDGA) in Creosotebush (*Larrea tridentata*)." *Biochemical Systematics and Ecology* 30:905–912.

Isenberg, Andrew C. 2000. *The Destruction of the Bison: An Environmental History, 1750–1920.* Studies in Environment and History. Cambridge: Cambridge Univ. Press.

Jackson, Donald, ed. 1962. *Letters of the Lewis and Clark Expedition, with Related Documents, 1783–1854.* Urbana: Univ. of Illinois Press.

James, Edwin. 1823. *Account of an Expedition from Pittsburgh to the Rocky Mountains . . .* 2 vols. Reprint of Philadelphia 1823 edition, March of America Facsimile Series, no. 65. Ann Arbor, MI: Univ. Microfilms, 1966.

Janzen, Daniel H., and Paul S. Martin. 1982. "Neotropical Anachronisms: The Fruits the Gomphotheres Ate." *Science* 215:19–27.

Jeffreys, Diarmuid. 2004. *Aspirin: The Remarkable Story of a Wonder Drug.* London: Bloomsbury.

Jelks, Edward B. 2005. *Handbook of Texas Online,* s.v. "Taovaya Indians," http://www.tsha.utexas.edu/handbook/online/articles/view/TT/bmt17.html (accessed January 24, 2005).

Jennison, H. M. 1931. "Further Anent 'Frost Flowers': An Explanation of Frost Crystals on Dried Plant Stems." *Torreya* 31(4):111–112.

Jessee, Jill. 1965. *Perfume Album.* 2nd ed. New York: Beauty Data.

Johansson, S., J. Gullbo, P. Lindholm, B. Ek, E. Thunberg, G. Samuelsson, R. Larsson, L. Bohlin, and P. Claeson. 2003. "Small, Novel Proteins from the Mistletoe *Phoradendron tomentosum* Exhibit Highly Selective Cytotoxicity to Human Breast Cancer Cells." *Cellular and Molecular Life Sciences* 60:165–175.

Johnston, Alex. 1970. "Blackfoot Indian Utilization of the Flora of the Northwestern Great Plains." *Economic Botany* 24(3):301–324.

Johnston, Eliza Griffin. 1972. *Texas Wild Flowers.* Austin: Shoal Creek Publishers.

Jordan, Terry G. 1978. *Texas Log Buildings: A Folk Architecture.* Austin: Univ. of Texas Press.

Joutel, Henri. 1998. *The La Salle Expedition to Texas: The Journal of Henri Joutel, 1684–1687.* Ed. William C. Foster, trans. Johanna S. Warren. Austin: Texas State Historical Assoc.

Kalm, Pehr. 1942. "Pehr Kalm's Observations on Black Walnut and Butternut Trees." Trans. and ed. Esther Louise Larsen. *Agricultural History* 16:149–157. Originally published 1767.

———. 1950. "Pehr Kalm's Description of the North American Mulberry Tree." Trans. and ed. Esther Louise Larsen. *Agricultural History* 24:221–227. Originally published 1776.

Kalteyer, George H. 1892. "Report and Analyses of Texas Sumach (*Rhus copallina*)." Geological Survey of Texas, Bulletin no. 1. Austin: Hutchings.

Kashiwada, Yoshiki, Hui-Kang Wang, Tsuneatsu Nagao, Susumu Kitanaka, Ichiro Yasuda, Toshihiro Fujioka, Takashi Yamagishi, et al. 1998. "Anti-AIDS Agents. 30. Anti-HIV Activity of Oleanolic Acid, Pomolic Acid, and Structurally Related Triterpenoids." *Journal of Natural Products* 61:1090–1095.

Katz, Alexander, Alvah G. Hall, Robert Petersen, E. N. Gathercoal, Walter D. Scott, Monroe C. Kidder, William H. Finney, et al. 1950. "Some Potential Sources of Important Plant Products in California." *Economic Botany* 4(1):3–36.

Kaufman, Peter B., Wilbur C. Bigelow, Rudolf Schmid, and Najati S. Ghosheh. 1971. "Electron Microprobe Analysis of Silica in Epidermal Cells of *Equisetum*." *American Journal of Botany* 58(4):309–316.

Kausch, Albert P., James L. Seago, Jr., and Leland C. Marsh. 1981. "Changes in Starch Distribution in the Overwintering Organs of *Typha latifolia* (Typhaceae)." *American Journal of Botany* 68(7):877–880.

Keasey, Merritt S., III. 1981. "Prickly Pear." *Pacific Discovery* 34(4):1–8.

Kellam, Laura L., Phillip J. Johnson, Joanne Kramer, and Kevin G. Keegan. 2000. "Gastric Impaction and Obstruction of the Small Intestine Associated with Persimmon Phytobezoar in a Horse." *Journal of the American Veterinary Medical Association* 216(8):1279–1281.

Keller, W. J., W. M. Bourn, and J. F. Bonfiglio. 1981. "A Folk Medicine for Diabetes Mellitus." *Quarterly Journal of Crude Drug Research* 19(2–3):49–51.

Kephart, George S. 1972. "Live Oak: The Tree with a Past." *American Forests* 78(6):36–39, 58–61.

Kernell, Judith L., and Gerald F. Levy. 1990. "The Relationship of Bald Cypress . . . Knee Height to Water Depth." *Castanea* 55(4):217–222.

Killingbeck, Keith T. 1990. "Leaf Production Can Be Decoupled from Root Activity in the Desert Shrub Ocotillo (*Fouquieria splendens* Engelm.)." *American Midland Naturalist* 124(1):124–129.

Kindscher, Kelly. 1987. *Edible Wild Plants of the Prairie: An Ethnobotanical Guide.* Lawrence: Univ. Press of Kansas.

———. 1989. "Ethnobotany of Purple Coneflower (*Echinacea angustifolia*, Asteraceae) and Other Echinacea Species." *Ethnobotany* 43(4):498–507.

———. 1992. *Medicinal Wild Plants of the Prairie: An Ethnobotanical Guide.* Lawrence: Univ. Press of Kansas.

Kingsbury, John M. 1964. *Poisonous Plants of the United States and Canada.* Englewood Cliffs, NJ: Prentice-Hall.

Kirkland, Forrest, and W. W. Newcomb, Jr. 1967. *The Rock Art of Texas Indians.* Austin: Univ. of Texas Press.

Kirkpatrick, Zoe M. 1992. *Wildflowers of the Western Plains: A Field Guide.* Austin: Univ. of Texas Press.

Kirtley, Guy. 1954. "'Hoping Out' in East Texas." In Boatright et al. 1954, 195–202.

Knauer, K. W., J. C. Reagor, E. M. Bailey, Jr., and L. Carriker. 1995. "Mescalbean (*Sophora secundiflora*) Toxicity in a Dog." *Veterinary and Human Toxicology* 37(3):237–239.

Kniffen, Fred B., and Malcolm L. Comeaux. 1979. *The Spanish Moss Folk Industry of Louisiana. Mélanges,*

no. 12. Baton Rouge: Louisiana State Univ., Museum of Geoscience.

Krenzelok, Edward P., T. D. Jacobsen, and John Aronis. 1997. "American Mistletoe Exposures." *American Journal of Emergency Medicine* 15(5):516–520.

Krochmal, Arnold, and W. Grierson. 1961. "Brief History of Grape Growing in the United States." *Economic Botany* 15(2):114–118.

Kuijt, Job. 2003. "Monograph of *Phoradendron* (Viscaceae)." *Systematic Botany Monographs*, vol. 66. Ann Arbor, MI: American Society of Plant Taxonomists.

Kumler, Donna J. 2005. *Handbook of Texas Online*, s.v. "Bois D'Arc Creek," http://www.tsha.utexas.edu/handbook/online/articles/view/BB/rhb25.html (accessed February 3, 2005).

Kuttruff, Jenna T., S. Gail DeHart, and Michael J. O'Brien. 1998. "7500 Years of Prehistoric Footwear from Arnold Research Cave, Missouri." *Science* 281(5373):72–75.

La Barre, Weston. 1989. *The Peyote Cult.* 5th ed, enlarged. Norman: Univ. of Oklahoma Press.

Lacey, Marc. 2004. "Sudan War Threatens U.S. Supply of Resin." *Austin American-Statesman,* Sunday, May 30. Reprinted from *New York Times.*

Laferriere, Joseph E., Charles W. Weber, and Edwin A. Kohlhepp. 1991. "Use and Nutritional Composition of Some Traditional Mountain Pima Plant Foods." *Journal of Ethnobiology* 11(1):93–114.

Lampe, Kenneth F., and Rune Fagerström. 1968. *Plant Toxicity and Dermatitis.* Baltimore: Williams & Wilkins.

Lampe, Kenneth F., and Mary Ann McCann. 1985. *AMA Handbook of Poisonous and Injurious Plants.* Chicago: American Medical Assoc.

Lancaster, Mark, Richard Storey, and Nathan W. Bower. 1983. "Nutritional Evaluation of Buffalo Gourd: Elemental Analysis of Seed." *Economic Botany* 37(3):306–309.

Langdon, O. Gordon. 1958. *Silvical Characteristics of Baldcypress.* U.S. Dept. of Agriculture Forest Service, Station Paper, no. 94.

Latorre, Dolores L., and Felipe A. Latorre. 1977. "Plants Used by the Mexican Kickapoo Indians." *Economic Botany* 31:340–357.

La Vere, David. 1998. *Life Among the Texas Indians: The WPA Narratives.* College Station: Texas A&M Univ. Press.

Lawson, Edwin R. 1990. "*Juniperus virginiana* L. (Eastern Redcedar)." In Burns and Honkala, 1990, s.v. "*Juniperus virginiana.*"

Lemus, I., R. García, S. Erazo, R. Peña, M. Parada, and M. Fuenzalida. 1996. "Diuretic Activity of an *Equisetum bogotense* Tea (Platero Herb): Evaluation in Healthy Volunteers." *Journal of Ethnopharmacology* 54:55–58.

Lentz, David L., Mary E. D. Pohl, Kevin O. Pope, and Andrew R. Wyatt. 2001. "Prehistoric Sunflower (*Helianthus annuus* L.) Domestication in Mexico." *Economic Botany* 55(3):370–376.

Lewis, Isaac M. 1915. *The Trees of Texas: An Illustrated Manual of the Native and Introduced Trees of the State.* Bulletin of the Univ. of Texas, no. 22. Austin: Univ. of Texas.

Lia, Veronica V., Viviana A. Confalonieri, Cecilia I. Comas, and Juan H. Hunziker. 2001. "Molecular Phylogeny of *Larrea* and Its Allies (Zygophyllaceae): Reticulate Evolution and the Probable Time of Creosote Bush Arrival to North America." *Molecular Phylogenetics and Evolution* 21(2):309–320.

Linares, Edelmira, Robert Bye, and Beatriz Flores. 1999. *Plantas Medicinales de México: Usos y Remedios Tradicionales.* Bilingual facing-page edition. Mexico, DF: Proyecto y Ejecución Editorial.

Lincecum, Gideon. 1949. *Journal of Lincecum's Travels in Texas, 1835.* Ed. A. L. Bradford and T. N. Campbell. Reprinted from *Southwestern Historical Quarterly* 53(2).

Lipe, John A. 1979. "Muscadine Grape Variety Trials in East Texas." *Texas Agricultural Experiment Station, PR-3557.* College Station: Texas A&M Univ. System.

Liu, Yong-Long, and T. J. Mabry. 1982. "Flavonoids from *Artemisia ludoviciana* var. *ludoviciana.*" *Phytochemistry* 21(1):209–214.

Lively, Jeanne F. 2005. *Handbook of Texas Online,* s.v. "Blanket, TX," http://www.tsha.utexas.edu/handbook/online/articles/view/BB/hlb33.html.

Loaiza-Figueroa, Fernando, Kermit Ritland, Jose A. Laborde Cancino, and S. D. Tanksley. 1989. "Patterns of Genetic Variation of the Genus *Capsicum* (Solanaceae) in Mexico." *Plant Systematics and Evolution* 165:159–188.

Lockett, Landon. 1991. "Native Texas Palms North of the Lower Rio Grande Valley: Recent Discoveries." *Principes* 35(2):64–71.

———. 1995. "Historical Evidence of the Native Presence of *Sabal mexicana* (Palmae) North of the Lower Rio Grande Valley." *Sida* 16(4):711–719.

———. 2004. "Identification of Palm Trees in the Austin, Texas, Area." *Native Plant Society of Texas News* 22(2):5–6.

Lockett, Landon, and Robert W. Read. 1990. "Extension of Native Range of *Sabal mexicana* (Palmae) in Texas to Include Central Coast." *Sida* 14(1):79–85.

Lomax, John A., and Alan Lomax. 1948. *Cowboy Songs and Other Frontier Ballads.* New York: Macmillan.

Loughmiller, Campbell, and Lynn Loughmiller. 1996. *Texas Wildflowers.* Austin: Univ. of Texas Press.

Mabry, T. J., J. H. Hunziker, and D. R. DiFeo Jr., eds. 1977. *Creosote Bush: Biology and Chemistry of* Larrea *in New World Deserts.* US/IBP Synthesis Series, no. 6. Stroudsburg, PA: Dowden, Hutchinson & Ross.

MacDougal, D. T. 1893. "Frost Plants: A Resume." *Science* 22 (569):351–352.

———. 1894. "Frost Plants." *Botanical Gazette* 19(3):120–121.

Mackay, Wayne A., Jerry M. Parsons, Greg Grant, Steve George, Tim D. Davis, and Larry Stein. 2000. "'Texas Maroon' Bluebonnet." *HortScience* 35(2):313.

Maguire, Jack. 1975. "When the Bluebonnet Came to Texas." *Southwest Airlines Magazine,* April, pp. 6, 8.

Malm, Olaf, Marlon De Freitas Fonseca, Paula Hissnauer Miguel, Wanderley Rodrigues Bastos, and Fernando Neves Pinto. 1998. "Use of Epiphyte Plants as Biomonitors to Map Atmospheric Mercury in a Gold Trade Center City, Amazon, Brazil." *Science of the Total Environment* 213(1–3):57–64.

Manaster, Jane. 1994. *The Pecan Tree.* Austin: Univ. of Texas Press.

Marcy, Randolph B. 1853. *Exploration of the Red River of Louisiana in the Year 1852.* Washington, DC: Robert Armstrong.

Marshall, George. 1984. "A Review of the Biology of *Equisetum arvense* L. (field horsetail)." *Aspects of Applied Biology* 8:25–31.

———. 1986. "Growth and Development of Field Horsetail (*Equisetum arvense* L.)." *Weed Science* 34:271–275.

Martin, Craig E., Kenneth W. McLeod, Carol A. Eades, and Angela F. Pitzer. 1985. "Morphological and Physiological Responses to Irradiance in the CAM Epiphyte *Tillandsia usneoides* L. (Bromeliaceae). *Botanical Gazette* 146(4):489–494.

Martin, George C. 1933. *Big Bend Basket Maker Papers No. 3: Archaeological Exploration of the Shumla Caves; Report of the George C. Martin Expedition.* San Antonio: Southwest Texas Archaeological Society, Witte Memorial Museum.

Martínez, Raymond J. [1968?] *The Story of Spanish Moss: What It Is and How It Grows.* New Orleans: Hope Publications.

Massey, A. B. 1945. "Native Grapes." *Bulletin of the Virginia Polytechnic Institute* 38(9):3–20.

Mathias, Mildred E. 1994. "Magic, Myth and Medicine." *Economic Botany* 48(1):3–7.

Matsui, Shichiro. 1930. *The History of the Silk Industry in the United States.* New York: Howes.

Mattoon, W. R., and C. B. Webster. 1928. *Forest Trees of Texas: How to Know Them.* Texas Forest Service, Bulletin no. 20. College Station: Texas Forest Service.

Maverick, Mary A. 1921. *Memoirs of Mary A. Maverick: Arranged by Mary A. Maverick and Her Son Geo. Madison Maverick.* Ed. Rena Maverick Green. San Antonio, TX: Alamo Printing.

Mayhall, Mildred P. 1962. *The Kiowas.* Norman: Univ. of Oklahoma Press.

Mazza, G., F. A. Kiehn, and H. H. Marshall. 1993. "*Monarda*: A Source of Geraniol, Linalool, Thymol and Carvacrol-Rich Essential Oils." In *New Crops,* ed. J. Janick and J. E. Simon, 628–631. New York: Wiley.

McAlister, Wayne H., and Martha K. McAlister. 1993. *Matagorda Island: A Naturalist's Guide.* Austin: Univ. of Texas Press.

McAllister, J. Gilbert. 1949. "Kiowa-Apache Tales." In Boatright 1949, 1–141.

McDonald, Andrew. 2004. "A Botanical Perspective on the Identity of Soma (*Nelumbo nucifera* Gaertn.) Based on Scriptural and Iconographic Records." *Economic Botany* 58 (Suppl.):147–173.

McLemore, B. F. 1990. "Flowering Dogwood." In Burns and Honkala, 1990, s.v. "*Cornus florida.*"

McLeRoy, Sherrie S., and Roy E. Renfro, Jr. 2004. *Grape Man of Texas: The Life of T. V. Munson.* Austin: Eakin Press.

McPherson, J. M. 1987. "A Field Study of Winter Fruit Preferences of Cedar Waxwings." *Condor* 89(2):293–306.

Merrill, William L. 1977. *An Investigation of Ethnographic and Archaeological Specimens of Mescalbeans (Sophora secundiflora) in American*

Museums. Technical Reports, no. 6. Ann Arbor: Univ. of Michigan Museum of Anthropology.

———. 1979. "The Beloved Tree: *Ilex vomitoria* Among the Indians of the Southeast and Adjacent Regions." In Hudson 1979, 40–82.

Meyer, Brian N., and Jerry L. McLaughlin. 1981. "Economic Uses of *Opuntia.*" *Cactus and Succulent Journal* (U.S.) 53(3):107–112.

Mielke, Judy. 1993. *Native Plants for Southwestern Landscapes.* Austin: Univ. of Texas Press.

Milanich, Jerald T. 1979. "Origins and Prehistoric Distributions of Black Drink and the Ceremonial Shell Drinking Cup." In Hudson 1979, 83–119.

Miller, Howard A., and Samuel H. Lamb. 1985. *Oaks of North America.* Happy Camp, CA: Naturegraph.

Mills, Anne H. 1996. "The Splendid Ocotillo." *Fremontia* 24(3):3–7.

Millspaugh, Charles F. 1974. *American Medicinal Plants: An Illustrated and Descriptive Guide to Plants Indigenous to and Naturalized in the United States Which Are Used in Medicine.* New York: Dover. Reprint of the 1892 ed. published in 2 vols., by J. C. Yorston, Philadelphia, under the title *Medicinal Plants.*

Missouri Botanical Garden. 1924. "Frost Flowers." *Missouri Botanical Garden Bulletin* 12(8):104–105.

Mitchell, Wilma A., Patsy A. Gibbs, and Chester O. Martin. 1988. "Flowering Dogwood (*Cornus florida*)." Section 7.5.9., *U.S. Army Corps of Engineers Wildlife Resources Management Manual.* Dept. of Defense Natural Resources Program, Technical Report EL-88-9. Vicksburg, MS: U.S. Army Corps of Engineers Waterways Experiment Station.

Mitich, Larry W. 1970. "The Ocotillo: Hallmark of the Desert." *National Cactus and Succulent Journal* 25(2):45.

———. 1988. "Common Lambsquarters." *Weed Technology* 2(4):550–552.

———. 1992. "Horsetail." *Weed Technology* 6(3):779–781.

———. 2000. "Common Cattail, *Typha latifolia.*" *Weed Technology* 14(2):446–450.

Moerman, Daniel E. 1998. *Native American Ethnobotany.* Portland, OR: Timber Press.

Moore, Michael. 1990. *Los Remedios: Traditional Herbal Remedies of the Southwest.* 2nd ed. Santa Fe, NM: Red Crane Books.

Moreno, Sylvia. 2005. "For Native Americans, Peyote Is Dwindling." *Austin American-Statesman,* Sept. 19, Sect. F.

Morgan, Mrs. A. L. 1941. "The Sky Fell on Texas: Bluebonnets Had Made History Before They Were Named Texas' State Flower." *Texas Parade* 5(12):13, 18.

Morgan, George R. 1983. "The Biogeography of Peyote in South Texas." *Botanical Museum Leaflets, Harvard University* 29(2):73–86.

Morton, Julia F. 1975. "Cattails (*Typha* spp.): Weed Problem or Potential Crop?" *Economic Botany* 29(1):7–29.

Mueller, Ferdinand von. 1884. *Select Extra-Tropical Plants Readily Eligible for Industrial Culture or Naturalization, with Indications of Their Native Countries and Some of Their Uses.* Detroit, MI: George S. Davis.

Muenscher, Walter Conrad. 1944. *Aquatic Plants of the United States.* Ithaca, NY: Cornell Univ. Press.

Muir, Andrew Forest, ed. 1958. *Texas in 1837: An Anonymous, Contemporary Narrative.* Austin: Univ. of Texas Press.

Nabhan, Gary Paul. 1979. "Southwestern Indian Sunflowers." *Desert Plants* 1(1):23–26.

———. 1991. "Desert Legumes as a Nutritional Intervention for Diabetic Indigenous Dwellers of Arid Lands." *Arid Lands Newsletter* 31:11–13.

National Research Council (U.S.) Panel on Amaranth. 1984. *Amaranth: Modern Prospects for an Ancient Crop.* Washington, DC: National Academy Press.

Naves, Y. R., and G. Mazuyer. 1947. *Natural Perfume Materials: A Study of Concretes, Resinoids, Floral Oils and Pomades.* Trans. Edward Sagarin. New York: Reinhold.

Neich, Roger, and Mick Pendergrast. 1997. *Traditional Tapa Textiles of the Pacific.* London: Thames & Hudson.

Nelson, Barney. 2000. *The Last Campfire: The Life Story of Ted Gray, a West Texas Rancher.* Marathon, TX: Iron Mountain Press.

Nesom, Guy L. 1998. *Trees of Huntsville and Walker County Texas and Big Tree Register.* Texas Research Institute for Environmental Studies, Sam Houston State Univ. Huntsville: Sam Houston Press.

Newberry, J. S. 1887. "Food and Fiber Plants of the North American Indians." *Popular Science Monthly* 32:31–46.

Newcomb, W. W., Jr. 1961. *The Indians of Texas: From Prehistoric to Modern Times.* Austin: Univ. of Texas Press.

Newkumet, Vynola Beaver, and Howard L. Meredith. 1988. *Hasinai: A Traditional History of the Caddo Confederacy.* College Station: Texas A&M Univ. Press.

Nobel, Park S. 1994. *Remarkable Agaves and Cacti.* New York: Oxford Univ. Press.

Nobel, Park S., and Edgar Quero. 1986. "Environmental Productivity Indices for a Chihuahuan Desert CAM Plant, *Agave lechuguilla*." *Ecology* 67(1):1–11.

Noguchi, Masami, Toshihiro Okabe, and Hisashi Tanaka. 1981. "Polishing of Wood with Tokusa (*Equisetum hiemale* [sic] L. var. *japonicum* Milde.). *Mokuzai Gakkaishi* 27(3):191–196.

Nokes, Jill. 2001. *How to Grow Native Plants of Texas and the Southwest.* Austin: Univ. of Texas Press.

Nuttall, Thomas. 1821. "A Description of Some New Species of Plants, Recently Introduced into the Gardens of Philadelphia, from the Arkansa Territory." *Journal of the Academy of Natural Sciences of Philadelphia* 2(1):114–123.

Nye, Wilbur Sturtevant. 1962. *Bad Medicine and Good: Tales of the Kiowa.* Norman: Univ. of Oklahoma Press.

Olmsted, Frederick Law. 1857. *A Journey Through Texas, or, a Saddle-Trip on the Southwestern Frontier.* Reprint of the 1857 ed. published by Dix, Edwards, New York. Austin: Univ. of Texas Press, 1978.

Olvera-Fonseca, Silvia. 2004. "Evaluation of the Bromatological Potential of Seeds and Fruits of *Sabal mexicana* Mart. (Areaceae)." *Economic Botany* 58(4):536–543.

Opler, Morris Edward. 1940. *Myths and Legends of the Lipan Apache Indians.* New York: American Folklore Society.

Ownbey, Marion. 1950. "The Genus *Allium* in Texas." *Research Studies of the State College of Washington* 18(4):181–222.

———. 1958. "Monograph of the Genus *Argemone* for North America and the West Indies." *Memoirs of the Torrey Botanical Club* 21(1):1–159.

Ownbey, Marion, and Hannah C. Aase. 1955. "Cytotaxonomic Studies in *Allium.* I: The *Allium canadense* Alliance." *Research Studies of the State College of Washington:* Monographic Suppl. No. 1.

Paine, Laura K., and Helen C. Harrison. 1992. "Mistletoe: Its Role in Horticulture and Human Life." *HortTechnology* 2(3):324–330.

Palmer, Edward. 1878. "Plants Used by the Indians of the United States." *American Naturalist* 12:593–606, 646–655.

Parks, H. B. 1937. *Valuable Plants Native to Texas.* Bulletin no. 551. College Station: Texas Agricultural Experiment Station.

Parsons, Elsie Clews. 1941. "Notes on the Caddo." *Memoirs of the American Anthropological Association* no. 57. Menasha, WI: American Anthropological Assoc.

Parsons, Jerry M., Tim D. Davis, Steven W. George, and Wayne A. Mackay. 1994. "'Barbara Bush' Bluebonnet (*Lupinus texensis* Hook.)." *HortScience* 29(10):1202.

Pasztor, Patty Leslie. 2003. "Texas Trees and Their Uses." Lecture, Lady Bird Johnson Wildflower Center, Austin, TX, February 16.

Peacock, Howard. 1982. "Just Plain Poke." *Texas Highways* 29(3):8–11.

———. 1985. "Pine Needle Art of the Big Thicket Indians." In *Folk Art in Texas,* ed. Francis Edward Abernethy, 141–153. Dallas: Southern Methodist Univ. Press.

Peattie, Donald C. 1953. *A Natural History of Western Trees.* Boston: Houghton Mifflin.

———. 1966. *A Natural History of Trees of Eastern and Central North America.* Boston: Houghton Mifflin.

Pellett, Frank C. 1976. *American Honey Plants.* 5th ed. Hamilton, IL: Dadant & Sons.

Penfound, W. T., and F. G. Deiler. 1947. "On the Ecology of Spanish Moss." *Ecology* 28(4):455–458.

Pénicaut, André. 1953. *Fleur de Lys and Calumet: Being the Pénicaut Narrative of French Adventure in Louisiana.* Trans. and ed. Richebourg Gaillard McWilliams. Baton Rouge: Louisiana State Univ. Press.

Pennington, Campbell W. 1958. "Tarahumar Fish Stupefaction Plants." *Economic Botany* 12:95–102.

Perttula, Timothy K. 2005. *Handbook of Texas Online,* s.v. "Caddo Indians," http://www.tsha.utexas.edu/handbook/online/articles/CC/bmcaj.html (accessed August 30, 2005).

Peters, Charles M., Joshua Rosenthal, and Teodile Urbina. 1987. "Otomi Bark Paper in Mexico: Commercialization of a Pre-Hispanic Technology." *Economic Botany* 41(3):423–432.

Pimienta-Barrios, Eulogio, Giuseppe Barbera, and Paolo Inglese. 1993. "Cactus Pear (*Opuntia* spp., Cactaceae) International Network: An Effort for Productivity and Environmental Conservation for Arid and Semiarid

Lands." *Cactus and Succulent Journal* (U.S.) 65:225–229.

Piña Lujan, Ignacio. 1972. "El Palmito." *Cactáceas y Suculentas Mexicanas* 17(3):84–92.

Pinchot, Gifford. 1907. *Black Walnut* (Juglans nigra). U.S. Dept. of Agriculture, Forest Service, Circular 88.

Pinckney, Pauline A. 1967. *Painting in Texas: The Nineteenth Century.* Austin: Univ. of Texas Press.

Pitcher, J. A., and J. S. McKnight. 1990. In Burns and Honkala, 1990, s.v. "*Salix nigra.*"

Pliny the Elder. 1938–1963. *Natural History, with an English Translation in Ten Volumes.* Loeb Classical Library. Cambridge, MA: Harvard Univ. Press. See especially vols. 6–7, trans. W. H .S. Jones.

Porcher, Francis Peyre. 1869. *Resources of the Southern Fields and Forests, Medical, Economical and Agricultural.* Charleston, SC: Walker, Evans & Cogswell.

Powell, A. Michael. 1988. *Trees and Shrubs of the Trans-Pecos and Adjacent Areas.* Austin: Univ. of Texas Press.

———. 1994. *Grasses of the Trans-Pecos and Adjacent Areas.* Austin: Univ. of Texas Press.

Powell, A. Michael, and James F. Weedin. 2004. *Cacti of the Trans-Pecos and Adjacent Areas.* Lubbock: Texas Tech Univ. Press.

Prendergast, D. V., Max J. Kennedy, Rosemary F. Webby, and Kenneth R. Markham. 2000. "Plant Portraits: Pollen Cakes of *Typha* spp. (Typhaceae), 'Lost' and Living Food." *Economic Botany* 54(3):254–255.

Prior, Sophia. 1939. *Mistletoe and Holly.* Field Museum of Natural History, Botany Leaflet 24. Chicago: Field Museum of Natural History.

Pulich, Warren M. 1976. *The Golden-Cheeked Warbler: A Bioecological Study.* Austin: Texas Parks and Wildlife Dept.

Pyatt, F. B., J. P. Grattan, D. Lacy, A. J. Pyatt, and M. R. D. Seaward.

1999. "Comparative Effectiveness of *Tillandsia usneoides* L. and *Parmotrema praesorediosum* (Nyl.) Hale as Bio-Indicators of Atmospheric Pollution in Louisiana (USA)." *Water, Air, and Soil Pollution.* 111(1–4-):317–326.

Quarles, William. 1995. "The Truth About Horsetails or Natural Plant Disease Protection from Silica." *Common Sense Pest Control* 11(2):18.

Radeleff, R. D. 1970. *Veterinary Toxicology.* 2nd ed. Philadelphia: Lea & Febiger.

Ranson, Nancy Richey. 1933. *Texas Wildflower Legends.* Dallas: Kaleidograph.

Ray, Sankar N., and Wesley J. White. 1979. "*Equisetum arvense*: An Aquatic Vascular Plant as a Biological Monitor for Heavy Metal Pollution." *Chemosphere* 8(3):125–128.

Rea, Amadeo M. 1991. "Gila River Pima Dietary Reconstruction." *Arid Lands Newsletter* 31:3–10.

Record, Samuel J. 1916. "Spanish Moss: The Source of a Valuable Upholstering Material." *Scientific American* 115:58–59.

Reid, Mrs. Bruce. 1964. "An Indian Legend of the Blue Bonnet." In *Legends of Texas: Publications of the Texas Folklore Society,* no. 3, ed. J. Frank Dobie, 197–200. Reprint of the original 1924 ed. of the Texas Folklore Society. Hatboro, PA: Folklore Associates.

Reiff, A. E. 1984. *Native Texans: Some Medicinal, Social and Philosophic Contexts of the Plants of Texas and the Southwest.* Phoenix: Newfoundland.

Reyes-Agüero, Juan Antonio, Juan Rogelio Aguirre-Rivera, and Cecilia Beatriz Peña-Valdivia. 2000. "Biología y Aprovechamiento de *Agave lechuguilla* Torrey." *Boletín de la Sociedad Botánica de México* 67:75–88.

Reyes Carmona, Ramiro, and Ana María García Gil. 1982. "El Uso Múltiple del Ocotillo (*Fouquieria splen-*

dens Engelm.) en las Zonas Áridas." *Ciencia Forestal* 7(36):3–18.

Rice, Dale. 2004. "Vines for Texas Climes." *Austin American-Statesman,* Nov. 10, Section E.

Richardson, Alfred. 2002. *Wildflowers and Other Plants of Texas Beaches and Islands.* Austin: Univ. of Texas Press.

Richardson, James B., III. 1972. "The Pre-Columbian Distribution of the Bottle Gourd (*Lagenaria siceraria*): A Re-evaluation." *Economic Botany* 26(3):265–273.

Ricklis, Robert A. 1996. *The Karankawa Indians of Texas: An Ecological Study of Cultural Tradition and Change.* Austin: Univ. of Texas Press.

Rivas, Maggie. 1994. "Seeking an Antidote: Officials Hope to Learn Prevalence of Jimson Weed Abuse, Avert New Tragedy." *Dallas Morning News,* Aug. 28, Section A.

Robertson, James A., trans. and ed. 1993. "The Account by a Gentleman from Elvas." In *The De Soto Chronicles: The Expedition of Hernando de Soto to North America in 1539–1543,* ed. Lawrence A. Clayton, Vernon James Knight, Jr., and Edward C. Moore. Tuscaloosa: Univ. of Alabama Press.

Roell, Craig H. 2005. *Handbook of Texas Online,* s.v. "Weesatche, TX," http://www.tsha.utexas.edu/handbook/online/articles/WW/hlw11.html (accessed August 21, 2005).

Roemer, Ferdinand. 1935. *Texas, with Particular Reference to German Immigration and the Physical Appearance of the Country.* Trans. Oswald Mueller. Reprint of 1935 edition. Special heritage edition. Austin: Eakin, 1995.

Rogers, George K. 1985. "The Genera of Phytolaccaceae in the Southeastern United States." *Journal of the Arnold Arboretum* 66(1):1–37.

Rogers, Ken E. 2000. *The Magnificent Mesquite.* Austin: Univ. of Texas Press.

Russell, Charles F., and Peter Felker. 1987. "The Prickly-pears (*Opuntia* spp., Cactaceae): A Source of Human and Animal Food in Semiarid Regions." *Economic Botany* 41(3):433–445.

Ryan, Julie. 1998. *Perennial Gardens for Texas*. Austin: Univ. of Texas Press.

Safford, William E. 1922. *Daturas of the Old World and New: An Account of Their Narcotic Properties and Their Use in Oracular and Initiatory Ceremonies*. From *The Smithsonian Report for 1920*, pp. 537–567. Publication 2644. Washington, DC: Government Printing Office.

Samuelsson, Gunnar. 1973. "Mistletoe Toxins." *Systematic Zoology* 22(4):566–569.

Sargent, Charles Sprague. 1947. *The Silva of North America: A Description of the Trees Which Grow Naturally in North America Exclusive of Mexico*. 14 vols. New York: Peter Smith.

Sauer, Jonathan D. 1950. "Pokeweed, an Old American Herb." *Missouri Botanical Garden Bulletin* 38(5):82–88.

———. 1952. "A Geography of Pokeweed." *Annals of the Missouri Botanical Garden* 39:113–125.

Scagel, R. F., R. J. Bandoni, J. R. Maze, G. E. Rouse, W. B. Schofield, and J. R. Stein. 1984. *Plants: An Evolutionary Survey*. Belmont, CA: Wadsworth.

Schaal, Barbara A., and Wesley J. Leverich. 1980. "Pollination and Banner Markings in *Lupinus texensis* (Leguminosae)." *Southwestern Naturalist* 25(2):280–282.

Schaffner, John H. 1898. "Observations on the Nutation of *Helianthus annuus*." *Botanical Gazette* 25(6):395–403.

———. 1900. "The Nutation of *Helianthus*." *Botanical Gazette* 29(3):197–200.

Schambach, Frank F. 2000. "Spiroan Traders, the Sanders Site, and the Plains Interaction Sphere: A Reply to Bruseth, Wilson, and Pertulla." *Plains Anthropologist* 45(171):7–33.

Schnetzler, Kent A., and William M. Breene. 1994. "Food Uses and Amaranth Product Research: A Com-

prehensive Review." In *Amaranth Biology, Chemistry, and Technology*, ed. O. Paredes-López, 155–184. Boca Raton, FL: CRC Press.

Schrimpff, Ernst. 1984. "Air Pollution Patterns in Two Cities of Colombia, S.A., According to Trace Substances Content of an Epiphyte (*Tillandsia recurvata* L.)." *Water, Air, and Soil Pollution* 21:279–315.

Schütze, Julius. 1884. "Seidenbau in Texas." *Schütze's Jahrbuch für Texas und Volks-Kalender für 1884*. Austin, TX: Albert Schuetze.

Schultes, Richard E. 1938. "The Appeal of Peyote (*Lophophora williamsii*) as a Medicine." *American Anthropologist* N.s. 40(1):698–715.

———. 1976. *Hallucinogenic Plants*. New York: Golden.

Schultes, Richard E., and Albert Hofmann. 1973. *The Botany and Chemistry of Hallucinogens*. American Lecture Series, no. 843. Springfield, IL: Charles C. Thomas.

Schultz, J. C., D. Otte, and F. Enders. 1977. "*Larrea* as a Habitat Component for Desert Arthropods." In Mabry et al. 1977, 176–208.

Schulz, Ellen D. 1928. *Texas Wild Flowers: A Popular Account of the Common Wild Flowers of Texas*. Chicago: Laidlaw Bros.

Schwartz, Owen M. 1986. "On the Vascular Anatomy of *Tillandsia usneoides* (Bromeliaceae)." *Journal of the Bromeliad Society* 36(4):154–158.

Seigler, D., F. Seaman, and Tom J. Mabry. 1971. "New Cyanogenetic Lipids from *Ungnadia speciosa*." *Phytochemistry* 10(2):485–487.

Seigler, D. S., S. Seilheimer, J. Keesy, and H. F. Huang. 1986. "Tannins from Four Common *Acacia* Species of Texas and Northeastern Mexico." *Economic Botany* 40(2):220–232.

Seiler, Elizabeth McGreevy. 2005. "Untwisting the Cedar: The Myths and Culture of the Ashe Juniper Tree," http://members.toast.net/juniper (accessed May 18, 2005).

Shafer, Harry J. 1986. *Ancient Texans:*

Rock Art and Lifeways Along the Lower Pecos. Austin: Texas Monthly Press.

Shah, Sachin A., Stephen Sander, C. Michael White, Mike Rinaldi, and Craig I. Coleman. 2007. "Evaluation of Echinacea for the Prevention and Treatment of the Common Cold: A Meta-Analysis." *Lancet Infectious Diseases* 7(7):473–480.

Sharma, Nirmal, Anu Shilpa, and S. S. Agrawal. 2000. "*Argemone mexicana*, the Dropsy Devil of Swaranshiri: A Review." *Hamdard Medicus* 43(1):110–118.

Sheldon, Sam. 1980. "Ethnobotany of *Agave lecheguilla* and *Yucca carnerosana* in Mexico's Zona Ixtlera." *Economic Botany* 34(4):376–390.

Shemluck, Melvin. 1982. "Medicinal and Other Uses of the Compositae by Indians in the United States and Canada." *Journal of Ethnopharmacology* 5(3):303–358.

Shen-Miller, J., Mary Beth Mudgett, J. William Schopf, Steven Clarke, and Rainer Berger. 1995. "Exceptional Seed Longevity and Robust Growth: Ancient Sacred Lotus from China." *American Journal of Botany* 82(11):1367–1380.

Sievers, A. F. 1947. "The Production of Minor Essential Oils in the United States." *Economic Botany* 1(2):148–160.

Silverthorne, Elizabeth. 1996. *Legends and Lore of Texas Wildflowers*. College Station: Texas A&M Univ. Press.

Simpson, Benny J. 1988. *A Field Guide to Texas Trees*. Austin: Texas Monthly Press.

Simpson, Beryl B. 1999. "A Revision of *Hoffmannseggia* (Fabaceae) in North America." *Lundellia* 2:14–54.

Simpson, Beryl B., J. L. Neff, and A. R. Moldenke. 1977. "Reproductive Systems of *Larrea*. In Mabry et al. 1977, 92–114.

Simpson, Beryl B., Jennifer A. Tate, and Andrea Weeks. 2004. "Phylogeny and Character Evolution of *Hoffmannseggia* (Caesalpinieae: Caesalpinioideae:

Leguminosae)." *Systematic Botany* 29(4):933–946.

———. 2005. "The Biogeography of *Hoffmannseggia* (Leguminosae, Caesalpinioideae, Caesalpinieae). *Journal of Biogeography* 32:15–27.

Sjoberg, Andrée F. 1951. "The Bidai Indians of Southeastern Texas." *Southwestern Journal of Anthropology* 7:391–400.

———. 1953. "The Culture of the Tonkawa, A Texas Indian Tribe." *Texas Journal of Science* 5(3):280–304.

Slotkin, J. S. 1951. "Early Eighteenth Century Documents on Peyotism North of the Rio Grande." *American Anthropologist* 52(3):420–427.

Small, John K. 1927. "The Palmetto-Palm, *Sabal texana.*" *Journal of the New York Botanical Garden* 28:132–143.

Smith, Bruce D. 1984. "*Chenopodium* as a Prehistoric Domesticate in Eastern North America: Evidence from Russell Cave, Alabama." *Science* 226 (4671):165–167.

Smith, Edwin B., and Hapton M. Parker. 1971. "A Biosystematic Study of *Coreopsis tinctoria* and *C. cardaminefolia* (Compositae)." *Brittonia* 23(2):161–170.

Smith, Huron H. 1928. "Ethnobotany of the Meskwaki." *Bulletin of the Public Museum of the City of Milwaukee* 4(2):175–326.

Smith, Jeffrey L., and Janice V. Perino. 1981. "Osage Orange (*Maclura pomifera*): History and Economic Uses." *Economic Botany* 35(1):24–41.

Smith, Lyman B., and Carroll E. Wood, Jr. 1975. "The Genera of Bromeliaceae in the Southeastern United States." *Journal of the Arnold Arboretum* 56(4):375–397.

Smith, Robert L. 1974. "Greenbriers." In *Shrubs and Vines for Northeastern Wildlife*, comp. and rev. John D. Gill and William M. Healy, 54–58. U.S. Dept. of Agriculture, Forest Service General Technical Report NE, no. 9. Upper Darby, PA: Northeastern Forest Experiment Station.

Smithers, W. D. [1964?] *Pancho Villa's Last Hangout on Both Sides of the Rio Grande in the Big Bend Country.* Alpine, TX. (See chapter "Nature's Pharmacy and the Curanderos.")

Smithwick, Noah. 1983. *The Evolution of a State or Recollections of Old Texas Days.* Comp. Nanna Smithwick Donaldson. Barker Texas History Center Series, no. 5. Austin: Univ. of Texas Press.

Solano, M. L., P. Soriano, and M. P. Ciria. 2004. "Constructed Wetlands as a Sustainable Solution for Wastewater Treatment in Small Villages." *Biosystems Engineering* 87(1):109–118.

Solís, Gaspar José de. 1931. "Diary of a Visit of Inspection of the Texas Missions Made by Fray Gaspar José de Solís in the Year 1767–1768." Trans. Margaret Kenney Kress. *Southwestern Historical Quarterly* 35:28–76.

Sperry, Brian. 1994. "A Toast to Thomas Volney Munson." *Neil Sperry's Gardens* 8(8):18–21.

Sperry, Neil. 1991. *Neil Sperry's Complete Guide to Texas Gardening.* Dallas: Taylor.

Spiller, Henry A., Danetta B. Willias, Susan E. Gorman, and Jayne Sanftleban. 1996. "Retrospective Study of Mistletoe Ingestion." *Clinical Toxicology* 34(4):405–408.

Spongberg, Stephen A. 1977. "Ebenaceae Hardy in Temperate North America." *Journal of the Arnold Arboretum* 58(2):146–160.

Stahle, David W. 1996–1997. "Tree Rings of Ancient Forest Relics." *Arnoldia* 56(4):2–10.

Stahle, David W., and John G. Hehr. 1984. "Dendroclimatic Relationships of Post Oak Across a Precipitation Gradient in the Southcentral United States." *Annals of the Association of American Geographers* 74:561–573.

Standley, Paul C. 1912. "Some Useful Native Plants of New Mexico." Annual Report of the Board of Regents of the Smithsonian Institution . . .

for the Year Ending June 30, 1911. Washington, DC: U.S. Government Printing Office.

———. 1920–1926. *Trees and Shrubs of Mexico.* Issued in 5 parts, paged continuously. U.S. National Museum, Contributions from the U.S. National Herbarium, vol. 23. Washington, DC: U.S. Government Printing Office.

Stanford, Geoffrey. 1990. "Regional Reflections on Ballmoss." *Journal of the Bromeliad Society* 40(2):82–84.

Stanley, Dick. 2004. "Long-Long-Lost Pines." *Austin American-Statesman,* Jan. 7, Section B.

Stein, John, Denise Binion, and Robert Acciavatti. 2003. *Field Guide to Native Oak Species of Eastern North America.* Morgantown, WV: U.S. Forest Service, Forest Health Technology Enterprise Team.

Sternitzke, Herbert S. 1972. "Bald Cypress: Endangered or Expanding Species?" *Economic Botany* 26:130–134.

Sterns, E. E. 1888. "Some Peculiarities in the Seed of *Smilax,* Tourn." *Bulletin of the Torrey Botanical Club* 15(6):162–164.

Stevenson, Dennis W. 1993. "Ephedraceae." In *Flora of North America: North of Mexico,* ed. Flora of North America Editorial Committee, vol. 2, 428–434. New York: Oxford Univ. Press.

Stevenson, Matilda Coxe. 1915. *Ethnobotany of the Zuni Indians.* Washington, DC: Bureau of American Ethnology. Thirtieth Annual Report.

Stewart, Omer C. 1980. "Peyotism and Mescalism." *Plains Anthropologist* 25(90):297–309.

Stoutamire, Warren. 1977. "Chromosome Races of *Gaillardia pulchella* (Asteraceae)." *Brittonia* 29(3):297–309.

Stransky, John J. 1990. "*Quercus stellata* Wangenh. (Post Oak)." In Burns and Honkala, 1990, s.v. "*Quercus stellata.*"

Sturtevant, William C. 1979. "Black Drink and Other Caffeine-Containing Beverages Among Non-Indians." In Hudson 1979, 150–165.

Stuzenbaker, Charles D. 1999. *Aquatic and Wetland Plants of the Western Gulf Coast*. Austin: Texas Parks and Wildlife Press.

Swan, Daniel C. 1999. *Peyote Religious Art: Symbols of Faith and Belief*. Jackson: Univ. Press of Mississippi.

Swanton, John R. 1929. *Myths and Tales of the Southeastern Indians*. Smithsonian Institution, Bureau of American Ethnology, Bulletin no. 88. Washington, DC: U.S. Government Printing Office.

Taylor, Col. Nathaniel Alston. 1936. *The Coming Empire; or, Two Thousand Miles in Texas on Horseback*. Revised ed. (original published 1877). Dallas: Turner.

Taylor, Richard B., Jimmy Rutledge, and Joe G. Herrera. 1997. *A Field Guide to Common South Texas Shrubs*. Austin: Texas Parks and Wildlife Press.

Terry, Martin, Kerry L. Steelman, Tom Guilderson, Phil Dering, Marvin W. Rowe. 2006. "Lower Pecos and Coahuila Peyote: New Radiocarbon Dates." *Journal of Archaeological Science* 33:1017–1021.

Texas Legislature. 1971. Senate Concurrent Resolution No. 31. 62nd Legislature, Regular Session.

———. 1995. House Concurrent Resolution No. 44. 74th Legislature, Regular Session.

———. 1997. House Concurrent Resolution No. 82, 75th Legislature, Regular Session.

Theophrastus. 1916. *Enquiry into Plants and Minor Works on Odours and Weather Signs*. Trans. Sir Arthur Hort. 2 vols. Loeb Classical Library. London: William Heinemann.

Thomson, William A. R., ed. 1978. *Medicines from the Earth: A Guide to Healing Plants*. New York: McGraw-Hill.

Thorstensen, Thomas C. 1993. *Practical Leather Technology*. 4th ed. Malabar, FL: Krieger.

———. 1995. "Leather." In *Encyclopedia of Chemical Technology*, ed. Jacqueline I. Kroschwitz and Mary

Howe-Grant. 4th ed. Vol. 15, 159–177. New York: John Wiley & Sons.

Timmermann, B. N. 1977. "Practical Uses of *Larrea*." In Mabry et al. 1977, 252–256.

Torrey, Raymond N. 1931. "Fantastic Frost Crystals on Dried Stems of Dittany." *Torreya* 31(1):10–12.

Troike, Rudolph. 1962. "The Origins of Plains Mescalism." *American Anthropologist* 64:946–963.

Tull, Delena. 1999. *Edible and Useful Plants of Texas and the Southwest: A Practical Guide*. Austin: Univ. of Texas Press.

Tunnell, Curtis. 1981. *Wax, Men and Money: A Historical and Archeological Study of Candelilla Wax Camps Along the Rio Grande Border of Texas*. Office of the State Archeologist Report 32. Austin: Texas Historical Commission.

Turner, B. L. 1994. "Taxonomic Treatment of *Monarda* (Lamiaceae) for Texas and Mexico." *Phytologia* 77(1):56–79.

———. 1996. "Synoptical Study of *Rhus virens* (Anacardiaceae) and Closely Related Taxa." *Phytologia* 85(5):368–376.

Turner, B. L., Holly Nichols, Geoffrey Denny, and Oded Doron. 2003. *Atlas of the Vascular Plants of Texas*. 2 vols. Sida, Botanical Miscellany, no. 24. Fort Worth: BRIT Press.

Turner, Ronald B., Rudolf Bauer, Karin Woelkart, Thomas C. Hulsey, and David Gangemi. 2005. "An Evaluation of *Echinacea angustifolia* in Experimental Rhinovirus Infections." *New England Journal of Medicine* 353(4):341–348.

Turner, Tressa. 1954. "The Human Comedy in Folk Superstitions." In Boatright et al. 1954, 230–253.

Turpin, Solveig A. 1986. "Bonfire Shelter: An Ancient Slaughterhouse." In Shafer 1986, 88–93.

Tveten, John, and Gloria Tveten. 1997. *Wildflowers of Houston and Southeast Texas*. Austin: Univ. of Texas Press.

Tweit, Susan J. 1995. *The Great Southwest Nature Factbook: A Guide to the Region's Remarkable Animals, Plants and Natural Features*. Seattle: Alaska Northwest Books.

Tyler, Varro E. 1993. *The Honest Herbal: A Sensible Guide to the Use of Herbs and Related Remedies*. 3rd ed. New York: Pharmaceutical Products.

U.S. Dept. of Agriculture. 1942. "Dogwood Needed for Mill Shuttles." Press Release. Forest Service and Extension Service Cooperating. September. Washington, DC.

U.S. Geological Survey Online. 2004. "Not Just for Kissing: Mistletoe and Birds, Bees, and Other Beasts," http://www.usgs.gov/mistletoe/index.html (accessed Dec. 10, 2004).

Upton, Roy. 1997. *Echinacea*. New Canaan, CT: Keats Publishing.

Van Auken, O. W. 1993. "Size Distribution Patterns and Potential Population Change of Some Dominant Woody Species of the Edwards Plateau Region of Texas." *Texas Journal of Science* 45(3):199–210.

Vane, John R., and Regina M. Botting. 1992. "The History of Aspirin." In *Aspirin and Other Salicylates*, ed. John R. Vane and Regina M. Botting. London: Chapman & Hall.

Vargas-Arispuro, I., R. Reyes-Báez, G. Rivera-Castañeda, M. A. Martínez-Téllez, and I. Rivero-Espejel. 2005. "Antifungal Lignans from Creosotebush (*Larrea tridentata*)." *Industrial Crops and Products* 22(2):101–107.

Vasek, Frank C. 1980. "Creosote Bush: Long-Lived Clones in the Mojave Desert." *American Journal of Botany* 67(2):246–255.

Veitch, F. P., and J. S. Rogers. 1918. "American Sumac: A Valuable Tanning Material and Dyestuff." *Bulletin of the U.S. Department of Agriculture*, no. 706.

Verástegui, M. Angeles, César A. Sánchez, Norma L. Herdia, and J. Santos García-Alvarado. 1996. "Antimicrobial Activity of Extracts of Three Major Plants from the Chihuahuan

Desert." *Journal of Ethnopharmacology* 52(3):175–177.

Vestal, Paul A., and Richard Evans Schultes. 1939. *The Economic Botany of the Kiowa Indians.* Cambridge, MA: Botanical Museum.

Vikramaditya, Manisha Sarkar, Rajat Rashmi, and P. N. Varma. 1993. "Differences Between Two Horsetails (*Equisetum hyemale* L. and *Equisetum arvense* L.) Used in Homoeopathic System of Medicine." *Journal of Plant Anatomy and Morphology* 6(2):131–135.

Vines, Robert A. 1960. *Trees, Shrubs, and Woody Vines of the Southwest.* Austin: Univ. of Texas Press.

———. 1984. *Trees of Central Texas: A Field Guide.* Austin: Univ. of Texas Press.

Wade, Maria F. 2003. *The Native Americans of the Texas Edwards Plateau, 1582–1799.* Austin: Univ. of Texas Press.

Wagner, Warren H., Jr., and William E. Hammitt. 1970. "Natural Proliferation of Floating Stems of Scouring-Rush, *Equisetum hyemale.*" *Michigan Botanist* 9:166–174.

Walker, Laurence C. 1996. *Forests: A Naturalist's Guide to Woodland Trees.* Austin: Univ. of Texas Press.

Walters, Terrence W., Deena S. Decker-Walters, Usher Posluszny, and Peter G. Kevan. 1990. "Understanding Grape (*Vitis,* Vitaceae) Cultivar Phylogenies." *Economic Botany* 44(1):129–131.

Ward, Hortense Warner. 1949. "Yellow Flower of Death." In Boatright 1949, 155–167.

Ward, John R., and Elray S. Nixon. 1992. "Woody Vegetation of the Dry, Sandy Uplands of Eastern Texas." *Texas Journal of Science* 44(3):283–294.

Warnock, Barton H. 1970. *Wildflowers of the Big Bend Country, Texas.* Alpine: Sul Ross State Univ.

———. 1974. *Wildflowers of the Guadalupe Mountains and the Sand Dune Country, Texas.* Alpine: Sul Ross State Univ.

———. 1977. *Wildflowers of the Davis Mountains and Marathon Basin, Texas.* Alpine: Sul Ross State Univ.

Waser, Nickolas M. 1979. "Pollinator Availability as a Determinant of Flowering Time in Ocotillo (*Fouquieria splendens*)." *Oecologia* 39(1):107–121.

Wasowski, Sally, and Andy Wasowski. 1997. *Native Texas Plants: Landscaping Region by Region.* 2nd ed. Houston: Lone Star Books.

Watson, C. C., S. R. Abt, and D. Derrick. 1997. "Willow Posts Bank Stabilization." *Journal of the American Water Resources Association* 33(2):292–300.

Watson, F. D. 1985. "The Nomenclature of Pondcypress and Baldcypress (Taxodiaceae)." *Taxon* 34(3):506–509.

Wauer, Roland H. 1980. *Naturalist's Big Bend: An Introduction to the Trees and Shrubs, Wildflowers, Cacti, Mammals, Birds, Reptiles and Amphibians, Fish, and Insects.* College Station: Texas A&M Press.

———. 1999. *Heralds of Spring in Texas.* College Station: Texas A&M Univ. Press.

Weaver, David K., Thomas W. Phillips, Florence V. Dunkel, T. Weaver, Robert T. Grubb, and Elizabeth L. Nance. 1995. "Dried Leaves from Rocky Mountain Plants Decrease Infestation by Stored-Product Beetles." *Journal of Chemical Ecology* 21(2):127–141.

Webb, Walter Prescott. 1931. *The Great Plains.* New York: Grosset & Dunlap.

Webber, John Milton. 1953. *Yuccas of the Southwest.* U.S. Dept. of Agriculture Monograph, no. 17. Washington, DC: U.S. Government Printing Office.

Weber, Carl. 1962. *Weber's Guide to Pipes and Pipe Smoking.* New York: Cornerstone Library.

Weekes, William D. 1979. "The Awesome Live Oak." *American Forests* 85(2):20–23, 56–59.

Wellmann, Klaus F. 1978. "North American Indian Rock Art and Hallucinogenic Drugs." *Journal of the American Medical Assoc.* 239(15):1524–1527.

Weniger, Del. 1984. *The Explorers' Texas: The Lands and Waters.* Austin: Eakin Press.

———. 1996. "Catalpa (*Catalpa bignonioides,* Bignoniaceae) and Bois D'Arc (*Maclura pomifera,* Moraceae) in Early Texas Records." *Sida* 17(1):231–242.

White, L. L. 1907. *Production of Red Cedar for Pencil Wood.* U.S. Dept. of Agriculture, Forest Service, Circular 102. Washington, DC.

Whitehouse, Eula. 1936. *Texas Flowers in Natural Colors.* Austin: Texas Book Store.

Whitenberg, D. C., and W. D. Hardesty. 1978. "Environmental Factors Affecting Growth and Development of the Texas Madrone, II: Interaction of Light Intensity and Water Stress." *Texas Journal of Science* 30(4):347–350.

Whitford, A. C. 1941. "Textile Fibers Used in Eastern Aboriginal North America." *Anthropological Papers of the American Museum of Natural History* 38(1):1–22.

Whittaker, Paul L. 1984a. "The Insect Fauna of Mistletoe (*Phoradendron tomentosum,* Loranthaceae) in Southern Texas." *Southwestern Naturalist* 29(4):435–444.

———. 1984b. "Population Biology of the Great Purple Hairstreak, *Atlides halesus,* in Texas (Lycadeniae)." *Journal of the Lepidopterists' Society* 38(3):179–185.

Wiersema, John H. 1997. "Nelumbonaceae." In *Flora of North America: North of Mexico,* ed. Flora of North America Editorial Committee, vol. 3, 64–65. New York: Oxford Univ. Press.

Wigginton, Eliot, ed. 1977. *Foxfire 4: Water Systems, Fiddle Making, Logging, Gardening, Sassafras Tea,*

Wood Carving, and Further Affairs of Plain Living. Garden City, NY: Anchor.

Wilke, Cindy. 2005. *Handbook of Texas Online*, s.v. "Onion Culture," http://www.tsha.utexas.edu/handbook/online/articles/OO/afo1.html (accessed July 15, 2005).

Williams, David G. 2004. *Perfumes of Yesterday*. Port Washington, NY: Michelle Press.

Williams, Robert D. 1990. "Black Walnut." In Burns and Honkala 1990, s.v. "*Juglans nigra*."

Williams-Dean, Glenna. 1978. "Ethnobotany and Cultural Ecology of Prehistoric Man in Southwest Texas." Ph.D. diss., Texas A&M Univ.

Wills, Mary Motz, and Howard S. Irwin. 1961. *Roadside Flowers of Texas*. Austin: Univ. of Texas Press.

Wilson, Hugh D. 1981. "Domesticated *Chenopodium* of the Ozark Bluff Dwellers." *Economic Botany* 35(2):233–239.

———. 1983. "Quinua: Significant Past, Questionable Future." *Herbarist* 49:115–120.

———. 1990. "Quinua and Relatives (*Chenopodium* sect. *Chenopodium* subsect. *Cellulata*)." *Economic Botany* 44(3 Suppl.):92–110.

Wilson, Hugh D., and Charles B. Heiser, Jr. 1979. "The Origin and Evolutionary Relationships of 'Huauzontle' (*Chenopodium nuttalliae* Safford), Domesticated Chenopod of Mexico." *American Journal of Botany* 66(2):198–206.

Winkler, A. J. 1949. "Grapes and Wine." *Economic Botany* 3(1):46–70.

Wood, B. W., and C. C. Reilly. 2004. "Control of Mistletoe in Pecan Trees." *HortScience* 39(1):110–114.

Wood, Horatio C., Jr., and Arthur Osol. 1943. *The Dispensatory of the United States of America*. 23rd ed. Philadelphia: Lippincott.

Wood, Virginia Steele. 1981. *Live Oaking: Southern Timber for Tall Ships*. Boston: Northeastern Univ. Press.

Woodhull, Frost. 1954. "Ranch Remedios." In Boatright et al. 1954, 254–264.

Wrede, Jan. 1997. *Texans Love Their Land: A Guide to 76 Native Texas Hill Country Woody Plants*. San Antonio: Watercress.

Wright, Colin W., ed. 2002. *Artemisia*. London: Taylor & Francis.

Wyeth Laboratories. 1966. *The Sinister Garden: A Guide to the Most Common Poisonous Plants*. Philadelphia: Wyeth Laboratories.

York, Harlan H. 1909. "The Anatomy and Some of the Biological Aspects of the 'American Mistletoe.'" *Bulletin of the University of Texas*, no. 120. Austin.

Zarling, E. J., and L. E. Thompson. 1984. "Nonpersimmon Gastric Phytobezoar: A Benign Recurrent Condition." *Archives of Internal Medicine* 144(5):959–961.

Zarling, J. M. 1990. "Inhibition of HIV Replication by Pokeweed Antiviral Protein Targeted to CD4+ Cells by Monoclonal Antibodies." *Nature* 347(6288):92–95.

Zhang, Daoning, and Fathi T. Halaweish. 2003. "Isolation and Identification of Foetidissimin: A Novel Ribosome-Inactivating Protein from *Cucurbita foetidissima*." *Plant Science* 164(3):387–393.

Zona, Scott. 1990. "A Monograph of *Sabal* (Arecaceae: Coryphoideae)." *Aliso* 12(4):583–666.

Index

Abbott, Carroll, 241
Acacia, 149, 261; *berlandieri*, 6; *farnesiana*, 3–6; *greggii*, 6; *senegal*, 5
Acoma Indians, 178, 224
acorns, 12, 78–79, 84. *See also* nuts
African Americans, 14; foods of, 266; medicines of, 23, 35, 73, 99, 219, 281
agarita, 114–117
Agave, 118, 119, 120; *fourcroydes*, 111; *lechuguilla*, 109–113; *parryi*, 113; *sisalana*, 111
agriculture, 142, 204
Akimel O'odham Indians: basketry of, 92; beverages of, 68; building materials of, 287; foods of, 70, 197, 230–231, 259, 275; medicines of, 124, 276; paints of, 286
Akokisa Indians, 247
Alabama-Coushatta Indians, 57
Alabama Indians, 22, 93, 135, 219, 271–272
Alamo (San Antonio de Valero mission), 53, 63, 85
Alarcón, Martín de, 106
algarrobo, 64, 70
Algonquin Indians, 207
allelopathy, 36, 141
Allium: canadense, 171–174; *drummondii*, 171–174
amaranth, 175–179, 197
Amaranthus, 175–179, 195; *blitoides*, 178; *hypochondriacus*, 177; *palmeri*, 176, 178; *retroflexus*, 178
American colonies. *See* colonies, American
American Revolution, 50, 82, 138
Anasazi Indians, 197
Andrews, Jean, 193, 240
animals. *See* dogs; livestock; wildlife
Apache Indians: beverages of, 68, 124; building materials of, 121; ceremonial items of, 121; cradleboards of, 121; folklore of, 173, 188–189; foods of, 73, 84, 116, 145, 163–166, 172, 178, 197, 227, 230–231, 254; medicines of, 69, 124, 132, 143, 254; musical instruments of, 121, 204;

paints of, 35, 286; rituals of, 166, 227; seasonings of, 148–149, 172, 193, 243; tattooing of, 254; weapons of, 22. *See also* Chiricahua, Lipan, Mescalero, *and* White Mountain Apache Indians
Appalachia: foods in, 100, 216; Native Americans of, 22, 30, 50, 197, 216, 243, 252
Arapaho Indians, 156, 236
Arbutus: menziesii, 10; *xalapensis*, 7–10
archaeological remains: animal effigies, 146; baskets, 121; bulbs, 172; coprolites, 18, 113, 148, 177, 227, 252–253, 286; fiber/cordage, 112, 121, 220; flowers, 113, 165, 227, 252; foliage, 41; fruits, 25, 116, 192, 295; marine shells (as cups), 135; mats, 121, 287; nuts/nutshells/hulls, 12, 35, 253; peyote, 234; pollen, 18, 286; sandals, 121, 220; seeds, 18, 25, 153, 159–161, 197, 198, 203, 206, 253; starchy staples, 119; stems, 251; weapons, 45, 121; wood, 41
Argemone: albiflora, 180–182; *mexicana*, 181–182; *polyanthemos*, 180–182
Arikara Indians, 288
Artemisia: absinthium, 186; *annua*, 185; *dracunculus*, 185; *filifolia*, 185; *herba-alba*, 185; *ludoviciana*, 183–186; *pallens*, 185; *pontica*, 186; *tridentata*, 183; *vulgaris*, 185
aspirin, history of, 93–94
Atakapa Indians, 279, 280
Austin, Stephen F., 85, 200, 218, 293
Aztec Indians, 177, 197, 206, 223, 255

Bach, J. S., 83
barberry: creeping, 117; red, 117; Texas, 117
Bartram, William, 270–271
basketry, 18, 41, 92–93, 97, 112, 113, 121, 145–146, 166, 287; waterproofing of, 143

baths, 132, 142; steam, 142, 145, 185. *See also* sweat lodges
beargrass, 121; as yucca, 163
bedding. *See* stuffing materials
Bedichek, Roy, 76, 85
beebalm, 244; lemon, 242, 243
beeplant, 178
bees/beekeeping, 6, 69, 114, 142, 152, 244, 258; carpenter, 130; pollinating, 241; sonicating, 277. *See also* honey plants
Berberis: haematocarpa, 116–117; *repens*, 117; *swaseyi*, 117; *trifoliata*, 114–117
bergamot: citrus, 243; wild, 243
Berlandier, Jean Louis, 25, 116, 137, 155, 226, 279–280, 290, 292
beverages (alcoholic), 50; absinthe, 186; aguardiente, 166; beers, 30, 100, 198, 272; cherry bounce, 73; colonche, 254; gin, 42; from goat milk, 275; from ground meal, 68; margarita, 116; mescal, 157; sotol mescal, 120; tequila, 120; tulbai, 259; vermouth, 186; wine, 25, 72, 73, 116, 294, 295–297
beverages (non-alcoholic), 50, 116, 145, 253; black drink, 135–137, 155, 219; coffee substitutes, 31, 79, 100, 116; from flowers, 70, 132, 201; from ground meal, 68; psychotropic, 207; soft drinks, 73, 100–101, 256, 272; sarsaparilla, 272; teas, 16, 70, 100, 124, 134–138, 243–244
Bidai Indians, 13, 84, 204, 247
biofilters/biological monitors, 216, 282, 283
birds, 18, 42, 50, 145, 268, 273, 288; bluebirds, 18, 97; bobwhites, 31; cardinals, 18, 265; chachalacas, 90; cedar waxwings, 18, 97, 265; doves, 18, 69, 179, 182, 255; flycatchers, 18, 265; grouse, 148, 273; hummingbirds, 129, 244; mockingbirds, 18, 265; pheasants, 148; prairie chickens, 148; quail, 6, 69, 114, 124, 131, 148, 179, 255, 258; roadrunners, 255; robins, 18, 97; sparrows, 18, 265; thrashers,

18, 255; thrushes, 18, 23; turkeys, 18, 23, 24, 27, 31, 69, 79, 84, 173, 179, 255, 273; warblers, 18, 43, 283; woodpeckers, 18, 23; wrens, 255, 288
Blackfoot Indians, 46, 155, 188, 224, 252
bluebonnet, 199, 221; Texas, 238–241
bois d'arc, 45–48
Bollaert, William, 30, 137, 218, 226, 280
Bouteloua: curtipendula, 188–190; *gracilis*, 187–188
boxwood: American 22, Turkish, 21
Bracht, Viktor, 8, 25, 161–162
Broussonetia papyrifera, 51
Buckelew, Frank, 18
buckeye, Mexican, 159–162
bulbs (edible), 172–173
butterflies, 18, 101, 244, 265; hairstreaks, 27, 97, 148, 265; Henry's elfin, 27, 162
Buxus sempervirens, 21

Cabeza de Vaca, Alvar Núñez, 13, 135, 137, 153–154, 204, 253, 255, 278–279
cactus: organ pipe, 255; peyote, 232–237; prickly-pear, 248–256; saguaro, 253; tasajillo, 257–259
Caddo Indians: basketry of, 18, 22, 35, 92; beverages of, 137; building materials of, 41, 93, 287; cordage of, 36; dyes of, 35, 268; and fire drills, 41, 50; folklore of, 31, 41; foods of, 13, 30, 50, 73, 84, 178, 227, 295; furniture of, 22; incense of, 41; medicines of, 22, 30, 155; musical instruments of, 204; psychotropics of, 154, 235–236; stuffing materials of, 62, 287; textiles of, 51; utensils of, 33–34; weapons of, 22, 45–46
Cahuilla Indians, 132
Cajuns, 100
Calocedrus, 39
camphorweed, stinking, 290
candelilla, 125–128, 131
candles, 126, 227, 252
Capoque Indians, 279
Capsicum annuum, 191–194
careless weed, 175, 178–179
carob tree, 70
Carrizo Indians, 235
Carya illinoinensis, 11–16
Castanea, 247
Castaneda, Carlos, 209
Catawba Indians, 135
catclaw, 6
cattail, 62, 284–288

caulking material, 287
cedar: eastern red-, 38–44; Pacific red-, 44; use of name, 43–44, 63; yellow, 44
Cedrus, 44
Celtis: laevigata, 17–21; *reticulata*, 17–21
Ceratonia siliqua, 70
Chamaecyparis, 44
chaparral, 139, 142
Charruco Indians, 153
Cheatham, Scooter, 162, 259
Chenopodium, 178, 195–198; *album*, 197; *ambrosioides*, 198; *berlandieri*, 195–197; *quinoa*, 198
Cherokee Indians: beverages of, 135; dyes of, 150, 201; foods of, 30, 271; medicines of, 22, 30, 73, 93, 99, 217–219, 243
cherry, 33, 66; black, 73–74
chestnut, 106; American, 149
Cheyenne Indians, 211, 236
chia, 198
Chichimeca Indians, 235
Chickasaw Indians, 93, 135, 292
Chihuahuan Desert, 109, 129, 166
chiltepín, 191–194
chinaberry, 97
chinquapin: Allegheny, 247; water, 245, 247
Chippewa, 100
Chiricahua Apache Indians, 53, 120, 178, 185, 230, 259. *See also* Apache Indians
Choctaw Indians: beverages of, 135; foods of, 271; medicines of, 99, 217–218, 292; pecan cultivation of, 13; seasonings of, 100; textiles of, 50–51
Chumash Indians, 207
cinchona tree, 94
citronella oil, 243
Citrus aurantium, 243
Civil War (American): and beverages, 100, 272; demise of wooden ships during, 83; and inks, 268; medicinal uses during, 22, 30, 35; and timber demands, 35
Cleome, 178
clothing: 50–51, 166, 287; decoration with beads, 154, 155–156; cloaks/robes, 50, 166; hats, 121, 166; sandals, 112, 121, 220, 287; skirts, 51
Coahuiltecan Indians, 13, 66, 112, 113, 154, 254
cochineal, 255–256
Cochiti Indians, 275

Cocopah Indians, 131, 230
colonies, American: beverages of, 50, 135, 243–244; cloth/cordage of, 51; foods of, 30, 172; grape cultivation in, 295–296; livestock forage in, 50, 52; medicines of, 99, 269; sericulture in, 52; wood uses of, 33–34, 50
Comanche Indians, 204; building materials of, 41; folklore of, 18, 241; foods of, 13, 18, 25, 30, 50, 68, 73, 120, 148, 172, 230, 247, 254, 295; insecticides of, 157; incense of, 185; medicines of, 16, 35, 69, 93, 145, 155, 181, 185, 211, 276; psychotropics of, 154, 235–236; rituals, 41, 167; saddles of, 93; smoking materials of, 145, 150, 273; soap of, 167; sweat lodges of, 145, 185; weapons of, 22, 46
coneflower, purple, 210–213
Cora Indians, 235
coral bean, 151, 153
cordage, 19, 36, 50, 51
Coreopsis, 223, *tinctoria*, 199–201
coreopsis, plains, 199–201
Cornus: drummondii, 22; *florida*, 20–24; *kousa*, 24; *mas*, 20; *nuttallii*, 24; *sanguinea*, 20, 24
Corpus Christi de la Isleta (mission), 295
Cortés, Hernán, 177, 224
cosmetics, 126–127, 243; coloring of, 256; scenting of, 40
cottonwood, 41, 59–63, 91, 287
cowboys: and chuck wagon, 47; and fuel, 67, 94, 121; medicines of, 142, 209; songs of, 63, 205, 227, 251
Crassulacean acid metabolism (CAM), 251, 255
Cree Indians, 93
Creek Indians, 35, 99, 135, 217
Cremony, John, 230
creosote bush, 139–143, 257
Crockett, David, 48
Cross Timbers, 75, 77–78
Crow Indians, 93, 211
Cucurbita foetidissima, 202–205
Cunila origanoides, 290
cypress, 246; bald, 50, 102–106

Dasylirion: leiophyllum, 118–121; *texanum*, 118–121; *wheeleri*, 118–121
dátil, 165–166
Datura, 206–209; *inoxia*, 206; *stramonium*, 206; *wrightii*, 206
da Vinci, Leonardo, 83
decorations: for Christmas, 134, 263, 283; on clothing, 154, 155–156

Delaware Indians, 30, 99, 236
De León, Alonso, 13
deliriants, 157, 206–207. *See also* hallucinogens
de Soto, Hernando, 13, 30; expedition of, 51
detergent. *See* soap
Dickens, Charles, 263
Dioscorides, 287
Diospyros: ebenum, 27; *texana*, 25–27; *virginiana*, 28–31
diseases, plant, 24, 106
diseases, human. *See* medicinal uses
dittany, common, 290
Dobie, J. Frank, 63, 104, 116, 205, 241
dogs, toxicity in, 157
dogwood, 30, 56, 94; flowering, 20–24; rough-leaf, 22
domestication, plant: 192, 197–198, 227–228
Druids, 263
Drummond, Thomas, 171, 223
Duval, John C., 172
dyes, 10, 19, 23, 31, 116, 201, 224, 255–256, 267, 273; for baskets, 35, 145, 227, 268; for blankets, 143; for cake frosting, 268; for cloth, 35, 97, 145, 150, 227, 255; for flags, 268; for hair, 16, 27, 35, 69; for leather, 5, 27, 35, 143, 150; in military uniforms, 48, 256; for wines, 268; for wood, 182

Echinacea: angustifolia, 210–213; *pallida*, 210; *purpurea*, 210
Elizabeth I, 28, 38, 80
Engelmann, George, 248
epazote, 198
Ephedra: antisyphilitica, 122–124; *equisetina*, 122; *intermedia*, 122; *sinica*, 122
Equisetum: arvense, 214, 216; *fluviatile*, 214; *hyemale*, 214, 216; *laevigatum*, 214
Erica arborea, 272
erosion control, 28, 92, 148, 188, 215
Eryngium: campestre, 217; *yuccifolium*, 217–222
Erythrina herbacea, 153–154
Euphorbia antisyphilitica, 125–128
explosives, 10, 16, 94, 127

Felipe II, of Spain, 192, 233
Ferguson, James E. "Pa", 205
fiber plants, 111–112, 166–167, 220, 287
fiber uses: bowstrings, 112, 166;

brooms, 112; brushes, 112, 166; ceremonial items, 167; cordage/twine 112, 166, 220, 227, 287; dishes, 167; mats, 112, 121, 167; mattresses, 166; nets, 166; paintbrushes, 167; rope, 112, 121, 166, 287; sacks/bags, 112, 220, 287; trays, 167. *See also* basketry; clothing; paper
fire, 42, 56–57, 65, 146, 258
fish: steamer, 252; stupefaction, 16, 37, 97, 112, 167
flavoring agents, 100, 186. *See also* seasonings
flowers: disks of, 211; in dried arrangements, 246; ingested as food, 62, 70, 113, 121, 132, 142, 163–165, 227, 252, 286; legends about, 223–224; pickled, 165; ritual use, 227; in sachets, 243; stalks of, 113, 121, 163, 167; state, 20, 163, 224, 228, 239–240, 261–262
folklore, 31; Texan: 19, 104, 150, 205, 223–224, 241, 263. *See also under specific Native American tribes*
food, natural. *See* bulbs; flowers; fruits; nuts; rhizomes/tubers; seeds
food, prepared: breads/ashcakes, 68, 84, 120, 177, 197, 198, 227, 247, 271, 285, 286; candies, 14, 100, 132, 145, 148, 177, 254; casseroles, 247; cheeses, 275; crackers, 19; fruit-breads, 25, 30; ground meal, 68, 79, 84, 132, 177–178, 197, 203, 227, 253, 254, 271, 285; jams/jellies, 25, 30, 50, 68, 72–73, 100, 116, 145, 254, 271, 294–295; leaf vegetables, 52, 178–179, 195–198, 266; nopalitos, 251; pemmican, 13; pies, 25, 30, 50, 73, 116, 267, 294–295; preservatives for, 143; puddings 25, 30; starchy staples (baked), 113, 119–120, 165; syrups, 18, 68, 254, 285; thickening agents, 100; vinegar, 69. *See also* fruits, seasonings
food preservative, 143
Fouquieria splendens, 129–133
French explorers and traders, 13–14, 30, 46, 50, 93, 280
frostweed, 289–292
fruits (edible): dried, 10, 30, 50, 53, 73, 165–166, 193, 253, 295; fresh, 10, 18, 25, 28–30, 35, 41, 49–50, 53, 73, 89, 114–116, 145, 165–166, 193, 252–254, 258–259, 294–295; as pods, 67–68, 165–166
fuel: flower spikes, 287; leaves, 167; seed floss, 286–287; seedpods, 167;

stems/stalks, 132, 167; whole plants, 121, 143, 280; wood, 5, 10, 18, 34, 36, 40, 41, 55, 62, 97. *See also* explosives
fungus, 8, 39

Gaillardia: aristata, 224; *picta*, 223; *pinnatifida*, 224; *pulchella*, 221–224
games, 152, 162
Garner, Cactus Jack, 239
German colonists, 8, 42, 162
glue and adhesives, 5, 58, 69, 126, 143; birdlime, 264
goldenwave, 199, 201
Goodnight, Charles, 47, 53, 62
goosefoot, 178, 195–198; pitseed, 195
gourd: bottle, 204–205; buffalo, 202–205; decorated, 138; Spanish, 205
grafting, 14, 37, 73
grama: blue, 187–188; hairy, 187; red, 187; sideoats, 188–190; six-weeks, 187; Texas, 187
grape: canyon, 295; champin, 295; El Paso, 295; fox, 296; frost, 296; graybark, 295; mission, 295; muscadine, 294, 296; mustang, 294, 296; pigeon, 295; scuppernong, 294; summer, 295; sweet mountain, 295; wild, 293–297
grass: curly-mesquite, 190; forage, 187–188; growth habits of, 42, 43, 190; mesquite, 190; sacaton, 254; stalks as brooms/brushes, 190; state, 188
Gray, Ted, 94, 255, 257, 258
greasewood, 139, 143
Greeks (ancient), 20, 94, 144, 147, 148
greenbrier, 100, 270–273
guajillo, 6
Guaraní Indians, 138
gum: for chewing, 58, 100, 126–128, 227, 273; as resin, 58, 69, 132
gum arabic, 5, 69, 83

hackberry, 17–19, 261
hallucinogens: 186, 206–209, 234; purported, 50, 153–156, 259
Han Indians, 279
Havard, Valery, 35, 53, 67, 95, 118, 120, 152, 156, 162
Havasupai Indians, 53, 124
hedges, 46–47
Helianthemum canadense, 290
Helianthus annuus, 225–228
heliotropism, 225–226
hemp, 166
henequen fiber, 111
Henry, Patrick, 46

Hernández, Francisco, 192, 193, 233
hickory, 11, 21, 35
Hidatsa Indians, 211
Hilaria belangeri, 190
Hispanics: beverages of, 120, 124, 275; and curdling agents, 275; dyes of, 27, 143; and fish stupefaction, 97; foods of, 14, 163, 166, 178, 230, 251, 275; housing of, 131–132, 287; medicines of, 35, 93, 123–124, 132, 142, 167, 184–185, 198, 224, 276; seasonings of, 191; soaps of, 95; and water clarification, 252
Hoffmannseggia glauca, 229–231
Hogg, James Stephen, 15, 24
Holley, Mary Austin, 52, 137–138, 200, 218
holly, Christmas, 134; English, 134
honey plants, 27, 69, 114, 162, 224, 244, 292. *See also* bees/beekeeping
Hopi Indians, 167, 227
horsemint, 70, 242–244; spotted, 244; yellow, 244
horsetail, 214–216
Houma Indians, 99, 271
Houston, Sam, 47, 83, 85, 226–227
Hualapai Indians, 132
Huichol Indians, 235
huisache, 3–6

ice formation (in plants), 289–290
Ilex: aquifolium, 134; *paraguariensis*, 138; *vomitoria*, 134–138
Inca Indians, 198
incense, 41, 185
Indian blanket, 199, 221–224, 262
Indian potato, 229–231
Indian rush-pea, 229–231
Indian spinach, 197
Indian tobacco, 289, 292
industrial uses of plants: acid-proofing agents, 126; additives in oil drilling, 36; brushes, 112; emulsifiers, 97; engine cleaners, 36; film developer, 143; filters, 36; foams, 97; illuminants, 182; insulation, 126, 287; linoleum, 126; lubricants, 127, 182; mattresses, 281, 287; polishing agents, 16, 127; paint, 16; paint strippers, 36; rubber preservative, 143; rust preventative, 143; scale remover, 143; surfactants, 95; water-proofing agents, 127, 132. *See also* cosmetics; explosives
ink, 5, 23, 27, 31, 58, 126, 268; iron gall/oak gall, 83, 268
insect repellents and deterrents, 100, 185, 243; ants, 36; bedbugs, 101, 201,

204; beetles, 204; cockroaches, 48; fleas, 201, 243; flies, 36, 213; lice, 69, 101, 157; mites, 243; mosquitoes, 213, 252; moths, 39, 101; termites, 39; weevils, 243
insects, associated with plants, 142, 143, 266, 292, 295; moths, 36, 168, 244. *See also* butterflies
Iroquois Indians, 99, 285
Isleta Indians, 276, 287

jacales, 39, 66, 131, 287
James I, of England, 52
Jefferson, Thomas, 14, 20, 23, 46, 194
jewelry: beads/beadwork, 96, 116, 154, 155–156, 162; necklaces, 96, 154, 268; rosaries, 177
jimsonweed, 206–209, 251
Juglans: major, 36; *microcarpa*, 35, 36–37; *nigra*, 32–36
Jumano Indians: basketry of, 92, 112; building materials of, 287; cordage of, 112; foods of, 113, 254; houses of, 62, 132; psychotropics of, 235
juniper: Ashe, 38–44, 78; berries, 35, 41–42
Juniperus: ashei, 38–44; *communis*, 42; *virginiana*, 38–44
jute, 166

Kalmia latifolia, 158
Karankawa Indians: adornment of, 89; beverages of, 135–137; building materials of, 93; clothing of, 279; foods of, 25, 84, 247, 254; musical instruments of, 204; psychotropics of, 235; seasonings of, 193; weapons of, 41
Keresan Indians, 276
Kickapoo Indians: beverages of, 121; cradleboards of, 93; deer calls of, 10; foods of, 13, 89, 172, 251, 254; hides of, 16; houses of, 132; medicines of, 6, 16, 69, 73, 125, 145, 173, 181, 184–185, 292; psychotropics of, 235; saddles of, 18; seasonings of, 193; tools of, 96–97
Kiowa-Apache Indians, 150, 185
Kiowa Indians: building materials of, 41, 93; combs of, 211; customs of, 188; dyes of, 35; folklore of, 62, 146, 224, 226; foods of, 18, 73, 78, 145, 163, 197, 216, 254; gum of, 227; and impediments to pursuit, 270; jewelry of, 268; medicines of, 16, 35, 42, 93, 96, 145, 167, 184–185, 252, 254; musical instruments of, 93; perfume of, 242; psychotropics of, 155, 235–236;

rituals of, 41, 62, 146; and smoke for cleansing, 41; smoking materials of, 145, 150; soap of, 167, 203; sweat lodges of, 93, 185; tanning materials of, 167, 276; and tattooing, 182; varnish of, 252; weapons of, 22, 46, 93, 254
Lagenaria, 204
Laguna Indians, 224
lamb's-quarters, 195–197
lamp wicks, 280
Larrea: divaricata, 141; *tridentata*, 139–143
larval host plants, 18, 27, 36, 97, 101, 148, 162, 265
La Salle expedition, 51, 88, 172, 254
Laurus nobilis, 158
lechuguilla, 109–113, 118, 119, 121, 151, 163, 166, 251; hearts of, 113
Lewis, Captain Meriweather, 46, 250
Lewis and Clark Expedition, 46
Liatris punctata, 219
Linceceum, Gideon, 69, 84
Lindheimer, Ferdinand, 152
Linnaeus, Carolus, 17, 109, 214, 278
Lipan Apache Indians: basketry of, 112; bedding material of, 41; cigarette papers of, 121; cordage of, 112; folklore of, 121, 155, 254; foods of, 13, 113, 120, 165, 254; psychotropics of, 155, 235; saddles of, 18, 93; tools of, 22; weapons of, 53. *See also* Apache Indians
livestock, disease: in horses, 31, 184, 204, 211, 269; in pack animals, 209; screwworms, 35
livestock, forage, 6, 67, 142, 173, 188; cattle, 10, 23, 31, 69, 90, 118–119, 124, 168, 173, 255, 258; fowl, 90; goats, 10; hogs, 31, 50, 52, 69, 84, 90, 229, 231; horses, 31, 48, 62, 69; mules, 69; poultry, 50; sheep, 255
livestock, toxicity, 74, 179; in cattle, 79, 111, 156–157, 173, 255, 275; in chickens, 157; in hogs, 269; in horses, 36, 216; in goats, 79, 111, 156, 275; in sheep, 79, 111, 139, 156–157, 275
Lockett, Landon, 88–89
longevity (in plants), 75, 104, 141, 261
Long expedition, 156, 173
Longfellow, Henry Wadsworth, 85
lotus, yellow, 245–247
Louis XVI, 268
Lungkwitz, Hermann, 63
Lupinus: havardii, 240; *subcarnosus*, 239; *texensis*, 238–241

Maclura pomifera, 45–48
madrone, Texas, 7–10
ma-huang, 122–123
Mandan Indians, 62
Maricopa Indians, 68
mats, 41, 112, 121, 167, 216, 287
medicinal uses of plants: abortifacients, 263, 292; analgesics, 62, 93, 182, 193, 209, 233, 281; anemia, 224; anesthetics, 209, 211; anthelmintics, 35, 99, 184, 186, 198; antibiotics, 213; antifungals, 16, 35, 37, 116, 142, 220, 244, 269; antimicrobials, 112, 116, 181; antiseptics, 22, 142, 173, 185, 186, 244; appetite stimulant/stomachic, 116, 185, 186; arthritis/rheumatism, 93, 96, 99, 123, 142, 167, 185, 186, 193, 209, 211–212, 233, 269, 272; astringents, 10, 16, 22, 30, 69, 73, 83, 93, 116, 123, 145, 181, 287; bites/stings, 123, 173, 185, 211–212, 217–220, 233, 244, 252, 276; blood cleaners, 123, 212, 272, 292; blood pressure, 209, 263, 281; blood thinners, 173, 292; burns, 182, 211–212, 233, 244, 252, 287–288; cancer, 142, 204, 264, 269; cholesterol, lowering, 193; colds, 73, 99, 123, 142, 145, 173, 184, 185, 193, 198, 212, 243, 276; colic, 145, 184; coughs, 73, 123, 132, 193, 211–212, 219–220, 243; cuts/wounds/sores, 6, 30, 35, 42, 62, 96, 99, 132, 142, 143, 173, 182, 185, 204, 209, 211–212, 233, 244, 252, 254, 272, 287; dandruff, 167; dental care, 19, 23; diabetes, 69, 185, 251, 281; diaphoretics, 99, 220, 272, 276, 292; diarrhea/dysentery, 22, 30, 35, 69, 73, 83, 99, 145, 184; diuretics, 10, 42, 99, 124, 216, 219, 243, 292; emetics, 135–136, 155, 157, 182, 204, 219–220, 269; epilepsy, 209; eye issues, 69, 93, 116, 181–182, 209, 276; fatigue, 132, 233; fever, 22, 30, 62, 73, 93, 96, 98, 185, 212, 220, 243, 272, 287, 292; gallstones, 254; gangrene, 212, 220; hangovers, 123; hay fever, 123; headache, 6, 22, 182, 209, 224, 233, 264; hemorrhoids, 30, 73; HIV, 264, 269; indigestion, 6, 62, 69, 99, 116, 142, 145, 184, 185, 193, 198, 243; infertility, 224, 263; inflammation, 62, 93, 132, 145, 167, 185, 211–212, 252; influenza, 6, 145, 212, 269; jaundice, 123; laxatives/purgatives, 123, 125, 182, 204, 276;

liver cleaners, 267; malaria, 22, 94, 98, 185; menstrual problems, 73, 99, 132, 182, 184, 185, 198, 292; milk production, stimulation of, 198, 276; pneumonia, 93, 99, 173; rabies, 211; respiratory disorders, 99, 123, 184, 185, 209, 227, 243; scurvy, 173; sedatives, 182, 276; sexual stimulants, 272; skin problems, 6, 62, 116, 142, 167, 173, 182, 185, 211–212, 244, 252, 269; sore feet, 132; sore throat, 30, 69, 73, 93, 99, 132, 173, 184, 211–212, 243; splints/casts, 62, 167; sprains, 182; sunblocks/sunburn/sunstroke, 69, 182, 227, 233, 252; thirst quenchers, 123, 233; thorn removal, 252; tonics/stimulants, 22, 73, 98, 123, 184, 186, 211–212, 220, 233, 243, 272; tonsillitis, 132, 276; toothache, 62, 93, 116, 211–212, 219, 252, 276; tuberculosis, 73, 219; ulcers, 96, 145, 212, 269; urinary/renal disorders, 96, 124, 132, 142, 212, 216, 224; venereal disease, 124, 125, 269, 272, 292; weaning infants, 202, 224; weight loss, 272
megafauna, Pleistocene, 48
Melia azedarach, 97
mescal: alcoholic beverage, 157; beans, 151–158, 160–161; buttons (peyote), 157–158; foodstuff, 113, 145
Mescalero Apache: basketry of, 166–167; building materials of, 93; foods of, 35, 53, 68, 113, 120, 165, 178, 254, 285, 295; medicines of, 116, 124, 252; psychotropics of, 235, 259; seasonings of, 185; weapons of, 53. *See also* Apache Indians
Meskwaki Indians, 155, 211, 217–218
mesquite, 64–70, 151, 257, 261
Mexican buckeye, 151–158
Mexican tea, 198
Mexico, traditional medicine of, 123, 125, 142, 181, 184–185, 227, 233, 276
Milam, Ben, 106
mistletoe, 114, 260–265; European, 260
Moctezuma, 177
Mojave: Desert, 141; Indians, 207
Momaday, N. Scott, 146
Monarda: citriodora, 242, 244; *clinopodioides*, 244; *didyma*, 243–244; *fistulosa*, 242, 243; *pectinata*, 243; *punctata*, 243–244
Monardes, Nicolás, 98, 242

Mormons, 18, 93, 124
Mormon tea, 122–124
Morus: alba, 49, 52; *microphylla*, 51, 52–53; *rubra*, 49–53
moss: ball, 282–283; Spanish, 85, 246, 278–283
mountain laurel: of eastern U.S., 158; Texas, 151–158, 209
Mountain Pima Indians, 10
mugwort, 186; common, 185; western, 183
mulberry: 41, 48; little-leaf, 51, 52–53; paper, 51; red, 49–53; white, 49, 52
Munson, Thomas Volney, 296–297

NASA, 16
Natchez Indians, 135
National Champion trees. *See under* trees
Native American Church, 236–237
Navajo Indians, 124, 165, 197, 236, 275, 276
Nelumbo: lutea, 245–247; *nucifera*, 245, 247
nightshade, silverleaf, 274–277
nutmeg, 101
nutritional value (of plants): antioxidants, 142; caffeine, 134; carbohydrates, 12, 69, 198, 285; cholesterol, 12, 173; fats, 12, 23, 84, 197; fatty acids, 12, 35, 90, 203; fiber, 68, 69, 177; protein, 35, 69, 84, 90, 175, 178, 188, 197, 198, 203, 247, 254–255, 273, 277, 285; sugars, 68, 253. *See also* vitamins and minerals
nuts: for eating, 12–14, 35, 36, 79; hulls for dyeing, 16, 35; milk from, 35; oils from, 35, 36, 84; shelling methods, 14, 37
nutshells: industrial uses, 16, 36
Nuttall, Thomas, 183, 199
Nymphaea, 245, 247

oak, 66, 261; blackjack, 77; English, 80; galls, 83; live, 80–86, 280; post, 75–79; use of name, 63; white, 81
ocotillo, 129–133
Ojibwa Indians, 155
O'Keeffe, Georgia, 206
Olmsted, Frederick Law, 14, 78, 104, 238, 280
Omaha Indians, 46, 211
onion: Canada, 171–174; Drummond's, 171–174; Texas 1015 SuperSweet, 174; wild, 171–174
O'odham Indians, 68, 178. *See also* Akimel *and* Tohono O'odham Indians

opium, 182
Opuntia: *engelmannii*, 248–256; *ficus-indica*, 254, 256; *leptocaulis*, 257–259; *lindheimeri*, 248; *phaeacantha*, 248–256; *streptacantha*, 254
Osage Indians, 46, 236
Osage orange, 45–48, 50, 52, 53, 78, 261
Oto Indians, 156, 236

paint, 16, 35, 36, 69, 227, 286; sizing, 252. *See also under* industrial uses of plants
paintbrush (plant), 199
Paiute Indians, 178, 207, 286
palm, sabal, 87–90
palmetto, dwarf, 87, 88
Papaver somniferum, 182
papaw, 290
paper, 50–51, 55, 61, 166, 227, 287; carbon, 126
parasites, 262–263
Parker, Quanah, 236
Pawnee Indians, 46, 211
Payaya Indians, 13
pecan: nut, 12–14, 35, 36; tree, 11–16, 68, 151, 263. *See also* nuts
pepper, 191, 193; bell, 191, 193, 194; black, 101; chiltepín, 191–194; jalapeño, 191, 194; habanero, 193; official state, 194
perfume, 4–5, 40, 100, 185, 243; for hair, 242
persimmon: common, 25, 28–31; Texas, 25–27
peyote, 156–158, 232–237; ceremonies/rituals, 41, 154, 185
Phoradendron: *californicum*, 265; *tomentosum*, 260–265
phototropism, 225–226
Phytolacca americana, 266–269
pictographs/petroglyphs, 153, 163, 207, 235, 251
pigweed, 175–179; prostrate, 178; redroot, 178, 179
pine: loblolly, 54–58; longleaf, 56–58; Sonderegger, 58; white, 57
Pinus: *oocarpa*, 132–133; *palustris*, 56–58; *taeda*, 54–58; x *sondereggeri*, 58; *teocote*, 132
pioneers: dental hygiene of, 23; foods of, 73, 165, 197, 247; housing of, 62, 78; and insect deterrents, 36; and nut preservation, 35. *See also* settlers (Anglo)
pioneer species, 91, 147
pipes. *See* smoking materials

pit houses, 132
pit ovens, 113, 119, 251
plant, official state, 248–250
Pleistocene, 13, 48, 56, 153
Pliny the Elder, 17, 36, 122, 125, 180, 214, 215, 240
Pluchea foetida, 290
plum: Chickasaw, 71–72; inch, 71–72; Mexican, 72–73; wild, 71–73
pods. *See* fruits
poison: antidotes against, 271; plants used for, 97, 112, 157, 160, 264. *See also* toxicity
poke/pokeberry/pokeweed, 266–269
polishing agents, 215–216. *See also under* industrial uses of plants
pollen, 43, 48, 286
Polk, James Knox, 269
Ponca Indians, 211
Ponce de León, Juan, 85
Populus deltoides, 59–63
Portulaca, 178
pottery, 5, 62, 69, 143
prickly pear (cactus), 111, 151, 163, 190, 248–256
prickly poppy: white, 180–182; yellow, 181–182
Prunus: *angustifolia*, 72; *mexicana*, 72–73; *serotina*, 73–74
psychotropic/psychoactive: compounds, 157; drugs, 160, 233; plants, 154, 206, 232–237; plants, purported, 154–156, 209, 247, 259
Puebloan Indians: beverages of, 145; building materials of, 287; fiber use of, 167; foods of, 178, 197, 230–231; and gourds, 204; medicines of, 123–124; musical instruments of, 61; paints of, 286; rituals of, 227; seasonings of, 243; soap of, 167; wood use of, 62. *See also specific tribes*
purification and cleansing agents (spiritual), 41, 167, 185
purslane, 178

Quapaw Indians, 236
Quercus: *ilex*, 134; *marilandica*, 77; *robur*, 80; *stellata*, 75–79; *virginiana*, 80–86
quinine, 22, 94
quinua, 198

ranchers: and drought forage, 66, 118, 255; and forage, 188; and medicines, 62, 142, 209, 252, 264; and toxic plant concerns, 109, 173, 275. *See also* cowboys

rattlesnake master, 217–220
rhizomes/tubers (edible): 216, 247, 285–286
Rhus: *aromatica*, 144–146; *copallinum*, 147–150; *coriaria*, 148–149; *glabra*, 147–150; *lanceolata*, 147–150; *trilobata*, 144–146; *virens*, 150
Roemer, Ferdinand, 104, 173, 200, 223
Romans (ancient), 20, 94, 144, 147, 148, 197, 220, 263
Roosevelt, Theodore, 239
Rose, Oklahoma, 262
rosin, 58

Sabal: *mexicana*, 87–90; *minor*, 87, 89
sage, white, 183–186
sagebrush, 183; white, 142, 183–186
Salix: *alba*, 94; *fragilis*, 94; *nigra*, 91–94
San Diego Indians, 276
Sapindus saponaria, 95–97
saponins, 95, 97, 112, 268, 272
sassafras, 98–101, 272
Sassafras albidum, 98–101
scouring agents, 112, 215
seasonings, 42, 100, 148–149, 172, 185, 191–194, 198, 243
seeds (edible), 203, 227, 247, 286; oils from, 227; oldest viable, 247; purportedly edible, 162. *See also* acorns; nuts
Seminole Indians, 53, 99, 219, 236, 271, 292
Seri Indians, 67
settlers (Anglo), 42; beverages of, 135; dyes of, 116, 143; and fencing, 66; foods of, 73, 163, 166, 178, 247, 254, 266, 295; gourd use of, 205; housing of, 131–132; livestock forage of, 84, 231; medicines of, 123–124, 167, 193, 212, 217, 254, 292; polishing agents of, 215; tools of, 66. *See also* colonies (American); pioneers
Shakers, 243
shampoo, 95, 167, 203; medicinal, 227
Shawnee Indians, 236
ship-building/boats, 33, 50, 57, 78, 81–83, 101, 287
Shoshone Indians, 181
silkworms/sericulture, 48, 52
Sioux Indians, 211; Dakota, 155; Lakota, 182, 201
sisal fiber, 111
skunkbush, 144–146
Smilax, 270–273; *bona-nox*, 270–271, 273; *glauca*, 270–271; *lanceolata*, 270; *laurifolia*, 270; *rotundifolia*, 271; *tamnoides*, 271

Smith, John, 29, 99

Smithwick, Noah, 18, 269

smoking materials and paraphernalia, 209; cigarette paper, 121, 273; pipes, 36, 41, 272–273, 292; tobacco additives, 145, 150; tobacco substitutes, 41, 252, 292

snakeroot, 210–211, 219; button, 217–219

snakeweed, 219

soap: 36, 58, 95, 112, 167, 182, 203, 227; as laundry detergent, 95, 112, 167, 203; scenting of, 40, 100

soapberry, 95–97

soapweed, 163, 167

soil: improvers, 23, 66, 240, 288; stabilizers, 76, 92, 288

Solanum elaeagnifolium, 274–277

Sophora secundiflora, 151–158

sotol, 111, 113, 118–121, 131, 163, 165, 167, 251

Spain: colonists from, 135, 276, 280, 295; dyes from, 255–256; explorers from, 13, 25, 42, 50, 73, 98, 109, 138, 172, 198, 287

spice. *See* seasonings

spines/thorns: glochids, 254, 259; useful, 182, 254

Sporobolus, 254

State Champion trees. *See under* trees

state flower/grass/tree. *See under* flowers; grass; trees

stems, uses for: animal effigies, 146; bast fiber, 92, 220; building/construction, 131; cradleboards, 146; erosion control, 92; fencing, 131; food (as shoots), 272, 285–286; fuel, 132; pouches/bags, 251; walking sticks, 132

stuffing/padding materials: 41, 185, 201, 279–281, 287

sugarberry, 17, 18

sumac: currier's, 149; flame-leaf, 147–150; fragrant, 35, 144–146; prairie flame-leaf, 147–150; Sicilian, 149; skunk berry, 146; smooth, 147–150

Suma Indians, 120

sunflower, 225–228

sweat lodges, 41, 93, 145, 185. *See also* baths

tanning, 19, 31, 48, 69, 83, 149, 167, 267; chrome, 149

tannins, 141; for dyeing 5, 35, 69; in foods, 78–79; for ink, 5; for medicinal purposes, 30, 69, 123; for tanning, 10, 149. *See also* tanning

Taovaya Indians, 204

Tarahumara Indians: and fish stupefaction, 16, 37, 167; psychotropics of, 207, 235; seasonings of, 193; soap of, 112

tarragon, 185

tasajillo, 257–259

tattooing, 182, 254

Tawakoni Indians, 140, 155, 204

Tawehash Indians, 155

Taxodium: distichum, 102–106; *mucronatum*, 104

Taylor, Nathaniel, 67, 79, 81, 149, 250, 294

tea (beverage). *See under* beverages (non-alcoholic)

tea (plant): Indian, 124; Mexican, 198; Mormon, 122–124

Tejas Indians, 279

Texas (cities, settlements, towns): Abilene, 228; Austin, 8, 40, 85, 226–227, 283; Bandera, 105; Bastrop, 56; Bend, 15; Blanket, 150; Boerne, 296; Bonham, 48; Brackettville, 53; Brownsville, 87, 89; Brownwood, 150; Corpus Christi, 89; Del Rio, 119; Denison, 296; El Paso, 120, 132, 209, 295; Falls City, 53; Fort Concho, 67; Fort Davis, 60; Fort Saint Louis, 88; Fredericksburg, 8, 39; Gonzales, 85; Grapevine, 297; Houston, 88, 226–227; Huntsville, 47; Jefferson, 47; Jourdanton, 6; Kerrville, 105; La Grange, 38, 226; Leakey, 70; Lewisville (site), 18; Lubbock, 228; Marble Falls, 18; Matamoros, 89; New Braunfels, 39, 106; Plainview, 19; Rockport, 86; Rock Springs, 41; Sabinal, 106; San Antonio, 14, 39, 63, 65, 66, 67, 88, 105, 154, 156, 167, 253, 287; Sanderson, 119; San Felipe de Austin, 97; San Saba, 15; Shafter, 53; Shumla, 157; Sisterdale, 104; Uvalde, 106; Victoria, 88; Weatherford, 16; Weesatche, 6; Ysleta, 295

Texas (bays, islands): Follet's Island, 279; Galveston Bay, 38, 222; Galveston Island, 86, 135, 153, 278; Lavaca Bay, 88; Matagorda Bay, 89, 137

Texas (mountains), 7, 10, 117

Texas (rivers): Brazos, 293; Colorado, 279; Devils, 35, 253, 295; Frio, 25; Guadalupe, 104, 280; Nueces, 4, 13; Pecos, 153, 177, 197, 204, 207, 227, 234–236, 253, 286; Red, 45, 48, 62, 296; Rio Grande, 87, 121, 127, 153, 204, 234, 236, 252; Sabinal, 106; Sa-

bine, 106; San Antonio, 53, 106; San Jacinto, 38; South Canadian, 62

Texas mountain laurel, 151–158

thatching, 89, 121, 131, 287

Thelesperma megapotamicum, 124

Theophrastus, 149, 180, 248, 270, 285

Thompson Indians, 93

Thoreau, Henry David, 39

Thuja, 44

thyme/thymol, 244

Thymus vulgaris, 244

Tillandsia: recurvata, 282–283; *usneoides*, 278–283

Timucuan Indians, 135

Tohono O'odham Indians: beverages of, 124; fiber uses of, 167; foods of, 53, 132, 178, 197, 251, 253; seasonings of, 193; weapons of, 53

Tonkawa Indians, 150; bedding materials of, 279; beverages of, 137; cordage of, 51; folklore of, 167; foods of, 13–14, 84, 247, 254; musical instruments of, 204; poisons of, 264; psychotropics of, 154–155, 235; seasonings of, 193; weapons of, 22

toothbrushes, 19, 23

toothpaste, 23, 100

toxicity (in humans), 74, 116, 156, 162, 269, 275; cardiovascular, 264; dropsy, 182; gastrointestinal, 50, 173, 264, 267; glaucoma, 182; hepatitis, 143; nervous disorders, 50, 186, 208; renal disorders, 143

trees: historic, 15–16, 48, 62, 79, 85–86, 104; as indicators of water, 60, 91; largest in Texas, 105; longevity of, 75, 104; as markers, 62, 104; National Champions, 6, 8, 27, 39, 46, 53, 70, 97; state, 15, 20, 63, 104; State Champions, 8, 16

tule, 284–288

Tull, Delena, 89, 150, 224, 259, 267

turpentine, 58

Typha: domingensis, 284–288; *latifolia*, 284–288

Ungnadia speciosa, 159–162

U.S. Constitution, 83, 268

U.S. Navy, 82, 166

USS *Constitution*, 82

varnish, 97, 127, 132, 252

*Verbesina: micropter*a, 292; *virginica*, 289–292

Viscum album, 260, 264

vitamins and minerals, 12; aluminum, 23; calcium, 13, 23, 68, 175, 178, 197,

251, 253; cobalt, 23; fluorine, 13; iron, 13, 23, 68, 178, 197, 203, 267; magnesium, 13, 23; manganese, 23; phosphorus, 13, 23, 178, 253; potassium, 13, 23, 178; silicon, 215; sodium, 12; sulfur, 23; vitamin A, 178, 193, 197, 251; vitamin B, 193; vitamin B-1, 173; vitamin B-2, 173, 197; vitamin C, 165, 173, 178, 193, 197, 253; zinc, 203
viticulture, 295–297
Vitis: aestivalis, 295; *arizonica*, 295; *berlandieri*, 295, 296; *cinerea*, 295, 296; *labrusca*, 296; *monticola*, 295; *mustangensis*, 294; *rotundifolia*, 294; *vinifera*, 293, 295–297; *vulpina*, 296

Waco Indians, 140, 155, 204
walnut (nut), 12, 13, 35–36, 253. *See also* nuts
walnut (tree/wood), 15, 21, 66, 261, 290; Arizona, 36; black, 32–36, 50, 74; English, 37; Texas black, 36–37
War of 1812, 82
Washington, George, 14, 20
wastewater treatment, 288
water, clarification of, 252
waxes, 125–128, 142
weapons: arrowpoints, 254; arrows, 22, 69, 93, 146; bows, 36, 41, 45–46, 53, 66; bowstrings, 112, 166; gunstocks, 34, 36, 66, 74; knife handles, 113, 121; in mythology, 121; polishing of, 215–216; spear shafts, 113, 121; wadding material, 281; war clubs, 66
White Mountain Apache Indians, 188, 201. *See also* Apache Indians
Whitman, Walt, 84
Wichita Indians, 22, 41, 73, 93, 154–155, 236
wickerwork, 93
wild: bergamot, 243; china, 97; grape, 151, 293–297; onion, 171–174
wildlife: alligators, 283; bats, 283; bears, 23, 84; bison, 13, 188; coyotes,

27, 69, 90, 131, 255; deer, 6, 10, 13, 18, 23, 27, 31, 69, 79, 84, 124, 148, 179, 255, 273, 288; foxes, 23, 27, 31, 255; hogs (feral), 69, 288; javelinas, 5, 27, 37, 69, 79, 84, 255; muskrats, 288; opossums, 31, 50; rabbits, 13, 31, 69, 179, 255; raccoons, 18, 23, 27, 31, 50, 90, 255; ringtails, 27; rodents, 79, 90, 116, 255; skunks, 31, 69, 255; snakes, 116; squirrels, 23, 37, 50, 79, 84, 254–255; tortoises, 255. *See also* birds
willow, 261; black, 91–94; withes of, 93, 146
windbreaks, 17, 39, 52
wine. *See under* beverages (alcoholic)
Winnebago Indians, 155, 211
wood: impermeability of, 78; resistance to decay, 34, 39, 47, 50, 78, 81, 89, 105; resistance to insects, 39, 47; resistance to shipworms, 88
wood uses: artificial limbs, 93; building/construction, 10, 16, 18, 33–34, 39–40, 41, 48, 55, 57, 62, 78, 89, 101, 105, 167; boxes/crates, 18, 55, 61, 92; cabinetry, 5, 27, 33, 34, 50, 74, 101; carvings, 116; cooperage, 50, 55, 78, 101; divining rods, 93; engraving/printing blocks, 27, 74; excelsior, 61; farm implements, 5, 16, 21, 61, 66; fencing, 18, 34, 36, 39–40, 47, 50, 66, 78, 101, 105; fillers, 16; fire drills, 22, 41, 50, 62; fish weirs, 92; flooring, 16, 18, 30, 57, 66, 78, 101, 105; furniture, 16, 18, 27, 33, 34, 39, 41, 61, 66–67, 74, 78; hand tools, 5, 10, 16, 21, 27, 30, 36, 66, 74, 96–97; hunting (animal) calls, 10, 48; inlay, 67; kitchen/eating utensils, 16, 33–34, 36, 61, 66; musical instruments, 27, 34, 41, 48, 61, 93; paving blocks, 48, 66; pencils, 39; picture frames, 27; piers, 40, 48, 83; propellers, 34; pulpwood, 55, 57, 61; railroad ties, 40, 48, 50,

78, 105; saddles, 18, 61, 93, 97; shoe lasts, 21, 30; splints, 167; sports equipment, 16, 18, 21, 30; stirrups, 10; telegraph poles, 40; in textile industry, 21–22, 30, 55; travois poles, 93; turnery, 27, 30, 78; veneering, 16, 34, 74, 78; walking canes, 27; wagons/wagon wheels, 47, 66, 83; water tanks, 106; waterwheels, 33, 83; wharf docks, 88, 105. *See also* flower stalks; fuel; resin; ship-building/boats; stems; turpentine
World War I: fiber demands during, 166, 287; medicinal uses during, 167, 173, 209, 244; timber demands during, 34–35; wax demands during, 127
World War II: fiber demands during, 166; medicinal uses during, 173, 209; sotol/mescal production during, 121; tannin demands during, 149; timber demands during, 22, 35; wax demands during, 127–128
wormseed, 198
wormwood: 184–185; common, 185–186; sweet, 185

Yaqui Indians, 46
yaupon, 134–138, 151, 155; tea, 100, 134–138, 219
Yavapai Indians, 167
yerba maté, 138
Yokut Indians, 207
yucca: 151; banana, 165–166
Yucca: 121, 163–168; *baccata*, 165–166; *elata*, 163, 165, 166, 168; *glauca*, 166, 168
Yuchi Indians, 135
Yuman Indians, 178, 207

Zuni Indians: beverages of, 124, 201, 275; building materials of, 287; dyes of, 201; foods, 165, 178, 197; medicines of, 124, 209, 276; psychotropics of, 207; sacred plants of, 209